THE POVERTY OF NATIONS

William W. Murdoch is professor of biology at the University of California, Santa Barbara. He is the editor of *Environment: Resources, Pollution, and Society,* second edition.

THE POVERTY OF NATIONS

The Political Economy of Hunger and Population

William W. Murdoch

THE JOHNS HOPKINS UNIVERSITY PRESS
Baltimore and London

The Johns Hopkins University Press, Baltimore, Maryland 21218
The Johns Hopkins Press Ltd., London

Library of Congress Cataloging in Publication Data

Murdoch, William W
  The poverty of nations.

  Bibliography: p. 367
  Includes index.
  1. Underdeveloped areas. 2. Underdeveloped areas—
Population.   3. Underdeveloped areas—Food supply.
4. Underdeveloped areas—Poor. I. Title.
HC59.7.M86   330.9172'4   80-16201
ISBN 0-8018-2313-7
ISBN 0-8018-2462-1 (pbk.)

For Stephen and Helen

CONTENTS

FIGURES

TABLES

PREFACE

Massive population growth, widespread hunger, and poverty are among the most critical problems of our time. Yet their causes are widely misunderstood. They are misunderstood in part because much of the popular writing obscures and distorts these problems, and in part because much of the best analysis is written by experts, for experts, in the esoteric jargon of their disciplines. In this book I have aimed to clear away the misconceptions, to bring within reach of the nonprofessional the wealth of evidence and analysis that illuminate the real nature of these problems, and to provide a synthesis, a unified explanation for the persistence of hunger, rapid population growth, and poverty.

I have tried to write a book that is both scholarly and accessible to a wide readership. Professionals in demography, agricultural economics, and development will not find here original research in their disciplines, but I hope they will find something useful in the connections I have drawn among those disciplines and in an outsider's view of their fields. However, I particularly hope to reach lay persons interested in these important problems and people responsible for policy. As a consequence, while much of the relevant literature uses statistical and formal economic analysis, I have discarded most of that methodology in presenting the material. I believe that the important issues and ideas can be presented in plain English.

The first five chapters analyze the food-and-population problem in a straightforward way. I have thought it important to analyze high fertility and the technical aspects of food production in depth in Chapters 2 and 5, respectively. These two chapters contain summary sections for readers who prefer to skip the details and concentrate instead upon the flow of the argument. Chapters 6 through 11 are intended to provide a conceptual framework for placing the problems of population and hunger in perspective. They take a broader and less detailed approach.

Writing this book has been a deeply interesting intellectual journey. I began, probably where many readers will begin, with a concern about world hunger, growing population, and increasing environmental degradation. But I was dissatisfied with the explanations commonly offered. The progression of chapters essentially charts my course toward what I believe to be a more satisfactory explanation. I hope that in following this journey the reader will share in some measure the fascination of discovery. I hope, too, that this process of discovery will prove as profoundly unsettling for the reader as it has been for me.

ACKNOWLEDGMENTS

I am grateful to my friends and colleagues at the University of California, Santa Barbara, who helped me while I wrote this book. Among those who commented on all or part of various versions of the manuscript, or who provided useful discussions, are Joe Connell, Rob Day, Elvin Hatch, Sally Holbrook, Robert Huttenback, Joan Murdoch, Carroll Pursell, Allan Stewart-Oaten, and members of the Graduate Population Ecology Seminar. I used the manuscript as a text for my Environmental Studies class and the students responded with enthusiastic insight. Scholars at other institutions who provided helpful criticisms and suggestions include Judith Bannister (East-West Population Institute, Honolulu), Martin Birley (Imperial College, London), John C. Caldwell (Australian National University), Robert Cassen (Institute of Development Studies, Brighton), Alain de Janvry (University of California, Berkeley), Barry Edmonston (International Population Program, Cornell University), William Felstiner (Social Science Research Institute, University of Southern California), Bruce F. Johnston (Stanford Food Research Institute), Michael Way (Imperial College, London), and Robert E. Asher (former Senior Fellow in Foreign Policy Studies, Brookings Institution). None of the above, of course, bears responsibility for the mistakes that remain.

A John Simon Guggenheim Fellowship enabled me to spend time in several developing countries during 1977 and 1978.

1

INTRODUCTION

Throughout the developing world the populations of poor people are expanding rapidly. These same poor people also do not have enough to eat. This book is devoted to analyzing the relationship between these two problems and to exploring the connection between them and widespread poverty.

Population and Food Supply: A Race

Only a recluse could have lived in a rich nation in the 1960s and 1970s without being informed that a race between population and food production was taking place in the poor nations of the world. The importance of such a race can hardly be overestimated. On its outcome rest the lives and well-being of hundreds of millions of people.

The outlines of the problem are well known and need only a brief sketch. For most of human history, population growth has been negligible: it took a million years before the discovery of agriculture for world population to reach 5 to 10 million people; during the next 10,000 years population doubled on average only every 2,000 years, reaching about 300 million at the birth of Christ; and the next doubling took 1,600 years. Thereafter the rate of population growth increased until by the onset of World War II it was 1 percent a year and the population of just over 2 billion had a doubling time of seventy years (table 1-1). This acceleration, however, was nothing compared to the spurt of growth that has occurred since 1940. In a mere twenty years the rate of increase doubled to almost 2 percent a year, the doubling time fell to thirty-six years, and a billion people were added to the population. In the next fifteen years another billion were added, giving a 1975 population of about 4 billion.

This modern population explosion is almost entirely a phenomenon of the less developed countries (LDCs). Their rate of increase *tripled* in thirty years, reaching 2.4 percent a year and yielding a doubling time of only twenty-nine years by 1970. Their population growth in the 1970s was more than three times faster than that of the rich nations, where population growth rates have declined in the past thirty years. At present there are roughly 1 billion people in the rich countries and 3 billion in the poor. Unless dramatic changes occur, by the year 2000 there will be some 6 billion people in the world, of whom about 80 percent, or almost 5 billion, will be in the underdeveloped countries—and population will still be expanding.

It should not be thought from this account that world population size has increased smoothly. It has been at times stationary. For example, although world population doubled in the 1,600 years after Christ, it probably changed little from A.D. 1 to 1000. At times world population has even declined. The uneven progression of the size of one particular population is illustrated in figure 1-1.

In the face of the modern explosive acceleration in population growth, world food production on average has not only kept up with but surpassed the growth of population. Even in the poor countries, growth in food production has on average equaled or exceeded growth in people.

Unfortunately, the key phrase here is "on average." Thus, while food supply in the poor countries during the first half of this century kept pace with population, on average, food production per head in India declined throughout the last five decades of British rule.[1] Although, on average, food production in the developing nations has increased slightly faster than population since 1960, it has lagged behind population in some fifty to sixty of these nations; as a result, huge numbers of people have inadequate and dwindling food supplies. Some estimates have put the number of malnourished people at over 1 billion in 1970, although the most widely accepted estimate is about 460 million.*

*See Chapter 5 for details of food production, the extent of malnourishment, and projections of future global food problems.

Table 1-1. World population growth and doubling times

Date	Population size	Annual growth rate (%)	Doubling time (years)	Factor of increase per century[a]
8000 B.C.	5–10 million	0.035	2000	—
1650 A.D.	600 million	0.35	200	1.4
1750 A.D.	800 million	0.40	170	1.5
1850 A.D.	1.3 billion	0.50	130	1.7
1950 A.D.	2.5 billion	0.80	87	2.2
1975 A.D.	4.0 billion	1.90	36	6.7
		Other doubling times		
		1.0	69	2.7
		2.0	35	7.4
		2.5	28	12.0
		3.0	23	20.0

[a]For example, at an annual exponential growth rate of 3 percent a population would increase by twentyfold in 100 years.

Sources: Ansley J. Coale, "The History of the Human Population," Scientific American 231 (1974): 40–51; John D. Durand, "Historical Estimates of World Population: An Evaluation," Population and Development Review 3 (1977): 253–96; United Nations, Department of Economic and Social Affairs, World Population Trends and Policies: 1977 Monitoring Report, vol. 1 (ST/ESA/SER.A/62), 1979.

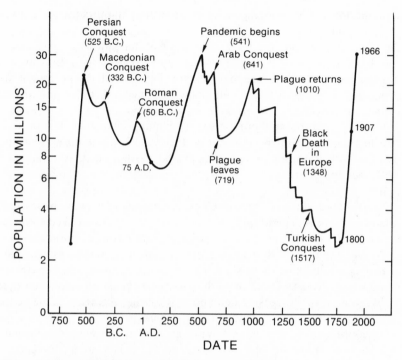

Figure 1-1 Population of Egypt, 664 B.C. to A.D. 1966

Source: Redrawn from Thomas Henry Hollingsworth, *Historical Demography* (London: Hodder and Stoughton, 1969), p. 311.

Glimpses of the probable future give even greater cause for gloom. Projections based on the past growth rates of LDC agriculture and on current information about population growth imply a total of about 1 billion malnourished people by the year 2000 (Chapter 5). A sophisticated and realistic model of the world food situation, created by a group in the Netherlands, projects that by the year 2010 the number of malnourished people will have risen to between 1.3 and 1.6 billion.[2] This is true even though aggregate world food production keeps up with or increases faster than population growth in all runs of the model.

Another cause for concern is that the balance between food and population is more precarious than long-term average growth rates suggest, because food production fluctuates from year to year. Shortfalls in production in some years can cause greatly increased hardship. They are especially serious when, as is often the case, bad weather causes simultaneous reductions in many parts of the world.

If food production in the poor countries has barely kept pace with population growth, it has failed abysmally to keep up with increasing *demand*.

Demand for food reflects the amount that would be purchased at a given price and income if the food were available, and so it increases with both the number of people and their income. Food demand in the poor countries has been growing at 3.5 percent per year, greatly outstripping growth in food production.[3] Notice that demand is not need. Many people are poor and their demand falls well below their need. The demand of rich people, on the other hand, may exceed their need.

The important point about increasing demand relative to local production in the poor countries is that the difference is made up by food imports, which often impose a very heavy burden on poor economies. By 1990 they may cost the less-developed countries $18 to $22 billion per year.[4]

The future performance required of food production in the poor countries over the next generation can be put quite simply. Just to keep food intake at current levels, production must grow initially at 2.3 percent a year (a doubling time of thirty years). This would mean that the same fraction of people would be malnourished, but of course the *number* of malnourished would increase. In the meantime, the cost of imports would continue to rise to meet the increasing demand of the richer segments of the population. An annual growth rate of about 4 percent, which requires a doubling of production every seventeen to eighteen years, is needed to keep up with demand, to reduce the number of malnourished (under the current pattern of distribution), and to contribute to improved economic growth. This is much higher than most rates achieved before.

These opening paragraphs sound a recurrent theme: *the problem conceptualized as a race between population and food supply.* They emphasize large numbers, exponential growth rates, the projection of growth rates into the future, and, in general, the relative performance of food and population. They provide the standard fare of the public debate on population and food.

This notion of food and population as a race has characterized the public debate and much of the writing on the problem, and it has probably become the standard way in which most of us think about it.[5] Typically, population "outruns" or "outstrips" food supply, or food supply "lags behind" population. Two quotations, from among the myriad available, will serve to illustrate this:

It is abundantly clear to anybody who has looked at the statistics of human population growth and who knows the problems of agriculture and what is happening to the environment of our planet, that the race between population growth and food production has been lost.

World food production cannot keep pace with the galloping growth of population.[6]

The way we conceptualize the problem is important because it determines the kind of explanations we seek and the sort of solutions we propose. Thus the idea of a race, which arises quite naturally from a comparison of exponential growth rates, leads us just as naturally to consider food and population as two separate, independent variables, *with separate mechanisms governing the growth of each.* And, while one variable clearly influences the other, we are led nevertheless to think of two different sets of procedures: one demographic, for slowing down population, the other agricultural, for speeding up food production. This separation can be seen clearly in recent analyses of the problem:

> We are being misled by those who say there is a serious food shortage. This is not true; world food production this decade is the greatest in history. *The problem is too many people.*

> Our main focus here is on world agriculture...But we consider that the primary issue for the longer-term future is reduction in the rate of growth of world population.[7]

James Echols, recent president of the Population Reference Bureau suggests that "without drastic population control measures, high fertility in the less developed countries will overtake food production."[8]

Agriculturalists striving to increase food production through the development of new strains and other techniques see themselves as providing time during which population experts, using *their* techniques, can struggle to control fertility. Lester Brown views the Green Revolution in cereals as "a means of buying time, perhaps an additional fifteen years, during which some way might be found to apply the brakes to population growth."[9]

Pursuit of the race analogy has also led to devastatingly callous recommendations for a solution to the population and food problem. Several observers have concluded that population must win, which is to say that people will lose, because "We have reached, or nearly reached, the limit of the world's ability to feed even our present numbers adequately."[10]

Given such a foregone conclusion to the race, it is but a small step of logic to give up on those who are stumbling hopelessly ever further behind and to help only those who have some hope of success. Hence we have "lifeboat ethics," which seek to make neglect of the poor a moral virtue, and "triage" policies that help us decide which developing nations do not need help, which we should help, and which we should leave to rot on the battlefield of the fight for survival.[11] And if the connection between the two variables of food and population is extremely simple—"more food means more babies"[12]—then there is all the more justification for the malign neglect of those who are faltering. According to this view, the problem will be best solved by our withdrawing food and other aid, or at most by giving it selectively to those developing countries that have some hope of solving their population problem.

In my view, the concept of the problem as a race, and the consequent separation of the two variables of population and food, are serious impediments both to understanding the issues and to developing an appropriate solution. On the contrary, it is essential to realize that rapid population growth and inadequate food supply have a *common* origin and a *joint* explanation. We will see that analyses like those above bear little relation to reality; that the problem is more complex than the simple analogies of a race, lifeboats, and triage will allow; that our tangled connections with the problem are strong, ubiquitous, and pervasive; that we in the rich nations have helped create and perpetuate the problem; that we continue to help perpetuate it; and that the simple withdrawal of aid will not solve the problem, nor will it eliminate those activities through which we make it more intractable.

It is certainly possible to solve the food and population problem. But its solution will require profound changes in both the poor and the rich nations.

Population and Food: A Single Problem

My basic thesis is that population and food problems are merely symptoms and that we must dig deeper to find their common causes. The examination of these underlying causes will take us into a wide range of disparate disciplines and occasionally complex analyses that are at times apparently distant from the issues of population and food supply. But I hope to show that a single explanation emerges from these analyses and binds them firmly together: the same political, economic, and social machinery both drives rapid population growth and constrains food production. That machinery has created and maintained the *structural poverty of rural populations* in the underdeveloped world. This single phenomenon is the cause of both rapid population growth and inadequate food supplies.

The emphasis on rural poverty is crucial because the rural population is the heart of the problem. In most developing countries, this segment of the population is the largest, the poorest, and has the highest birth rates, so it is the dynamo that drives population growth. Inadequate food supply is obviously an agricultural (rural) problem and, as we will see, the failure of development is basically the failure of agriculture. This is not to say that the basic causes of rural poverty lie solely or even mainly in the countryside, only that the condition of the rural population must be the major focus of our concern.

By "structural" poverty I mean poverty that is the result of the man-made political and economic framework in which the poor exist. This framework consists of those arrangements and institutions that give rise to and help maintain the present distribution of political and economic power. It includes, for example, the patterns of land ownership, of access to credit, capital, and modern technology, and the form of the relationships between poor and rich nations. The term structural also implies that poverty is *not* the result of poor soils, poor climate, inadequate natural resources, or other physical or biological conditions.

Part I of this book explores how poverty, particularly rural poverty, causes the population explosion. Part II shows how rural poverty limits food production. In turn, low food production and an inappropriate pattern of production lead, in a vicious circle, to persistent rural poverty. Part III then seeks a still deeper explanation for the persistence of poverty, that is, for the failure of development. It shows that it is the biases built into the economic structure of the poor countries, and into their relationships with the rich countries, that have created and maintained rural poverty and have suppressed the dynamic mechanisms of development. Part III also discusses those changes in the structure of LDC economies that are needed to solve these joint problems. (The reader who would like to preview how these various parts of the argument fit together could turn first to the "Synthesis" in Chapter 11.)

Why Is Population a Problem?

It is obvious that an inadequate food supply is a problem. So is poverty. But is there a "population problem?" The mere raising of this question may seem to many people heretical, or even ludicrous. Virtually all of the debate on population simply assumes that population is a problem; it is generally recognized as one of the two or three major issues of our time. But whether or not there is a population problem is a question of both values and of the interpretation of facts.

Mamdani put the dilemma well.[13] It has been said that one has only to step into the hordes on Calcutta's streets to know there is a population problem. But, asked Mamdani, would one also conclude there was a population problem from encountering crowds just as large in London? Or, if you prefer, at the Kennedy Center in Washington? Isn't it mass *poverty*, rather than masses of people, that strikes with such sickening force in the streets of Calcutta?

Indeed, a great difficulty affecting discussion of population is that it *seems* so simple and straightforward: populations are growing rapidly and these same people are underfed; therefore there are too many people for the food supply, i.e., population growth is the cause of malnutrition. Poor

countries have very high population growth rates, and each extra person is
an additional burden on the economy, so population growth causes poverty. Populations are expanding in a finite world and therefore we are in
danger of depleting resources and destroying our life support systems.

Yet the issues are not so simple. I will try to show that rapid population
growth does not *cause* the food problem—they share common causes.
Again, it is not at all certain that rapid population growth prevents increases in average incomes. Birdsall, reviewing various economic model-
ing studies, concluded that high fertility did suppress average income two
or three decades later.[14] However, other studies show that both historically
in the rich nations, and more recently in the poor nations, countries with
more rapidly growing populations have tended to have more rapidly growing average incomes. One must hasten to add that the correlations are
weak. In a highly detailed analysis, using both real data and models,
Simon argues that moderate population growth in poor countries in the
long run increases per-person income faster than either zero population
growth or very rapid growth.[15]

Whatever its long-run effects, rapid population growth does pose economic problems in the short term. A major difficulty is that a population
experiencing rapid growth is a very young population. The ratio of productive workers to dependents therefore tends to be low. This not only
spreads the product of each worker over more dependents but raises the
per-worker cost of educational and other social services. Rapid population
growth can also make it more difficult to achieve widespread improvement
in economic well-being. The difficulty of finding useful employment for
the expanding labor force can be a tremendous problem; the need for
social services (education, health, housing) expands very rapidly. These
problems affect the poor most, and so a major short-term consequence of
rapid growth is often an increase in poverty. (We need to be careful here;
that such problems are visited largely upon the poor is not an inexorable
law of nature but the consequence of particular political and economic
conditions.)

If it is not certain that population growth is inevitably an economic mis-
fortune, it is also not always clear that present populations are too large.
Here we run into questions of different values and of disagreements over
the facts. For those who have a very pessimistic view of the extent of physical resources, most countries are already overpopulated. But for economists with even a modestly optimistic view of resources, some nations have
too small a population and others are too sparsely populated to be capable
of steadily increasing their economic well-being.

The question of pressures on limited resources is not straightforward.
The historical fact is that, although population has grown faster than exponentially in the past century, so has the recognized supply of resources.

Historically, increased demand for resources has induced a larger supply: "Though paradoxical, supplies of natural resources may be expected to *increase* indefinitely, and the long-run resource outlook is good."[16] This claim is not a fact, but it rests upon detailed analysis of the issue and, in the light of past experience, it cannot merely be brushed aside (Chapter 10).

In the final analysis, it is the uncertainty surrounding each of these issues that makes untramelled population growth such a threatening problem. Whatever our previous experience, there *is* uncertainty about future resources—food, minerals, energy; there is uncertainty about the ability of environments to sustain damage and still function, and about the ability of land to continue producing ever greater amounts of food. The conservative procedure in the face of such uncertainty is to make possible the control of population size and growth. This can be done humanely only if high fertility is no longer the inevitable outcome of the conditions in which people live in the LDCs.

The Poor

Since poverty is a central issue, we need a brief description of the poor. About 1 billion people live in the rich countries, or the "developed world" —North America, Europe (including the USSR), Japan, Australia, and New Zealand.* Although some of these people are malnourished or poor, or both, they are not our focus here. About 3 billion people live in the poor countries in Africa, Asia, and Latin America. Of these, about 1 billion live in Communist Asia, almost all in China, and—as we will see—they are a special case. The remaining 2 billion live almost entirely in non-Communist developing countries, and of these 40 to 50 percent, about 800 million to 1 billion people, are the truly poor.

Some of these poor live in the slums, shanty towns, and streets of the developing world's cities—Lima, Bogota, Nairobi, Calcutta, Bombay, Delhi. There they exist on the fringe of the urban economy, only fitfully employed, cut off from the countryside yet not absorbed into the city's economic life. Probably the greatest poverty can be found in pockets of these cities. Certainly, exposed each day to the high standard of living of other urbanites, they must be the most acutely aware of their poverty.

---

*The division of the world into developed and less developed countries (LDCs) is always somewhat arbitrary. Argentina, Israel, and some additional small nations are sometimes included in the developed world. Greece and Spain are often categorized as LDCs in analyses dealing with the 1960s and earlier periods. "Poor," "developing," "underdeveloped," and "less developed" are used interchangeably throughout this book.

However, the great bulk of the poor (80 percent or more is a reasonable guess) live in the countryside.

Throughout this book I will refer to "the poor" as if they were a single homogenous group of people. Of course they are not. This book is too short to discuss at each point the various groups of poor people, but it is well to bear in mind that many different groups do exist. In the country-side, the poorest are often the landless resident or migrant laborers, employed only intermittently at very low wages. There are poor tenant farmers with small plots who may pay rent, share their crop with the land-lord, or labor for him. There are small landowners, who in some cases may be even poorer than the tenant, small businessmen, and artisans in the village. In Africa poor herdsmen and nomads are ubiquitous. All of these lead very different lives from the urban squatter.

The poor of all sorts, however, share much in common. Around 1970, about half of them had incomes of less than $50 per head per year (in 1971 U.S. dollars), and most had annual incomes of less than $75.* Probably about half are malnourished and the remainder have diets that could be greatly improved. Life expectancy is less than fifty years. More than fif-teen out of every hundred children born die before they are a year old, and most families will experience the death of at least one child. Sickness is

---

*Hollis Chenery et al., *Redistribution with Growth* (London: Oxford University Press, 1974), p. 12. These and other U.S. per capita income figures given for the LDCs are mislead-ing. This is because official exchange rates (converting, say, Indian rupees to U.S. dollars) underestimate the real purchasing power of incomes in the developing countries. The reason is that the price of a given good, converted to dollars, tends to be lower in the LDCs than in the United States, and this difference is not fully reflected in the official exchange rates (Irv-ing B. Kravis, Alan W. Heston, and Robert Summers, "The Real GDP Per Capita for More than One Hundred Countries," *The Economic Journal* 88 [1978]: 215–42). It is clear, for ex-ample, that $50 would not buy enough food in America to maintain one person for one year, yet people in the LDCs do survive, however poorly, on incomes officially pegged at $50 per year.

Kravis and his co-workers have found that real per capita incomes in the LDCs, that is, in-comes in terms of purchasing power, are generally two or three times larger than the official (nominal) income in U.S. dollars. Furthermore, the degree of underestimation tends to be greater for poorer countries. Roughly speaking, up to nominal per capita incomes of $185 (in 1970), real per capita income was two and a half to three times larger than the nominal in-come. Between nominal per capita incomes of $185 and $500, real per capita income was two to two and a half times higher. Above $500, real per capita income was generally less than twice as high as nominal per capita income. Nominal per capita incomes are used throughout this book.

This difference between real and nominal incomes does not mean that the figures given in Chapter 1 overestimate the prevalence of poverty. On the contrary, it is quite likely that the often-quoted World Bank estimate that 40 percent of the Third World's population is in ab-solute poverty is an underestimate by any generally accepted criterion of poverty. Richard R. Fagen ("Equity in the South in Context of North-South Relations," in Albert Fishlow et al., *Rich and Poor Nations in the World Economy* [New York: McGraw Hill, 1978]) argues that a nominal income of $50 to $75 is too low a threshold to serve as a demarcation of poverty. For example, while only 20 percent of Brazil's population had an income of less than $75 in 1969, an estimated 44 percent of its population was malnourished.

rife, intestinal parasites common, and energy low; yet medical help is essentially unobtainable.

The family, which is likely to include grandparents and other relatives, will be large but will live in a cramped hovel or hut, often with only one room and usually without sanitation, fresh water, or electricity. Typically the poor have had little or no schooling and virtually all of them are illiterate.

The circumstances of the poor are not only appalling; they have not noticeably improved over the last few decades, and for some they have worsened. Almost everywhere their position has become worse relative to the small segment of the population whose incomes and wealth have increased.

It is important to realize that the poor are relatively, as well as absolutely, poor. By any measure, inequality is much greater in the developing than in the developed countries. Thus, while the poorest 40 percent of the population receives 25 percent of the national income in developed Communist countries and 16 percent of the income in the developed capitalist countries, they receive only 12.5 percent of the much smaller income in the developing capitalist countries and, in half of these countries, only 9 percent.[17] In most poor countries urban incomes are several times larger than rural incomes. In Brazil, for example, the 1974 average annual income for the whole country was about $800, while for the 30 million people of the rural northeast it was $200. In Colombia the average urban income in 1970 was nine times the average rural income.[18] Finally, in spite of low average incomes, there are small segments of the population whose standard of living far exceeds that reached by most people in the West.

We will turn for the next three chapters to a discussion of how this prevalent poverty influences fertility and population growth in the developing world.

I

POPULATION

2

POPULATION AND POVERTY

During most of its existence the human population has been virtually at zero population growth (ZPG). Average completed family size in this long period was probably about six to seven children, but these births were balanced by a crushing mortality rate, especially in infants and children (table 2-1). Average life expectancy was roughly twenty years. Probably fewer than half of the children born survived to have any children of their own. Of those women who did have children, a large fraction would not survive to the end of their reproductive life.

The developed nations are now once again very close to zero population growth.[1] Now, however, the average life span is about seventy years, and almost all infants survive to maturity. To prevent population growth, average completed family size must therefore be not more than about two children, and in the developed nations family sizes of one, two, and three children are the norm. Indeed, in some nations completed family size has

Table 2-1. Demography of premodern, modern, and future populations

	Fertility		Mortality			
	Average completed family size[a]	Crude birth rate	Life expectancy at birth	Crude death rate	Infant mortality per 1,000 births	Population under 15 years (%)
Zero population growth (ZPG) in premodern[b] populations	6.5	50	20 years	50	greater than 300	35
Developing non-Communist countries	5.7	40	less than 50 years	15	140	44
Developing Communist countries[c]	4.0	30	62 years	11	?	35
Rich nations	2.3	17	71 years	9	27	27
Eventual ZPG conditions	2.1	13	75 years	13	10	20

(Developing non-Communist countries, Developing Communist countries, and Rich nations bracketed as "around 1970")

Sources: Ansley J. Coale, "The History of the Human Population," *Scientific American* 231 (1974): 40–51; United Nations, Department of Economic and Social Affairs, *World Population Prospects as Assessed in 1973* (ST/ESA/SER.A/60), 1977.

[a]Total fertility rate.

[b]Premodern here means poulations living before the marked increase in population that began roughly 300 years ago.

[c]Mainly China.

fallen below the level needed to maintain the population over the long run. In the United States, for example, family size was fewer than two children in the late 1970s. Such populations continue to increase only because the population has a high fraction of people in their reproductive years or because immigration exceeds emigration. (Measures of fertility and the effects of age distribution are discussed in more detail in appendix A.)

The fertility of the developing nations provides a startling contrast. Families with eight or more children, rare aberrations in the rich nations, are quite normal in poor countries, where the average completed family size of about five children is more than twice that of rich nations. Even that average hides the fact that in large areas of the underdeveloped world most people have seven children or more. In rural Uttar Pradesh in India, for example, the average woman marries at age thirteen, has her first child at age sixteen, and has had eight children by the time she is over forty. The birth rate is fifty per thousand per year, and 20 percent of all infants die before they are a year old.[2]

Although large families are startling in the modern context, it must be stressed that they are the historical norm. Parents in poor countries are not having larger families than previously. On the contrary, it is the shift to low death rates that is the crucial break with the past in the developing world. The important numbers for comparing the rich and poor countries are in table 2-2.

Persistent high fertility in poor nations is the driving force of population growth. Therefore, the crucial task is to understand the fertility behavior of parents: why do they have large families in some circumstances and small families in others? In particular, we need to understand rural parents, for these not only constitute the great majority of parents in poor nations, but they also have larger families than their urban counterparts.

There is a well-developed body of theory attempting to explain the fertility behavior of parents; it has emerged since Notestein proposed the demographic transition theory in 1945.[3] We will examine that theory in this chapter but first will look briefly at the historical evidence on which it is based.

Table 2-2. Demography of rich and poor countries in 1975

	Crude birth rate	Crude death rate	Annual rate of population growth (%)	Population in billions
Developed countries	16.1	9.6	0.7	1.1
Less developed countries (LDCs)	35.9	13.4	2.3	3.0
LDCs excluding China	39.7	15.1	2.5	2.0

Source: U.S. Bureau of the Census, *Current Population Reports,* Special Studies Series P-23, no. 79 (Washington, D.C.: U.S. Bureau of the Census, 1979).

A THEORY OF FERTILITY CONTROL

Background: The Demographic Transition in the Rich Nations

By the end of World War II, the nations of the world were divided into two clearly separate demographic categories. The rich nations had low death rates and low birth rates. Each year about 10 out of every 1,000 people in the population died, a *crude death rate* of 10. Each year there were about 23 births for every 1,000 people in the population, a *crude birth rate* of 23. The difference, about 13 per 1,000 people, gave an annual rate of increase of about 1.3 percent. The poor nations showed a range of death rates that were much higher (generally 20 to 30 per thousand) but were declining precipitously. They had high birth rates—usually greater than 40 and often close to the historical level of 50 per thousand. Very few countries were intermediate; Japan was one of the few.

It was known that fertility in the rich nations had declined over the past three-quarters of a century. The demographic transition theory developed in the 1940s and early 1950s explained that decline as a response to an earlier fall in the death rates and to improved economic conditions. Various changes in social structure, including the effects of urbanization and industrialization, were also thought to be important.

Western Europe was the first region to pass through this transition. The example of Sweden is shown in figure 2-1. Death rates had declined over several centuries and had sunk below 30 per thousand by the late nineteenth century. Lifespan increased correspondingly. For example, in Sweden it increased from thirty-three years in 1778 to fifty years in 1878. Death rates continued to decline to their current level of about 10 per thousand per year. With life expectancy now over seventy years, the death rate is unlikely to decline much further, and indeed will rise to 13 or 14 per 1,000 as the age distribution becomes older (appendix A).

Before 1870, Western Europe's birth rate had also fallen gradually, largely because many women did not marry and those who did married late. Thereafter, fertility *within* marriage also fell (figure 2-2). Fertility decline accelerated during the first part of the twentieth century and crude birth rates were low by the 1930s. In other parts of the developed world, fertility decline did not begin until the twentieth century but proceeded faster than in Western Europe (Chapter 4).

After World War II, fertility increased briefly in many western countries (the "baby boom"), although birth rates were still low in comparison with those in poor countries. The increase was caused in large part by earlier marriage (and therefore in the timing of births relative to the mother's age) and by a reduction in the proportion of women who remained single.[4]

Figure 2-1 Demographic transition in Sweden

Source: Nathan Keyfitz and Wilhelm Flieger, *Population: Facts and Methods of Demography* (San Francisco: W. H. Freeman and Co., 1971), p. 101.

Even though death rates usually fell before birth rates, Europe rarely experienced population growth rates in excess of 1 percent a year. By contrast, most of the developing world is now experiencing growth of more than 2 percent a year.

By the 1950s, as Japan was joining the rich nations and also experiencing rapid fertility decline, there seemed to be a fairly clear correspondence between economic development and reduced fertility. More recent analysis of European records, however, shows that the pattern was not entirely consistent. In some local areas fertility declined *before* death rates did and while the population was still rural, poor, and mainly illiterate. Nonetheless, the correspondence between increased economic welfare and lower fertility remains broadly valid, and while development may not always have been a *necessary* condition, it appears to have been a *sufficient* condition in the demographic history of the rich nations.[5]

I am not suggesting that the European demographic experience neces-

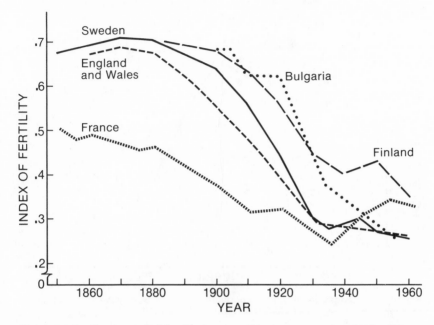

Figure 2-2 Decline in marital fertility in some European countries, 1850–1960

Source: Redrawn from Ansley J. Coale, "The Decline of Fertility in Europe from the French Revolution to World War II," in Samuel J. Behrman, Leslie Corsa, Jr., and Ronald Freedman, eds., *Fertility and Family Planning: A World View* (Ann Arbor: University of Michigan Press, 1969), p. 23.
Note: The index of fertility can range from 0 to a maximum of 1.

sarily provides a reliable guide to the present or future demography of the poor countries. Conditions are now altogether different from those in Europe over the past century or so. The European experience led to the formulation of the demographic transition theory, but the relevance of that idea to the modern poor countries must be judged on the modern evidence.

Variations in Fertility: A Conceptual Framework

Although economic theory attempts to explain the entire range of fertility behavior, we will be concerned here with only a part of that range. Figure 2-3 attempts to summarize the different sorts of variation in fertility that occur. Four types of variation that will *not* concern us are: relatively small variations through time in extremely poor countries; variation among such countries; relatively small variations through time in affluent countries; and variation among such countries.

What we will try to uncover are the mechanisms that move a poor coun-

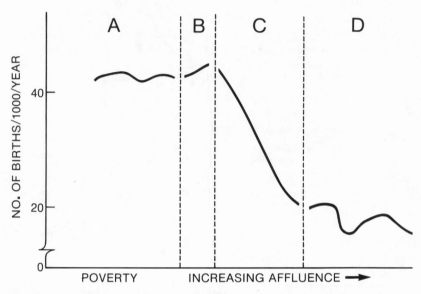

Figure 2-3 Changes in fertility as populations move from poverty to affluence through time

try from stage A in figure 2-3, where the birth rate is generally 40 or more, to stage D, where the birth rate is 20 or less. By choosing an arbitrary "goal" of 20 births per thousand, I do not mean to imply that a nation's population problems are solved once its birth rate reaches that level. Clearly, population growth will then still continue. Nonetheless, the crucial transition appears to be from around 40 to around 20; once this transition has been made, a reversal to very high fertility is unlikely and population increase is much more manageable.

A word of warning is necessary. We can never be certain that any particular explanation of fertility is correct. Well-controlled experiments are generally impossible; many factors vary together and we are forced to select some, ignore others, and to correlate changes in birth rates with changes in our selected variables. We can ask people about what motivates them to have children, but we can never be sure of getting the "real" answers. Motivations are complex, and no single factor is likely to explain all variations in birth rates. However, we can hope to discover the major factors that account for most of the variation in fertility.

Our analysis will be strengthened if we begin with a hypothesis about what drives high birth rates. Such a hypothesis will guide us to select certain variables and ignore others, rather than leaving us merely to rummage through the data until we discover something that "fits." A number of economists have given a good deal of thought to providing an economic theory of fertility. Among them there is general agreement on the broad issues, although there is some disagreement over details.[6] The discussion below largely follows Leibenstein's approach, which is both direct and testable.

The fundamental notion is that family size is largely determined by parents' *motivation,* and that this motivation reflects rational, and broadly economic, decisions (table 2-3). Family size is not seen as an accident, as the expression of religious beliefs, or as a result of the availability of birth control technology, although family planning can certainly affect family size.

The crux of the theory is that parents balance economic benefits against economic costs in deciding whether to have another child, especially a fourth or later child. (The first two or three births do not cause population growth, and our concern is therefore with the extra children that characterize families in the developing nations.) The theory assumes that the benefit/cost ratio for extra children is high for poor families in poor societies and that this motivates poor parents to have large families. It assumes that as circumstances change and the economic welfare of families improves, the balance of costs and benefits also changes; costs come to exceed benefits and parents become motivated against having these extra children. Thus, as the level of economic well-being increases, the rationale and motivation for large families disappear.

The theory assumes three types of benefits:

1. "Consumption benefit." The child is wanted for itself, for the pleasure and emotional satisfaction it brings. This benefit is assumed not to vary with the level of the parents' economic welfare (though, clearly, it may vary with the number of children already in the family).
2. Work and/or income benefits. It may be difficult for those who live in an industrial society to appreciate that in poor countries children

Table 2-3. Factors affecting motivation to have a large family as economic well-being increases

	Motivation of poor parents	Motivation of richer parents
Benefits		
1. Consumption benefit	does not change	
2. Labor and/or income benefit	high	low
3. Security benefit (old age)	high	low
Costs	low	high
Competition from "other consumption"	low	high

can be an important source of labor and income. But from a very
early age children in poor countries, especially in rural areas, carry
out crucial work: gathering firewood, collecting water, moving livestock around the countryside, helping with household chores, and
providing extra labor in the fields, especially at critical periods such
as harvesting.

The labor and income benefits from children increase with their
age and are reaped as long as they are associated with the parents'
household. In extended families this may be well into adulthood.
For example, older children who have left the household and mi-
grated to the city often send home cash.
3. Security benefit. In the absence of a social security system, children
are the main source of security in old age. This security may take the
form of cash or of food and shelter. Recently this idea has been extended to include security against emergencies that occur before old
age.

Some economic benefits are hard to measure and do not fit neatly into
any one category. For example, when extended families are the rule, children establish extensive ties when they marry. These ties can be a source
of additional work and security benefits, but they can also provide a more
general sort of economic benefit that derives from the size of the family.
Caldwell describes this situation in Nigeria where "in rural Yoruba society
it is still taken as one of the immutable facts of existence that [extended]
family numbers, political strength, and affluence are not only interrelated
but are one and the same thing." More generally, he notes that "in traditional societies nearly all parents have social and usually economic gains
which increase almost indefinitely with the size of the family."[7]

Against these benefits must be balanced the costs of raising a child.
There are two types: maintenance costs and "opportunity" costs. In poor
societies food is the major maintenance cost. As economic development
proceeds, work for women becomes available and child rearing then im-
poses an opportunity cost equal to the income the mother could earn doing other work.

The economic motivation for having an extra child is that the benefits
accrued from the child exceed the costs when both are calculated over the
years that the child is attached to the household or is sending help to the
parents. The theory does not claim that parents in poor countries actually
make such detailed calculations explicitly. Indeed, they would be very difficult to make in any straightforward way. First, food and shelter or a few
dollars sent to parents in a year when they are too old to support themselves would need to be weighted in the calculation much more heavily
than the same help given them in their mid-life; such old-age support

might well make the difference between life and death and the benefit would be essentially incalculable.

Secondly, peasants are not western businessmen; their desire to increase production or profits is strongly tempered by the need to avoid catastrophe, which is ever-threatening. They are, in economic jargon, "risk-averse." In the general absence of access to modern means of saving, the peasant can prepare to avert catastrophe mainly by accumulating children. Sometimes this can also be done by accumulating land, but usually this also requires a large amount of family labor. Such risk avoidance is certainly an economic benefit, but for parents facing a highly uncertain future, it is extremely difficult to calculate the likelihood of such risks, or the benefits. In these circumstances, we might expect risk to affect family size through the accumulated experience of the community as embodied in its "folk wisdom." Parental motivation can thus have a deep economic rationality even though parents may not be able to draw up a balance sheet of projected costs and benefits.

It is important to realize that the "level of economic welfare" that influences motivation encompasses more than current income level, though current income obviously is an important aspect of economic well-being. People's motivations and attitudes arise out of their backgrounds, which for the bulk of reproductive parents covers a previous period of twenty to thirty years. Furthermore, it is not mere income but the goods and services income can buy, or those provided in some other way, that constitute economic welfare. So the theory in table 2-3 is concerned not only with current income but with a broadly defined concept of welfare, or economic well-being, averaged over a period of at least a decade.

The theory postulates that changes in the level of well-being change people's behavior. In particular, parents at different socio-economic levels have different *backgrounds, desires,* and *preferences.* These profoundly affect both the likely benefits they can derive from children and how they view expenditures, including those for children. Parents at different levels of economic development thus have very different views of the economic utility of children.

It is easy to see how the value of children changes as families and societies in general become richer. As income rises it is possible to replace child labor by using some labor-saving machinery and by employing seasonal labor. As family income rises the child's contribution is likely to be less significant in the total family income. In addition, the child's income is likely to decline because, as the society becomes richer, it becomes more difficult for the child to gain employment, partly because of the changing types of jobs available and partly because economic development is generally accompanied by compulsory education and by child labor laws. Similarly, the need for children, especially male children, to provide economic security to the parents in old age also declines as the parents' economic welfare increases.

The cost of raising a child will clearly rise with income because the child will share a better house, diet, and general standard of living. The child will attend school rather than work. As development proceeds, women are able to join the labor force but a mother may have to forego income to stay home and care for her child. Within a society undergoing economic development, increasing education generally leads to the individual's receiving more income, and there is pressure to concentrate educational expenditure on fewer children. It is not clear that such costs per child necessarily increase faster than income, though they may well do so. However, even if they merely increase proportionately, the decreasing benefits will ensure that, as income increases, the balance will move toward fewer children.

Perhaps as important as the increasing cost of rearing children is the increasing competition provided by rising consumption standards during development. Economic development provides an increasing flow of new goods and new ways to spend money, which can substitute for expenditures on extra children. Leibenstein has also suggested that the higher the socio-economic status of the parents, the higher the expenditure on "status goods." These goods involve services disproportionately, and their costs rise disproportionately as development proceeds.*

We need to add three more components to make a complete framework for understanding fertility. First, parents desire *surviving* children, not births. Thus, when childhood mortality is lower, fewer births are needed to produce a given number of survivors. Second, Easterlin and others have pointed out that when fertility is depressed for medical reasons, the parent's "demand" for births can exceed the "supply." For example, lowered fertility owing to ill health was common in poor countries before incomes started to increase and is still common in parts of sub-Saharan and West Africa. This is partly caused by disease-induced sterility and by poor parental health, which lowers the chances of conception and of successfully carrying the fetus to term.† Thus, in a poor society increased income

---

*The theory as I have presented it is close to Leibenstein's original ideas, published in 1957. I have chosen to do this for two reasons. First, the theory is being used to predict and not to explain with hindsight, and most of the relevant data on poor countries have been published since 1957. Second, much of the recent refinement adds to the model details that are of interest to the economic theoretician but are not salient to our purposes.

†An alternative or additional explanation of relatively low fertility in parts of Africa is that births are intentionally spaced far apart to increase the chances of child survival. In much of sub-Saharan Africa, this spacing may be accomplished by postnatal sexual abstinence (John C. Caldwell and Pat Caldwell, "The Role of Marital Sexual Abstinence in Determining Fertility: A Study of the Yoruba in Nigeria," *Population Studies* 31 [1977]: 193–213).

and associated better health can be expected initially to *raise* the birth rate. This is the general explanation for segment B in figure 2-3.

Finally, family size is strongly influenced by the age at which parents, especially women, marry. In high-fertility countries family size is smaller where the age at marriage is older, for the obvious reason that the woman is exposed to pregnancy for fewer years. A reasonable estimate is that family size would be reduced by about two children if women married at age twenty rather than at fifteen.[8]

An increase in the age at marriage has been one of the first signs of fertility decline in LDCs and has accounted for roughly 35 to 40 percent of the fertility decline observed there in the period from the early 1960s to around 1975.[9] Two recent and striking examples are in Tunisia, where the average age at marriage rose from nineteen in 1956 to over twenty-three in 1975, and in West Malaysia, where the age rose from nineteen to twenty-two in fifteen years. In Sri Lanka the age in 1975 reached 25.1 years. These ages should be compared with those in high-fertility countries such as Bangladesh (fifteen years), Nepal (fifteen years), and Pakistan (sixteen years), and with the U.S. in 1975 (21.1 years).[10]

Age at first marriage and motivation for family size are affected by economic development in a similar way.[11] Marriage is likely to be postponed as both family and national income increase, as the importance of education (especially women's education) grows, and as opportunity for women's employment increases.

I have presented an almost purely economic theory of fertility. The reader may feel that any theory is lacking that omits cultural aspects such as religion, family structure, degree of openness to other cultures, and so on. I will discuss these cultural aspects later when we compare the theory with the actual evidence. For the present it is worth mentioning two points.

First, the cultural matrix may strongly influence what does and what does not make good economic sense. For example, the benefits to be derived from children probably are greater in an extended family than in a nuclear family because children in the former are expected to help parents and grandparents more than those in the latter. We should not be surprised, therefore, if a family size that makes good economic sense in one society at a given level of economic welfare makes poor economic sense in another society at the *same* level of welfare. However, although the culture helps determine the structure of costs and benefits and thereby influences fertility, the decision to have the extra child remains an economic one.

Second, our aim is to explain the major changes in fertility, not all changes. To a surprising degree, economic factors are able to do this. One reason is that economic changes also bring about cultural changes—for example, the extended family tends to break down in the face of industrialization. Variables regarded primarily as economic, such as income, degree of industrialization, and general level of health or education, therefore carry hidden within them statements about culture. Thus, although discussion of cultural conditions will be omitted here most of the time, it should not be assumed that culture has no influence on fertility. Deeper explanations of economic motivation will generally require a cultural component.

We turn next to examining the evidence. The theory presented here claims, in brief, that the great mass of poverty-stricken peoples of the world have large families because they are poor and *because having a large family is the economically rational decision for poor parents to make*. In the following sections we will first look briefly at the evidence on costs and benefits. Then we will try to discover if people's motivations vary as we have assumed they do, and for the postulated economic reasons—that is, we will try to test directly the assumption of economic rationality. Finally, we will ask if family size and birth rate actually vary as a function of economic welfare in the way the theory predicts.

EVIDENCE ON THE ASSUMPTIONS OF THE THEORY

Costs and Benefits

There are two questions to be asked about the costs and benefits of children: in poor countries do the benefits that poor parents derive from children exceed the costs? Second, do the costs increase relative to the benefits as development proceeds and as the level of economic welfare of families increases?

Most students of poor societies agree that children there are a net economic asset to their parents over the long run. A highly detailed study in Bangladesh has substantiated these ideas.[12] It demonstrated that male children begin to provide labor and/or income at about age six. The value of their production exceeds that of their consumption from the time they are twelve (at the latest); their cumulative production exceeds their cumulative consumption by the time they are fifteen, and it exceeds their own and one sister's cumulative consumption by the time they are twenty-two. By age thirteen, boys are working more than nine hours a day and during almost four of these hours they are either earning wages or are engaged in trading.*

*Eva Mueller has claimed that peasants' perceptions are wrong and that children in peasant societies are, on balance, an economic burden on their parents. Mueller reached this

Turning to our second question, there is no doubt that the costs of raising children increasingly outweigh the benefits as the level of economic welfare increases. Parents in developed countries gain almost no economic benefits from their children and the costs of rearing them are very high. In the United States in 1977 the direct maintenance cost of raising a child to age eighteen ranged from $31,675 to $58,255. In 1975 it cost an additional $18,416, on the average, to send the child through four years of college. This will have increased to about $50,000 by the 1990s. There is also an opportunity cost represented by income lost during child rearing. If the mother rears the child, the lost earnings are $26,562 to $54,347 at 1977 pay rates.[13]

Mellor shows, for Indian villages, how the value of child labor and income is lower, and the costs of child rearing are greater for parents with higher incomes. The children of poor parents are needed at home for work and, especially at harvesting time, they are out earning income. The fraction of these children that goes to school is therefore very small. In addition, the labor they do requires no formal education. By contrast, the children of richer parents are not needed to work on the farm or to earn outside income, and a high proportion attends school, which costs money.

However, as rural development proceeded in the study areas, and average income increased, so too did the types of employment that were available. In particular, there was an increased demand for educated labor. But in order to get such employment, the costs of education had to be borne, and these were quite sizeable. So the farmer, as he and his community rose from poverty, had to begin to spend more on raising each child in order to participate in development, and at the same time lost the child's labor and income. It is worth noting as an aside that these costs were sometimes so high that the peasants' children were excluded from the development process:

conclusion by assigning to each age both costs ("consumption") and benefits ("production") and then calculating that, over the parents' married life, children's consumption exceeded their production. See "The Economic Value of Children in Peasant Agriculture," in Ronald G. Ridker, ed., *Population and Development: The Search for Selective Interventions* (Baltimore: Johns Hopkins University Press, 1976).

There are quite serious problems with this analysis. It does not tackle the problem of risk avoidance; it assumes that once children marry, they no longer help their parents; it takes no account of those difficult-to-measure indirect effects that stem from increasing the size of the extended family, which we noted above. Finally, the basic data are inadequate in several ways (see John C. Caldwell, "The Economic Rationality of High Fertility," *Population Studies* 31 [1977]:9). The labor that was measured greatly underestimates the complexity of the peasant economy (for example, it excluded time spent in trading); estimates of production and consumption were very indirect, and they were not made in a single society but derived from dispersed and fragmentary data from different countries. Cain's study in Bangladesh overcame these difficulties by directly observing villagers producing and consuming (see note 12).

In the outlying areas, in order to obtain economic rewards, further schooling must follow primary education. For additional education, a large proportion of rural people would have to move their children to an urban area. In 1971, according to Shortlidge's survey in Badaun district, the total of direct and indirect costs to send a child to primary school was Rs. 168 per year, or approximately three-quarters of the average landless laborer's annual per capita income; for attending middle school, the total cost rose to Rs. 343—more than the average laborer's annual income.[14]

In summary, large families are an economic advantage to poor parents in poor countries. This advantage disappears as economic welfare increases.

Parental Motivation

Before asking if parents are motivated by these cost/benefit considerations, we need to know if they make *any* decisions about procreation or if it is purely accidental. There can be no rationality without knowledge, and it has often been claimed that people in poor countries are breeding themselves into ever greater poverty out of sheer ignorance of even the reproductive functions.

This notion is false. The connection between sexual intercourse and pregnancy is understood almost universally. Africa is the touchstone in these matters: it is the poorest, least developed, and most undereducated region in the world, yet Morgan and Ohadike claim that all tropical Africans know that abstinence from sexual relations will prevent conception, nearly all know that withdrawal before ejaculation greatly reduces the chances of conception, and nearly all know about abortion. Caldwell and Caldwell show that, in Africa south of the Sahara, births are spaced about four years apart on average, to increase the health of the child, and that this is done mainly, and consciously, through long periods of sexual abstinence.[15]

There is no doubt that parents all over the world take the economic costs and benefits of children into account in making decisions about family size. Studies in poor countries consistently show that economic considerations (both expected benefits and expected costs) are of primary importance in parental decisions about family size. Attitudes toward restricted fertility (including family planning) become more favorable as income and education increase. In addition, in poor areas with high childhood mortality, fear of that mortality is a major cause of opposition to family planning. Simon has presented and summarized the extensive evidence for economically rational parental behavior, and a readily available and readable summary of studies on parental motivation has been published by the Population Reference Bureau.[16] In addition, Caldwell has written:

Over two decades in Asia and Africa...I have not met any lower level of rationality in explaining behavior than I have in most modern industrialized countries. Each society has some people who are more capricious or less careful than others, but the proportion is higher in the more affluent industrial ones where some risk can be afforded. Cultural and linguistic barriers may at first cause a peasant or an urban shanty town dweller to give the impression that he is less rational or more illogical than the *Western* intruder, but when these barriers are broken it turns out that this is not the case. Peasants are notoriously hardheaded everywhere. Their social aspirations are often different, but they are understandable and are not masochistically based on supernatural injunctions. Within these aspirations, their economic behavior is absolutely rational...They usually do not even exhibit high fertility at personal economic cost.[17]

Even where the parents' stated object is to have as many children as possible ("as many as God sends"), the children's economic value as labor—to allow more land to be rented or worked, and as a source of income and future security—is explicitly stated as the rationale.[18]

Perhaps the nicest piece of evidence about motivation comes from Freedman's studies in Japan on the importance of children in providing security for old age.[19] Between 1950 and 1961 the Japanese economy expanded very rapidly and changed the country's status to that of a developed nation. Every two years during this period the Mainichi press asked a representative cross-section of the population: "Do you expect to depend on your children in your old age?" In 1950, more than half (55 percent) answered "definitely yes." This proportion declined steadily as economic welfare improved dramatically over the next decade, and in 1961 reached only 27 percent. Over the same period the birth rate fell from 28 to 17.

In a study in Taiwan, where birth rates have been declining rapidly as income has grown, Mueller showed that over three-fourths of the husbands interviewed were concerned about the economic disadvantages of a large family and commented on the economic advantages of a small one. She also showed that the amount of economic benefit expected from the children was smaller where the husband and wife's education and family income were greater. Similarly, at higher levels of education and "consumption aspirations," parents were more sensitive to the large educational cost of raising children. Hermalin noted that in Taiwan, wives who expect both to live with and get financial assistance from their sons desire larger families than those who do not expect such help.[20]

Turning to Africa, in Nigeria the very small group of parents who use modern contraceptive techniques to restrict family size put great stress on the cost of raising children, especially educating them.[21] These parents, who are educated and highly "upwardly mobile," also expect to receive no financial gain from their children.

An intensive and thorough analysis of motivation done by the East-

West Population Institute examined parental motivation in six countries. In each country the investigators interviewed large numbers of young parents from the urban middle class, the urban poor, and the rural (i.e., poor) population. Four of the areas already had moderate-to-low birth rates (Hawaii, Japan, Korea, and Taiwan), while Thailand and the Philippines still had high birth rates.

Tables 2-4, 2-5, and 2-6 exemplify the sorts of results obtained during the study. Notice how the economic motivation for children consistently declines from the poorest to the richer countries (although U.S. Filipinos are somewhat exceptional).

The study showed that parents in different socio-economic classes have different motivations, although they all share the view that children are a source of happiness and they all take costs into account. However, urban middle class parents in the richer populations stress the emotional benefits of having children and give almost no weight to economic benefits (table 2-6), whereas they rate financial costs, especially opportunity costs, as the severest disadvantage. As we move from the urban middle class through the urban lower classes to the rural parents in the poorer countries, the economic benefits of children, especially their contribution to old-age security, become primary, and opportunity costs become unimportant.

Parents in the two poorest countries showed the greatest concern about childhood mortality, and this concern was greatest in the two poorer classes. In every country at least 70 percent of rural parents expected some financial help from their children in old age (table 2-5), and in the two poorest nations economic benefits, including old-age security, ranked first in the rural population (table 2-6).

In summary, formal surveys and the general experience of scholars in

Table 2-4. Percentage of Filipino parents in three socio-economic classes who expect help from their children

	Rural poor	Urban poor	Urban middle class
Children very important for security in old age	80	56	47
Expect to rely on children in old age	89	85	71
Expect children to provide income	87	64	58
Expect household/farm help from children	50	39	36
Percentage who finished high school	26	54	82
Income/month (₱)	270	310	650

Source: Rodolfo A. Bulatao, *The Value of Children, A Cross-National Study: Vol. 2, Philippines* (Honolulu: East-West Population Institute, East-West Center, 1975), pp. 16, 109, 110.
Note: This study was done from 1972 to 1973.

the field confirm that parents consider the economic costs and benefits in arriving at a desired family size. Further, the actual and perceived ratio of benefits to costs declines as we move from the poorest rural populations to the richest urban populations. Childhood deaths in poor families also influence the desire for large numbers of births. Thus, as far as we can find out by exploring stated attitudes and actual costs and benefits, the assumptions of the theory are confirmed.

Table 2-5. Percentage of parents who expect to rely upon their children for financial support in old age

| | | Socio-economic class | |
	Rural	Urban lower class	Urban middle class
Thailand	90	83	26
Philippines	89	82	73
Taiwan	92	80	47
Korea	72	62	25
Japan	73	31	29
U.S. (Hawaii)			
Filipinos	80	62	—
Japanese	—	25	19
Caucasians	—	23	2

Source: Fred Arnold et al., *The Value of Children, A Cross-National Study, Vol. 1, Introduction and Comparative Analysis* (Honolulu: East-West Population Institute, East-West Center, 1975), p. 42.
Note: This study was carried out in the early 1970s. The countries are listed from poorest (Thailand) to richest (United States).

Table 2-6. Percentage of parents who rank economic benefits, including security in old age, as major advantage of children

| | | Socio-economic class[a] | |
	Rural	Urban lower class	Urban middle class
Thailand	60 (4.2)	66 (5.6)	6 (13.8)
Philippines	60 (7.0)	46 (9.8)	30 (12.6)
Taiwan	36 (4.7)	9 (6.0)	3 (12.2)
South Korea	21 (6.2)	11 (8.0)	3 (15.4)
Japan	11 (10.6)	3 (11.4)	2 (12.3)
U.S. (Hawaii)			
Filipinos	63 (7.0)	15 (10.7)	—
Japanese	—	3 (12.3)	1 (13.6)
Caucasian	—	2 (11.7)	2 (13.9)

Source: Arnold, et al., *The Value of Children* vol. 1, pp. 28, 29, 50.
Note: This study was carried out in the early 1970s.
[a]Years of education in parentheses.

EVIDENCE ON PREDICTIONS OF THE THEORY

The theory set forth here predicts that family size will decline as the economic welfare of the family increases, although we expect a lag between increased welfare and the parent's perception that conditions have really improved. On a larger scale, the theory predicts that the birth rate of the nation will decline as national economic development occurs.

Perhaps the best evidence would be a study in detail of the stated motivations and actual fertility behavior of large numbers of parents in different countries as they become increasingly developed. This is exceedingly difficult to obtain, but there are several alternatives. First, we can look at fertility differences between rich and poor countries, on the assumption that the economic differences have caused the fertility differences. Second, we can *look at differences among poor countries that are now at different points along the transition to low fertility,* to see if these differences are correlated with differences in socio-economic conditions. Third, we can look *within* poor countries at families with differing levels of economic welfare, to see if those that are better off have lower fertility, as the theory predicts. Our assumption is that if increases in economic welfare have lowered fertility for richer families or richer countries, they will do the same in the future for those who are now poor. We thus hope that these cross-sectional analyses will tell us about future fertility behavior.

Our main interest is in a decrease in fertility, as in section C of figure 2-3, but we will also look briefly at the tendency for fertility in some very poor countries to increase at the onset of economic development (section B of figure 2-3).

An impressive and varied array of evidence that has become available since the 1950s is overwhelmingly in support of the theory. In bringing order to these results I will first deal with differences in national birth rates, particularly among the poor nations, and the relationship between these differences and broad measures of the level of economic development in each nation. Then I will deal with variation in fertility in relation to particular aspects of economic welfare, both among poor countries and among socio-economic classes within poor countries.

Differences among Countries and States

The simplest indicator of a nation's level of economic development is its annual per capita income. Figure 2-4 presents data for 116 countries and shows that the birth rate in 1970 was 40 or more in almost all of the poorest nations, less than 25 in almost all of the richest nations, and decreased

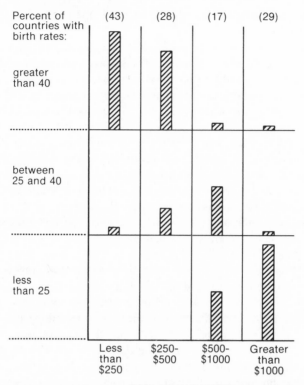

Figure 2-4 Declines in birth rate as per capita income increases

Source: Dudley Kirk, "A New Demographic Transition?" in National Academy of Sciences, *Rapid Population Growth: Consequences and Policy Implications* (Baltimore: Johns Hopkins University Press, 1971).

Note: Each column is the percentage of countries in a given income class with birth rates of greater than 40, between 25 and 40, or fewer than 25 births per thousand per year. The number of countries in each income class is shown above the columns.

to less than 40 somewhere between $250 and $500 annual income per head. Yotopoulos has made a similar point and has also demonstrated that the total fertility rate (see appendix A) falls with increasing per capita income.[22]

The overall trend of fertility with income is clear. However, we will always get a negative correlation between fertility and income, or some other indicator of development, if we include the rich nations, since they all have low fertility. So a more powerful test of our theory is to compare fertility and income among only the developing nations. Even when we restrict the analysis in this way we still find that, on a global scale, birth rate is strongly and negatively correlated with average per capita income (figure 2-5).[23]

Yotopoulos has subdivided the LDCs by geographic region and has also shown that within each region, fertility (measured by total fertility rate) decreases as average per capita income increases.[24] However, the correlation between birth rates and average income is by no means perfect, as figure 2-5 illustrates. In fact, only about half of the variability in birth rates among poor countries is "explained" by differences in average income (appendix B elucidates the idea of "explaining" a fraction of variability). Average income is a relatively poor predictor of birth rates because it fails to measure many aspects of economic welfare and does not take account of the *distribution* of welfare (Chapter 3). The remainder of this chapter explores additional aspects of economic welfare.

We need a broader and more sophisticated measure of the general level of economic welfare than is provided by per capita income. Such a measure has been developed by Oechsli and Kirk. Their "index of development" combines ten variables that measure GDP (gross domestic product), degree of urbanization and industrialization, general level of education and health care, and the development of communication channels (newspapers, telephones). The index is affected by how even the distribution of development is across the population. For example, it measures the proportion of the population that is literate and the proportion in primary and secondary schools.[25]*

Kirk had shown earlier that we can expect regional differences in the degree to which particular variables are important.[26] For example, the income level needed for declining birth rates seems to be higher in Latin America than in Asia. He therefore restricted his analysis to twenty-five Latin American and Caribbean countries, which is also a region for which the data are generally available. Each country can be assigned to a point on the index scale, measuring the level of development, and its birth and death rates are then plotted against this level of development (figure 2-6). The development index is calculated for roughly eight years earlier than

---

*The ten socio-economic variables used in this study were: literacy (%); primary school enrollment (%); secondary school enrollment (%); life expectancy at birth; number of hospital beds per 1,000 population; gross domestic product per capita; male labor force not in agriculture (%); percentage of population urban; newspaper circulation per 1,000 population; number of telephones per 1,000 population. Notice that some of these variables are socioeconomic, rather than purely economic. Clearly, government decisions about how much to spend on health and education and whether to emphasize widespread literacy rather than higher education are social and political as well as economic decisions. Child labor laws, discussed earlier, are another example of important socio-economic conditions. Thus, although the theory is fundamentally an economic one, based on parental decisions at various levels of economic welfare, social and political factors help determine the level of economic well-being experienced by the family.

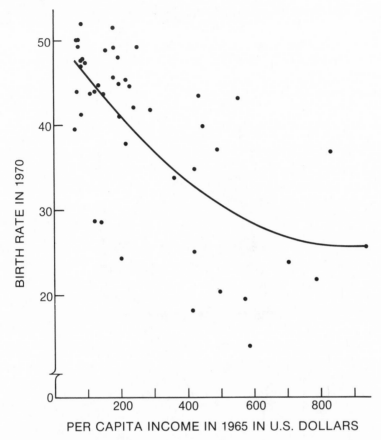

Figure 2-5 Birth rate compared to per capita income in developing countries

Source: appendix B
Note: The curve is explained in appendix B.

the birth rate, to allow for the expected time lag between increasing welfare and declining birth rate.

Birth rates clearly decline as the level of economic development increases; the curve drawn through the birth rates "explains" (in a statistical sense, see appendix B) about nine-tenths of the variability in birth rates among these different nations. Furthermore, with the exception of the three countries where birth rates were already around 20 per thousand, all countries with a positive development index showed declines in their birth rate of a half-point or more per year during the 1960s.

Two Latin American countries show clearly how fertility in different states within a country is determined by their level of economic develop-

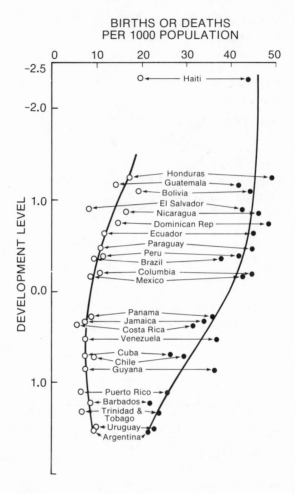

BIRTHS OR DEATHS
PER 1000 POPULATION

Figure 2-6 Fertility and development in Latin America and the Caribbean

Source: Redrawn from F. W. Oechsli and D. Kirk, "Modernization and the Demographic Transition in Latin America and the Caribbean," *Economic Development and Cultural Change* 23 (1975): 412.

Note: The 1970 birth rates (•) and death rates (o) are plotted against the level of economic development in 1962 for twenty-five countries.

ment. First, the range of birth rates in different regions of Brazil is almost as great as the range that occurs between the poorest and the richest countries on the Latin American continent. The states in the least developed region of Brazil (the northeast) have birth rates of 40 to 46; the two regions of intermediate development have birth rates between 30 and 40; finally, the two most highly developed regions (including Rio de Janeiro and São Paulo) have birth rates between 20 and 30.[27]

Venezuela also illustrates this relationship nicely, as Edmonston and Oechsli show.[28] They analyze changes in fertility, state by state, between 1950 and 1971, as a function of the percentage of literacy among people over ten years of age. (This was the only one of the ten indicators of development used by Oechsli and Kirk that was available for all states. As we will see later, educational level is the most important and reliable economic indicator of fertility.)

The percentage of literacy increased in every Venezuelan state between 1950 and 1961. In this period fertility also increased, as it did in most of Latin America as the health and survival of parents increased.[29] However, increases in fertility were smaller in the most developed states, so that by 1961 the most literate states tended to have the lowest fertility, which was negatively correlated with the percentage of literacy. From 1961 to 1971 literacy again increased in all states, but each state now showed a decrease in fertility. The greatest reductions in fertility were in the most literate states, so that by 1971 the negative correlation between fertility and literacy had become much stronger (figure 2-7).

The studies by Kirk and his co-workers at Stanford (cited above) have also shown that the time lag between the onset of sustained development and the beginning of a sustained fertility decline seems to be quite short— on the order of a decade.[30]

Our analysis so far can be summarized by saying that variation in fertility among countries and states is closely correlated with their general level of economic welfare, especially when welfare is measured about a decade earlier than fertility.

Fertility and Various Aspects of Economic Welfare

We turn now to explore those aspects of economic welfare that seem to be most important in causing lowered fertility. In doing so, we can make further tests of the theory. We will look mainly at comparisons of different groups within countries, but also at comparisons among countries.*

*The discussion of the fertility of parents in different socio-economic classes applies to countries that have begun to experience economic development and, consequently, some decline in fertility in at least some socio-economic classes. By contrast, historical differences in fertility have been observed between parents in different socio-economic classes in "pre-transition" societies, and some of these still persist in societies where there has been negligible improvement in the standard of living. Naturally, good data on this subject are hard to find, since demographers have not been measuring fertility for most of history.

In such pretransition societies we might expect greater fertility in the higher socio-economic classes, mainly because the poorest parents in the society would have difficulty producing as many children as they desired because of poor parental health. This seems to have been the case, for example, in rural China before 1930 (G. W. Barclay et al., "A Reassessment of the Demography of Traditional Rural China," *Population Index* 42 [1976]: 606–35).

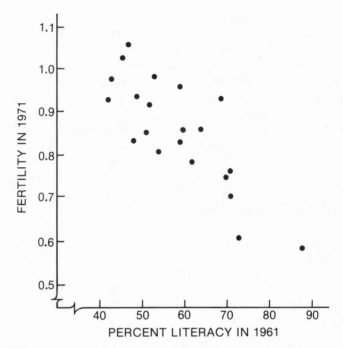

Figure 2-7 Fertility in 1971 compared to percentage of literacy in 1961 in the states of Venezuela

Source: Barry Edmonston and Frank W. Oeschsli, "Fertility Decline and Socioeconomic Change in Venezuela," *Journal of Interamerican Studies and World Affairs* 19 (1977): 385, 386.
Note: Fertility is measured by the ratio of children aged 0–4 to women aged 15–44 in each state.

There, peasants had relatively modest fertility (completed family size about 5.5) in spite of early marriage. The same situation persists today in rural West Africa. See John C. Caldwell et al., eds., *Population Growth and Socioeconomic Change in West Africa* (New York: Columbia University Press, 1975).

An alternative explanation for similar data, which show that families with more land had more children in some pretransition rural societies, is that larger families were able to work more land. However, the data in these studies are not always reliable.

There is now one example in which the data do seem to be reliable and the causes have been explained. See Terence H. Hull and Valerie J. Hull, "The Relation of Economic Class and Fertility: An Analysis of Some Indonesian Data," *Population Studies* 31 (1977): 43–58. In Java the level of the mother's formal education is a good indicator of her economic status. Two studies showed that the number of births to women of a given age around 1970 *increased* with the level of primary education (it decreased again for the small number of women who had gone to secondary school). The increase was negligible for young women but quite marked for older women. It must be stressed that these differences were small (about one child per family), occurred in a high-fertility society (five to six children per family), and most of the children were born before the society underwent economic development.

The authors show that the differences are caused by three main factors: (1) Marriages in the poorest families are much more frequently disrupted, mainly by divorce. Women in this group thus spend almost a quarter of their reproductive lives outside of marriage, where almost no children are ever born. (2) Poor diet and disease reduce the fecundity of the poorer women. (3) Poor women pay more attention to traditional strictures against sexual intercourse following the birth of a child.

When many socio-economic variables are analyzed both separately and together, certain types are consistently shown to be closely linked with fertility. These are various measures of education (especially women's education), health, and some aspects of the work force.[31] From our point of view, levels of health and education are highly appropriate measures because they reflect the general level of economic well-being experienced over the past ten or twenty years. For parents in the midst of creating their families, this is the period when attitudes about fertility will have been formed. These measures are therefore actually preferable to current income.

On the other hand, treating the various socio-economic measures separately attributes to the components of development and welfare a discreteness that does not exist. As development proceeds, changes in such variables as education, income, urbanization, job structure, population distribution, and health care all occur together. These variables are usually highly correlated with one another, since people with more money are also likely to live in the city, have better health and education, and so on. This correlation among variables can be seen very nicely in the tiny group of parents in Ibadan, Nigeria, who are having small families in the midst of high-fertility parents.[32] This innovative behavior was much more likely if the wife had a secondary education and the husband and wife both had a nonmanual occupation. In turn, the wife was 150 times more likely to have a nonmanual job if she had a secondary education and more likely to have such an education if her father had a nonmanual job.

Various statistical devices exist for trying to separate the effects of different variables upon fertility (see, for example, appendix B). However, there is really no technique that will definitively assign in a truly causal way a specific amount of change in fertility to a particular change in any one variable.

Let us now look at these variables one by one.

Current Income Level

As we have seen, variation in average income level explains much of the variation in fertility among countries, although the correlation is by no means perfect (figure 2-5). Within each poor country, there is also a huge range in incomes, with some rich urban groups having large incomes even by western standards. We would expect to find a negative correlation between income and fertility within poor countries. Table 2-7 shows one out of many examples of this relationship, which occurs wherever it has been looked for.*

---

*Increasing income is associated with a decrease in fertility over the long run through its influence on the outlook, tastes, and preferences of parents. Simply put, family size de-

We turn now to those variables that better reflect the level of long-term economic well-being. These variables are preferable to income for another reason: when they are used *first* to explain fertility, and the effect of income is then *added* to the analysis, income alone has little or no additional effect. However, when income is used first and then the other variables are added, they do have additional explanatory power. In other words, the main effects of income upon parental behavior occur through other variables, such as education.

Education

The best single variable for explaining variation in fertility is level of education. It is easy to see why this should be so. A parent aged twenty-five or thirty who has had, say, twelve or more years of education, has been raised in a family that was sufficiently well off to send him or her to school over that extended period. This higher level of education implies a greater ability to earn now and in the future, and so implies an enhanced sense of economic well-being now, and of present and future security. In turn, such a parent is more aware of the economic advantages of an extended educa-

Table 2-7. Relationship between income and fertility in Santiago, Chile (1959)

Income (pesos)	Number of children born to women aged 35–40
Less than 9,000	5.9
9,000–14,999	3.7
15,000–20,999	3.0
21,000–26,999	2.6
27,000–39,999	2.2
40,000 and over	2.4

Source: Leon Tabah, "A Study of Fertility in Santiago, Chile," *Marriage and Family Living* 25 (1963): 22.

creases with socio-economic status. The exceptions are the very poorest families, where demand for children remains high and increased income improves health, and the very richest families, which sometimes have marginally higher fertility than the next richest class. There is evidence that the immediate *short-term* effect of an increase in income may be to cause a small increase in fertility. See Julian L. Simon, *The Effects of Income on Fertility* (Chapel Hill, N.C.: Carolina Population Center, 1974), and Julian L. Simon, *The Economics of Population Growth* (Princeton, N.J.: Princeton University Press, 1977). For example, parents marry and tend to have babies at high points of the business cycle and to postpone marriage and births at the low points. This is really a matter of the timing of births and does not affect average fertility. However, *within* a socio-economic class an increase in income may enable parents to afford the number of children they desire, thus causing a real, if small, increase in fertility. The desired number of children, however, does not increase with such increases in income. The evidence for this positive short-run effect is stronger in rich than in poor countries.

tion for his or her own children, and this is likely to motivate the parent to have fewer children so that each can be educated. The direct effect of schooling upon tastes, preferences, consumption patterns, attitudes, and openness to new ideas is also likely to redirect motivation toward a smaller family. If the wife's education has led to employment, then these motives will have even greater force because the mother would lose income while raising the child. As a corollary, illiteracy is an adjunct of poverty.[33]

At the national scale, a high average level of education implies that the nation is sufficiently wealthy to have made the necessary investments in a pervasive educational system, or, if the country is poor, that the government has subsidized education and has committed resources to the social goal of improving the welfare of its people. In the latter case we would expect that other broad social goals are also being pursued, thus raising the general welfare of the population. This indeed is what we find (Chapter 3).

The evidence that education is linked to lowered birth rates in poor countries is ubiquitous and powerful; indeed, education is frequently used by itself as a good predictor of fertility when additional and more complex measures of development and economic welfare are not available. The great effect of education on fertility is obvious both within countries and when different poor countries are compared. A sample of the within-country data is presented in table 2-8. In many poor countries, while the least educated groups have close to the socially maximum possible number of children, the most educated group has close to replacement family size (about two children).

Not only is education in general the most important single variable affecting fertility, *the educational level of females is the strongest and most consistent predictor of fertility.* A wide range of studies from both rich and poor countries shows that the wife's educational level is a better predictor of fertility than is the husband's, and Srikantan's highly detailed studies of family planning show that women's education strongly determines their demand for family planning services. The paramount importance of female education has been reaffirmed by the recent World Fertility Survey.[34]

More education for women can be expected to reduce fertility by increasing the age at marriage, modernizing the woman's outlook and so making her more likely to accept and use family planning, raising the aspirations she has for her children (and so adding to the cost of rearing them), increasing the chances of survival of her previous children, and increasing her opportunities for employment. Unfortunately, the education of women world-wide continues to lag behind that of men: in 1970, 40 percent of adult women were illiterate, compared with 25 percent of adult men.[35]

Although family size generally declines as the level of the parents' education increases within a country or particular area, there are of course differences in the overall level of fertility from place to place. For example, Edmonston and McGinnis show that as the educational level of parents goes from zero to college level, completed family size changes from 6.1 to 3.6 (Bogota), 5.5 to 3.0 (Mexico City), and 4.9 to 2.8 (Rio de Janeiro). However, the average fertility of different places also varies with their average educational level. Edmonston and Oechsli show how the educational level of the different states of Venezuela is a powerful predictor of their differing fertility rates (figure 2-7). On a continental and even global scale, the educational level of the population has consistently been shown

Table 2-8. Fertility and education

	Level of Education				
Country and group	None	Some primary	Primary complete	Some secondary	Secondary complete	University
A. Number of births to women in various educational categories in developing countries						
San Juan, Puerto Rico, 1960						
Married women aged 35-44						
All women	5.8	5.6	4.5	3.3	2.4	2.3
Economically active women	4.6	4.9	4.0	2.9	1.9	2.0
Economically inactive women	6.0	5.7	4.6	3.4	2.6	2.7
Cauqenes, Chile, 1960						
Married women	4.9	3.4	1.3	1.2	1.7	—
India, 1961						
Women over age 47	6.7	6.9	6.6	5.0	4.6	2.1
Sri Lanka, 1971						
Married women aged 40-44	6.0	5.7[a]		5.1	3.6	3.1
Thailand, 1960						
Married women	4.4	4.1[a]		3.3[a]		2.3
B. Fertility rate for						
Taichung, Taiwan, 1962						
Women aged 35-39	5.7	5.2	5.3	4.5	3.6	—
Ghana, 1960						
Total fertility rate	6.2	6.4[a]		2.9[a]		4.1
Completed fertility	6.2	5.5[a]		2.1[a]		0.4

Sources: Anne D. Williams, *Effects of Economic Development on Fertility: Review and Evaluation of the Literature* (Washington, D.C. and Santa Barbara, Calif.: General Electric Co.-Tempo, 1974), GE74TMP-32, pp. 18, 20; William Rich, *Smaller Families Through Social and Economic Progress,* (Washington, D.C.: Overseas Development Council, 1973), Monograph no. 7, p. 11; United Nations, Department of Economic and Social Affairs, *World Population Trends and Policies: 1977 Monitoring Report,* vol. 1, (ST/ESA/SER.A/62) 1979, p. 220; Ronald Freedman, John Y. Takeshita, and T. H. Sun, "Fertility and Family Planning in Taiwan: A Case Study of the Demographic Transition," *American Journal of Sociology* 70 (1964): 23; S. K. Gaisie, "Population Growth and its Components," in John C. Caldwell, et al., eds., *Population Growth and Socioeconomic Change in West Africa* (New York: Columbia University Press, 1975), p. 343.

[a]Breakdown not available. Numbers reflect all women who attended primary or secondary school, whether they finished or not.

to have a strong effect on fertility. This was shown for Latin America and the Caribbean by Beaver and by Oechsli and Kirk. In analyses and summaries of previous work, Williams and Simon confirm that educational level explains much of the differences in fertility among countries.[36]

There are exceptions to the general correlation between more education and lower fertility. These exceptions fit the pattern we would expect. In very poor societies, the introduction of a few years of elementary education may have no effect on fertility, or may even increase it. This effect is analogous to those caused by increases in general economic well-being, which we expect to lead to higher fertility in the poorest countries (segment B in figure 2-3). In Nigeria, for example, a few years of schooling is associated with an increase in parental health and the reduction of disease-caused sterility.[37]

Finally, increases in the education received by children are associated with reductions in the number of subsequent births. This is reflected generally in negative correlations between the current percentages of school enrollment and fertility.[38]

Female and Child Employment

Working women in poor societies have fewer children than do nonworking women. Since working women tend to be better educated, their lower fertility can be explained in part by their higher educational level. However, employment has an additional suppressive effect on family size beyond that attributable to education, although the effect is not as strong as that of education.[39] The additional effect is nicely illustrated in table 2-8 by data from Puerto Rico.

Presumably female employment reduces family size by making it more costly for the mother to take time off to rear children. In addition, employment generally enhances a woman's status and sense of self-worth and provides an alternative role to motherhood. There is evidence from China, Kerala (in India), and Sri Lanka that an increase in the social status of women reduces fertility (see Chapter 3). Women in new roles become eager to control their fertility and are able to do so because they play a strong role in making decisions in the family.[40]

The effect of employment in "modern" jobs is quite clear. There is, however, some doubt about the effect of female employment in agriculture or in "cottage industry" in rural society. The answer probably is that any type of employment will tend to reduce fertility, provided the women cannot simultaneously do the work and look after children, and provided the work brings improved status. Work in rural societies, including work in agriculture, can certainly create a separation of roles and can reduce fertility, and China provides an excellent example of women gaining in status through rural employment.[41]

By contrast with working women, and precisely as our theory would predict, working children are associated with *increased* fertility in all studies. Where children are economically productive, parents have large families.[42]

Childhood Mortality

Numerous studies have shown that in poor countries fertility declines with improvement in various indicators of health: life expectancy, number of hospital beds or medical personnel per person, infant or child survival.[43] The last of these is especially important, since childhood and infant mortality rates are staggeringly high in some parts of the world. Among the poor in poor countries it is common for at least 15 percent of infants to die in their first year. In West Africa, for example, more than 30 percent of children die before they are five years old, while in northern Nigeria about half the children born do not survive to adulthood.[44]

Fertililty studies have consistently demonstrated that couples give birth to fewer children when fewer of their children die. When a broad range of countries is compared, fertility is found to be lower where the childhood death rate is lower, both when only developing countries are considered and when the entire range of countries is examined. Birdsall noted that there is no country with a high infant mortality rate (over 150 per 1,000) and a low birth rate (less than 30 per 1,000).[45]

Although there is generally a lag between decrease in childhood mortality and a decrease in fertility, that lag is quite short. Beaver's analysis of twenty-four Latin American and Caribbean countries, over a twenty-year period, showed that childhood mortality was strongly correlated with fertility levels ten years later.[46] In Puerto Rico fertility is most highly correlated with the death rate of the previous one to four years.

The World Health Organization carried out a study of the relationship between infant mortality and birth rate for fifty-three countries in Asia, Africa, and Latin America, in all the five-year periods between 1945 and 1970.[47] The study found that the faster the postwar infant mortality rate fell, the shorter was the time lag between the decrease in infant mortality and the onset of fertility decline—in fact, the correlation was almost perfect. The average time lag was again about a decade.

A reduction in childhood mortality can reduce the number of births in two ways. First, when an infant does survive in a poor country, the mother usually breast-feeds it. The chances of conception are then less, both because of the physiological effects of lactation and also because there are sometimes cultural constraints on intercourse during lactation. Furthermore, new pregnancies may be avoided for some time to allow the mother to focus on the present child's health.[48]

The second probable effect is through motivation. Parents may feel less need to maximize the number of births when they know their children are likely to survive. Attitude surveys in poor countries regularly show that one major reason for having large families, and for resisting family planning services, is fear of childhood deaths. Srikantan has shown that higher infant mortality is associated with lower demand for family planning. Parents' motivation is affected not only by the deaths of their own children but also by childhood deaths in their community.[49] The World Health Organization studies show that both the actual death of a child and the fear of childhood deaths appear to increase the subsequent fertility of couples, regardless of their income or actual family size. Although it is clear in principle how this second motivational mechanism can reduce fertility, and although interviews confirm that motivations are affected, it is not possible to disentangle statistically the biological and motivational effects that infant and childhood mortality have upon fertility.

Although lower infant mortality leads to a lower birth rate, it can lead to an *increase* in the final number of surviving children and hence in the rate of population growth. There are two forces that operate when childhood mortality is reduced: on the one hand a higher proportion of children survives to become adults, but on the other hand these same improvements lower the subsequent number of births. It is therefore not immediately clear whether the population grows faster or more slowly when a higher fraction of children survive. In fact, the result is likely to depend on the general level of welfare in the population.

In the very poorest of the poor countries, increased child survivorship seems to lead to a higher total number of surviving children: the death rate is lowered more than the birth rate is lowered. This is because poor parents desire more surviving children than they are able to have when childhood mortality is high and deaths reduce the size of the completed family. The "demand" for children exceeds the "supply," both because the demand is high and because, through poor health, the supply is low. In these countries, improved childhood survival can thus be expected to lead to a temporary increase in the growth rate of the population (figure 2-3, segment B).

By contrast, in developing countries that are not extremely poor, a reduction in the fraction of children who die will both directly reduce the number of births (through its effects on lactation) and indirectly reduce the total number of surviving children (through its effects on motivation). Schultz showed this nicely by analyzing differences among several hundred small regions in Taiwan.[50] He showed that as one moved from areas of high to low childhood death rate, the birth rate (three years later) also declined, and it declined *faster* than did the death rate, so that as the childhood death rate became lower, the completed family size also decreased.

In general, then, we can expect the population to grow faster when infant and childhood deaths are reduced in the initial stages of development, as indeed it has done historically. Analyses by Chenery and Syrquin suggest that as a general rule, the reduction in birth rate caused by development exceeds the reduction in death rate in countries where the average 1970 gross national product (GNP) per capita was $200 or more.[51]

In summary, lower childhood mortality is consistently associated with lowered birth rates. We can expect this to result in a temporary increased rate of production of surviving children, and hence in an increase in the rate of population growth, in the very poorest nations. However, in all but the poorest countries an improvement in childhood survival will lower the rate of population increase.

It seems clear that lowered infant and childhood mortality, like increased education, is a powerful determinant of fertility. An intriguing possibility is that such critical socio-economic factors may interact synergystically to reduce fertility. This was suggested in a recent analysis of the combined effects of education and the infant mortality rate on the 1975 birth rates in eighty-eight developing countries.[52] Glassman and Ross showed not only that some 68 percent of the variation in birth rate among LDCs could be explained statistically by the joint action of these two socioeconomic variables, but that the effect of education on fertility increased as infant mortality decreased, and vice versa.

One final comment on childhood mortality is needed. In Chapter 1 we saw that one commonly held view is that improving the nutrition of poor people (through food aid or other means) will lead to higher birth rates ("more food means more babies"[53]). This is clearly *not generally the case.* Food shortage is visited more heavily on children (Chapter 5) and contributes strongly to childhood deaths: malnutrition probably is a primary or contributing factor to half of infant deaths in poor countries.[54] Improved childhood nutrition will therefore lead to lower childhood death rates, but in turn this leads to fewer births. Only in the very poorest societies is improved nutrition, by improving *maternal* health, also likely to cause a tendency toward increased fertility.

Urbanization

Birth rates tend to be higher in rural than in urban populations in the developing world. This difference is crucial, since the majority of people in the LDCs live in the countryside. It is especially evident in Latin America (table 2-9). In Asia, urban fertility is lower than rural fertility in Malaysia, Indonesia, Lebanon, and Turkey, in addition to the countries listed in table 2-9.[55] In Africa there is some scattered evidence of lower urban fertility in addition to that in the table. However, we would not expect marked differences in countries when there has been little or no fertility decline. Indeed, in some parts of Africa there is evidence for higher *urban* fertility, probably because parents are healthier in the towns.

Early writers on the demographic transition considered that the effects of urbanization and industrialization on fertility were important in and of themselves. And, as we have noted earlier, job opportunities for women increase while those for children decrease in towns, and these changes do result in lower fertility. However, it now seems clear that in developing countries the lower fertility of urban dwellers *mainly reflects their higher level of economic well-being.* Urban incomes are generally higher than rural incomes, often by a factor of three or more; medical and other serv-

Table 2-9. Urban versus rural fertility in developing countries: Average number of children born per woman aged 45 to 49

Country	Year	Urban	Rural	Urban as percentage of rural
Puerto Rico	1970	3.7	6.1	61
Dominican Republic	1969–71	5.6	8.5	66
El Salvador	1971	5.2	7.3	71
Guatemala	1973	5.5	7.2	76
Mexico	1970	5.9	7.1	83
Argentina	1961	2.1	3.4	62
Chile	1970	4.1	6.3	65
Brazil	1970	4.8	6.7	72
Colombia	1969	5.6	6.8	82
Ecuador	1974	5.7	6.9	83
Paraguay	1972	4.8	7.2	67
Peru	1971	5.3	6.4	83
Venezuela	1961	4.8	7.1	68
S. Korea	1970	5.0	6.0	83
Thailand	1969–70	5.3	6.7	79
Philippines	1968	no difference		
Bangladesh	1961	5.1	5.8	88
Pakistan	1968–69	5.5	5.4	102
Sri Lanka	1969–70	5.3	5.9	90
India	1964–65	5.8	5.8	100
Iran	1965–66	6.0	7.6	79
Syria	1970	7.7	8.1	95
Algeria[a]	1969	7.3	8.1	90
Morocco[a]	1973	6.7	7.9	85
Egypt[a]	1966	5.7	6.8	84

Source: United Nations, *World Population Trends.*
[a]Number given is the total fertility rate.

ices are better; education is more available (see table 2-10 on urban/rural fertility and education); and the illiteracy rate in the countryside is twice as high as in urban areas.[56] Even in China, where great efforts have been made to improve rural conditions, health care, education, and incomes are all better in the cities, and birth rates have fallen faster and further in the cities (Chapter 3).

In general it appears that, contrary to earlier ideas, urbanization per se has little or no effect on fertility. Chenery and Syrquin showed that, over a broad range of underdeveloped countries, urbanization does not have a significant effect on the birth rate after the separate effects of education, income, and infant mortality have been taken into account. There may, however, be some effects in some areas. For example, in Latin America, urbanization appears to lower fertility even after such factors as education are taken into account.[57] One possible way that cities could have such an effect is through changes in the cultural milieu. The "modern" environment may weaken the bonds of the extended family, expose parents to more "progressive" ideas, to a wider range of consumer goods, and to family planning propaganda.

One result that is crucial to the argument of this book is that *urban-rural differences in fertility can be wiped out when increased economic welfare is extended into the countryside.* This has been shown in parts of India, in China, Taiwan, and Sri Lanka. This point will be taken up in more detail in Chapter 3.

Table 2-10. Relative influence of education and place of residence on fertility

A. *Puerto Rico, 1960.* Fertility compared to mother's education[a]

		Primary			Secondary		College
Years:	None	1-4	5-6	7-8	1-3	4	1 or more
San Juan	6.9	6.0	5.1	3.9	3.0	2.4	1.9
Other urban	6.5	5.9	4.9	4.1	3.3	2.5	1.9
Rural	7.8	7.6	6.9	5.3	4.5	2.7	1.9

B. *Egypt, 1960.* Fertility compared to father's education[a]

	Illiterate	Elementary	Primary	Secondary	College
Large towns	8.0	6.1	5.3	3.3	2.7
Rest of Egypt	7.2	6.6	5.9	3.7	2.7

Source: Julian L. Simon, *The Effects of Income on Fertility* (Chapel Hill, N.C.: Carolina Population Center, 1974), p. 117.

Note: Each entry for Puerto Rico is the number of children already born to women who were over 45 years of age at the time of the study. Each entry for Egypt is the number of children born to married women who had completed their families at the time of the study.

[a]Notice that differences associated with education are much greater than those between urban and rural parents.

Fertility and Cultural Differences

By culture, I mean religious beliefs, family or community structure and traditions, and values or other beliefs that distinguish one racial, ethnic, or religious group from other such groups. One of the more persistent and widely held beliefs about fertility is that various aspects of culture, particularly religious beliefs, not only influence fertility but are great obstacles to reducing the birth rate. Yet the evidence is quite clearly against this thesis.

Culture surely has *some* effect on fertility, as we will see. In particular, some small differences in fertility are directly attributable to cultural differences between people, and cultural features, especially family structure, may modify the way socio-economic factors influence parents. However, cultural conditions change radically under economic development and become less important in influencing fertility during this process. Cultural conditions may affect the timing of the onset of fertility decline, but they are not a great obstacle and do not delay it indefinitely.

Let us look first at religion. Simon's survey of the evidence led him to conclude that religion is unimportant in determining fertililty;[58] indeed he believes that, in the long run, family structure and other cultural features can also be ignored as determinants of family size. He has shown that religious beliefs also make very little difference in the use of family planning techniques. Even when the Catholic Church has campaigned strongly against birth control, as in Puerto Rico, there has been no appreciable effect on the extent to which birth control is practiced. The prevalence and high frequency of abortion in Latin America is also powerful evidence against the success of the church in determining birth control practices. Beaver has shown that in Latin America no systematic association exists between religion and fertility,[59] and studies in West Africa suggest at most only a slight difference in fertility levels among religious groups (table 2-11).

Table 2-11. Religious differences and fertility in Ghana

Religion	Total fertility rate[a]	Completed fertility[a]
Christian	6.4	6.2
Moslem	5.8	5.3
Traditional	6.1	6.1
No religion	6.1	6.3

Source: Gaisie, "Population Growth and its Components," in Caldwell, et al., eds., *Population Growth in West Africa,* p. 344.

[a]Total fertility rate is the number of children a woman would have in her lifetime if she had children at the prevailing rates for women of all reproductive ages (see appendix A). Completed fertility is the number of children actually borne by women who had reached the end of child bearing at the time of the study.

One recent study in Lebanon, however, has found that religion does have a small but significant effect on family size.[60] *Among poor parents* (completed family sizes around five to seven children), the religious group with the highest fertility (the Moslem Shi'as) has, on average, about one and a half more births than the group with the lowest fertility (non-Catholic Christians). These differences persist even when corrections have been made for income and other variables. However, *such fertility differences disappear among the richer classes, among whom fertility is low for all religious groups.* This study thus shows that, in the face of increasing economic welfare, religion is not a barrier to reduced fertility and that the small effects it may have had before fertility decline are swamped by the effects of increasing affluence.

Poston and Singlemann, in a detailed study in North India, showed that different "value orientations" also did not cause differences in fertility when individuals in the same socio-economic class were compared.[61] These "values" included religious beliefs and attitudes toward marriage and divorce.

Although religious beliefs and other values seem to have only a small effect on fertility, there is evidence that some other aspects of culture are important. It is not always clear what these cultural features are. For example, I alluded earlier to differences among continents in the level of development needed to initiate natality decline. Moslem countries also tend to have higher fertility levels than one would expect from their income levels. This may be caused by factors we have already discussed: low status and educational level of women and the fact that few women work outside the home.

Figure 2-6 and table 2-12 suggest that those countries in Latin America and Asia that are most clearly into the demographic transition generally have a strong European (Latin America) or Chinese (Asia) heritage, and it has been suggested that these cultures are particularly open to outside (especially western) influence. Western ideas such as the nuclear family, a strong interest in consumer goods, and an emphasis on formal education may act to lower fertility.

Beaver suggested that within the twenty-four Latin American and Caribbean countries he examined, the openness of the culture to outside influences was greatest in those countries with strong European influences (e.g., Argentina, Uruguay), less where the major influence was African and East Indian (e.g., Guyana, Jamaica), and least where the culture was largely American Indian (e.g., Bolivia, Paraguay). The extent of the demographic transition does indeed correlate fairly well, although not perfectly, with such a classification (figure 2-6). He suggested, as has Caldwell, that such cultural differences may cause variation in the *time* of onset of fertility decline once the economic conditions are appropriate for such a decline.[62]

The difficulty here is that economic and cultural change generally occur together and interact. In fact, those very cultural features that character-ize lower-fertility countries have also been important in determining the

Table 2-12. Fertility declines since 1960 in developing countries

Country	Birth rate per thousand (1960)	(1965)	(1975)	Annual decline in birth rate 1965-1975	Decline in total fertility rate (%) 1968-1975
Africa					
Egypt	43	42	35	0.7	23
Mauritius	39	36	26	1.0	32
Reunion	44	43	28 (1973)	1.9	33
Tunisia	46	43	34	0.9	15
Latin America					
Barbados	31	27	19	0.8	24
Chile	38	35	23	1.2	28
Colombia	45	44	33	1.1	35
Costa Rica	47	42	29	1.3	31
Cuba	30	35	21	1.4	26
El Salvador	50	47	40	0.7	15
Guadeloupe	38	35	28 (1973)	1.0	—
Guyana	42	40	32	0.8	27
Jamaica	42	39	30	0.9	13
Martinique	38	35	22 (1973)	1.6	—
Mexico	46	44	40	0.4	13
Panama	39	38	31	0.7	14
Puerto Rico	32	31	22	0.9	—
Trinidad and Tobago	40	33	23	1.0	28
Asia					
China	40	38	25	1.3	24
Hong Kong	36	30	18	1.2	27
Indonesia	47	44	40	0.4	29
S. Korea	43	31	24	0.7	18
Malaysia	45	38	31	0.7	14
Mongolia	41	42	38	0.4	10
Singapore	38	30	18	1.2	28
Sri Lanka	37	33	27	0.6	14
Taiwan	39	32	23	0.9	28
Thailand	46	44	36	1.0	17
N. Vietnam	42	42	32	1.0	18
Oceania					
Fiji	40	36	28	0.8	41

Sources: United Nations, Department of Economic and Social Affairs, *Levels and Trends of Fertility Throughout the World, 1950-1970* (ST/ESA/SER.A/59), 1977; United Nations, *World Population Trends;* W. Parker Mauldin, "Patterns of Fertility Decline in Developing Countries 1950-1975," *Studies in Family Planning* 9 (1978): 75-84. For estimates of China's birth rates, see Chapter 3. The change in total fertility rate, 1968 to 1975, is from Amy Ong Tsui and Donald J. Bogue, "Declining World Fertility: Trends, Causes, and Implications," *Population Bulletin,* vol. 33 (Washington, D.C., Population Reference Bureau, 1978), pp. 1–56.

Note: Table includes only countries that have shown substantial fertility declines. Ex-cluded from the table are those countries that showed no significant decline before 1965 and have had a decrease in the total fertility rate, 1968 to 1975, of less than 10 percent.

extent of economic development that has occurred. Beaver concluded for Latin America that culture affected fertility mainly through its influence on economic development.[63]

Perhaps the most important manifestation of a culture's openness to external influence is its family structure—whether or not the extended family is the rule. Here again, there is ambiguity in the evidence and disagreement among workers in this area. Caldwell has suggested that family structure—that is, the nature of family ties—may be *the* feature, at least in Africa, that determines when it becomes economically rational for parents to control fertility.[64] Caldwell's hypothesis is that the crucial process affecting motivation for family size is whether, within families, income flows from children to parents and grandparents, or whether it flows in the opposite direction, from parents to children. The direction of this flow depends on both the level of economic development and on family structure. Within the extended family, income tends to flow from children to older generations, whereas in the nuclear family that flow is reversed. Thus Caldwell contends that children in extended families remain economic assets to their parents and to other members of the older generation further into the development process than do children in nuclear families. The extended family structure may thus delay the beginning of the decline in family size, though family size still remains a response to economic conditions.

While cultural differences may lead to variation in the timing of fertility decline or in the level of economic development needed to initiate the decline, it is also clear that economically mediated decline in fertility has occurred in an enormous variety of populations, regardless of culture. Table 2-12 shows how wide that range is. Fertility has decreased in response to increased welfare for the Singhalese in Ceylon; the Indians in Singapore; blacks in the Caribbean; Punjabis and Keralans in India; the Chinese populations of Asia; the Indians, Pakistanis, and Goans of Uganda and Kenya; and the Indians, Chinese, and Malays in Malaysia.[65] The powerful effect of improved economic welfare upon fertility thus cuts across cultural differences within and between populations.

In summary, the basically economic motivations that explain fertility behavior develop within a cultural setting and are affected by it. In particular, family structure and other characteristics that affect the openness of the population to outside influence appear to influence the level of economic development at which it becomes economically rational for parents to have smaller families. Thus culture may affect the time of onset of fertility decline. However, religious beliefs and other culturally determined values seem to have little influence on birth rate, especially over the long term.

Fertility and Family Planning Programs

In the 1960s the response of governments and organizations in the developed countries to the population explosion was to "launch massive schemes involving the export of new birth control technology, in the hope that indigenous governments would distribute these techniques within the framework of a more or less integrated national family planning program."[66] This was consistent with the view that food and population are in a race and that the population problem requires separate, control-oriented solutions. It also reflected western belief in the power of the technological remedy. As recently as 1976, the then government of India reaffirmed its belief in this approach in its national population policy statement. (It also added the idea of compulsory sterilization, which led to terrifying experiences for many Indians.[67])

A huge amount of experience with family planning programs has now been accumulated. By 1977 government-supported programs had spread to sixty-four developing countries containing 92 percent of the developing world's population; hundreds of studies of the efficacy of such programs have now been carried out. *There seems little doubt that such programs have an important part to play in reducing fertility.* However, the view that the fertility of the LDCs can be controlled by the spread of family planning alone is almost certainly incorrect. Such a view rests on two mistaken assumptions: that poor people in poor societies want small families, and that they lack the techniques of fertility control.[68]

It has often seemed quite reasonable to make these mistaken assumptions. For example, villagers in the Khanna Study in the Indian Punjab initially expressed almost universal approval and interest when asked about modern contraception. But this was largely out of a sense of politeness; when contraceptives were actually made available, acceptance rates were very low and use rates even lower. Indeed, in the village with a population program, birth rates fell no faster than in the control village.[69] It also must not be assumed that parents who use modern family planning techniques will necessarily have smaller families. More than 75 percent of the women users in Ibadan, Nigeria, wanted more children fairly soon; they were using contraception as a device to space their children and as a replacement for sexual abstinence. Reduction of fertility was not their primary aim.[70]

A basic difficulty in evaluating the contribution of family planning is that there is no way of assigning with certainty a given amount of decline in fertility to a given factor. For example, countries with strong fertility declines often have strong programs. But countries with strong programs tend also to be more economically developed—i.e., there is a correlation between those socio-economic factors that reduce fertility and the strength of the program.[71] Different evaluations are obtained even when the data are good because the data can be analyzed in different ways by scholars with different views of the causal mechanisms. Taiwan provides a good illustration.

Taiwan's program is generally considered the outstanding example of an effective family planning program.[72] However, Taiwan's birth rate and total fertility rate fell markedly from 1956 onwards even though the program began only in 1964. Li concluded that "the evidence shows that Taiwan's fertility was neither induced nor accelerated by the programme. This fact was especially obvious in Taichung City, where the action programmes were concentrated." Instead, he concluded that improved education and childhood survival led to reduced fertility. By contrast, Schultz estimated that the program *did* cause declines in fertility in its initial years, but that the effect has lessened markedly with time. Srikantan also concluded that, although fertility decline began in response to economic improvements, the program then caused a large fraction of that decline in the period from 1965 to 1971. Hermalin, after analyzing changes in different areas of Taiwan during the period from 1968 to 1972, concluded that the program accelerated a fertility decline that was already underway. This seems the most likely explanation.[73]

The effects of family planning programs in other countries are also ambiguous. Some studies show no effect. For example, Conning reviewed the evidence from Latin America up to 1970 and concluded that family planning programs there had no direct effect on fertility. On the other hand, Freedman and Berelson suggest that differences in the strength of family planning programs throughout the developing world can "explain" 8 to 15 percent of the variation in birth rates beyond the 60 percent or so that is "explained" by differences in such socio-economic variables as infant mortality, educational level, and per capita GNP. Overall they feel that, "if the fertility effect of family planning programs were always of overwhelming magnitude it would shine through; if it were always zero the question would not survive. In middle-ground cases, while problems of data and measurement remain, we find plausible evidence that family planning programs made a difference that matters."[74]

It is possible to make sense out of this apparent confusion. First, to reiterate the overall claim made at the start of this section, there is as yet no evidence that a family planning program *by itself* can initiate or cause a decline in fertility.* Second, substantial and sustained declines in fertility

---

*Of the recent declines in fertility, the one that provides the strongest evidence that a family planning program can itself cause fertility to decline is that in Indonesia. It has been claimed that the recent and rapid decline in fertility in Java and Bali has been caused by the

have occurred in the absence of family planning programs (Turkey provides a recent example). Thus, family planning clearly is neither necessary nor sufficient for fertility decline. We do know, however, that improvement in economic well-being does cause sustained fertility declines. This knowledge allows us to evaluate the part that family planning programs can play, and this evaluation has been done most thoroughly by Srikantan.[75] He points out that improved welfare creates the desire for fewer children, a desire that is equivalent to demand for family planning services. Within this context, a family planning program can then contribute to fertility decline by making fertility control easy, effective, and cheap, and by educating the population on fertility matters and making contraception and family planning socially acceptable. Economic progress and

---

extensive family planning program there. See Terence H. Hull, Valerie J. Hull, and Masri Singarimbun, "Indonesia's Family Planning Story: Success and Challenge," *Population Bulletin,* vol. 32 (Washington, D.C.: Population Reference Bureau, 1977). Hull and his co-workers concluded that the strong family planning program, which got underway seriously in 1971, was a spectacular success and was responsible for roughly two-thirds to three-quarters of the fertility decline observed between 1967/71 and 1976.

By 1977 the family planning program was spending about $80 million per year. By 1976 just under a quarter of all married women aged fifteen to forty-four were using contraception. The decline in fertility ranged from 15 percent in parts of Java to over a third in Bali. Fertility within marriage fell by about 10 percent (Jakarta, Central and East Java) to 33 percent (Bali). Elsewhere in Indonesia (in Yogyakarta, West Java, and the Outer Islands), fertility decline has been small or absent.

The relationships among fertility, socio-economic factors, and family planning in Indonesia have yet to be studied in detail. It is not clear, however, that the family planning program achieved the fertility reduction in the absence of the usual change in parental motivation stimulated by socio-economic changes. Asian societies have typically reduced their fertility at levels of average per capita income that are lower than elsewhere, except where extreme inequality has created great poverty for the majority. By the late 1960s, Indonesia, although poor, was at a level of development that led the United Nations to predict an imminent fertility decline there. See United Nations, Department of Economic and Social Affairs, *World Population Prospects as Assessed in 1968* (ST/SOA/SER.A/53), 1973. Since then national income has risen rapidly from the sale of oil. Between 1965 and 1974, per capita GNP grew at the very high rate of 4.1 percent per year and reached $180 in 1975. See International Bank for Reconstruction and Development, *World Bank Atlas* (Washington, D.C.: World Bank, 1976). What *is* surprising is that fertility declined while infant mortality has apparently remained high (around 140/1,000 in 1971).

There is also evidence that fertility decline had begun before the family planning program began in 1971 (see Cho and Retherford, "Comparative Analysis"). More important, changes were occurring before 1971 in the pattern of marriage; these changes typify the onset of fertility declines everywhere and cannot be attributed to a family planning program. Age at marriage was increasing in the 1960s, continued to increase in the 1970s, and contributed significantly to the fertility decline. In Bali, where the decline has been greatest, a large fraction of women work outside the home, and collective working of much of the land reduces the value of children as labor (see Hull, Hull, and Singarimbun, "Indonesia's Family Planning Story").

Indonesia's fertility data are notoriously inadequate and much analysis remains to be done. Clearly, the final word is not yet in on the contribution made by family planning in that country. It appears, though, that the program has been remarkably efficient and that it may have made a major contribution to the observed decline in fertility.

the program can also interact—for example, development provides an infrastructure that can make the program more effective.

Srikantan was able to show, in an analysis of LDCs with well-developed programs, that the programs strongly enhance the effects of economic development. They cause fertility to fall faster than it would in their absence. He also confirmed that the most important economic changes that create the demand for family planning are in health care (e.g., infant mortality) and education, especially female education.

These conclusions about the role of family planning programs in helping fertility declines rest upon evidence that describes the situation in the LDCs up to about 1970. In 1977 and 1978 new evidence became available that quite widespread and rapid declines had occurred in the LDCs by 1975 (table 2-12 and Chapter 4). Tsui and Bogue have analyzed these data. They show that most of the variation in 1975 levels of fertility among LDCs can be explained statistically by the 1968 levels—i.e., countries with lower fertility in 1975 generally had lower fertility in 1968. The small amount (24 percent) of remaining unexplained variation in 1975 fertility levels in different countries is caused by different *rates* of fertility decline between 1968 and 1975. One-fourth of this variation can be explained by differences in the 1968 levels of socio-economic indicators in different countries, and another one-fifth can be explained by differences in the strength of family planning programs in different countries.[76]

This analysis clearly confirms our earlier conclusions about family planning programs. They can have a separate additional effect on fertility and, in particular, they can increase the speed of fertility decline. Since they do not "explain" a very large fraction of the variation in 1975 fertility, or of the change in fertility between 1968 and 1975, this conclusion must be applied with caution to particular countries. India, for example, experienced only a slight decline in fertility, yet it has had an official program to reduce fertility since 1952, and in 1975 its government spent twice as much on family planning as it did on health care.[77]

Tsui and Bogue go on to draw the startling conclusion that the family planning "campaign has been a major force for social change and has been successful in arresting a major world catastrophe," and further that future "world fertility may be determined in large part by the size, quality, and spread of the family planning campaign."[78] These conclusions are not justified by the evidence. An adequate explanation of recent fertility declines will require both additional data and, as always, several thorough analyses that look at the data from different points of view. Nevertheless, it seems clear that, while family planning programs have an effect on fertility, the new evidence does not remove socio-economic factors from their position as prime movers.*

*A detailed statistical analysis of the relationships among 1975 fertility, economic development, and family planning programs is beyond the scope of this book. Some comments on

CONCLUSIONS

Our theory claims that the number of children desired by parents is greatly influenced by rational decision making, based on the balance between expected economic costs and benefits. The major benefits to be expected by poor parents in a poor nation are the labor, earnings, and future security the child will provide. Costs include both direct costs and opportunity costs, such as the income that might be forgone by a working mother.

The theory assumes, therefore, that parental decisions about children are largely economic and are determined by the parents' long-term average level of economic welfare. The level of welfare determines the parents' background, desires, preferences, and motivations. As income increases during economic development, these motivations change in favor of smaller families; the costs of children increase and the benefits decline;

Tsui and Bogue's ánalysis, however, may be useful. Their conclusions rest upon the fact that, after the effect of 1968 levels of development have been taken into account, an additional 19 percent of the *remaining* variation in the amount of decline between 1968 and 1975, in different countries, can be explained by the strength of the family planning program in each country. Stronger programs tend to be associated with more rapid declines in fertility.

There are two problems. One concerns the interpretation of these results, the other concerns the details of the analysis. It makes sense to interpret these new results against the huge amount of evidence that already exists. This evidence says that family planning programs operate within a socio-economic framework and, specifically, that once motivation for small families occurs, we can expect the program to influence the rate of fertility decline. The results are quite in line with this framework. There is no evidence that the program *substituted* for socio-economic factors in motivating parents to have smaller families. For example, the new data do not show that fertility is declining first in poorer rather than in richer families. Indeed, the standard pattern persists: the more affluent classes lead the fertility decline (see, for example, recent World Fertility Surveys). Again, the recent declines are characterized, as usual, by increases in the age at which women marry, and this age has not been shown to be determined by family planning programs.

Turning to the analysis itself, I will discuss a few important details. First, the changes in fertility between 1968 and 1975 should be treated as a continuation, albeit an intensification, of existing processes. In fact, Tsui and Bogue show that the change in fertility between 1968 and 1975 is strongly correlated with 1968 levels of socio-economic status.

Second, Tsui and Bogue's analysis demonstrates that the 1968 levels of fertility were the best predictors of 1975 fertility levels (they explained 76 percent of the variation in 1975 fertility levels). Now, we know from our earlier analyses that the differences in fertility levels around 1968 are explicable largely in terms of differences in socio-economic variables that reflect the level of welfare of the population. Thus, these socio-economic variables remain the best predictors of 1975 fertility. These results are, therefore, quite in line with our previous findings about the major significance of levels of welfare.

Third, there are problems with the particular variables chosen by Tsui and Bogue. In particular, little emphasis was placed on variables that measure the *distribution* of economic welfare. For example, no measure of the distribution of income was used. Yet in Chapter 3 we will see that this is a crucial variable that explains a large amount of the variation in fertility among LDCs. Again, one of the crucial socio-economic indicators is percentage of literacy, but a value for this variable was missing for roughly half of the LDCs in 1968 and had to be excluded from the analysis, along with life expectancy. The point is that when crucial socio-economic variables are left out of the analysis, the total amount of variation explained by such variables is bound to be reduced.

children begin to compete with other goods and services; and old age becomes economically more secure. Various structural changes also accompany development—in education, job opportunities, etc.—and these also make children less desirable. These processes, occurring during the shift from great poverty to relative affluence, are responsible for the major transition in birth rates during development, from around 40 per 1,000 per year to around 20 per 1,000 per year.

The economic costs and benefits can be shown to change with economic well-being, as the theory assumes. The evidence available from varied cultures throughout the developing world also substantiates the assumptions about parental motivation.

The major prediction of the theory, that fertility should fall with increasing economic welfare, is also borne out by all the various types of evidence that it is possible to bring to bear on it. This is true throughout the developing world, within countries over time, among socio-economic classes within countries, among regions within countries, and among countries at different stages of economic development. The best single estimator of welfare seems to be the level of education of the parents, especially of the mother.

Cultural values seem to be of minor significance, except that the culture, especially through family structure, may help determine when it becomes economically sensible to reduce family size.

Family planning programs can accelerate the rate of fertility decline, but they cannot, by themselves, cause the onset of such a decline.

3

FERTILITY AND EQUALITY

In countries that have gone through the demographic transition, there has been a more or less steady decline in the national birth rate. At the start of this process, parents have been poor and family size has been large; by the end of the process, economic well-being has increased and the typical family has only two or three children. An important question is: can the process be speeded up by spreading the benefits of economic development evenly across the population?

The analyses in Chapter 2 support the idea that parental motivation moves from large to small families as economic well-being increases and parents become aware that the costs of children have come to outweigh the benefits. Recall, however, that income in the LDCs has in general been much more unevenly distributed than in the developed countries. In addition, increases in income and benefits have tended to accrue mainly to those who are already better off (Chapter 9). We might expect this bias to slow down fertility declines, since it gives additional welfare to those who already have incentives for small families and withholds welfare from those who don't. By contrast, if future increases in income and benefits were to be directed to the poorer segments of society, a larger fraction of the population would be motivated to have small families, and we could expect a greater decline in the birth rate for a given increase in aggregate income. Moreover, since the mass of poor people lives in the countryside, where birth rates are highest, we would expect in particular that national fertility will be lowered more rapidly when special attention is paid to the well-being of the rural population.

There may, of course, be some national income level that is so low that no degree of even-handedness will lower the birth rate—there is simply not enough welfare to be spread around. Thus the effect of evenness of distribution can be expected to weaken or even disappear among the most poverty-stricken nations. At the other extreme, in the richest nations almost everyone is rich enough to desire few children, and we would not expect the distribution of income to have much effect on the national birth rate. However, our expectation that fertility will be lower when the distribution of welfare is more even, at a given average level of welfare, should hold for the entire group of developing countries except for the very poorest.

FERTILITY AND INCOME DISTRIBUTION

You may recall from Chapter 2 that Oechsli and Kirk showed that the degree of economic equality appeared to influence fertility in Latin America. Their index of economic development was strongly affected by how evenly economic benefits were spread across the population, and that index explained almost all of the variation in birth rates among Latin American and Caribbean nations.

We start here by looking at fertility and income distribution over a broad range of developing countries. Figure 2-5 showed that birth rates tend to be lower in those developing countries with higher average incomes. Figure 3-1 presents these same data. In this figure, the curve shows the birth rate that would be expected at each level of average income. The dotted lines show the difference (deviation) between each country's actual birth rate and this expected birth rate (appendix B explains how the curve is obtained).

Now, if equality is important, we should find that those countries with uneven income distributions will also have birth rates that are too high for their average income level. In other words, the countries lying above the curve in figure 3-1 should tend to have uneven income distributions. Similarly, countries that have more even income distributions should have birth rates that are relatively low for their average income—i.e. these countries should tend to be below the curve.

We can test this idea using the Gini coefficient, a number that increases when income becomes more *unevenly* distributed. If everyone in the nation had the same income, Gini would be zero. If a single group had all the income, Gini would be 1. In most developed countries income is relatively evenly distributed and Gini is .35 or less, whereas in most LDCs Gini is over .40, and some have been measured over .65.

First we go to figure 3-1 and measure how much larger or smaller the birth rate of each country is than we would expect on the basis of the country's *average* income. That is, we measure the distance from the curve to each point, as shown in figure 3-1. Then we graph each country's *deviation* against its Gini coefficient. As figure 3-2 shows, in countries where income is evenly distributed the birth rate tends to be lower than expected on the basis of average income; in countries where the income is unevenly distributed the birth rate tends to be higher than expected. Thus, at a given level of average income, the birth rate is lower the more evenly income is distributed. Our prediction is confirmed.

Notice that this analysis is actually telling us about the importance of the welfare of the poorer majority of society. Their absolute incomes are determined by two things: the average income in the country, and the fraction of that income that they receive. The Gini coefficient is high when

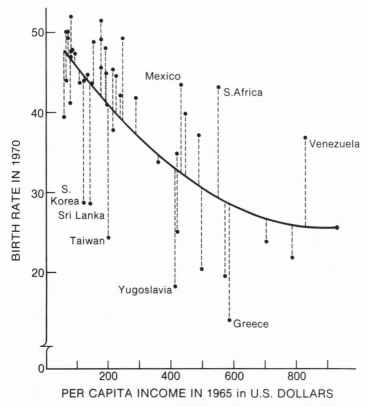

Figure 3-1 Birth rate in 1970 compared to per capita income in 1965

Source: appendix B
Note: The dashed lines show the difference (deviation) between the actual birth rate and the birth rate expected on the basis of average income.

the lower income majority receives a small fraction of national income and decreases when it gets a larger fraction of the national income.

This analysis allows us to make another powerful point. The correlation between the birth rates of these forty-six countries and their average incomes, shown in figures 2-5 and 3-1, "explains" 46 percent of the variation in birth rates among the countries, leaving 54 percent of the variation not explained. However, when we also take the distribution of income into account, as we have just done, we are then able to "explain" 73 percent of the variation in birth rates (appendix B elucidates the notion of "explaining" some percentage of the variability). This is an astonishing result considering the difficulties of measurement, the tremendous variety of nations examined, the fact that only two variables are examined, and that income

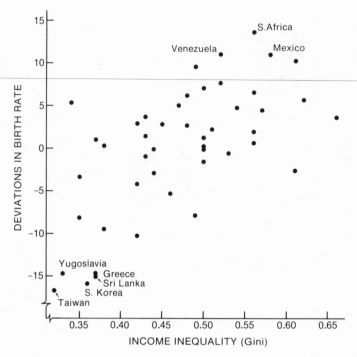

Figure 3-2 Birth rate and inequality

Source: appendix B
Note: The actual birth rate is lower than expected when incomes are even and higher than expected when incomes are uneven. These are the same forty-six countries represented in figure 3-1.

does not catch all aspects of economic well-being. Our analysis tells us that most of the differences in birth rates between countries can be explained by the fact that their levels of income differ and, in particular, by the fact that the poorer segments of each country have different levels of income.

Another way of showing the importance of the distribution of income is to analyze birth rates compared to the actual income of the poorest 40 percent of the population.* Two-thirds (65 percent) of the variation in birth rates is explained by this single variable (figure 3-3 and appendix B). Thus the welfare of the poorest people in a country is a powerful predictor of national birth rate.[1]

---

*Ideally we would like to look at a majority, say 60 percent, rather than 40 percent. These data were not available. However, it is known that the two measures, income of the poorest 40 percent and the poorest 60 percent, are highly correlated.

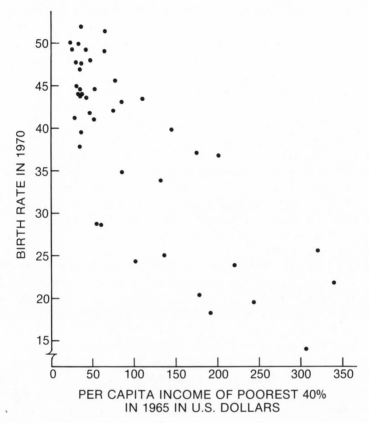

Figure 3-3 Birth rate in 1970 compared to the average annual income of the poorest 40 percent of the population in 1965

Source: appendix B

Notice that I am *not* claiming that high birth rates result from *relative* poverty. Unevenness of income distribution in poor countries causes the poor to be absolutely poorer than they would be if the same national income were evenly distributed. This is what causes their high fertility.

What we have shown here is that, to the degree that income measures economic welfare, most of the variability in fertility among developing nations can be explained by the level of economic welfare of the poorer majority of families in each nation. But income level undoubtedly does not catch all the components of economic welfare. For example, it may not reflect the level of health and educational services, or of nutritional supplements provided free or at low cost by the government. (We will see later that there can indeed be important nonincome contributions to economic welfare that drive down fertility.) On the other hand, there is almost certainly a correlation between the evenness of the income distribution and the effort by government to spread crucial services to all of the population.

MEXICO: AN EXCEPTION?

Mexico has recently undergone rather rapid economic growth. By 1970 its per capita GNP had reached $670 and by 1975 $1,190, higher than most Latin American nations. From 1960 to 1974, its GNP increased at more than 6 percent per year and its per capita GNP at more than 3 percent a year. In spite of this sustained aggregate economic growth, Mexico's crude birth rate remained at about 44 per 1,000 between 1950 and 1970. There was some argument as to whether a tiny decline in fertility of about 5 percent had occurred between 1960 and 1970, but the errors in the data were too large to tell.[2]

The persistence of high birth rates in the midst of rapid economic growth has led some observers to conclude that Mexico constitutes a massive exception to the demographic transition theory that relates declining fertility to economic development.[3] Certainly Mexico shows that rapid aggregate economic growth is not necessarily followed closely by declining fertility. But does it provide an exception to the theory?

From figure 3-1, it can be seen that Mexico's birth rate is clearly "too high" for its 1965 income level. Even allowing for a longer time lag, the 1972 birth rate of 44.7[4] was still higher than one would expect on the basis of average 1965 income. However, as soon as we examine the distribution of income, Mexico ceases to be an anomaly. Figure 3-2 shows that Mexico's 1970 birth rate lies almost exactly where it is predicted to be on the basis of income inequality. The simplest explanation for Mexico's high birth rate is that the benefits of economic growth have not reached the large majority of the population, for Mexico's already unequal income distribution became more uneven over the past two decades.[5]

In fact, Mexico's birth rate in 1970 was very close to the level predicted by Oechsli and Kirk in their study relating fertility to a broad index of level of development in 1962 (figure 2-6). Recall that this index is heavily influenced by the degree to which economic benefits are spread across the population. Mexico thus appears not to be an exception. Indeed, its demographic history seems to fit rather well into the framework developed here. We can test this in one more way: the uneven distribution of income means that a small fraction of the population is affluent, and they should show low birth rates. This is the case. Fertility is lowest in the most advanced states (Mexico City has the lowest) and highest in the most backward states, and its regional variation is explained by the usual development indexes. The same is true within Mexico City itself, where (after the first five years of schooling) family size decreases strongly as the parents' educational level rises.[6]

The earliest draft of this chapter was written in 1976. It contained the following passage:

> These results, and Oechsli and Kirk's analysis, suggest that sustained fertility decline ought to begin soon in Mexico, in spite of the uneven distribution of welfare. Mexico in the 1960s was not far below the threshold levels of development postulated by Kirk in 1971. In the period 1960 to 1964, four high-birth-rate countries (Costa Rica, Guyana, Jamaica, and Venezuela) were in the threshold range for five of the eight variables and Mexico for three variables. All but Mexico have begun a clear fertility decline. Mexico thus seems poised on the brink of the transition.

Since then, new data for Mexico have become available. One estimate puts the 1975 birth rate at 40 and another at 42.[7] It appears that Mexico has indeed finally begun its fertility decline, as predicted.

FERTILITY AND URBAN-RURAL INEQUALITY

A major cause of the uneven income distribution in developing countries is that incomes typically are much higher in urban areas.[8] In addition, the availability of medical, educational, and other services is much greater in urban areas. An analysis of a large group of countries demonstrates how this inequality affects fertility.

Bhattacharyya analyzed data from around 1950 from fifty-two countries, including some now-developed nations. He first grouped countries according to average income level and then, within these groups, according to the degree of inequality between urban and rural incomes. Table 3-1 shows clearly how birth rate falls with rising income, which we have established already. It also shows how, *at a given level of average income,*

Table 3-1. Average birth rate compared to average per capita income

	Average birth rate	
Average per capita income	Rural and urban incomes less equal	Rural and urban incomes more equal
Up to $200	40.7	34.8
$200 to $500	37.2	28.7
Above $500	31.2	21.3

Source: Amit Kumar Bhattacharyya, "Income Inequality and Fertility: A Comparative View," *Population Studies* 29 (1975): 5–19.
Note: Each number is the average birth rate of countries in a given income class and income distribution class.

birth rates are lower when income is more evenly distributed between city and countryside. This confirmation of our hypothesis is especially important, since in poor countries the great majority of the population and the highest fertility are in the countryside. It emphasizes that the various issues in this book come together around the problem of rural poverty.

FERTILITY AND EQUALITY IN TWO GROUPS OF DEVELOPING COUNTRIES

The important contribution to reduced fertility that can be made by increasing the welfare of the rural majority is further illustrated by both Kocher and Rich, who have separately presented details of the spread of income and benefits in two very different groups of developing countries (see tables 2-8 and 3-2). They showed that, by 1970, sustained and often rapid declines in fertility had occurred in that group of countries which had concentrated on spreading the benefits of economic growth to the majority of the population, and especially to the rural poor, even though average income was low. By contrast, birth rates had remained stubbornly high in a second group of nations in which the distribution of benefits was extremely skewed and little effort had been made to improve the welfare of

Table 3-2. A comparison between relatively equitable and inequitable developing countries

Relatively equitable countries	$ GNP per capita 1961	$ GNP per capita 1970	Inequality (Gini)	Decline in birth rate	Time span
China	83	160	—	40–30	1960–70
Costa Rica	380	560	.43	47–33	1960–70
Japan	42 (1947)	211 (1955)	—	28–19	1947–55
S. Korea	106	250	.36	43–29	1960–70
Sri Lanka	123	110[a]	.37	37–29	1955–70
Taiwan	116	390	.32	46–27	1955–70
Inequitable countries					
Brazil	268	420	.61	41–38	1950–70
India	70	110	.46	45–42	1960–70
Mexico	297	670	.58	45–44	1950–70
Philippines	188	210	.50	45–43	1960–70
Thailand	101	200	.50	42–40	1960–70

Sources: Modifed from James E. Kocher, *Rural Development, Income Distribution, and Fertility Decline* (New York: The Population Council, 1973), pp. 64–65. Income data before 1970 are from Kocher and United Nations *Statistical Yearbooks.* The 1970 income data are from the *World Bank Atlas* (1972). Gini values from Hollis Chenery and Moises Syrquin, *Patterns of Development, 1950–1970* (London: Oxford University Press, 1975), p. 103. Birth rates are from various sources in the text.

[a]According to data in the World Bank files, income in Sri Lanka in 1970 was around $130.

the rural poor. (Chapters 6 and 7 present additional details about the degree of rural equality in several countries from both groups.)

The first group of nations includes Japan (before it became a developed nation around 1960), China, Taiwan, South Korea, Sri Lanka, and Costa Rica.* The second includes the Philippines, Thailand, India, Mexico, and Brazil. Notice that the Philippines and Thailand had by the 1970s clearly passed the income levels at which other Asian nations had shown strong fertility declines.

*Kocher's original analysis (James E. Kocher, *Rural Development, Income Distribution, and Fertility Decline* [New York: The Population Council, 1973]) included Malaysia among the more egalitarian countries. The available data suggested that its income distribution in 1961 was less even than Korea's, Japan's, or Taiwan's, but much more even than India's. From 1957 to 1958 one estimate of its Gini coefficient was 0.37, which is low for a developing country. During the period 1956 to 1970 the birth rate dropped (from 47 to 36 in peninsular Malaysia, where most of the population lives). Thus, although detailed information on the distribution of benefits to the rural population in Malaysia was not available, it seemed as if this was another good example of equality accelerating a fertility decline.

On the other hand, Malaysia's income has been exceptionally high for a developing country. In 1965 per capita income was $258, about twice that of Thailand and the Philippines and greater than Taiwan's; in 1975 it was about $720, still twice as high as Thailand's, the Philippines', and China's. We would therefore expect, simply on the basis of *average* income, that its birth rate should decline earlier and faster than in most other Asian nations, and the observed decline cannot really be used as evidence in support of the equality hypothesis.

In fact, Malaysia's fertility decline has not been as great as the declines in those Asian countries that have a high level of both economic equality and rural development (figure 3-5). South Korea, China, and Sri Lanka are poorer than Malaysia but have lower birth rates. Taiwan's per capita income is only about 20 percent higher than Malaysia's, but its birth rate is about ten points lower. Contrary to our first impression, therefore, Malaysia's fertility decline has been *relatively* unimpressive by Asian standards. When we turn to examine equality in Malaysia, we find that its relatively poor demographic performance is not surprising. On the basis of its income distribution in 1970, Malaysia was classified as a "high-inequality" nation (Hollis Chenery et al., *Redistribution with Growth* [London: Oxford University Press, 1974], p. 8), and several estimates of its income distribution in the 1960s and 1970s give, by Asian standards, very high Gini coefficients—well over .50 (S. Jain, *Size Distribution of Income: A Compilation of Data* [Washington, D.C.: World Bank, 1975]; Sudhir Amand, *Income Distribution in Peninsular Malaysia*, unpublished manuscript, 1979). Although it has been claimed that there has been a strong trend since 1957 to 1958 towards increasing inequality (e.g., J. T. Thoburn, *Primary Commodity Exports and Economic Development: Theory, Evidence, and a Study of Malaysia* [London: Wiley, 1977]), it appears that earlier and later estimates of inequality are not comparable (Amand, *Income Distribution*).

Because of the high average income level, relatively few Malaysians live in absolute poverty; in 1969 only 11 percent of the population received less than $50 per year (U.S. currency), compared with 36 percent of Asian populations in general (Chenery et al., *Redistribution with Growth*). Nonetheless, the rural Malays who work very small plots of land are an impoverished group (Thoburn, *Primary Commodity Exports*). The pattern of fertility decline fits these observations. The decline has been mostly in the towns, has been very slight in the countryside (United Nations, Department of Economic and Social Affairs, *Levels and Trends of Fertility Throughout the World, 1950–1970* [ST/ESA/SER.A/59], 1977), and has been least among the Malays (see Lee-Jay Cho and R. D. Retherford, "Comparative Analysis of Recent Fertility Trends in East Asia," International Population Conference, Liege [1973], vol. 2, pp. 163–81). Malaysia thus fits the equality hypothesis but, unfortunately, not in the way that Kocher had thought.

Kocher and Rich present a wealth of detailed analysis, and I can do no more here than summarize the main points and add some information. The first group of nations is characterized by serious attempts, including land reform, at raising the welfare of the rural population. Successful efforts have been made to spread health services to the poor and the countryside, rather than concentrating on advanced medical care for the urban elite. They have worked at raising both literacy levels and the proportion of the population that receives schooling; expenditure on education has been concentrated at the primary level, where most people will benefit. Income distributions are relatively even and characteristically have been becoming more even.[9]

In the second group of nations, in spite of occasional lip service, there has been no far-reaching attempt at land reform or rural development. Land distribution remains highly uneven. Strong inequalities pervade these societies, and income distribution is not only highly skewed but has been becoming increasingly uneven.[10] These regressive changes have occurred at the same time as these nations have benefited from the Green Revolution and, in the cases of Brazil, Mexico, and Thailand, as they have been experiencing rapid economic growth. Indeed, averaging Brazil's birth rate and other Brazilian statistics obscures the fact that Brazil is really two countries; in one of these, in the south, most people share a reasonable standard of living and have low birth rates; the other, the vast northern hinterland, is neglected, poverty ridden, and has high birth rates. The second group of countries has also concentrated educational expenditures on higher education for a small fraction of the population. Advanced medical care is available for an urban elite, while even rudimentary health services are not available in rural areas.

The demographic results reflect these differences (table 3-2). In the first group, fertility decline began early and proceeded rapidly. By contrast, in the process of growth, countries in the second group left behind the mass of their people. As a result, while a small urban elite passed through the demographic transition, the rest of the population maintained high birth rates.

There is now evidence that the Philippines, Thailand, and even India have belatedly begun their fertility decline, as family size has decreased in the higher socio-economic classes.[11] By 1975 the Philippines, with a per capita GNP of $370, and Thailand, with a per capita GNP of $350 and a 4.6 percent growth of per capita income from 1960 to 1974, both had a birth rate of 36. India, with a per capita GNP of $150, had a birth rate of about 38. Other figures in the same year, for comparison, were: Taiwan, $890 and 23; S. Korea, $550 and 24; China, $350 and 24; Sri Lanka, $150 and 27.

FERTILITY AND EQUALITY: SOME KEY SAMPLES

In the remainder of this chapter, I look in detail at the relation between fertility and the distribution of economic welfare in a few selected populations. These examples are particularly valuable because they show how even quite poor nations can lower their fertility by concentrating on the welfare of the poor in their population, particularly the rural poor. And they show how concentrating on those variables we know to be important (health, education, old-age security) can have dramatic effects on fertility.

The Case of Sri Lanka

The once British colony of Ceylon (now Sri Lanka) still suffers, as does its neighbor India, from the heritage of a century of British rule. Its development, especially its rural development, was severely depressed. In Sri Lanka this arose largely from the colonialist policy of concentrating on the production of estate cash crops (tea, rubber, coconuts) while neglecting food production and relying instead upon food imports (Chapters 8 and 9). While neither country has recovered economically from this heritage, India and Sri Lanka have dealt very differently with the problems of a low average standard of living (in 1970 they both had a per capita annual income of $110 in 1970 U.S. dollars).[12] In India inequalities have increased and the rural poor have been largely ignored (Chapter 7), while successive governments in Sri Lanka have concentrated on equalizing welfare across the population of 14 million.* The consequent difference in birth rates is dramatic: in 1975 India's was around 38, while Sri Lanka's was 27.

How has Sri Lanka achieved this demographic feat in the face of such low national income? The crux of the matter is that successive governments have developed what is essentially a poor man's welfare state. The government has provided food subsidies, free education, and free health care, and it has imposed a progressive tax structure. Other schemes provide security for wage earners and protect the tenure of small farmers. This is not to suggest that Sri Lanka is a perfectly egalitarian society. While income is quite evenly distributed, wealth and access to productive resources such as land remain unevenly distributed, as they are in most poor countries. But Sri Lanka has gone a long way toward equalizing the

---

*This pattern changed in 1977 with the election of a more conservative government and with the decision, reached in conjunction with the World Bank and the International Monetary Fund, to reduce spending on welfare programs and to aim at a more thoroughly capitalist, growth-oriented mode of development.

availability of the basic requirements of a healthy and secure life for the majority of its population.[13]

Mortality has declined since the war, owing to the control of malaria, the spread of health care facilities, and improved nutrition. Declines in the mortality of infants and mothers have been particularly marked. The infant mortality rate was reduced from 150 deaths per 1,000 births in 1946 to 42 in 1970. This is a very low rate for a poor nation—the average for the developing countries in 1970 was about 140; in India it was still about 130 in 1978. In fact, an infant mortality rate of 42 is lower than that of migrant agricultural workers in the United States, where in 1970 some 60 out of every 1,000 infants died. Life expectancy around 1970 was sixty-eight years in Sri Lanka, which approached the average for rich countries (seventy-one years) and greatly exceeded the average in India (forty-seven years) and in the developing world in general (fifty-one years).

Sri Lanka has achieved these astounding results by improving well-being on a broad front. Adequate diets have been assured by government programs that provide to the poorest people free supplementary rations of rice and some other items, and additional supplements at reduced prices. Figure 3-4 shows that as a result the poor in Sri Lanka get much more to eat than their counterparts in India.

The government has spent a relatively large fraction (7 percent) of its budget on health care, which has been free and, most important, available. Almost 100 health care units are spread throughout the island, so that even the rural population has easy access to medical care. These units emphasize preventive medicine, health education, and mother and child care.

Education also has been not only free but freely available to the whole population, and has accounted for a relatively large fraction of government spending. Except for the million or so Indian Tamils who live and work in the tea estates, educational levels are high: more than 80 percent of the population receives primary education and almost 40 percent aged fifteen to twenty-four are still students. In 1970 over 83 percent of the population was literate, compared with 29 percent in India and 32 percent in the developing nations on average.

Not only has income distribution become more and more even, but direct and indirect taxes have acted to redistribute income. In addition, there are minimum wage laws, job security laws, and in particular old-age security schemes that directly reduce a major incentive for high fertility. Small farmers have secure tenure to their land, and government policies have ensured reasonable prices for farm products.

In addition to all of this, it must be stressed that women in Sri Lanka enjoy a much higher status than is the rule in South Asia, and this has helped reduce fertility (see Chapter 2). By 1971, the enrollment of girls in

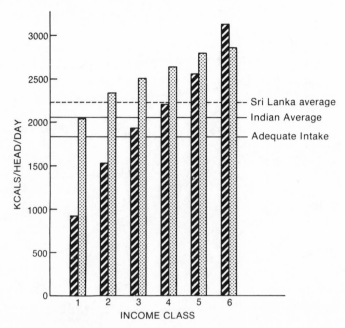

Figure 3-4 Food intake and income in Maharastra, India, and in Sri Lanka

Sources: Frederick C. Roche, "The Demographic Transition in Sri Lanka: Is Development Really a Prerequisite?" Cornell Agricultural Economics Staff Paper, no. 76-5(1976); United Nations, World Food Conference, Assessment of the World Food Situation: Present and Future (E/Conf. 65/3), Rome, 5–16 November 1974.

Note: Food intake in Sri Lanka (stippled bars) is more evenly distributed across income groups than in India (striped bars).

primary and secondary schools almost matched that of boys, and by 1977 they actually formed the majority of university students. Women expect to work outside the home, wage-earning wives are preferred, and education is viewed as important preparation for work. Ironically the growing unemployment in Sri Lanka reinforces the tendency to postpone marriage:[14] neither set of parents would approve of marriage by an unemployed son; at the same time, daughters need to help earn a dowry before they marry, and educated girls want to wait until they have a job before marrying.

The consequence of this spread in welfare, even at low average income, has been a steady decrease in fertility since the 1950s (figure 3-5). Two mechanisms have produced the fall in fertility.[15] First, the average age at first marriage increased from 22.5 in 1953 to 25.1 in 1975. This late age at marriage is strongly associated with high levels of female education. Second, fertility within marriage decreased 30 percent between 1953 and 1970 and fell more sharply between 1970 and 1974. Most important, the trend towards fewer children has been stronger in younger parents (a decline of

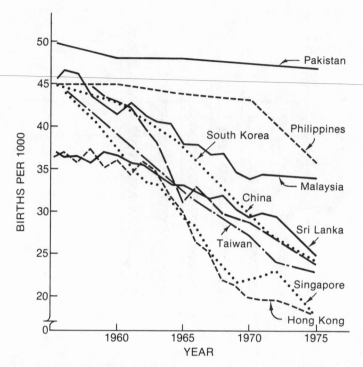

Figure 3-5 Twenty years of fertility change in Asia

Sources: United Nations, Department of Economic and Social Affairs, *Levels and Trends of Fertility Throughout the World, 1950–1970,* Population Studies no. 59 (New York: United Nations, 1977); Te-Hsiung Sun, Hui-Sheng Lin, and Ronald Freedman, "Trends in Fertility, Family Size Preferences, and Family Planning Practice: Taiwan 1961–76," *Studies in Family Planning* 9 (1978): 55; W. Parker Mauldin, "Patterns of Fertility Decline in Developing Countries, 1950–75," *Studies in Family Planning* 9 (1978): 76, 77; see text for China estimates.

45 percent compared with 30 percent), indicating that family size is likely to go on decreasing. These small family sizes correspond with a widely stated desire for only two or three children.

The rate of fertility decline increased in the first half of the 1970s. The World Fertility Survey has shown that the total fertility rate fell at 2.5 percent per year from 1963 to 1970 and then at 5.7 percent per year between 1970 and 1974. Within this framework of declining fertility, family sizes in Sri Lanka conform to the patterns we have observed in Chapter 2. Fertility is lower at higher income levels, in higher socio-economic classes, and in parents with higher levels of education.[16] There is no way to *prove* that Sri Lanka's socio-economic policies have caused the decline in fertility, but that is certainly the most reasonable explanation.

The pattern of fertility decline in Sri Lanka illustrates a further important point. Throughout the developing world, the greatest contribution to population growth comes from the poverty-ridden rural masses. In Sri Lanka, however, the government has ensured that the well-being of the rural population has increased together with that of urban dwellers and *fertility has been declining faster in the rural than in the urban population.* [17]

Sri Lanka's fertility has fallen as a result of the even distribution of a very modest national income. The decline has *not* been associated with a surge of economic development, as it has been in Malaysia, for example. In fact, Sri Lanka's economy has stagnated since the 1950s; in real terms per capita income has grown at about 1 percent a year for two decades. Only the translation of that income into broadly spread benefits has increased rapidly.

Sri Lanka faces severe difficulties in speeding up the process of development, including growth of the total national income. There is thus a real possibility that without increased development, the fertility decline may falter or continue only very slowly. This is not the place to discuss Sri Lanka's development problems in detail (see Chapters 6 to 9). But it is worth noting here briefly that the unusually even distribution of benefits in Sri Lanka rests upon a distorted pattern of *production* that does not differ from that of the rest of the developing world. Sri Lanka is poor in resources and depends for much of its income on a few cash crops, mainly tea, for which prices have generally fallen relative to imports. These cash crops have dominated the economy, which has failed to develop in a balanced and integrated manner. Sri Lanka's slow economic development stems from these basic structural problems. A particularly severe problem is unemployment, which is worst for the educated young people.

The government elected in 1977, together with the International Monetary Fund and the World Bank, decided that the welfare programs have been too costly and have been preventing economic growth. Instead, an all-out effort for growth is being made, helped by large injections of foreign aid.[18] Welfare programs are being scaled down; industrial goods are being imported from the developed countries; and to encourage foreign investors, a free trade zone has been set up and investors are being allowed to export their profits and avoid all taxes.

The later chapters of this book will argue that this "western" strategy is a poor one for the developing countries in general. But the island population of Sri Lanka may be small enough to become another Hong Kong. It will be fascinating to see how fertility in Sri Lanka changes in response to these dramatic economic alterations.

The Case of Kerala

India has been almost everyone's favorite example of a demographic basket case: hundreds of millions of people, low average income, great inequality and pervasive poverty, a birth rate that has declined late and very little in spite of highly organized and expensive family planning programs. It is all the more striking that within India there is a beautiful example of the power of equality to lower fertility rapidly and in a sustained fashion.

Kerala, in the southwest, is one of India's smallest states, both by size and by population (a mere 21.3 million in 1971). The state was formed in 1956, following a period in which inequality, especially in the rural areas, had generally increased. In the two decades before the state's creation the increase in rural inequities (increasing rents, the eviction of tenant farmers) gave rise to mass movements for radical agrarian reform and to radical political movements. The Communist Party was elected to the state government in 1956 but was deposed in 1959 by a presidential decree from the central Indian government. A more centrist coalition then governed until 1969, when a leftist coalition came to power. Since creation of the state, successive governments have set about spreading economic benefits to all classes within it and have also tried to bring about land reform.[19]

After several abortive attempts, some real implementation of land reform acts began in 1964, resulting in improvement in tenure. The most effective reform occurred in 1969, when the new government abolished tenancy so that landlords could no longer charge rent, and those who worked the land were given ownership to it. Landless laborers were given small plots. This land reform and increased wages in agriculture (achieved mainly by agricultural unions) have undoubtedly improved the distribution of income over the past two decades and have benefited the rural population in particular. Real wages in agriculture are higher than in most other states, and since 1956 they have increased faster than in any other state. A major distributional problem, however, is the high rate of unemployment, as in Sri Lanka.

Kerala has also had great success in equalizing the distribution of other benefits. The state's health and educational systems are exceptional. Health care is free and hospitals and health care units have been distributed throughout the state on the basis of population, thus assuring equal and easy access to medical care. The Keralans, as a consequence, have the highest rate of using health care facilities in India, and their death rate has declined much faster than the Indian average. Kerala now has the lowest death rate and the longest life expectancy (sixty-one years in 1971) in India, where the average life expectancy was forty-seven years in 1971. Yet as recently as 1940, life expectancy in Kerala was only thirty-four years. In a nation where women live shorter lives than men in spite of their innately greater potential longevity, women in Kerala live longer than men, reflecting their generally good health and high status. The effect of the even-handed distribution of health care is a remarkably small difference between rural and urban death rates in Kerala (the smallest difference in India). Finally, Kerala's infant mortality rate (about 50 per 1,000 live births in 1971) is the lowest in India and, like Sri Lanka's, is lower than the rate among U.S. migrant farm laborers.

Kerala's educational system is also very broadly based and concentrates on the lower and middle levels of schooling. Free schooling has recently been extended from elementary levels to high school. The result of the state's educational policies is that education is much more evenly distributed in Kerala than in the rest of India. The percentage of the population in school is three times the Indian average, and is especially high among girls. More than 60 percent of the population is literate (India's average is 29 percent), and the improvement during the 1960s was rapid, so that illiteracy has been almost eliminated among the population under forty years of age.

The average intake of calories in Kerala seems to be above the overall Indian average. The diets of the poor are improved through two government programs. The first of these provides a free cooked mid-day meal to all elementary school children whose parents request it. This program reaches the poorest three-quarters of the children in the population. The second program distributes cereals at prices controlled below the market price. This rationing system reaches virtually everyone in the state and provides about 40 percent of the cereals eaten.

Finally, various public works have also spread benefits. About 100,000 houses were built for poor families in the early 1970s, and since 1973 some locally directed labor-intensive projects have been started, one of which allowed three crops of paddy rice to be grown per year instead of two.

The consequence of these improvements in general welfare upon Kerala's birth rate has been exactly as we would expect. Between 1931 and 1960, before these improvements began to take effect, Kerala's birth rate declined the negligible amount of one point, from 40 to 39 per thousand. However, between 1965 and 1974 the birth rate declined twelve points, to 27. In a similar period India's birth rate declined about four points and in 1975 was probably close to 38. A significant aspect of Kerala's fertility decline, as in Sri Lanka's, is that rural fertility has declined together with urban fertility. Indeed, the rural birth rate is slightly lower than the urban birth rate.

Kerala's success in improving the welfare of its people and in achieving fertility decline cannot be explained by exceptional affluence in the state. On the contrary, the per capita income in Kerala is in fact *lower* than the average for all Indian states.

The Case of China

China is an unusual case. This palpable truth seems to be used in some discussions as grounds for ignoring the insights we can gain from China's economic, social, and demographic achievements since 1949. Yet China is particularly relevant here because of the consistent emphasis, since its revolution began, upon equality, an emphasis that has included reducing geographic and rural-urban as well as class differences. China's achievements can be illuminated by contrasting its recent history with India's. The two nations were similar in many respects when India became independent in 1947 and China's revolution succeeded in 1949. Per capita incomes were about the same. Both nations were predominantly agricultural. Although agricultural productivity was higher in China, India was more industrialized, and in 1949 China's economy had been disrupted and fragmented by the Japanese war and the civil war.[20] Poverty was extreme in both countries. Health care and education were hopelessly inadequate. Finally, by any measure of equality, "China and India were among the most unequal societies in the world. Vast differentials of income prevailed; large numbers of people were unemployed or under-employed; health and education facilities were inadequate or nonexistent for much of the population; and social mobility was very limited."[21]

China's performance has been better than India's by the usual measures of mere growth.[22] Its average annual rate of per capita economic growth of almost 4 percent has been roughly three times faster than India's and its industrial growth has been almost twice as fast. This has occurred in spite of the continual flow of western financial and technical aid that India has received. By contrast, China has received no external aid since 1960 and in fact has developed its own foreign aid program. Depending upon the period of measurement, China's food production has increased at about the same rate or faster than India's, in spite of the fact that India in the 1950s had much lower yields and per capita production than China, has a more favorable agricultural environment, and has had an externally developed Green Revolution. China's grain production per head in the period 1970 to 1978 (about 290 kg. per person) has been 70 percent greater than India's (about 170 kg. per person). Some of this production is fed to pigs, so that not only is the average caloric intake some 16 percent higher than in India but the average protein intake is almost 30 percent higher.[23]

However, it is in the even-handed distribution of economic welfare and in the removal of ancient, deep-seated inequalities that China has excelled. Such inequality is built into the very structure of developing countries and is by no means easy to correct (Chapter 9). Indeed, the general pattern in the developing nations has been for inequality to increase, as can be seen in India, Brazil, Mexico, and numerous other nations. But China has maintained a commitment to increased equality that was firmly established by Mao from the beginning. Differences in income have been greatly reduced, and it appears that in the 1970s income differences in industry were about the same as in developed countries, but much less than in typical LDCs. For example, the top of the engineering and management salary scale was about three to six times the average blue collar worker's wage. In India, by comparison, top managers receive net incomes that are typically twenty to thirty times that of the average worker.[24]*

A host of government measures in China has distributed welfare more evenly than even the data on wages suggest.[25] There is job security and almost full employment. Sick leave pay is 60 to 100 percent of wages for six months and thereafter is given at a lower rate, and there is 60 percent disability pay for life. Prices have been stable or declining. House rents are well below cost and run only 4 or 5 percent of monthly wages. Retirement is at fifty-five or sixty at 60 to 70 percent of the last month's salary, so that old-age security is not a cause for concern. The distribution of wealth is, of course, much more uneven in India than in China, where wealth is held communally.

Public health, including preventive medicine and environmental hygiene, has been a major priority. There are extensive immunization programs, and special emphasis is placed on child and mother health care. Medical care is free to employees and well below cost to dependents. Furthermore, China's ability to get health care spread throughout the rural population is by now famous and well-attested to by recent visitors, in strong contrast to India's very biased system.[26] The result is low death rates and an average life expectancy of about sixty-four years.

Education is largely free and broadly available to both young and old. Just after World War II only 10 percent of China's population was literate (15 percent in India). Since then the fraction in China has increased to 50 percent, while India has reached only 29 percent. Education to age fifteen is universal, and in the cities the age is seventeen.[27]

Perhaps the most striking and fundamental difference between China and India is in the organization of their agriculture and in the lives of the rural population. While India's land distribution is not the most unequal in Asia, it is highly skewed. Furthermore, in some states there is an almost feudal relationship between landlord and farm tenant, such that tenants are essentially in bondage to a master. Even in the modern Punjab, tenure

---

*Income inequality in India is much greater than any official estimates. The reason is that a great deal of business is transacted in cash and is never recorded. For example, the Indian government has a rule that the president of a company may not pay himself more than a certain salary (about $8,000 per year in 1978). But while they conform to this law on paper, businessmen circumvent it with ease in practice. Extra income is simply taken in cash. One businessman I came to know in a large city in India paid each of his many family members (whether working or not) $1,000 a month in cash, paid himself more than this in cash, and bought many of the goods for all of these households with his company's money. His official income was clearly only a small fraction of his real and virtually untaxed total income.

to the land is often insecure, and landlords and moneylenders have great power (Chapter 6).[28] The result is millions of rural Indians living brief lives in great poverty.

Before 1949 China's peasants also led lives of extreme poverty and oppression, punctuated in part by almost annual "natural" disasters of flood and drought (which were actually the result of an oppressive system that kept the peasants from maintaining dykes and taking other preventive measures). Famines were frequent and arose not only from difficult farming conditions but because any surplus produced in good years was removed by landlords and the ruling classes. Of the 1930s Tawney wrote that the rural population:

> is taxed by one ruffian who calls himself a general, by another, by a third, and, when it has bought them off, still owes taxes to the Government; in some places actually more than twenty years' taxation has been paid in advance. It is squeezed by dishonest officials. It must cut its crops at the point of the bayonet, and hand them over without payment to the local garrison, though it will starve without them. It is forced to grow opium in defiance of the law, because its military tyrants can squeeze heavier taxation from opium than from rice or wheat, and make money, in addition, out of the dens where it is smoked. It pays blackmail to the professional bandits in its neighborhood; or it resists, and, a year later, when the bandits have assumed uniform, sees its villages burned to the ground. . .
>
> There are districts in which the position of the rural population is that of a man standing permanently up to the neck in water, so that even a ripple is sufficient to drown him. The loss of life caused by the major disasters is less significant than the light which they throw on the conditions prevailing even in normal times over considerable regions.[29]

It was a major aim of the Agrarian Reform Law of 1950 to eradicate such misery. That act took land from landlords and some rich peasants (perhaps a total of 10 to 20 million people) and redistributed it together with farm implements, draft animals and so on, to 300 million peasants. Thereafter, though landlords still owned land, they could not rent it out but had to cultivate it themselves. Since then agriculture has been successively changed so that now there is local and communal ownership of most land and farm implements. These changes, together with rationing of essential food and massive investment in producing fertilizer, have led to adequate food production and a well-fed rural population.

Although the living standards of the rural population are, almost inevitably, lower than those in the city, great efforts have been made to reduce the difference (see also Chapter 7): "The Chinese have achieved a social security framework of schooling, health, security in old age and employment which has transformed the life of the agricultural worker." Rural wages are now about 80 percent of urban wages. Health care is being rapidly extended to the countryside, and it has been claimed that by 1975, 85 percent of China's production brigades and communes had implemented a cooperative health plan.[30]

None of the above should be taken to imply that China has achieved the perfection of egalitarian harmony. Obviously it has not, and inequalities remain. People in high posts have various perquisites in addition to their incomes. There are geographic differences in industrial wages and differences between different parts of industry. Bonus systems are being reintroduced and these will probably increase unevenness of income. Inequalities also exist among different rural production teams within communes, as well as in different regions of the country.[31] Political turmoil, as in 1960 to 1961, has occasionally disrupted food production and led to widespread hardship (Chapter 7).

Strong attempts have been made to iron out massive regional inequality, which had been deepened by earlier foreign influence. Industrial capacity had been concentrated in the northeast and in a few coastal areas. In 1949 large areas of the country were essentially without health care, education, and other important social services. These attempts at redistribution have been partly successful. Light industry is now widespread, as are health and other social services. "If China's leaders had not adopted the policy favoring inland areas, China most certainly would have developed as a dual economy." However, there has been very little evening out of the distribution of heavy industry, and, as noted above, marked regional differences in living standards are still common.[32]

The remaining shortcomings, however, do not change the fact of the remarkable Chinese success. Before the Revolution, the conditions of the mass of Chinese seem to have changed little from those that had prevailed for centuries. Disease, starvation, and extreme poverty were the lot of the general population.[33] Now:

> The basic, overriding economic fact about China is that for 20 years she has fed, clothed and housed everyone, has kept them healthy, and has educated most. Millions have *not* starved; sidewalks and streets have *not* been covered with multitudes of sleeping, begging, hungry and illiterate human beings; millions are *not* disease-ridden. To find such deplorable conditions one does not look to China these days but rather to India, Pakistan, and almost anywhere else in the underdeveloped world.[34]

China's Fertility

China's social and economic revolution has been followed by an equally profound demographic revolution. It is not possible to state precisely what China's birth rate is or has been, but we can get reasonable estimates. A survey of Chinese farmers done in 1929 to 1931 has now been reanalyzed.

There was a population census in 1953, and a population tally of some sort in 1964. There is good evidence that a thorough population count was also made sometime during the early to mid-1970s. Bannister has evidence that the count was made throughout China at the end of 1972 and that it included all births and deaths that occurred that year (although Aird believes it was probably not done simultaneously throughout the country). Finally, it appears from radio news items, wall posters, and visitors' reports that population registration or updating of population information was being done in the late 1970s by all provinces, but with variable reliability. From these sources we can piece together a history of China's fertility changes (figure 3-5).[35]

The survey of 1929 to 1931 sheds light on traditional China, for it covered only rural farmers, who were the most traditional group. Among these farmers marriage was almost universal and, on average, women were married by seventeen years of age. However, fertility within marriage was only moderate—completed family size averaged about 5.5 children. This most likely resulted from very poor parental health, which depressed fertility much as it now does in parts of Africa (Chapter 2). The generally poor health of rural farmers was reflected in appalling mortality statistics: 300 infants out of every 1,000 died by age one, life expectancy was only 24 years, and the death rate was more than 41 per 1,000 per year. The birth rate was also over 41. These farmers presumably suffered greater mortality and worse health than the rest of the Chinese population, and the national birth rate was probably close to 45. (These new analyses show that previous estimates of China's pre-Revolutionary birth rates, which have sometimes been less than 40, must be revised upwards. A major reason that earlier estimates were low is that female births were frequently not recorded.) Orleans estimates the birth rate around 1950 to be 43, which is also likely to be an underestimate. Even in Shanghai, for example, it was still 45 in 1957.[36]

By 1953 the death rate in China had fallen to the low or mid-20s, and it is likely that the birth rate began to decline sometime around 1960. Four years later, there was evidence of fertility decline in some cities and in Kiangsu, demographically the most advanced province. By this time the Chinese leadership had also agreed that birth planning was essential. By 1964, however, the birth rate was still likely to have been not much less than 40. For example, in Kiangsu it was 35 to 38.[37]

China's birth rate has declined precipitously since 1964. By 1972 it was officially claimed to be 26 to 27 per thousand, although it may have been as high as 30 per thousand. The death rate was officially 7.6 but may have been 8 or 9 per thousand, so that in 1972 the annual rate of population increase was around 19 per thousand, or 1.9 percent. China's birth rate thus declined somewhere around eight to twelve points in eight years and it has continued to decline. By 1976 the birth rate could have been as low as 21 and was probably around 24. Even Aird, who has made estimates consistently higher than other scholars, concludes that the 1976 birth rate had declined to 28.[38]

It is worth comparing China's performance with that of India. Indian estimates are also subject to error and revision, the most reliable probably being that of Adlakha and Kirk.[39] Their estimates show a very modest decline from about 45 in 1951 to 41 or 42 in 1971. There probably was a further decline to around 38 or so in 1975. Thus both China and India entered the 1950s with birth rates around 45 per 1,000 and China, by any estimate, has done much better than India.

The Chinese experience underlines again the importance of improving the lot of the rural masses. It is not possible, given an age distribution like China's, to achieve a birth rate below 30 unless a very large fraction of the population is limiting its fertility. More than 80 percent of the Chinese are still rural, and clearly this segment of the population is participating in the fertility decline.

The importance of increases in rural living standards in reducing fertility is demonstrated by China's "model" province of Kiangsu.[40] This largely rural province in East China, on the Yangtze river, has about 60 million people and would be one of the world's ten most populous countries if it were an independent nation. Around 1930 its death rate was about 47, life expectancy was twenty years and its birth rate was about 45. The area was torn by the Japanese invasion and the civil war. In 1938 it was severely flooded by Chiang Kai-shek, whose army dynamited the dikes on the Yangtze river, causing the deaths of perhaps a million people.

The province is fertile, however, and it surrounds Shanghai so that it is in the mainstream of China's communications. Since the Revolution in 1949, it has become one of the most prosperous provinces, and peasant incomes there are relatively high. Health care has spread rapidly into the countryside from the cities, and the death rate had declined to perhaps 25 by 1954 and 8 to 10 by 1964. Education has also been greatly expanded and by 1972, 92 percent of all elementary-age children were in primary school; among people age twenty-five to fifty, 75 percent were literate. The birth rate has shown a correspondingly rapid decline—from around 45 at the Revolution to between 35 and 38 in 1965, 22 to 24 in 1972, and 18 to 19 in 1974. In seven years (1965–1972) the birth rate thus fell 13 to 18 points! By the mid-1970s the province had almost passed through its demographic transition.

China and the Demographic Transition Theory

China, in spite of its uniqueness, provides strong support for the theory of fertility behavior presented in Chapter 2. The same variables have been important in lowering fertility there as elsewhere.[41] Fertility has fallen first and furthest in those cities (e.g., Shanghai, Peking) and provinces (Kiangsu, Hopei) where living standards are highest and medical care is most advanced. The poorer provinces (e.g., Szechwan, Tibet) still have high birth rates. Reduced fertility is clearly linked to the high status of women, whose liberation has been a major goal of the (male) leaders of the country since 1949. Women occupy posts of seniority and responsibility and most Chinese women work. China also illustrates the importance of providing modern birth control facilities once the demand for fertility control exists.[42]

One important way in which China *is* unique is the way birth planning takes place. Fertility planning is integrated into overall economic planning and takes place at all levels, from national through province, county, district and ward, commune, brigade, and production team. Local committees organize educational and motivational meetings at which the importance of late marriage and small families is stressed. Local meetings discuss national fertility plans (as they discuss economic planning). Social pressure is brought to bear on peasants who have excess children, and in some cases there is actually a process of deciding which couples will have children in the following year.[43]

There is evidence that such planning is voluntary and largely not the result of coercion. The key is that there is broad participation in reaching important economic decisions, including fertility decisions, at the local level. The local production team of perhaps 30 to 50 households makes decisions about the distribution of labor, resources, and income, following guidelines set by the central government. These decisions are reached communally so that "individuals see their fertility plans as an integral part of the (overall development) plan for their area."[44] Thus individual and collective interests are reconciled through this participation. There may well be some coercion, subtle or not, on these matters, but there does not appear to be extensive evidence to confirm it.

RURAL DEVELOPMENT: THE CRUX

Chapters 2 and 3 have demonstrated that the solution to the population problem is to increase the level of economic well-being of the vast majority of families. Aggregate economic growth may not cause this (e.g., Brazil, Mexico), but economic development with broad participation will and is therefore a sufficient condition for sustained fertility decline. The economic well-being of the poor can also be increased with very little aggregate economic growth if the available benefits are spread evenly across the population. This has been a successful strategy from a demographic point of view in Sri Lanka and Kerala—at least so far. However, low average income levels make well-being very vulnerable to fluctuations in the economy, and Sri Lanka's strategy is precarious in that it has not been able to generate aggregate economic growth through the broad participation of the population in productive work. In later chapters I will show that such broad participation, especially in agriculture, is not only the key to reduced fertility but is a crucial component of overall economic development.

It is clear also that the major demographic problem is in the countryside. Here lives the majority of the population; here is the greatest poverty and hence the highest fertility. There are, of course, burgeoning populations in the cities, and these result in part from the high fertility of poor city dwellers. But the urban problems in the poor nations are to a great extent merely the displaced problem of rural poverty. People have been driven by a lack of economic opportunity from the destitute countryside into the towns, where conditions, however bad, in general offer greater hope: "Without question, the phenomenon of accelerated rural-urban labor migration has been the principal cause of both the high rates of urban population growth and the rising levels of urban unemployment." Part of the rural poverty problem is simply transferred: "In spite of higher rural fertility, the rural populations of Africa, South Asia, and Latin America grew by only 16 percent between 1960 and 1970, while over the same decade urban populations grew by 60 percent in Africa, 52 percent in Latin America, and 51 percent in South Asia."[45]

There is usually no possibility of creating urban jobs fast enough to employ these rapidly growing populations. Instead, the rural problems need to be solved in the countryside where they arise, and they need to be solved in such a way that the inequalities between town and countryside are reduced. This demands the development of a dynamic and productive agriculture that will provide employment for the rural population, for agriculture is directly and indirectly the source of rural economic welfare. Indeed, agriculture employs 60 to 80 percent of the labor force in many poor countries.

Rural poverty persists because the poor are denied access to productive resources; it results from unemployment, underemployment, and from the low wages and low incomes of those who do work. The solution therefore requires the creation of *productive* employment in agriculture in such a way that the poorest classes (the landless laborers and subsistence farmers) benefit. From the point of view of population control, then, the central policy of most developing nations, and of those developed nations that would help them, should be to bring about the development of agriculture in the poor nations in a strongly egalitarian way.

4

FUTURE POPULATION GROWTH

To predict future population growth in the less developed countries, it is most important to know how fertility will change. This is mainly because there is a great deal of room for reduction in fertility: at some time in the future in the LDCs both average family size and the birth rate are likely to have fallen by more than twofold, from five to two children and from 36 to 14 births per 1,000. Fertility is critical also because, while it may decline very rapidly, there can be wide variability in the rate of decline.

By contrast with fertility, there is relatively little opportunity for decline in mortality and for increases in life span. The death rate in the LDCs is already down to about 13 per 1,000 and could sink to around 6 or so only temporarily before rising again to 14 (appendix A). Life expectancy in the LDCs in 1975 was already around fifty-five years, only about 20 percent lower than that in the developed countries, where it was about seventy-one years.[1]

Patterns of Fertility Decline and Future Population Growth

A glance back at table 2-12 will remind the reader that the birth rate in a large array of developing countries has decreased in recent years. The history of demographic change has been that fertility declines, once begun, have generally proceeded until the birth rate is low. It is true that some countries with birth rates below 20 per thousand have experienced temporary increases above this level. The postwar "baby boom" in the West provides examples. But this was largely a question of the timing of births within a generation; there are no examples of countries reverting to traditionally high fertility levels after they have passed through the demographic transition. Given that the LDCs will experience some economic development in the future, the major questions are therefore when, and how quickly, will birth rates fall throughout the developing world?

How soon and how fast fertility declines will make a great difference to the future world population size. This can be shown by comparing population projections that make different assumptions about future fertility changes. In 1974 the United Nations made projections based on three different assumptions about fertility. In general the "medium" projection assumed that fertility in a particular country would begin to decline five years later than it would in the "low" projection; the "high" projection assumed it would begin yet another five years later. It was assumed that the *rate* of decline would be the same for almost all developing countries, and that fertility would be cut in half roughly thirty years after the decline began.

Table 4-1 shows that this relatively small difference *only in the timing* of the onset of fertility decline would have an enormous effect on world population size. By 2075, when the population would be approaching zero growth, the high projection shows about 6 billion people more than the low projection. This difference is roughly the projected total world population in the year 2000! To provide an idea of extreme possibilities, table 4-1 also shows what would happen if fertility had been reduced to replacement family size by 1970 and, in contrast, if no reduction in fertility were to occur at all.

Frejka has made various population projections in which he has examined the consequences of a range of assumptions about the *rate* of fertility decline. He showed that if world fertility were to decline rapidly from an average of 4.7 children per woman in 1970 to a replacement 2.2 children in the year 2000, world population would eventually reach about 8 billion and would stop growing about the year 2100 (table 4-1). But if fertility were to decline slowly so that replacement fertility did not occur until 2040, world population would eventually level off at almost 16 billion in

Table 4-1. Long-range projections of populations under different assumptions about future fertility behavior

UN projections	World population in 2075 A.D. (in billions)
Low	9.5
Medium	12.2
High	15.8
Instant fertility decline	5.6
No fertility decline	80.0

Frejka's projections	Population in 2100 A.D. (in billions)		
	World	Developed countries	Less developed countries
Rapid decline	8.4	1.6	6.8
Slow decline	15.8	1.9	13.9

Sources: United Nations, Department of Economic and Social Affairs, *Concise Report on The World Population Situation in 1970–75 and its Long-Range Implications* (ST/ESA/SER.A/56), 1974; Thomas Frejka, *The Future of Population Growth: Alternative Paths to Equilibrium* (New York: John Wiley and Sons, 1973).

the twenty-second century, giving a difference between the two projections of more than 7 billion people.[2]

Notice that almost all future population growth in these projections is contributed by the LDCs (table 4-1). The developed world reached replacement fertility in 1975, and its population is expected to grow very little.[3]

We can summarize the probable future as follows. Even under optimistic assumptions about fertility, world population is likely to double before it stabilizes. Under more pessimistic assumptions, the eventual world population will be about four times its present size. Neither of these sets of assumptions is unreasonable in the light of recent changes in fertility; unless unforeseen changes occur in the future, it is unlikely that world population will stabilize at less than 8 billion or much more than 16 billion. The outcome hinges almost entirely on changes in fertility in the LDCs.

The past three decades have provided some interesting contrasts between projected and actual population sizes. In the 1950s and 1960s, population consistently grew faster than the UN had projected. This tendency was reversed in 1970, when the actual world population was estimated to be 21 million fewer than the UN had projected, on the basis of data available in 1968. This was because in the 1960s fertility had declined somewhat faster and mortality somewhat slower than predicted.

The UN also projected world population in the year 2000, on the basis of data available in 1968. However, a new UN projection of world population in the year 2000, made in 1977 and based on data available in 1973, gives a projection of 240 million fewer people than the previous estimate, a difference equal to the current total population of the United States and Canada.[4]

Still more recent data suggest that the 1977 UN projection is itself too high; fertility by 1975 had again declined faster than expected.[5] The Community and Family Study Center has now estimated world population in the year 2000 at almost 5.9 billion, or 370 million fewer than the 1977 UN medium projection (table 4-2). The Center's calculations also suggest that the developing world as a whole could be close to replacement fertility by 2000 A.D., which would make eventual world population much closer to 8 billion than to the UN's medium projection of 12 billion. Of course, these projections may easily miss the mark, just as previous figures have.

Recent Patterns of Fertility Change

The size of the future population depends upon how fertility changes in the future in the LDCs. Will fertility decline begin soon in those LDCs where it has not yet done so? Will the decline be rapid in LDCs with high fertility, and will rapid decline be sustained? The only source of evidence we can turn to is past and current fertility behavior, especially in the developing world. This behavior provides both encouraging and discouraging evidence, since different groups of countries have shown markedly different behavior.

Declines began in the 1950s in a small group of LDCs: Barbados, probably China, Guadeloupe, Mauritius, Puerto Rico, Reunion, Singapore, Sri Lanka, Trinidad and Tobago, and Taiwan. (In Latin America, in the meantime, fertility generally *increased,* largely because parents in their reproductive years were living longer.) These areas were joined in the early 1960s by a second wave: Chile, Costa Rica, Fiji, Guyana, Hong Kong, Malaysia, and South Korea. Finally, fertility began to decline substantially in a wide range of LDCs between 1965 and 1975. This group includes Colombia, Cuba (fertility already rather low), Egypt, El Salvador, Indonesia, Jamaica, Martinique, Mexico, North Vietnam, Panama, Thailand, Tunisia, and Venezuela.[6] The remaining LDCs have shown no, or only small, declines in fertility. Some of the poorest LDCs can even be expected to show increases in the future as parental health improves.

Two encouraging sets of evidence come from the history of fertility decline. First, there has been a strong historical tendency for fertility to decline faster as time progresses. This is illustrated by some examples in figure 4-1. Further, Kirk has analyzed the rate of fertility decline starting with the demographic transition in Europe at the end of the nineteenth century.[7] He calculated the average length of time taken by groups of na-

Table 4-2. Various estimates and projections of future populations (in billions)

Area	Year	U.S. Bureau of the Census	United Nations	World Bank	Community and Family Study Center, University of Chicago
World	1975	4.090	3.968	4.033	4.017
	2000	6.350	6.254	6.054	5.883
Developed regions	1975	1.131	1.132	1.134	1.133
	2000	1.323	1.360	1.346	1.314
Less developed regions	1975	2.959	2.836	2.899	2.884
	2000	5.027	4.894	4.707	4.569

Source: U.S. Bureau of the Census, *Illustrative Projections of World Populations to the 21st Century,* Special Studies Series P-23, no. 79 (Washington, D.C.: Bureau of the Census, 1979), p. 92.

Note: These are the "medium" estimates and projections. The "low" and "high" projections of population in the developed regions for the year 2000 are generally 5 percent less or greater than the medium projections. The low and high projections for LDC population in the year 2000 range up to 10 percent lower and higher than the medium estimate.

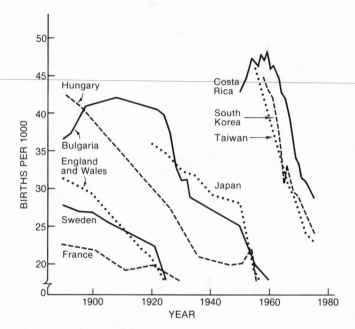

Figure 4-1 Demographic transition through time

Sources: Nathan Keyfitz and Wilhelm Flieger, Population: Facts and Methods of Demography (San Francisco: W. H. Freeman and Co., 1971); R. R. Kuczynski, The Measurement of Population Growth: Methods and Results (New York: Gordon and Breach, 1969); W. Parker Mauldin, "Patterns of Fertility Decline in Developing Countries 1950–75," Studies in Family Planning 9 (1978): 76, 77; Thomas McKeown, R. G. Brown, and R. G. Record, "An Interpretation of the Modern Rise of Population in Europe," Population Studies 26 (1972): 345–82; M. Muramatsu, Japan: Country Profiles (New York: Population Council, 1971); Te-Hsiung Sun, Hui-Sheng Lin, and Ronald Freedman, "Trends in Fertility, Family Size Preferences, and Family Planning Practice: Taiwan 1961–76," Studies in Family Planning 9 (1978): 55; United Nations, Department of Economic and Social Affairs, Levels and Trends of Fertility Throughout the World, 1950–1970 (ST/ESA/SER.A/59), 1977.
Note: Fertility has declined faster as the transition has spread from western Europe.

tions to move from birth rates of 35 to 20 per thousand, i.e., for the birth rate to drop by fifteen points, reasoning that a birth rate as low as 35 could be taken as a signal that the nation was fully into the transition. Nine nations (Austria, Australia, England and Wales, Finland, Italy, the Netherlands, New Zealand, Scotland, and the United States) began the process between 1875 and 1899. They took an average of forty-eight years to drop fifteen points. Seven countries (Argentina, Czechoslovakia, Germany, Hungary, Japan, Portugal, and Spain) reached a birth rate of 35 between 1920 and 1924. They took an average of thirty-eight years to reach 20 per 1,000. Between 1925 and 1949 another five countries (Bulgaria, Poland, Romania, the Soviet Union, and Yugoslavia) reached 35 births per 1,000 and took an average of thirty-one years to reach 20 per 1,000.

Kirk also recognized six countries as having entered the transition between 1950 and 1960: Sri Lanka, Chile, Hong Kong, Puerto Rico, Singapore, and Taiwan. Of these, only Hong Kong (1970) and Singapore (1975) had dropped fifteen points or more by 1975, thus completing the transition in less than fifteen years. If fertility in the other four areas were to continue to decline as it did up until the mid-1970s, this group would complete the transition in an average time of about seventeen years. Finally, Kirk has also shown that the rate of decline itself tends to increase during the transition within a given nation.

Another way of showing that declines have greatly speeded up is to look at the average yearly drop in fertility. In Western Europe and the United States, from the time at which fertility began declining until it stopped in the mid-1930s, it took a decade to lose three points off the birth rate. Thus, each year, on average, the birth rate fell by 0.3. Although this average rate increased with time, no country entering the demographic transition before World War II exceeded an average rate of decline measuring 0.5 of a point per year. (Bulgaria was the fastest at 0.49.) These rates should be compared with average declines of one point and more per year for modern declines, as shown in table 2-12. These show that fertility can decline in modern poor countries at rates two and three times the historical record, and four or five times faster than occurred in Western Europe. Table 2-12 also shows that such high rates have occurred in a wide range of countries.

The second encouraging fact is the one stressed in Chapter 3, namely that sustained rapid fertility declines can be achieved by countries with low average incomes, provided that income and benefits are well distributed.

The bad news is that a number of countries, including some large ones, have shown very late fertility declines, very slow declines, or both, even though they have achieved average income levels at which nearby countries have experienced rapid declines. Some of these countries are listed in table 4-3.

In evaluating table 4-3, we must remember that, for reasons that are not entirely clear, while Asian countries that had early fertility declines did so at annual per capita incomes around or below $100, in Latin America even the demographic front runners, such as Chile and Costa Rica, have not shown declines until incomes reached about $300. Presumably this is partly because incomes are typically distributed more unequally in Latin America than in Asia (appendix B). In any case, it makes sense to compare nations with those that are similar and nearby. Thus, while India's fertility, or even that of the Philippines, might not appear high in comparison with richer Latin American countries, it is high in comparison with those equally poor or poorer Asian nations that have managed to achieve a sustained reduction in fertility.

The most discouraging examples are to be found in Latin America. The richer segments of Brazil's highly inequitable society have reduced their fertility (Chapter 2), but the *national* birth rate has declined only very slowly over a period of sustained economic growth and industrialization. The country has tremendous resources and potential for development; by 1970 its GNP per capita was $420 and by 1975 it was $1,010. Per capita GNP grew at 4 percent a year from 1960 to 1974. Mexico is an equally dramatic case. Per capita GNP in 1970 was $670, in 1975 $1,190, and it grew at 3.3 percent from 1960 to 1974. Yet Mexico has only just begun its fertility decline. Venezuela, with huge revenues derived from oil, had a per capita GNP of $980 in 1970 and $2,220 in 1975, but did not begin its fertility decline until the late 1960s.

In Asia we have already noted India's poor performance in comparison with those of Sri Lanka and China. Pakistan lags even more, and by East Asian standards, average income in the Philippines has long been high enough to stimulate fertility decline, which has occurred only recently. In Thailand, Colombia, and Venezuela, the late decline at least seems to be substantial. The question raised by these late but rapid declines is, will the poor majority of people in such countries reduce their fertility soon and quickly, or will the process of national fertility decline slow down once the more affluent segments of the population have achieved small-sized families?

Future Trends in Fertility and Rates of Population Growth

Clearly, there is no simple answer to the question posed at the start of this chapter: when and how quickly will birth rates fall in the developing

Table 4-3. Selected developing countries showing late or slow fertility declines, or both

Country	Late and slow declines Percentage of decline in family size, 1968-1975[a]	Per capita 1975 GNP, in U.S. $	Country	Late declines Percentage of decline in family size, 1968-1975[a]	Per capita 1975 GNP, in U.S. $
Brazil (38)[b]	6	1,010	Colombia (33)	35	550
India (38)	8	150	Thailand (36)	17	350
Mexico (40)	13	1,190	Venezuela (37)	17	2,220
Nigeria[c] (49)	−1	310			
Pakistan (47)	4	140			
Philippines (36)	7	370			
Turkey (34)	4	860			

Source: Amy Ong Tsui and Donald J. Bogue, "Declining World Fertility: Trends, Causes, and Implications," *Population Bulletin*, vol. 33 (Washington, D.C.: Population Reference Bureau, 1978), pp. 1–56.
[a]Family size here is the total fertility rate, which is not affected by age distribution.
[b]1975 birth rates are in parentheses.
[c]Notice that Nigeria's fertility increased slightly.

world? It depends upon how rapid economic development is, how egalitarian the pattern of development is, and, within this context, how well family planning programs operate. The pattern of future development therefore will have enormous demographic significance.

A commitment to equality and to rural development, coupled with steady economic growth, could produce sustained rapid fertility declines on the order of those seen in table 2-12. At these rates much of the developing world's population could be nearing replacement fertility of about 2.2 children per couple by the year 2000. By way of illustration, table 4-4 provides a series of low fertility projections which assume that family size will decrease by about one child every ten to twelve years in most of the developing world. This rate is equivalent to an annual decline in the birth rate of about 0.7 or 0.8 per year, a rate of decline that has been equaled or exceeded over long periods by a number of countries (table 2-12).

On the other hand even steady economic growth, in the absence of such a commitment, could lead in many countries to slow declines that would leave fertility far from the replacement level by the year 2000. Table 4-4

Table 4-4. Current and projected fertility in various regions and in the 12 most populous LDCs

Region or country	Population in 1975 (millions)	Family size[a] 1975	Projected family size[a] in 2000	
			Low estimate	High estimate
World	4,090	4.3	2.7	3.9
Developed countries	1,131	2.1	1.9	2.6
Less developed countries	2,959	4.8–5.1	2.9	4.2
China	935	3.2–4.1	1.9	3.1
India	618	5.3	2.9	4.5
Indonesia	135	4.6–5.3	2.2	4.0
Brazil	109	5.0–5.7	2.5	5.0
Bangladesh	79	6.3–7.0	4.1	5.0
Pakistan	71	6.3–6.9	3.8	5.0
Nigeria	63	6.7	4.9	6.4
Mexico	60	5.7–6.4	3.4	4.7
Vietnam	46	5.1	—	—
Philippines	43	5.1	2.6	3.8
Thailand	42	5.1	2.2	3.9
Turkey	40	5.4	2.3	3.5
Total	2,241			

Sources: Population sizes from U.S. Bureau of the Census, Current Population Reports, Special Studies Series P-23, no. 79 (Washington, D.C.: U.S. Bureau of the Census, 1979); Vietnam and Turkey data from Tsui and Bogue, "Declining World Fertility." Estimates of family size in 1975 from U.S. Bureau of the Census and Tsui and Bogue; both estimates are given only where they differ significantly. Low estimate of fertility in 2000 A.D. from Tsui and Bogue, high estimate from U.S. Bureau of the Census.

[a]Total fertility rate.

also provides a series of high fertility projections which assume that it will take about seventeen years for average family size in the LDCs to decrease by one child. This is equivalent to an annual decline in the crude birth rate of less than 0.5 per year. At this rate, replacement fertility would not occur until somewhere around 2030 A.D., which, as discussed earlier, would put the eventual world population much closer to 16 billion than to 8 billion.

It should be emphasized that the estimates of future fertility in table 4-4 are no more than best-informed guesses. They bracket the range of fertility that demographers feel might occur—given current fertility, the relation between fertility and socio-economic conditions, and probable economic growth in the future. The recent rash of fertility declines has led some demographers to believe that the lower estimate is more likely to be borne out. However, most LDCs are experiencing only modest economic growth, most of them are highly inequitable, and most are doing little to bring about rural development (Chapters 6, 7, and 9). Furthermore, inequality typically increases as economic growth occurs.[8] Substantial fertility decline has yet to occur in several large countries—India, Pakistan, Bangladesh, Philippines, Brazil, and Mexico—and in most of Africa. Countries that have not yet had substantial declines contained about 1.5 billion people in 1975. Thus the demographic future does not appear as bright as recent fertility declines might suggest.

In summary, future growth rates will depend heavily upon how the poorest people in the world's poor countries fare in the coming decades. That, in turn, will depend upon the degree and pattern of development that is achieved, especially in agriculture, and on the relation between agriculture and the rest of the economy. Parts II and III examine these issues.

FOOD SUPPLY AND AGRICULTURE

5

FOOD SUPPLY, HUNGER, AND
THE PHYSICAL LIMITS TO PRODUCTION

Widespread hunger has been common throughout modern history. The present, in spite of great technological advances, is no exception. It is the thesis of this chapter, however, that the nations of the world are quite capable of feeding adequately all of their people, both now and in the future. We will substantiate this claim by examining the physical and technical aspects of, the limits to, and the potential for, increased food production. Let us first examine why huge numbers of people are hungry now.

MALNUTRITION: THE PROBLEM OF POVERTY

Widespread malnutrition exemplifies in a straightforward way the general contention of this book that problems of food and population are fundamentally economic, social, and political, and not merely a matter of too many mouths searching for too little food. That many millions of people are malnourished is an incontrovertible fact. That they are malnourished because food supplies are inadequate is a reasonable first hypothesis, but it is in most instances false, and the persistence of malnutrition in the midst of plenty should alert us to the possibility that the obvious superficial explanations of food and population problems may not be correct.

It is not at all certain just how many people in the world are malnourished. In the late 1960s and early 1970s, the FAO estimated that approximately 1.5 billion people were undernourished or malnourished, and that protein deficiency was a distinct problem affecting hundreds of millions who had sufficient calories. But in 1974 the FAO estimated that around 1970 less than half-a-billion people were suffering from inadequate diets. They also concluded that protein deficiency is not a separate additional problem, except in regions where the main staple is cassava or some other starchy crop. Otherwise, those who have enough calories (mainly from cereals) probably have enough protein. Unfortunately, the greatly reduced estimate of the number who are malnourished does not reflect improved diets—merely changed definitions. As they have learned more about human physiology, nutritionists have gradually reduced their estimate of the amount of both calories and protein required for an adequate diet.[1]*

In 1977, the FAO once again estimated the number of undernourished in the LDCs at somewhere over 400 million people (table 5-1). The estimate is in some respects conservative.† It is based on a calorie requirement that takes no account of the energy needed for activities such as farming, and Scrimshaw and Young have evidence that even when allow-

*There are two different hunger problems: famine and chronic malnutrition. Although famine is more apparent, it is now less important than chronic malnutrition. Famines have become less frequent, less severe, and more efficiently solved since World War II. They have often been caused by the dislocations of war or other man-made difficulties, although drought and other natural catastrophes are still important. In the short term they can be solved by proper communication and modern transportation and by a proper system of food reserves, the cost of which is not particularly large. This is not to say, of course, that either donor countries or local governments and distributors have always responded in time, efficiently, or fairly (L. Wiseberg, "An International Perspective on the African Famines," in M. H. Glantz, ed., *The Politics of Natural Disaster* [New York: Praeger, 1977]), or that the necessary steps will be taken to respond to future famines.

Famine, like chronic malnutrition, affects the poor more than the rich. For example, in a study area in Bangladesh during the 1974 to 1975 famine, the death rate for landless families was three times higher than in families with three or more acres of land; the death rate of young children was five times higher in landless families than in those with three or more acres (A.K.M. Alauddin Chowdhury and L. C. Chen, "The Interaction of Nutrition, Infection, and Mortality During Recent Food Crises in Bangladesh," *Stanford Food Research Institute Studies* 16 [1977]: 47–62).

Famine, again like chronic malnutrition, affects infants and children the most. In fact, famine accentuates the effects of chronic malnutrition. In the same study area in Bangladesh, by the end of the 1971 war-induced famine, 140 children had died—out of 1,000 children who were severely malnourished at the start. Of 1,000 children who had normal diets before the famine, only 30 died. As in the case of chronic malnutrition, the actual immediate cause of death is usually infectious disease (diarrhea, cholera, dysentery, measles, smallpox, and others).

†The calculations in 1977 were based on a more conservative estimate of nutritional requirements than in 1974. The estimate was made as follows. First, from extensive laboratory studies FAO calculated the minimum number of calories that will suffice to maintain the body weight of a person who is resting most of the time but does require some energy for a minimum of activity—eating, dressing, washing, and so on. This critical minimum requirement is stated for a reference person in each country and takes into account the climate; differences among children, men, and women; and the age distribution of the population. For most LDCs the critical requirement is around 1,500 to 1,600 calories per day (this is 1.2 times the average basic metabolic rate or BMR; the estimates in 1974 used 1.5 times BMR). Actual requirements for an active person are likely to be close to 2,000 calories.

The number malnourished in a given country is then estimated by calculating how many people receive less than this minimum requirement. This is done by first calculating the number of calories available per capita in the particular country, with a fraction subtracted for loss and wastage. There is some information available about what fraction of the food in each country goes to each fraction of the population (the poor receiving the least and the rich the most), and this is used to estimate how many of the available calories each group receives.

These critical calorie requirements should not be confused with FAO's per capita calorie requirement for a given *country*. The latter (generally around 2,200 to 2,400 for LDCs) represents the per capita calories needed to provide adequate diets in the country when wastage, moderate level of activity, *and uneven food distribution* are taken into account.

ance is made for such activities, the FAO requirements may still be understated. Using somewhat different methods and criteria, Reutlinger and Selowsky calculated that 840 million people were malnourished in the mid-1960s; for 1975 their estimate rises to 932 million.[2]

On the other hand, there is evidence that FAO has overestimated the prevalance of malnutrition. Poleman has pointed out that there is a tendency in the LDCs to underreport food production, perhaps by as much as 15 percent. Surveys also tend to underestimate actual food consumption. For example, even sophisticated nutrition surveys in India probably underestimate the food available by 10 to 34 percent.[3] These factors lead to overestimates of the number malnourished.

There is, in fact, no sound way to arrive at a "correct" figure for the number malnourished, partly because of inadequate data and partly because "malnutrition" is hard to define. A National Academy of Sciences study concludes that "we do not know...how many calories are needed for people to live their daily lives." However, a minimum estimate of the number of malnourished can be obtained by examining medical surveys in the developing countries. These surveys estimate directly the number of people showing clinical symptoms of malnutrition. The World Health Organization, using a large number of such surveys of children in many countries in the mid-1960s, estimated that 100 million children aged zero to five years were suffering from moderate to severe malnutrition (table

Table 5-1. Estimated number of people suffering from malnutrition

Region	Total population (millions)		Percentage of population suffering		Total number suffering (millions)	
	1969–1971	1972–1974	1969–1971	1972–1974	1969–1971	1972–1974
Non-Communist developing countries						
Africa	278	301	25	28	70	83
Far East	968	1,042	25	29	256	297
Latin America	279	302	16	15	44	46
Near East	167	182	18	16	31	20
(Most seriously affected countries)	(954)	(1,027)	(27)	(30)	(255)	(307)
All developing countries	1,692	1,827	24	25	401	455
Developed countries	1,070	—	3	—	28	—

Sources: Data on developing countries are from the Food and Agriculture Organization, *The Fourth World Food Survey,* Statistics Series no. 11 (Rome, FAO, 1977), p. 53; data on developed countries are from the United Nations, World Food Conference, *Assessment of the World Food Situation: Present and Future* (E/Conf. 65/3), Rome, 5–16 November 1974, p. 66.

Note: From the available accounts it appears that there is no significant malnutrition in the Communist developing countries. No estimates were made for the developed countries for 1972 to 1974. See appendix C for list of most seriously affected countries.

5-2).[4] Thus, in spite of the difficulties of estimation, it is clear that at least 100 million people, and probably hundreds of millions, are chronically malnourished.

What is the cause? Certainly not inadequate global supplies of food. For example, in the 1970s world foodgrain production was great enough to provide the average person in the world with more foodgrain than is consumed by the average Japanese, and the Japanese are a well-nourished population. The extra food needed to provide adequate diets for the malnourished of the world is not even very large in relative terms. The deficit in calories is equivalent to about 37 million tons of grain.[5] This was one-fiftieth of world grain production and is less than 10 percent of the amount of grain fed to livestock in the rich countries.

Couching the problem in terms of *global* production, however, is misleading. Although global production would be more than adequate if it were evenly distributed, both production and consumption per head are much greater in the developed countries, where the average person consumes 50 percent more calories and 70 percent more protein than the average person in the poor countries, and directly and indirectly uses three times as much grain.[6] Clearly, global food supplies are not evenly distributed, nor are they likely to be. In fact, global redistribution is not a satisfactory solution, even if it were politically likely and economically possible, because it would suppress the development of local agriculture in poor nations (Chapter 6). The widespread discussion of a *world* food problem actually obscures the fact that it is really a question of a large number of *national* problems.

What is more striking than malnutrition in the presence of adequate global supplies of food is that even within each country, food supplies would in general be adequate *if they were evenly distributed.* Even if we ignore local underreporting of food production, only in a handful of small

Table 5-2. Children with moderate or severe forms of protein-energy malnutrition in mid-1960s

Area	Number of affected chilren aged 0–5 years (millions)	Percentage of the population aged 0–5 that is affected
Latin America	9.0	20.5
Africa	19.5	30.9
Asia	71.0	33.4
Total	99.5	

Source: E. M. de Maeyer, "Protein-Energy Malnutrition," in G. H. Beaton and J. M. Bengoa, eds., *Nutrition in Preventive Medicine,* World Health Organization Monograph Series no. 62, 1976.

Note: Severe malnutrition = 60 percent or less of standard weight for age; moderate malnutrition = 60 to 75 percent of standard weight for age.

countries does *average* food consumption per person fall below that required for an adequate diet. Malnutrition results instead from the uneven distribution of food *within* nations.[7]

In particular, hunger is the lot of the poor. Figure 3-4 shows diets in India as a function of income. Although the amount of food available per person in India is, on average, more than what is required for an adequate diet, the poorest are on starvation diets while the rich eat better than most westerners. Similar data are available from other areas of the world; table 5-3 provides an example. Even during times of severe shortages, as in India in 1965 and 1966, it is often unequal *distribution* of food, not inadequate production, that causes hunger.[8]

Hunger persists then, because poor people cannot afford to buy more food (or to produce it—a problem I will return to) and not because supplies are inadequate in some absolute sense. In 1978 India produced in its record rice and wheat harvests more grain than it could store. It exported more than a million tons of wheat, yet 20 to 40 percent of the population was still unable to get enough for an adequate diet. The point is surely made most clearly in the overfed rich nations where hunger still persists (table 5-1).

The malnourished are found mainly in the "most seriously affected countries" (MSAs). This is a group of forty-five developing nations that were most seriously affected by the economic and food crises of the 1970s. It includes most of the least developed countries and accounts for about 56 percent of the population of the capitalist developing countries. The MSAs are concentrated mainly in Africa but also include India and Bangladesh (appendix C).

Within countries, the groups that suffer most frequently are the urban poor and, in rural areas, the landless laborers, subsistence farmers, and nomads. Within these groups, small children and lactating mothers are most affected;[9] in the most seriously affected countries one-quarter to one-half of young children suffer from malnutrition (table 5-4).

The most acute result of malnutrition is high death rates, especially in infants and young children. Hunger and disease interact to cause appalling losses from "minor" childhood diseases such as diarrhea and measles. For example, in Guatemala in 1965, the childhood death rate from measles was 1,000 times the rate in the United States. The interaction is synergistic in that malnutrition impairs the body's ability to respond to disease and disease frequently reduces the body's ability to assimilate food.[10]

Malnutrition probably is the biggest single contributor to the high childhood mortality in the developing countries, although the data are hard to secure and the immediate cause of death is usually a disease. In Latin America malnutrition is a primary or contributory factor in over

Table 5-3. Income and diet in different regions of Brazil

Income (cruzeiros per household per year)	Northeast				East				South			
	Urban		Rural		Urban		Rural		Urban		Rural	
	House-holds (%)	Calories per capita/day	House-holds (%)	Calories per capita/day	House-holds (%)	Calories per capita/day	House-holds (%)	Calories per capita/day	House-holds (%)	Calories per capita/day	House-holds (%)	Calories per capita/day
Less than 100	9	1,240	18	1,500	5	1,180	7	1,420	1	1,480	4	2,380
100–149	13	1,500	14	1,810	5	1,530	10	2,100	3	1,740	4	2,900
150–249	26	2,000	25	2,140	17	1,880	20	2,210	11	1,970	16	2,500
250–349	17	2,320	13	1,820	14	2,090	15	2,720	13	2,050	15	1,860
350–499	14	2,420	10	2,228	17	2,220	13	2,670	20	2,360	18	2,970
500–799	11	2,860	11	2,370	20	2,630	13	2,920	22	2,470	21	3,000
800–1,199	5	3,310	5	3,380	11	2,820	8	3,060	14	2,780	9	3,780
1,200–2,499	4	4,040	3	2,870	9	3,270	11	3,040	12	3,080	10	4,160
More than 2,500	1	4,290	1	2,900	2	3,750	3	4,100	4	3,170	3	4,770

Source: FAO, Fourth World Food Survey, p. 35.

half the deaths of children under five. Those who survive malnutrition are small, weak, susceptible to disease, and have difficulty with tasks requiring good coordination. The FAO reports that more than 300 million children in the LDCs have grossly retarded physical growth as a result of poor diets.[11] Perhaps most serious, mental health may be irreversibly damaged, since the brain completes most of its growth and development in the first two years.

The massive cost of malnutrition in terms of human suffering is certainly reason enough to seek solutions, but there is the additional reason that, by its effects upon death rates (especially childhood death rates) and upon economic welfare, malnutrition almost certainly contributes to high fertility and rapid population growth, as we saw in Chapter 2.

THE WORLD FOOD SITUATION

Food Production, Trade, and Aid

We will discuss only standard agriculture. For the remainder of this century agriculture is unlikely to be replaced by "new foods," marine algae, or other novel sources as the main provider of the world's nourishment. Even world fisheries provide only 1 percent of the calories and about 4 percent of the protein consumed. Furthermore, for most of our discussion we will concentrate on grains, especially wheat, rice, and corn (the main crops). Grain is by far the most important food; it supplies over 60 percent of the calories and 50 percent of the protein in the developing world. The

Table 5-4. Percentage of children suffering from malnutrition in some of the "most seriously affected" developing countries

		Percentage suffering		
	Age group covered (years)	Severe malnutrition	Moderate malnutrition	Total
Guyana	0–4	1.3	30.8	32.1
Haiti	0–5	6.0	25.0	31.0
El Salvador	0–4	3.1	22.9	26.0
Guatemala	0–4	5.9	26.5	32.4
Burundi	0–5	2.2	28.7	30.4
Cameroon	0–5	4.4	36.4	40.8
Central African Empire	0–5	3.0	36.4	39.4
Kenya	—	1.0	25.0	26.0
Rwanda	0–5	9.8	44.9	54.7
India	1–5	2.0	52.7	54.7

Source: FAO, *Fourth World Food Survey,* p. 30.

trends for food production as a whole are similar to those for grain production.[12] Since 95 percent of the meat in international trade goes to the
rich nations, trade in meat products is of little direct relevance to consumption in poor countries, which are net exporters of meat to the developed countries.

Annual world grain production in 1978 was roughly 1.5 billion tons. Of
this, about 400 million tons were produced by the non-Communist developing nations, which have roughly half of the world's population. This indigenous production accounts for over 90 percent of the food consumed in
these nations. Almost 100 percent of the food eaten in Communist developing countries is produced locally. Thus, although trade and aid are important, the great bulk of food eaten in the LDCs is produced there, and
in their agriculture lies the solution to the food problem.

The difference between consumption and production is made up by
trade and aid, mainly by the former. In 1974 the poor nations imported
about 30 million tons from the rich nations (mainly the United States). In
1975 they imported 37 million tons, and in 1976, 35 million tons. Even
these large quantities represent less than 10 percent of the local grain
production in the non-Communist LDCs, although for the importing developing countries as a whole, imports represented about 15 percent of
consumption.

Food imports by the poor nations, although large, are not the major
fraction of world trade in food. I have already commented that 95 percent
of all meat products flow to the rich nations. In addition, most of the trade
in grains is among the rich nations, and especially from the United States
to the U.S.S.R., Europe, and Japan (figure 5-1). Trade is about 12 percent of total world production and is dominated by the United States,
which from 1971 to 1975 exported almost 60 percent of its wheat crop,
almost 20 percent of its corn, and over half of its soybeans. In 1978 over
half the world's grain exports came from the United States. Indeed, grain
exports recently have been the major earner of foreign exchange for this
country.

Finally, food aid from the developed countries has contributed the
smallest amount to consumption in the poor nations. At its peak during
the 1960s, food aid averaged about 12 million tons per year and contributed about 3 percent of consumption. Food aid declined rapidly in the
1970s and was about 5 million tons per year from 1973 to 1974. By 1975
and 1976 it was between 8 and 9 million tons per year. Notice again that
although such aid is important, it represents only about 2 percent of consumption in the non-Communist poor nations.

The United States has been the main supplier of food aid. Its food aid
program emerged in essence as a solution to a problem that has plagued
American farmers since about 1930—excess production (Chapter 6). In

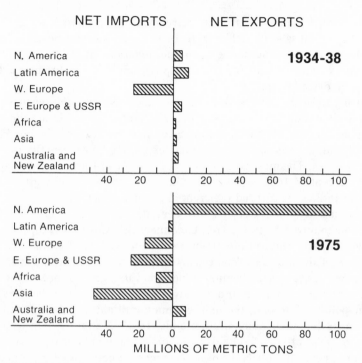

Figure 5-1 World trade in grain

Source: Sterling Wortman and Ralph W. Cummings, Jr., *To Feed This World: The Challenge and the Strategy* (Baltimore: Johns Hopkins University Press, 1978), p. 22.

the 1950s and 1960s, the United States had a glut of cheap grain stored at high cost—by 1959 government-owned stocks had reached $7.7 billion worth. Two or three decades ago there was no huge world demand to buy this grain, as there has been in the 1970s. The food aid program provided the necessary outlet.

Public Law (P.L.) 480, passed in 1954, institutionalized previous food aid programs. Its major purpose was the disposal of surplus U.S. production, but it was seen as serving several purposes:

1. getting rid of surplus stocks;
2. maintaining U.S. farm incomes;
3. developing markets abroad for U.S. farm products;
4. gaining political influence abroad; and
5. serving humanitarian purposes.

Title I of P.L. 480 authorized sales of surplus food to "friendly nations" for local currency rather than for foreign exchange. The Food for Peace

Act of 1966 stipulated that local currency sales be phased out and replaced by credit sales for dollars and other convertible currencies. Titles II and III of P.L. 480 authorized genuine donations of food, initially for emergency relief and special nutrition programs, later as broader aid to economic development.

During the 1950s and early 1960s, food aid was able simultaneously to achieve all of the purposes listed above. Humanitarian and U.S. economic and political ends were compatible, given the great excess of food. Food aid, of course, was not given without extracting some benefits for the United States. The massive U.S. food aid to India in 1965 and 1966 (equal to 15 percent of India's production in 1965) was given only after U.S. firms in India were assured preferential arrangements.[13]

Quite suddenly, in the early 1970s, demand increased from nations that were able to buy U.S. grain. This, combined with some minor dips in production, greatly reduced the amount of grain available for aid—even in the form of dollars sales financed by long-term credit. In this squeeze, U.S. priorities came clearly into perspective. First, grain went to those nations that could pay for it and was given to gain leverage in the world of power politics.[14] Second, the reduced amount of aid was clearly used for political rather than humanitarian ends. In 1972 South Korea was the main recipient of U.S. food aid, and four of the top five major recipients did not appear on the UN list of nations most in need; in 1971, 1973 and 1974, South Vietnam received the most food aid; and in 1974 South Vietnam and Cambodia received almost 80 percent of the Title I food aid, while millions of people went hungry on the Indian subcontinent.

Some important changes have occurred since the early 1970s. Legislation passed in 1977 requires U.S. food aid to go mainly to truly needy countries. In addition, the American role is now less dominant; its share of food aid declined from 94 percent in 1965 to around 60 percent from 1975 to 1976.[15]

There is a clear need for properly managed international food aid. However, care must be taken to ensure that it does not suppress local production, by driving down prices or by allowing the local government to use it as a substitute for developing local agriculture. These effects have certainly occurred in the past, although the record is mixed and the consequences of food aid depend very much on related government policies.[16]

Food aid is crucial for truly emergency situations following very bad weather or some other temporary disaster. Since such aid need be given only intermittently it should not in general drive down local production. Food aid can also help in development by serving as wages in public works projects or in special nutrition programs. However, the danger with all such aid is that governments can use it as a palliative instead of making fundamental changes in the structure of the economy that would increase both food production and the incomes of the poor (Chapters 6, 7, and 9). It is therefore not possible to claim that even this latter type of aid, which is distributed directly to the poor, is always to their benefit.

A major problem for both recipient and donor nations is that there is a great deal of uncertainty about food aid from one year to the next. The weather and other factors cause strong annual fluctuations in production everywhere. Fluctuations in production, trade, and the need for aid are therefore inevitable and largely unpredictable. In addition, food aid is given on a year-to-year basis. There is clearly a need to iron out this uncertainty by having an international system for taking advantage of good years to build up stocks for use in bad years. Such a system would need a standing stock of 10 to 20 million tons of wheat for famine relief.[17] At the average 1975 to 1977 prices of $137 per ton, this would require an initial outlay of about $2 billion. Maintenace costs thereafter would be quite low —about $210 million per year for a 20 million ton reserve.

There may also be great advantages in expanding such a system beyond famine needs so that it could be used to stabilize prices and assure supplies for international trade. In good years grain could be stockpiled, thus maintaining the farmers' prices, and in poor years supplies could be drawn upon, thus keeping down prices paid by consumers. Stocks for this purpose would need to be perhaps as large as 30 million tons each of wheat and corn, which would cost about $640 million per year to maintain.[18] Both of these types of reserves would be held in addition to "working stocks," which are about 10 percent of annual production (i.e., about 150 million tons). World-wide grain stocks by 1978 were in fact adequate to fulfill these needs, but there has as yet been no agreement on an appropriate international system for maintaining them. One difficulty is that the poor countries have inadequate facilities for storing grain. For example, the surplus from India's 1976 grain crop exceeded its storage capacity of about 17 million tons.

The World Market and Food for the Poor

Markets, prices, and production often respond in ways that are not intuitively obvious, and it is worth noting the probable international effects of various actions that the rich countries might take. These are depicted particularly well by the detailed economic model of world agriculture developed in the Netherlands.

First, although it may appeal strongly to one's moral sense, it probably will not help the poor in the LDCs if people in the rich countries reduce their intake of food in general, or of meat in particular (unless the money saved is somehow directly transferred to the poor). In fact, the reduction in demand would probably lower world market prices and thus lead to a *decrease* in food production in both the rich and poor countries.[19]*

Second, a deliberate policy of stabilizing world market prices for food (for example, through appropriate stockpiling) would stimulate food production in the poor countries, provided the average price is relatively high. Third, *policies that raise total production in the poor countries will not have much effect on hunger* because "hunger is caused above all by the unequal distribution of income within the developing countries." The same conclusion was reached by the FAO, which noted that even a 4 percent a year increase in food production would have little effect on hunger unless accompanied by income redistribution.[20]

By contrast, the Netherlands model shows that income redistribution toward the agricultural population in the LDCs would encourage food production and reduce the need for imports. Redistribution of income *within* the urban and rural populations would also reduce hunger—indeed, is necessary for reducing hunger.

The international effects noted above flow from the relative positions of the poor and rich nations in the world markets. Food consumption in the rich nations is not very sensitive to changes in the price of food in world markets. There are several reasons: individuals are rich enough to pay more as the price increases, the national prosperity of the rich nations is not affected much by the price of food imports, and the governments of developed countries protect domestic food prices from international fluctuations. This insensitivity to price increases the instability of the world market. For example, food consumption in the rich nations does not decrease in years of poor harvests. These instabilities are therefore visited most heavily upon poor importing countries. There, domestic prices go up when world prices increase, thus causing the poor to eat less, and they fall heavily in world surplus years, thus impoverishing small farmers and interfering with future food production. So those countries and groups of people who are at least able to withstand such fluctuations bear the brunt of them.

The Performance of Agriculture

Amidst the clamor of bells tolling for world agriculture, it is easy to overlook the fact that for almost three decades world food production has grown faster than world population (figures 5-2 and 5-3, and tables 5-5

---

*The question of whether or not the poor would gain by reduced diets in the rich countries is not straightforward. A model developed in the United Kingdom predicts that food production in the rich countries would decline if food intake there declined. However, the LDCs might gain *some* additional food. This would occur if the reduced price in the United States allowed the LDCs to buy the food more cheaply and if the increased imports did not suppress local production (H. Wagstaff, "Food Policies and Prospects: Insights from Global Modelling," *Food Policy* 4 [1979]: 155–68).

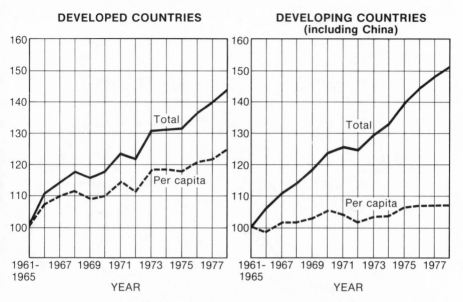

Figure 5-2 Index of total and per capita food production in developed and developing countries from 1961/65 to 1978

Source: Food and Agriculture Organization, *The Fourth World Food Survey*, Statistics Series no. 11 (Rome: FAO, 1977), p. 5; Food and Agriculture Organization, *Monthly Bulletin of Statistics*, no. 11 (1978): 17, 19.

and 5-6). Even in the developing nations, *on average,* food production has been increasing faster than population, and indeed faster than in the developed countries. (Note that data on food production in many LDCs are of poor quality.)

This apparently encouraging overall picture breaks down, however, for particular groups of people. The amount of food per head has actually decreased in Africa since the late 1960s and in the 45 "most seriously affected" countries in the 1970s. Recall too, that these fluctuations occur around average levels of per capita food production that vary from one area to another. Thus the daily supply of calories per person (which includes imports) during the early 1970s was:[21]

Developed countries	3,348 to 3,391
Non-Communist LDCs	2,147 to 2,197
Latin America	2,525 to 2,555
Near East	2,412 to 2,464
Far East	1,999 to 2,100
Africa	2,099 to 2,157
Communist Asia	2,223 to 2,331

The laggardly production in Africa and the Far East is thus particularly serious. (Appendix C lists the countries in each group.)

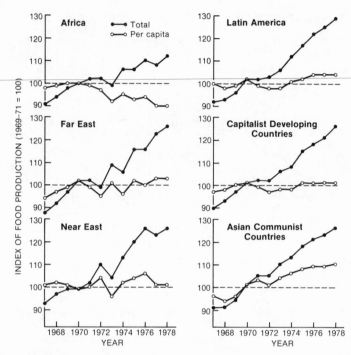

Figure 5-3 Total production and per capita production of food, 1967–1978

Source: Food and Agriculture Organization, *Monthly Bulletin of Statistics,* p. 19.
Note: Production in 1969 to 1971 is set at 100, and production in all other years is expressed as a percentage of that in 1969 to 1971. Data for 1978 are preliminary. The Far East includes only non-Communist countries: India, Bangladesh, Indonesia, etc. A list of countries in each group is in appendix C.

The average regional trends in figures 5-2 and 5-3 also obscure differences among countries within regions. Thus between 1952 and 1972 the annual rate of increase in food production was 6.1 percent in Venezuela but only 0.8 percent in Uruguay. It was 5.4 percent in Togo but only 0.8 percent in Tunisia, and 5.3 percent in Thailand but only 0.1 percent in Nepal.

During the 1960s, per capita food production declined in 56 out of 128 LDCs. During the 1970s this number rose to 69 countries and came to include the highly populated nations of India, Pakistan, Mexico, and Egypt.[22] Thus, in spite of quite sizable average increases in total food production, the diets of a large fraction of the population of the developing world have improved only very slightly, or not at all, and have worsened in many cases. A second disturbing pattern is that the rate of increase of both total food production and of food per person has been declining in the developing countries (tables 5-5 and 5-6).

Table 5-5. Average annual growth rates of population, total food production, and per capita food production, 1952–1976

Region	Population growth (%)			Growth of total food production (%)			Growth of per capita food production (%)		
	1952–1962	1961–1970	1970–1976	1952–1962	1961–1970	1970–1976	1952–1962	1961–1970	1970–1976
Developed nations	1.3	1.0	0.9	3.1	2.4	2.3	1.8	1.4	1.4
Non-Communist developing nations	2.3	2.5	2.4	3.1	3.3	2.8	0.8	0.8	0.4
Most seriously affected LDCs	—	2.4	2.5	—	3.1	2.1	—	0.7	– 0.4
Communist Asia	2.2	2.1	1.8	3.2	2.7	2.4	1.0	0.6	0.6
World	1.9	2.0	1.9	3.1	2.7	2.4	1.2	0.7	0.5

Sources: United Nations, *Assessment of the World Food Situation,* p. 66; FAO, *Fourth World Food Survey,* p. 4; United Nations, Department of Economic and Social Affairs, *World Population Prospects as Assessed in 1973* (ST/ESA/SER.A/60), 1977; U.S. Bureau of the Census, *Current Population Reports,* Special Studies Series P-23, no. 79 (Washington, D.C.: U.S. Bureau of the Census, 1979). For China's population growth rate, see Chapter 3.

Table 5-6. Average annual growth rates of total and per capita cereal production, 1961–1976

Region	Growth in cereal production (%)		Growth in per capita cereal production (%)	
	1961–1965 to 1970	1970–1976	1961–1965 to 1970	1970–1976
Developed nations	2.8	2.5	1.8	1.6
Non-Communist LDCs	3.7	3.0	1.1	0.6
Most seriously affected LDCs	3.9	2.0	1.4	– 0.4
Communist Asia	2.9	2.5	1.1	0.7
World	3.1	2.7	1.2	0.7

Sources: FAO, *Fourth World Food Survey,* p. 7; table 5.5.

Growth of food production in the poor nations on average certainly did not keep up with growth in the *demand* for food, which has been 3.5 percent per year.* The excess of demand over local production means that foreign exchange is spent to import food. The relationship between food production and food demand is therefore crucial to the question of overall economic development. One might pause to wonder why the increasing demand has failed to stimulate the necessary production, a question we will confront in Chapter 6.

Projections of the Future Food Supply Problem

Several projections of the future world food supply problem have been made.[23] They take account of previous information about rates of growth of income and productivity, and the relations among demand, prices, trade, and so on. However, they are only projections and are based on the assumption that the future will be largely the result of the continuation of past trends.

The various studies agree in broad outline but differ in detail: through 1985 (and thereafter for the forseeable future), aggregate world food supply will be able to keep up with world demand. However, although the Asian Communist countries will be largely self-sufficient, the poorest non-Communist LDCs will see no improvement or a decline in per capita food supply, while in the rest of the developing world food production will either keep pace with or will exceed population growth. The number of malnourished people is generally projected to increase.[24] These projections thus do not offer much hope of improvement for the countries and regions that have done badly in the recent past.

The projections also agree that in the non-Communist LDCs demand will continue to exceed supply, and in general the gap is expected to increase. Since the difference will be made up largely by imports, the LDCs are expected to face an increasing drain on their foreign currency, which may interfere with development in some cases.

The most recent projections are that the total deficit of staple food crops in the non-Communist LDCs in 1990 will be 120 to 140 million tons.[25] This deficit would be made up of 40 percent in Asia, 25 percent in North Africa and the Middle East, over 20 percent in Sub-Saharan Africa, and over 10 percent in Latin America.

---

*Recall that demand for food is the total amount that would be bought at a given price if it were available. Thus demand increases as the population does. It also increases as per capita income increases, since poor people spend on food at least half of any extra income they receive.

The most severe problem is projected for the poorest LDCs—those with per capita GNP in 1973 of less than $300. This group of nations has two thirds of the total population of the non-Communist LDCs; 75 percent of them live in Asia. Their aggregate food deficit is projected to increase from 12 million tons in 1975 to between 70 and 85 million tons in 1990, which would cost $10.5 to $12.5 billion at prices prevailing in the late 1970s. Simply to maintain 1975 levels of per capita consumption in 1990 would require 35 million tons more than projected production. Table 5-7 shows the current and projected food deficits of the largest of these poor countries.

To reiterate: *these are merely projections.* They do not take into account possible changes in government policies and agrarian structures (discussed in Chapter 6), that could radically alter the future. They do suggest what will happen in the absence of fundamental change.

A further problem, which we take up in Chapter 7, is that future economic development in the poor countries requires food production to grow more rapidly than it has done before—perhaps on the order of 3.5 to 4 percent a year. None of the above projections suggest that this rate will be achieved. Yet such rates have been achieved, and maintained, by developing countries. The rest of this chapter and the next will show that they are well within the capacity of most of the developing countries. The question is whether governments are willing to make the fundamental changes that are needed.

Table 5-7. Actual and projected food deficits in selected LDCs

| | Actual 1975 | | Projected 1990 | |
	(million metric tons)	(percentage of consumption)	(million metric tons)	(percentage of consumption)
India	1.4	1	17.6–21.9	10–12
Nigeria	0.4	2	17.1–20.5	35–39
Bangladesh	1.0	7	6.4– 8.0	30–35
Indonesia	2.1	8	6.0– 7.7	14–17
Egypt	3.7	35	4.9	32
Sahel group	0.4	9	3.2– 3.5	44–46
Ethiopia	0.1	2	2.1– 2.3	26–28
Burma	(0.4)[a]	(7)[a]	1.9– 2.4	21–25
Philippines	0.3	4	1.4– 1.7	11–13
Afghanistan	—	—	1.3– 1.5	19–22
Bolivia and Haiti	0.3	24	0.7– 0.8	35–38

Source: International Food Policy Research Institute, *Food Needs of Developing Countries* (Washington, D.C.: International Food Policy Research Institute, 1977), Research Report no. 3, p. 18.
[a]Surplus

PHYSICAL AND TECHNICAL CONSTRAINTS AND THE POTENTIAL OF AGRICULTURE IN THE DEVELOPING WORLD

In 1974 the Environmental Fund stated that "We have reached, or nearly reached, the limit of the world's ability to feed even our present numbers adequately." By contrast, two years later Revelle wrote of the earth's arable land:

> Making the conservative assumption that lower-quality soils and uneven topography would limit the average yields to half those obtained in the U.S. Midwest, 11.4 billion tons of food grains or their equivalent in food energy could be grown on this potential gross cropped area, enough for a minimum diet of 2,500 kilocalories per day for nearly 40 billion people. . .[26]

Somebody must be wrong.

It can easily be shown that the first quotation is completely wrong. It is always possible, of course, that a catastrophe will occur. But failing that, there is no known physical, biological, or technical reason why the food production of the developing nations cannot be increased by severalfold in the forseeable future. Revelle's estimate may be too high, but we are never likely to have to put it to the test because total world population is not likely to exceed 8 to 16 billion (Chapter 4).

In this section we will examine the constraints upon and the potential for increased food production and will give an estimate of cost. We will see not only that the poor countries are far from the limits of their food-producing capacities but that the present constraints on food production are not physical or technical.

To provide an idea of the potential for increased food production, we will look at the major resources required. These are land and the factors that determine yield per unit of land: water supply, fertilizer, energy, and technology. As a guide to future costs we will look at FAO's estimates of the cost of increasing LDC food production at about 3.6 percent per year, since a rate of increase between 3.5 and 4 percent per year would allow agriculture to fulfill its appropriate role in development (Chapter 7).

Land Resources

Throughout the world a total of about 1.4 billion hectares of land is now cultivated, slightly more than half of it in the developing countries. Several recent studies have analyzed the opportunities for cultivating new land. These studies all agree that large amounts of extra land are available, but they differ as to how much. The lowest estimate (by Mesarovic and Pestel) of total potential cutivable land—i.e., not including grazing land—is 2.4 billion hectares,[27] just under twice the existing total. This is certainly an underestimate. Norse estimates the potential total at just over 3.1 billion hectares. The highest estimate, by Buringh and his co-workers, is 3.4 billion hectares, which is well over twice the existing total (table 5-8). These last two estimates exclude land that is unsuitable for physical reasons such as poor climate, permanently unfavorable soil, and inadequate water, and they assume the use of currently available technology. They are both based on detailed geographic surveys. Their estimate of available land is very close to that obtained by the PSAC committee, and it is likely that they give a good indication of the true potential.[28]

There is general agreement among the various studies on the distribution of new arable land. The really huge reserves of new land are in the LDCs. Whereas the total cultivable land in the rich countries can be increased by between 50 and 100 percent, in the developing countries it can be increased by threefold and is potentially twice the total in the developed countries. Within the LDCs the main reserves of land are in Africa and South America. Asia, on the other hand, has 58 percent of the world's population but only 26 percent of the cultivable land, and 77 percent of this area is already under cultivation. This is therefore the first major distinction to be made among the developing countries: Africa and South America have vast tracts of additional cultivable land, while Asia is relatively land poor.

Land Quality

Most of the poor countries of the world are tropical or semi-tropical. This has led to the impression that their agriculture must always be unproduc-

Table 5-8. Distribution of presently cultivated and potentially cultivable land (in millions of hectares)

Region	Total land area	Percentage of land area potentially cultivable	Total area potentially cultivable	Area now cultivated	Percentage of arable land now cultivated
North America[a]	2,420	25.9	627.5	273.4	44
South America	1,780	33.5	595.6	78.3	13
Africa	3,030	23.5	711.3	157.5	22
Europe	1,050	37.9	398.7	212.1	53
Asia	4,390	20.2	886.9	684.8	77
Australia and New Zealand	860	23.2	199.1	33.5	17
World	13,530	25.3	3,419.1	1,439.6	42

Source: National Research Council, *Supporting Papers: World Food and Nutrition Study,* vol. 2, Study Team 4, *Resources for Agriculture* (Washington, D.C.: National Academy of Sciences, 1977), p. 68.
[a]Includes Central America and Caribbean Islands

tive because of leached soils, low nutrient levels, "lateritic" soils that become brick-like when exposed to the sun, and other problems. This impression is wrong.[29] Tropical and temperate soils are more similar than is often supposed: the average amount of organic matter is roughly the same; the patterns of erosion and deposition are roughly the same; and only about 7 percent of the tropics has lateritic soil, which also occurs in the United States. The temperate zone, like the tropics, has a large fraction of unusable land—vast areas in North America, Australia, and the U.S.S.R. are inherently poor for agriculture, being very dry and/or very cold. Indonesia, Bangladesh, and India, on the other hand, contain some of the most fertile soils in the world.

In general, tropical soils are older and thus tend to be somewhat less fertile than temperate soils. However, the tropics has the advantage in many areas of suitable year-round growing conditions. There are four main ecological zones in the tropics, determined largely by climate. Tropical rain forest covers 24 percent of the land area and is marked by rather even rainfall throughout the year. Frequently the soils are leached, are low in humus, have only large particles near the surface, and are low in nutrients. However some rain forest soils that are near rivers, are over a limestone base, or are developed from volcanic material are very fertile.

Savanna, the most common ecological type, covers 49 percent of the land area and is characterized by a dry season of at least three months. It is found mainly in South America and Africa, though smaller areas occur in Asia and Australia. Savanna soils in East and West Africa tend to be well supplied with bases (e.g., calcium), while those in South America are generally low-base (acidic) soils. Desert (16 percent of the land mass) and semi-desert (11 percent) have highly variable soils, some of which are very fertile. The major problem here is low and very variable rainfall.

In general, the soils of Asia are younger and more fertile than those of Africa and South America, the last being on average the poorest. Asia has a high proportion of very good soils that are alluvial or of volcanic origin. Indeed, some of the most fertile soils in the world are in Asia. Thus the low quantity of Asian land is offset by its generally higher quality.

The best and naturally most fertile soils are those that are high in bases. They have developed from alluvium, sediments, or volcanic debris and are rich in calcium, magnesium, and potassium. If they do not have high nitrogen, this is fairly easy and cheap to correct. The great tropical centers of population and the successes of the Green Revolution are on these soils, which cover about 18 percent of the tropical land area.

Although populations are concentrated on good farming areas in the tropics, this does not mean that such areas are fully exploited. Several startling examples illustrate this.[30] The southern half of the Sudan is an extraordinarily well-endowed region for agriculture, with good soil and abundant sunshine and water. But a large capital investment would be needed for drainage, infrastructure, and so on, and the Sudan simply cannot afford that. Yet, according to Hopper, the southern Sudan alone could produce perhaps as much food as the entire world agriculture now does!

The Indus-Ganges-Brahmaputra plain of Pakistan, Northern India, and Bangladesh encompasses 40 million hectares of naturally very fertile soil. There is also adequate water, but it has not been brought under control. It has been estimated that an annual yield (counting multiple crops) of twenty tons of grain per hectare (compared with current yields of two tons or less) is a reasonable expectation for this area, at a cost of $2 billion per year spread over about twenty-five years. This production would be equivalent to more than half of the world's current grain production, and the annual increments could alone increase world grain production by more than 4 percent a year. Although the cost is high, the return on the investment would make this a profitable enterprise. A study of the Mekong drainage basin in Southeast Asia suggests it has a potential grain output equal to that of North America.[31] Even if these claims are somewhat overoptimistic, they indicate that enormous potential exists in these areas.

It must be stressed that good soils in the tropics can be more productive than good soils in the temperate region because of the more favorable climate. Indeed, it is likely that once the appropriate research has been done, the most productive agriculture in the world will be primarily in the tropics, as are the most productive natural ecosystems.

The largest fraction (about 70 percent) of the potentially usable, but as yet unused, land in the tropics has low-base soils. These occur mainly in South America and Central Africa, with smaller but important areas in Indonesia and Malaysia. At the present time they are mainly either covered by natural vegetation or are used for grazing or shifting agriculture. However, the climate is generally ideal for year-round crop production, most areas having quite short dry seasons. Also, many areas have excellent topography and physical soil properties.[32] The major problem is that the soils are acid and generally low in some nutrients, therefore requiring lime and fertilizer.

Similar low-base soils dominate the eastern United States from New Jersey to Texas. They are also common in eastern China, and in both countries they support intensive cropping following the addition of lime and fertilizer. There is every reason to believe they can also become highly productive in the tropics. They produce high yields of export crops in the state of São Paulo in Brazil. Projects in jungle areas of Peru and Nigeria on these soils can continuously produce two or three grain crops per year, with each crop producing 80 percent as much as in the United States— that is, per year they produce 150 to 200 percent of production in the temperate zone. The same has been found in Colombia.[33] (In the drier Savanna areas, however, only one crop per year would be possible without irrigation.) The difficulty is in the cost of fertilizing large areas. There is therefore a need to develop more effective and cheaper fertilizers and tolerant plant varieties.

The important point is that "poor" soils need not remain poor, as farmers in the temperate zone have shown. It seems to be frequently overlooked that farming has generally greatly *increased* the productivity of such soil. Theodore W. Schultz has pointed out that:

> The original soils of western Europe, except for the Po valley and some parts of France, were, in general, very poor in quality. They are now highly productive. The original soils of Finland were less productive than most of the nearby parts of the Soviet Union, yet today the croplands of Finland are far superior. The original croplands of Japan were inferior to those of Northern India. Presently, the difference between them is greatly in favor of Japan.[34]

This is not to say that new land can be cultivated easily or cheaply. Low-base soils in particular must be cleared and maintained properly or erosion or other forms of deterioration will occur. However, although research could improve the use of such soils, the technology for managing them (e.g., liming, the periodic use of legumes, mulching, etc.) is known.[35]

The land used for grazing in the world, about 3 billion hectares, is much greater than the area that is now cultivated. Again, the area of grazing land can be increased, although it is not clear just how large the potential is (probably twice the amount now in use, or about 6 billion hectares). Much of the land not used at present is dry and would need watering places. In other areas animal diseases prevent development as grazing land—for example, in mid-and East Africa 5 million km² of grazing land is unusable because of sleeping sickness transmitted by the tsetse fly.[36]

Increasing Production through Higher Yields

Potential for Increased Yields

In the rich nations farmers have made a clear decision that it is cheaper to increase production through increased yields than through cultivating more land.[37] Increases in food production over the past few decades have come almost entirely from increased yields, and in fact in the United States a large fraction of arable land has been retired from production. Higher yields came in part from greater fertilizer use, but also from the application of an ever-changing "technological package" that has combined more efficient management with improved technology in crop strains, irrigation, and so on. The various parts of the "package" interact. For example, the productivity of a unit of fertilizer has increased with time because of changes in the crop strains and cultivation techniques. In the rich countries this has caused the yield *from a given amount of fertilizer* to increase each year by almost 2 percent. This means that farmers are not stuck on a curve of diminishing returns, but keep moving to higher curves.

The truly remarkable result of such technological innovation—for example, in the production of ever-cheaper fertilizers combined with the increased use of (previously) cheap fossil fuels—is that the increasing total production in the rich countries has been brought about without an increase in total costs. That is, the real cost of food production has decreased. The American experience in figure 6-1 illustrates this process.

The recent history of food production in the developing nations has followed a different pattern. In the 1950s, more than half of the increased production was created by cultivating more land. Since the 1960s the balance has shifted somewhat, and increasing yields have accounted for 60 percent of the increased production. However, new land has still been important, and has grown at just over 1 percent a year throughout this period. While the expansion of cultivated land will continue to contribute to increased production, it is likely that in most places in the developing world it will be cheaper to increase production by increasing yields. This is particularly the case in land-scarce Asia.

Yields of food grains in the LDCs are generally very low in comparison with the developed nations. This was not always the case. In fact, before World War II grain yields were the same in both regions, at approximately 1.15 tons per hectare.[38] However, yields in the developed countries have since increased much faster and are typically two to about three times larger than those in the LDCs (table 5-9).

It is clear that there is enormous potential for increases in yields in the LDCs. A comparison with yields in the rich nations and with maximum yields that have been achieved gives some idea of how large that potential

Table 5-9. Average yields in rich and poor countries and record yields, around 1975

Crop	Developing countries	Developed countries	World record
Wheat	1.3	3.25 (W. Europe)	14.5
Rice	1.8	5.5	14.4
Corn	1.3	5.4 (U.S.A.)	21.2
Sorghum	0.9	3.0	21.5

Sources: National Research Council, *Resources for Agriculture,* p. 97; Wortman and Cummings, *To Feed This World,* p. 147.

Note: Yields are in metric tons per hectare per crop and do not take multiple cropping into account.

is (table 5-9). Indeed, the differences *within* the rich nations show how yields can increase in response to need (figure 5-4). In the United States, land is abundant and yields are relatively low (though still much above LDC yields[39]). By contrast, land in Japan is scarce and yields are about ten times greater.

Rice, the major crop in land-scarce Asia, provides a good example of how yields increase in response to intensive farming. In the developing nations the average yield per harvest per hectare is 1.8 tons, whereas in Japan it is over six tons per hectare and is likely to reach eight tons in the near future.[40] Figure 5-5 shows how rice yields in various poor countries compare with Japan's historical performance. The fact is that most rice farmers in the developing countries remain at the level of technology that has existed for hundreds of years.

Yields in the LDCs are also low compared with those that we know *can* be achieved there. India, where agriculture is often regarded as hopeless, is a good example. I noted earlier that grain yields in the Gangetic plain might be increased about tenfold. Mellor has noted that "India...is the fourth largest grain producer in the world and has one of the largest potentials of any nation for future increases in grain production."[41]

Maximum Indian crop yields are only a small fraction of what has been produced on the *average* by Indian experimental stations, which produce seven times as much rice per hectare as the Indian farmer. Nor are such yields possible only on experimental stations. In the early 1950s, yields of fifteen to seventeen tons per hectare were achieved by farmers in production contests.[42] Yields almost as high have been achieved by farmers in the Philippines using strains that produce two crops per year (thus in some areas a year-long total of almost thirty tons per hectare is possible).

There is also great scope for increasing multiple cropping by growing two or even three crops per year instead of one. It is estimated that the number of crops grown per year in the LDCs can be roughly doubled.[43] Of course, multiple cropping cannot be done everywhere; it requires either a long wet season or irrigation.

The Green Revolution, which is merely the application of standard plant-breeding techniques, has shown that these potential increases in yields are not mere wishful thinking. It has been quite common for yields to increase three- to fourfold with the introduction of new strains. When this is done two or three times per year, as the rapidly maturing strains allow, total annual yield increases four- to eightfold. By the early 1970s the Green Revolution had reached only about 10 percent of the grainland in the developing countries. Moreover, its spread is frequently prevented by institutional rather than physical constraints (Chapter 6), and there is a steady accumulation of new strains and associated technology that is suitable for application in the tropics.[44] Thus it is quite realistic to assume that huge increases in yields are physically and technically possible.

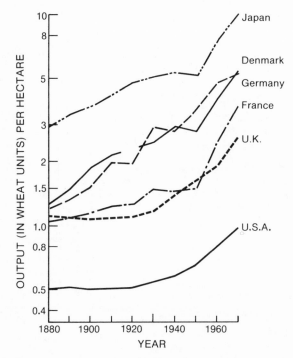

Figure 5-4 Yields per hectare in six countries, 1880–1970

Source: Redrawn from Hans P. Binswanger and Vernon W. Ruttan, *Induced Innovation: Technology, Institutions, and Development* (Baltimore: Johns Hopkins University Press, 1978), p. 50.

Note: The yield of crops in each country has been converted to equivalent "wheat units" by dividing the value of the crop by the price for one ton of wheat. Notice that yield is on a logarithmic scale.

Requirements for Increased Yields

The physical and technical factors that lead to increased yields are well-known—irrigation, fertilizers, improved strains, and so on. While there is great scope for research aimed at improving the use of these factors in the particular conditions of the LDCs, we certainly know enough now to increase yields greatly, and current research will undoubtedly improve this ability in the ensuing years and decades. A survey of the variety of ways of increasing yields will indicate the scale of changes that are needed and their probable cost.

Irrigation

Irrigation is important in food production quite out of proportion to the amount of land involved. Although it constitutes only about 14 percent of

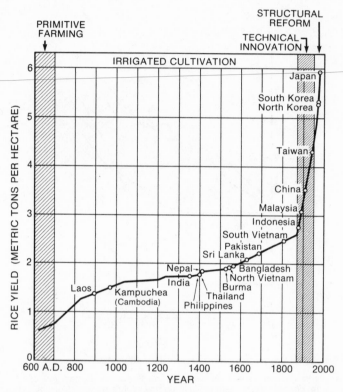

Figure 5-5 Comparison of the historical trend in rice yields in Japan with yields in other Asian countries in the early 1970s

Source: Redrawn from W. David Hopper, "The Development of Agriculture in Developing Countries," *Scientific American* 235 (1976): 200.

the land under cultivation, irrigated land produces (in value) almost as much food as nonirrigated land.[45] The yield from each crop is typically twice as high on irrigated land and, of course, multiple cropping is much more common than on nonirrigated land. Yields are higher because irrigation allows plants to be more closely spaced and enables them to take up more fertilizer.

Of the 200 million or so hectares of land now irrigated, roughly 75 percent is in the LDCs. The area irrigated could be more than doubled, with most of the extra potential lying in the LDCs. Fortunately, much of the potential for expanded irrigation is in Asia, including India and Bangladesh, where land is scarce.[46]

Production from irrigated farming can be increased by improving the efficiency of existing systems, as well as extending the area. In fact, improving existing systems is probably the better investment. Currently, irrigation systems in the LDCs are generally extremely inefficient. The UN estimated that half of the irrigated area in the LDCs was working at less than 50 percent efficiency, and the Asian Development Bank estimated that rice yields on irrigated land in Asia could be more than doubled simply by managing existing systems better. The technology of irrigation is well established, and inefficiency generally stems from institutional and economic rather than technical problems[47] (see also Chapter 10).

Irrigation has spread rapidly, at about 3 percent per year, in the past two decades, especially in Asia. The UN believes that continued expansion is crucial to meeting food needs, though it considers that improving existing systems should have first priority. The U.S. National Academy of Sciences reckons that, over ten years, improved and expanded irrigation could reasonably be expected to contribute an additional 200 to 400 million tons of foodgrains (roughly 20 percent of current world grain production); further improvements could yield three to four times this amount by 2000 A.D.[48]

Expanding irrigation by tubewells is relatively cheap, on the order of a few hundred dollars per hectare. But much of the new irrigation will be expensive, and an initial investment of $2,000 per hectare may be required on average. However, an increase in yield of only one ton per hectare per year would provide a profitable return. By contrast, rehabilitating existing irrigation systems costs only $200 to $300 per hectare.[49]

Operating costs have been increasing wherever pumps are required, since energy costs are increasing. This is an area that cries out for the development of innovative small-scale technology to make use of solar, wind, or other nonconventional sources of energy (see Chapter 10).[50]

Fertilizer
Fertilizer is probably the single most important physical input for raising yields. Although chemical fertilizer use in the developing nations has been growing extremely fast, it is still very low compared with use in the developed countries (it was 26 percent of world consumption in 1975). Excluding China, in 1970 the average cultivated hectare in the developing countries received less than one-seventh of the amount of fertilizer added to a hectare in the capitalist developed countries. Average rates, in kilograms per hectare around 1970, were Africa 5, Asia 20, and Latin America 30, compared with over 80 in the United States, almost 200 in Western Europe, and over 400 in Japan. Commonly half of the fertilizer used in the LDCs is applied to nonfood cash crops; in Latin America only 10 percent is used on basic food crops.[51]

Fertilizers are also used much less efficiently by farmers in the developing countries. This is because water is poorly controlled, the fertilizers are not adapted for tropical conditions or plants, farmers have not been educated in their optimal use, and so on. Improving the efficiency of fertilizer use could roughly double the yield from a given rate of application.[52]

The UN projects that by the year A.D. 2000, LDC consumption of chemical fertilizers will increase fivefold, from the 1975 level of 21 million tons to 122 million tons. Over the same period, world consumption is expected to increase from 81 million tons to 307 million tons. These calculations do not take account of possible increases in the efficiency of fertilizers in the tropics or of possible alternatives to inorganic fertilizers, both of which would greatly reduce the amount of conventional fertilizers needed by the LDCs (see below). However, it is worth asking if this amount of inorganic fertilizer can be made available and whether it will be prohibitively expensive.

There is no foreseeable absolute shortage of the materials required for fertilizers, either in the short or long term. Indeed, over the short term there are likely to be temporary gluts of fertilizer, since some LDCs have built too much production capacity. Over the long term, phosphate reserves are enormous relative to needs and are adequate for many centuries.[53] Nitrogen, of course, occurs in the air in essentially infinite quantities and the potential problem for nitrogen fertilizers is the supply of usable hydrogen, which usually comes from natural gas "feedstock." This conventional source will be adequate until the turn of the century; in fact, until recently each year the Middle East countries burned up ("flared") five times more natural gas than will be needed for fertilizers by the developing countries in 1985. Coal is likely to become a more important source as the price of natural gas increases. Global coal resources are, of course, much greater than those of petroleum.

Even though steadily increasing use of commercial fertilizer would place larger demands on conventional energy sources, it is important to keep in mind that fertilizer production uses only 1 or 2 percent of the world's energy. Given this relatively small demand and the crucial need for fertilizer, it is hard to argue seriously that energy for fertilizers would be physically in short supply for the forseeable future.

The more important question concerns the price of fertilizers. Over the short term, the price of fertilizer should not present difficulties to the LDCs. Reidinger's analysis of fertilizer production capacity showed production in the developing countries as a group growing even faster than consumption, so that in the early 1980s their imports of fertilizer should be low. These trends will be most marked in China, India, Brazil, Indonesia, Mexico, Venezuela, and several Middle East countries. However, over the longer term, as energy and other costs rise, fertilizer prices are expected to increase somewhat, thus reversing the historical trend to ever lower prices in response to technological innovation.[54] This could be a particular problem for those LDCs with poor energy resources (but see section on nonconventional sources of energy).

The issues of the cost of fertilizers, its relation to energy costs, and the implications for LDC food production are widely misunderstood. Concern over these problems arises mainly from the huge price increases for fertilizer in 1974 and 1975 (figure 5-6) and from persistent and large increases in the price of fuel. However, to a large extent this concern is misplaced.

Let us examine first the cost of fertilizer and its relationship to the price of energy—especially of natural gas, the "feedstock" for fertilizer production. It is quite wrong to assume that the three- to fourfold increase in fertilizer prices between 1972 and 1974 was caused by the increase in oil and gas prices.[55] Prices rose because too few fertilizer factories had been built, and they fell as excess production became available; these fluctuations were very little influenced by energy and natural gas prices. In fact, because fertilizer prices are affected by many factors other than the price of energy and feedstocks, it is estimated that an 800 percent increase in the price of natural gas would lead to only a 50 percent increase in fertilizer price; these are about the same price changes that have occurred since the early 1970s. It must be remembered that improving technology keeps decreasing the cost of producing fertilizer. Thus with late 1970s prices for natural gas, the cost of producing fertilizer with mid-1970s technology would be less than the cost with *free* natural gas and 1960 technology.[56]

The modest changes in the price of fertilizer since 1975 have confirmed these analyses. Between 1975 and 1979 the price of nitrogen fertilizer (urea), the one most affected by energy costs, moved gradually from around $120 per ton to around $165 per ton, compared with prices of over $350 per ton in 1974 (figure 5-6).[57]

The second point is that increased fertilizer prices need not pose severe problems to LDC farmers. Fertilizer costs are a very small fraction (less than 10 percent) of the total costs of producing food, although in the LDCs they are often the only purchased input and farmers are therefore sensitive to their price.

Third, and most important, farmers in LDCs already pay much higher prices for fertilizer than they should. Changed policies in the LDCs, at no extra national cost, could easily lead to much lower fertilizer prices, even as energy and other costs are increasing. The reason for this is that fertilizer prices in the LDCs are kept artificially high: nitrogen-producing factories operate at 60 to 70 percent of capacity; bringing them up to world standards would reduce the price significantly. A variety of government policies keep fertilizer prices high, and the consequence is that

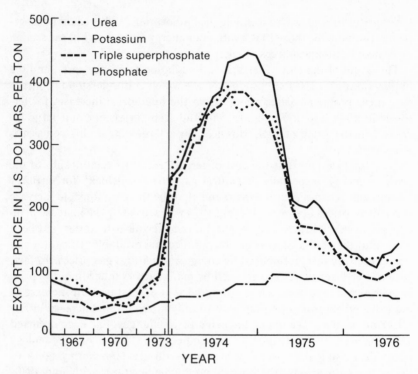

Figure 5-6 Export prices for some major fertilizers, 1965–1976

Source: Redrawn from Food and Agriculture Organization, *The State of Food and Agriculture 1976,* Agricultural Series no. 4 (Rome: FAO, 1976).

farmers in the LDCs can buy much less fertilizer with the food they produce than can farmers in the developed countries. This issue is discussed in detail in Chapter 6. It is enough here to note that these distortions in pricing outweigh the likely increases in the real costs of producing fertilizer that may occur in the forseeable future.

The effects of price increases could also be mitigated by an increase in the efficiency of fertilizers applied in the tropics and by using alternatives to conventional inorganic fertilizers. Research aimed at producing more appropriate fertilizers would be quite inexpensive and should quickly be successful.[58] A doubling of yields at a given rate of application is quite likely. The substitution of organic wastes (animal and human manure, crop residues) for inorganic fertilizers could also make a huge contribution to increasing food supply. For example, in the developing world 103 million tons of nutrients (N, P, and K—mainly cattle manure, and not including crop residues) are produced as organic waste each year.[59] The nutrient content of this material is about eight times greater than all of the inorganic fertilizers used in the LDCs. Although not all of these nutrients could be recaptured economically, they represent an enormous potential supply. China until very recently depended mainly on such recycling for its fertilizer, and it is still widely used there. There is no doubt that such non-conventional sources, together with crop residues, could make a major contribution to increased food production. One technique that combines fertilizer and energy production is discussed below in the section on non-conventional energy sources.

Energy Resources

It is important, first, to get agriculture's use of energy into perspective. Agriculture is a relatively small user of energy. Even the highly mechanized agriculture of California, including all farm operations and the manufacture and transport of fertilizer, pesticides, and machinery, uses only 5 percent of all energy consumed in the state. World-wide, agriculture accounts for only 3.5 percent of total commercial energy use, and in the LDCs agriculture uses only 4 percent of total energy consumed.[60]

In the developed countries there is a further large expenditure of energy in the processing, distribution, and preparation of foods; indeed, in the United States, food preparation alone uses more fossil fuel than food production! The entire food system in the developed countries probably accounts for about 13 percent of their total energy use, or about four times as much as is used in producing the food. Processing, distribution, and preparation in the LDCs use much less energy, perhaps about the same as food production.

In the LDCs fertilizers account for about 70 percent of farm energy use, compared with about 40 percent in the developed countries. The difference arises mainly from the low use of machinery in the LDCs, which, on half of the world's arable land, operate only 6 percent of the world's tractors.

The actual amount of commercial energy used in agriculture in the LDCs is, of course, much less than that in the rich nations. The developed capitalist countries use more than ten times as much commercial energy per hectare as the LDCs and, considering only food *production,* the LDCs (with 72 percent of the world's population) use only 18 percent of the commercial energy used in world agriculture. If we include processing and preparation, the fraction probably drops to about 8 percent. Finally, if we consider total commercial world energy use, *food production in the LDCs accounts for only about one-half of one percent of the total.* Clearly, LDC food production could increase its use of commercial energy by severalfold without having a large impact on total world energy demand.

There is no doubt that enough energy will be available in the world to supply agriculture's needs as far as one can see into the future. The problems are the the cost of energy (particularly the amount of foreign exchange required by importers) and assuring an uninterrupted supply.[61] Surprisingly, the LDCs as a whole, even excluding the OPEC countries, are expected to do quite well in the 1980s. Oil and natural gas production are expected to grow in a large number of non-OPEC developing countries, and coal production is expected to increase in India and South Korea, which have extensive coal reserves. The non-OPEC developing countries as a whole may even become net oil exporters in the 1980s. However, a large number of energy-poor LDCs will need to import increasing amounts of oil, if they insist on depending upon conventional energy sources. It would still be worthwhile for these poor nations to pay for such imports, since the value of the extra food produced will exceed the cost of the additional energy by a factor of ten or so.[62] Such increased food production could also save large amounts of foreign exchange that would otherwise be spent on food imports. In addition, most of these countries could find the needed foreign exchange by reducing imports of nonessential goods (Chapters 6 and 9).

Nonconventional Energy Sources

The discussion above assumes that the energy needed for fertilizer and power in the LDCs will be supplied by conventional sources. But for energy-poor LDCs there are many reasons for meeting these and other energy needs from nonconventional sources: these sources require almost no foreign exchange, they reduce dependence on oil-producing nations, they will often be cheaper, and they will generally create more employment. In the case of recycling of organic waste they will also produce much-needed fertilizer.

The salient fact is that agriculture in the LDCs produces more energy in its crops than is needed to fuel all agricultural activities, and this energy can be obtained and used economically. The energy stored in crop residues (e.g., plant stalks) during photosynthesis, plus the energy in weeds, dung, and other biological materials can be converted to useful energy in the form of methane gas by the process of biogasification.[63] Briefly, water and biological wastes are mixed in an underground pit and methane gas is produced by bacteria that decompose the material in the absence of oxygen. The gas is collected and piped to storage tanks or wherever it is needed. It can be used to drive machinery, or for cooking or lighting. The technology is well understood, and thousands of biogas plants are in use now in China, Taiwan, and India. They do require daily attention (thus generating productive employment), and care must be taken to assure mixing and the maintenance of the correct temperature.[64]

Biogas has been shown to be economically competitive with alternative energy sources such as natural gas and kerosene. A problem in some areas, such as India, is that the cost of a biogas plant is $200 to $300, so that poor farmers would need quite sizable loans to buy an individual plant. However, mass production in China has reduced the price to about $15 to $20, showing that the initial cost need not be a serious obstacle.[65]

A second problem is that the farmer needs several cows to produce enough dung to fuel a plant that would meet the family's energy needs. In India only 10 to 15 percent of the rural population own as many as three to five cows, so most poor farmers are excluded from producing biogas in individual plants. An obvious solution is to build a larger plant that can be used by the whole village. Such plants are both technically and economically workable. However, in India, where much of the technology has been pioneered, it is difficult to assure cooperation among different classes in the village and an even distribution of benefits.[66]

China's successful biogasification program has shown that these economic and organizational problems can be overcome. The number of plants (both family plants and large digesters that run farm machinery and power electrical generators) expanded very rapidly in the 1970s. By 1976 there were over 4 million biogas plants in China. The design has been improved, and gas stoves and lamps adapted to use them have been mass produced.[67]

This nonconventional source of energy is adequate for *all* LDC agricultural needs at present, and it has the advantage of increasing as crop production increases, and therefore as the need for energy does. LDCs facing foreign exchange problems could thus increase their energy use in agriculture without needing to resort to imports of fossil fuels. Indeed, in high-density areas agriculture could produce excess energy for use in industry. Given proper support and research, this is a technology that is likely to be developed first in the LDCs and later transferred to the developed nations. (Other nonconventional sources of energy that can be important include wind, water, and solar energy, as discussed in Chapter 10. That chapter also discusses other aspects of better energy technology for the LDCs.)[68]

The great additional advantage of biogasification is that it is also a superior way of producing organic fertilizer from wastes, provided an appropriate ratio of animal manure is used in the process. Many biological waste materials are now burned in open fires in the LDCs. This is not only a very inefficient use of the energy, but also results in a loss of valuable nutrients. Biogasification, on the other hand, since it is anaerobic, conserves the nitrogen in the manure much more effectively than does adding manure directly to the fields. The slurry that remains after biogasification is a medically safe fertilizer that has the advantage over inorganic fertilizers of improving the soil's physical characteristics.[69]

The discussion of fertilizer and energy requirements of agriculture in the LDCs can be summarized briefly. Overall, even if conventional commercial sources are used, there is little doubt that the energy and fertilizer needed will be physically available for the forseeable future (which goes well beyond the turn of the century). Even if the prices of both increase, the LDCs are likely to be able to pay for these requirements, though a reordering of priorities might be necessary. However, for a variety of reasons, many energy-poor LDCs would be better advised to develop their very large nonconventional sources of fertilizer and energy.

The Technological Package

The key to the modern technological revolution in agriculture is not merely the application of more and better fertilizer, the extension of irrigation, the development of more productive crop strains, or any other single item; it is instead the combination of these improvements in an optimal mix, so that each component of the technology package enhances the performance of the other components. For example, the grains of the Green Revolution have short stiff straws, so that when fertilizer is applied in heavy doses, the heavy grain that results does not bend the straw. They allow for more efficient use of fertilizer, though a good water supply is needed to allow the plant to take up extra fertilizer. The new strains also ripen more quickly and so increase the chances for multiple cropping, which in turn increases the productivity of irrigation systems, machinery, and labor.

A commonly expressed fear about the new strains of grain is that they are more susceptible to diseases and pests and less able to tolerate drought than are the local varieties. They are also said to have too narrow a genetic makeup, and too-large areas are allotted to a single strain. All of these features would make the new strains more likely to suffer widespread catastrophic losses of production.

Some of these criticisms have certainly been valid, as might be expected in the first generation of new strains. However, a good deal of work has been done to improve subsequent generations.[70] The genetic basis has been greatly broadened by crossing with local strains, and the new strains have a good deal of pest and disease resistance bred into them. High susceptibility to drought has been largely corrected. The second phase of rice breeding (strains IR20 and IR22) has raised the quality of the actual rice grains, which was a problem initially.

This is not to say that the ecological problems, particularly the insect pest problems, of the high-yielding varieties (HYVs) have been solved. A particular difficulty is that pests can evolve to overcome resistance in the plants, and so the breeder must try to keep one step ahead. The HYVs use more pesticides, in large part because it now pays farmers to protect their more valuable crops. These ecological problems are of course common also in the developed countries, and they have not placed limits on food production there. A particular difficulty in the LDCs is that there are relatively few scientists to develop a broad range of locally adapted cereal strains or to develop and manage complex integrated pest control programs. (The environmental issues are discussed in more detail in Chapter 10.) In spite of the difficulties, the HYVs have made an important contribution to increased production, and there is every reason to believe that this contribution will grow, as it has in the developed countries.

Research and development, however, require money. For example, in the United States in 1976 almost $1.9 billion was spent on research in food production by a complex set of public and private institutions.[71] This is almost $9 for each person in the country. By contrast, of the $3.7 billion spent on agricultural research in the world (excluding China) in 1974, only $355 million was spent in countries where per capita income was less than $400 per year. Of this amount almost half was spent on export crops such as cotton, sugar, and cattle. Thus in the mid-1970s roughly eleven cents was spent on food research for each of the 1.6 billion or so people in these poor countries; this is only slightly more than 1 percent of the per capita expenditure in the United States! The major research in tropical food crops is done at the ten International Agricultural Research Centers, and their 1977 budget was still only $79 million.

While the lack of research has so far unfortunately constrained food production, it also means that there is enormous unexploited potential. Only very recently has tropical research been extended from export crops to food crops, and the great majority of food-producing agriculture in the LDCs remains untouched by modern technology. There has been virtually no research into the special features of subsistence farming, including the common practice of growing together two or more crops, such as beans and corn.

A recent five-volume study by the National Academy of Sciences describes the enormous array of opportunities for research that would yield large increases in food production in the LDCs.[72] A few examples, some of which we have discussed, are:

1. Management and improvement of low-base soils;
2. Better plant strains, including greater response to fertilizers, greater tolerance to poor soils, drought, and pest resistance;
3. Alternative energy sources;
4. More appropriate machinery and technology, e.g., solar energy grain dryers and wind-driven irrigation pumps;
5. Water conservation and management;
6. Irrigation;
7. Intercropping; and
8. Nitrogen-fixing strains of cereals and grasses.

The economic case for investment in technological innovation is very strong, since the rate of return is likely to be high; indeed, the UN estimated that two or three times as much growth can be obtained from each dollar invested in agricultural research in developing countries as from any other investment there. It has been estimated that every dollar of basic agricultural research in the LDCs generates an annual benefit of $80 after eight to ten years, suggesting that annual return on investment from the start is 40 to 60 percent per year.[73]

Finally, the transition from subsistence farming to producing excess food for sale in the market requires the development of new facilities—extension services to farmers, markets, storage places, roads, centers for buying new seeds and fertilizers, a credit structure, and so on. These facilities and institutions are poorly developed in the LDCs, and their absence is in large part the result of distorted policies, a subject discussed in Chapter 6.

Potential Food Production

Taking all of these physical and technical factors into account, just how large is the potential food production of the LDCs? A quite modest claim is that yields could be tripled. The expansion of multiple cropping could almost double again a given annual output. Thus, *without adding new land*, roughly a fivefold increase in production is physically and technically possible. Furthermore, the amount of land cultivated could be more than doubled. Most other estimates of physical potential are at least this large. Revelle's conservative estimate suggests that current world production can be increased about tenfold, most of the increase occurring in the tropics. Buringh and his co-workers, in their exhaustive analysis, estimated that the full development of all arable and irrigable land and the full use of modern technology would produce a maximum of almost forty times the present annual crop production.[74] Again, most of the increase would be in the LDCs.

Even gloomy projections of future population growth suggest that these potential limits will never be approached for the LDCs as a whole. Pessimistic projections of the population of LDCs show it roughly doubling in 30 years and increasing less than fivefold over a period of 100 years before stabilizing. More probably it will double in closer to 40 years and will not increase more than about threefold before stabilizing.[75]

Under pessimistic assumptions only a few large LDCs, in which annual population growth rates are around 3 percent, will double their populations in less than twenty-five years. Under these pessimistic assumptions, the populations of these countries (Bangladesh, Pakistan, Nigeria, Brazil, and Mexico) would increase by five- to ninefold in a century or so before achieving stability. Of these, Bangladesh would be most likely to get close to physical limits. It has a relatively small amount of arable land per head (about the same as China's and twice as much as Taiwan's), and almost no new land to cultivate. On the other hand, potentially it is extraordinarily fertile and its yields relative to potential are among the lowest in the world.[76] More optimistic projections show Bangladesh's population eventually increasing by less than fourfold.

It is thus clear that physical and technical problems do not set the limits to food production and will not set such limits in the forseeable future for virtually all of the developing world. However, these conclusions should not be taken to imply that we can be optimistic about feeding future populations better than we feed people now. It is one thing to note that physical resources are adequate, but quite another to claim that they will be used to improve diets.

Estimated Costs of Agricultural Growth

At the 1974 World Food Conference, it was estimated that the total annual cost of the inputs and programs needed to increase food production in the LDCs by 3.6 percent per year was about $20 billion, and that roughly one-third of the investment would need to come from foreign sources, at an approximate annual cost of $7 billion, while the remainder could be found within the poor countries themselves. (The poor nations already contribute 85 percent of the investment in their agriculture.) In 1976 annual external aid needed was estimated at $8.5 billion per year, whereas aid to food-producing agriculture was $3.6 billion, leaving a gap of about $5 billion.[77]

While $7 billion or $8 billion may sound like a large sum of money, it is a minor expense compared with other annual expenditures—$8 billion is one-sixth of 1 percent of the 1974 GNP of the developed nations and about 2 percent of annual global expenditures on armaments. Even if the cost were to be borne by the U.S. alone, $8 billion is much less than 1 percent of the U.S. GNP and only about 2 percent of U.S. government spending. Unfortunately, the United States is now one of the most tight-fisted of the rich nations, giving less than one quarter of 1 percent of its GNP in aid.

The point here is not that $8 billion of aid per year would solve the world's food and population problem. It most certainly would not. As I shall show, the food problem is not one that can be solved by the mere infusion of large amounts of money. The point is that the economic sacrifice necessary to provide the physical and technological inputs is quite minor— indeed, a reordering of priorities would make it no sacrifice at all. We should be clear that the cost is one we could easily bear.

Environmental Costs

We have largely ignored the potential for degradation of land through efforts to increase the food supply, though clearly some environments have deteriorated and continue to do so under the pressure of agriculture. This topic is discussed at length in Chapter 10; here only two summary points need be made. First, even under current practices, environmental degradation is not likely to pose a major threat to agricultural production. Deterioration tends to be greatest in marginal areas that support rather few people, not in highly productive farmlands; furthermore, much of the deterioration in both good and marginal land is reversible, and the economic benefits would exceed the costs. This is not to deny, of course, that environmental degradation is a serious problem for some agricultural populations.

Second, when farmers are given access to the necessary productive inputs, i.e., when they are not rendered impotent by poverty, they are likely to improve rather than degrade the land. Indeed, as I noted earlier, the general historical trend is for the productivity of farming land to improve with time.

CONCLUSIONS

In the absence of marked improvement in current trends of food production in the poor nations, two existing problems will remain and probably become more severe. First, the number of malnourished people is likely to increase. Second, increasing population and aggregate incomes will result in more demand for food, and the LDCs will be forced to import larger amounts of food. Estimates of the probable amounts of these imports vary but range up to more than 100 million tons in 1990, at a cost of about $20 billion per year. This would be a severe drain on the very limited foreign exchange that many of the poorest LDCs can earn and would be a serious obstacle to their economic growth.

The major conclusion of the second part of the chapter is that there is no physical, biological, or technical reason why these problems should not be solved within this century. The natural resources—land, adequate soil, water—are not constraints on greatly increased food production. Everywhere in the developing world, including those countries where land is in short supply, there is enormous potential for increasing output per hectare, and neither the availability nor the cost of the required inputs need be a serious barrier to greatly increased yields. Even long-term increases in fuel prices need not constrain production and will have relatively little effect on the real cost of producing food. The claim that we have reached or are approaching the world's capacity to feed current and projected populations is simply wrong.

Local and temporary food shortages are probably inevitable, given the variability of the weather and some of the locally severe environmental problems in marginal grazing land. But these do not present insurmountable organizational or financial difficulties.

An annual increase of 3.5 to 4.0 percent in the production of food in the developing world is within physical and technical constraints and is also economically possible. Such a rate of increase is large enough to meet the projected food needs of the developing world and would be adequate for rapid economic development (Chapter 7). However, even at such high growth rates, a redistribution of income would be needed to reduce malnutrition significantly.

Unfortunately, it is not enough to have adequate resources *in the aggregate*. It is distortions in the distribution of these resources, in the access to productive resources, and in income that are the real constraints on food production, as they are the real causes of malnutrition. The next chapter discusses these distortions in detail and shows how inadequate food production derives from the structural poverty of the agrarian population.

6

STRUCTURAL CONSTRAINTS ON FOOD PRODUCTION

One of the facts that many of us find hard to accept is that the level of food production is determined to a large extent by economic rather than by biological, physical, or more obviously agricultural factors. The standard picture is of a poor peasant tending scrawny crops with primitive tools, eking out a mere subsistence living from poor soil. Superficially it looks as if the poverty of the soil and other natural features explain the farmer's poverty, and this may be partly true. But it is also true that the poor quality of the "natural" factors results in part from the farmer's poverty. Most of the natural features are no more immutable than are the primitive tools; both can be enormously enhanced. The farmer's economic well-being and the quality of his land, crops, and implements form a strongly linked feedback system. Improving the level of each component leads to improvement in the other parts, and a dynamic positive feedback can be set in motion that drives the farmer and his farm out of a condition of poverty and into a highly productive state.

Ultimately, of course, physical, biological, and technical factors must impose an upper limit on productivity. But as we saw in the last chapter, the agriculture of even the developed countries is so far below such a limit that those factors are essentially irrelevant to the question of why food production is now so low.

This chapter outlines the basic distortions in the economic and political structures underlying agricultural productivity.* It is these distortions that both restrict productivity and further undermine the usefulness of technological and other improvements. As we shall see in Chapter 7, the effects of these distortions ramify beyond agriculture to the entire structure

---

*By using the word "distortion" I mean to suggest, quite explicitly, that for each developing country there is a possible economic structure, or a range of economic structures, that would result in balanced and sustained economic growth and development, and that the actual economic structure is generally so different from the optimum that both economic growth and real development are impeded. The structure of the economy includes such features as the way land and other productive resources are distributed and how much different sectors, such as agriculture and industry, interact or are integrated. The thesis presented is that the dynamics of the economy are determined mainly by its structure, rather than, for example, simply by the total amount of capital available for investment.

of the developing nation's economy, interfering with the whole process of economic development. In this chapter we will concentrate on their effects upon agriculture itself.

The primacy of economic over physical and biological factors in determining food production should be obvious to those of us who live in the developed world. Perhaps the best evidence comes from the recent history of U.S. agriculture, which shows how the economic structure can promote *excess* food production.

U.S. AGRICULTURE: A CASE STUDY

The central problem in the history of U.S. agriculture since 1930, apart from a few exceptional years, has been how to deal with the virtually unmanageable *overproduction* of the U.S. farm.[1] This excess production has altered the shape of American farming communities, has dominated international agricultural trade, has been an important tool of U.S. foreign policy, and has led to the mixed blessing of food aid to poor countries. It has arisen from two major forces: relentless technological innovation and equally relentless economic pressure on farmers. The former has been created mainly through governmental spending on agricultural research in universities and research institutions, the latter from a combination of government policies and the fact that the U.S. farmer has been an almost unique being in our corporate capitalist society—an entrepreneur in a largely free enterprise system. (This system has been changing with the spread of agribusiness production, processing, and marketing.)

The role of government-supported research in creating continuous technological innovation is straightforward, but its consequences for farmers, and the subsequent economic pressure upon them, are perhaps less clear. Of special importance is the fact that there are so many farmers. As a consequence, no farmer can affect total food production by controlling his own output, and no farmer can increase the price he receives by producing less and thus reducing the supply. In economic jargon, he is a "price taker." Therefore, the only way farmers can make more money, or the same amount of money if prices fall, is to produce more. They can do this only if their costs per unit of output decrease. And they can do that only by adopting technological innovations that allow them to produce more for the same total costs.

Thus the U.S. farmer has been under pressure to adopt new technology and has done so with amazing speed. As a result, production has increased rapidly. Unfortunately for the individual, virtually all farmers have had to do precisely the same thing. When almost all farmers rapidly adopt the new technology, total production goes up, and prices are depressed. Indeed, because food consumption is relatively inelastic in rich countries, a 1 percent increase in supply relative to demand has tended to cause a 5 percent decrease in prices to farmers. The fall in prices that follows increased output drives farmers to adopt new technology, which increases both individual output and total output, which lowers the prices they receive...and so on. The fact is that there has been an excess of agricultural resources producing too much agricultural produce.[2]

These structural conditions have had a great effect upon farm communities. Those farmers who could not afford the new technology lost money, sold their farms, and went to the city. These invariably have been the poorer farmers, a bias that has been accentuated by government policies and the practices of most institutions involved in agriculture. In 1920 there were 32 million farmers (including their families) on this treadmill; by 1970 there were only 8 million.

The striking consequence of this process is that while farm output has roughly doubled since 1940, *total costs in real dollars have remained virtually the same* (figure 6-1). That is, the real cost per unit of food produced has been halved. The actual technological changes that have caused this decline include the substitution of cheap fossil fuels for labor, improvements in genetic strains of crops, better irrigation, cheaper fertilizers resulting from innovations in their manufacture, better management, and the combination of these different components of technology.

The U.S. government responded to overproduction by creating special farm legislation from the 1930s onward. The aims of this legislation were to support farmers' incomes, which tended to decline because of declining prices caused by excess production, and to restrict production to maintain prices. The two main mechanisms were (1) price supports, i.e., excess production was bought by the government at a guaranteed price, and (2) acreage allotments, that is, price supports were paid only if the farmer agreed not to produce a certain crop on a given percentage of land. This latter mechanism was meant to restrict production. In fact, the policy did succeed in maintaining farm incomes, which without the support prices would have been about 75 percent of their actual level. But they failed to constrain production. Indeed, they led to the accumulation of excess food, especially in the 1950s and 1960s, which was dumped on world markets at low prices or given away as food aid. The annual cost of such support programs reached $7 billion in 1972.

The world "food crisis" of 1972 led to a large increase in foreign demand for U.S. grain and therefore to an increase in its price, which persisted until 1974. Supply control programs were scrapped. But the situation for the U.S. farmer has now returned to the historical norm, and price supports have been reinstated even though exports continue to increase.

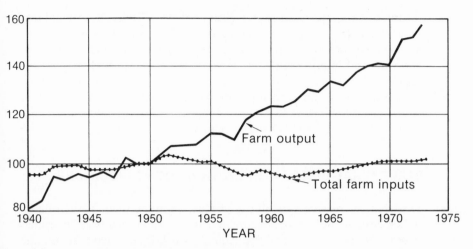

Figure 6-1 U.S. farm productivity, 1940–1973

Sources: Redrawn from Willard W. Cochrane, The City Man's Guide to the Farm Problem
(Minneapolis: University of Minnesota Press, 1965), p. 46. See also Willard W. Cochrane and
Mary E. Ryan, American Farm Policy, 1948–1973 (Minneapolis: University of Minnesota Press,
1976), p. 4.
Note: Shown is an index of the value of inputs and outputs, with the value in 1950 set at 100.

While the policy of reducing the amount of acreage in production may
have somewhat reduced total output, it actually increased greatly the incentive to produce more on the allotted acreage—i.e., it greatly increased
the incentive to adopt yield-increasing technology. Farmers responded to
restrictions on the use of productive land by greatly increasing the yield
per cultivated acre. A different set of policies on the funding of research,
on farm incomes, and on controlling supply would have resulted in a very
different level of yields. Yields and output have thus borne relatively little
relation to the natural endowment of the land.

As we will see, in the developing countries, government policies, the
economic structure of agriculture, the overall economic structure, and international relationships have all operated to have precisely the opposite
effect to that which occurred in the United States. Indeed, an indirect
consequence of U.S. policy has been that each year U.S. taxpayers have
paid several billion dollars to maintain price supports that in turn have led
to the dumping of cheap food on markets in poor countries. At least in
some instances, this has caused a reduction in the prices received by farmers there and hence a suppression of their food production, a consequence
of their tax dollar rarely contemplated by the U.S. citizen.[3]

The U.S. case should alert us to the importance of economic, social,
and political structures in determining the level of food production, and to

the relative unimportance of biological or physical limits. Nor should it be thought that the American case is unique. The European Economic Community countries are continually embarrassed by "lakes" of excess milk and wine and intermittently by "mountains" of excess beef, butter, and eggs.

In considering the agriculture of the poor nations, I shall examine structural distortions at two levels: within agriculture, and between agriculture and other sectors of the economy.

STRUCTURAL DISTORTIONS WITHIN LDC AGRICULTURE

The key to increasing agricultural production in the LDCs is to bring together three main "factors of production": labor, which is an enormous resource in most poor countries; capital, which is very scarce there; and land, which is scarce in some areas and plentiful in others. The mere bringing together of these three factors does not alone lead to increased production, of course. In addition, seeds, fertilizers, and other inputs must be available for purchase; there must be a market for the produce and a price that makes it worthwhile to produce it; and research and extension institutions are needed. But agriculture cannot begin to approach its potential productivity until the three factors are brought together in an efficient and, if possible, optimal mix.

The fundamental problem within the agriculture of the developing countries is that the great labor resources are kept separated from the scarce capital and even from most of the productive land. What capital exists is used in unproductive ways. The result is lowered productivity, increased unemployment, increased poverty, the misallocation of scarce capital, and inhibited economic development.

The details vary from country to country, but certain features are common throughout the developing countries. The basic distortions are in land distribution and land tenure, and these give rise to and are accentuated by extreme unevenness in the distribution of wealth and political power. These distortions in turn lead to extreme inequality in the access to and cost of additional capital in the form of credit. I will now deal with each of these problems separately.

In this discussion I will talk of the poor and rich farmer, and the landlord, as if the characteristics of these groups of people were invariant throughout the developing world. Of course they are not. For example, China, Taiwan, South Korea, Cuba, and Tanzania are exceptional, and highly instructive. Nonetheless, there is a remarkable similarity in the structure of agrarian societies throughout most of the developing countries, and the distortions in that structure are virtually universal. Detailed analyses have been made in a great range of developing countries in Asia, Latin America, and Africa.[4] I will mention specific countries mainly by way of illustration.

1. Land Distribution

The distribution of land among farmers in developing countries is startlingly uneven. In 1965 official data showed that 94 percent of the available land in Latin America was owned by only 7 percent of the landowners, and even these numbers underestimate land concentration.[5] Latin America is notorious for its inequality, and it comes as no surprise that some farmers own thousands of hectares while millions of peasants survive on only a few hectares or less. What is surprising is that even in most of the land-scarce countries of Asia, most of the land is owned by a small proportion of the rural families. In Java, where half of the households own less than half a hectare, the top 1 percent of landowners own about a third of the land; in India the top 8 percent of the rural population owns more than half of the arable land; and in the Pakistani Punjab almost one-quarter of the land is owned by less than 1 percent of the rural population. In Kenya in 1970, 13,000 square miles in the highlands, constituting 20 percent of the best land in the country, were owned by only 3,175 farmers out of a rural population of over 10 million.[6]

Since some farmers who do not own land can rent it, the distribution of land among farmers is more even than the distribution of land among owners. Even then, however, land distribution is still grossly uneven. For example, in the Philippines a thousand farms average over 600 hectares (6 square kilometers) each while 250,000 farms are smaller than 1 hectare; in Pakistan there are 14,000 farms that average 350 acres each and 740,000 that are less than 1 acre; in Colombia there are almost 7,000 farms greater than 500 hectares each and over 600,000 less than 3 hectares. Typically, less than 10 percent of the rural population farms more than half the land and a majority of the labor force is crowded onto a small fraction of the land. In some cases, especially in Latin America, the skew is much worse than this; for example in Peru 1 percent of the population farms more than 80 percent of the land.[7]

There are a few LDCs in which land is evenly distributed. In addition to those in which land is held communally—for example China, Cuba, and Tanzania—land distribution is also even in Taiwan and South Korea. Johnston and Kilby have termed this pattern of distribution "unimodal."[8] Thus, in Taiwan virtually all farms are small, most farms are very close to the average size (80 percent are within one acre of the average size), and most farmers work farms of intermediate size (figure 6-2).

Figure 6-2 also shows, in contrast, the "bimodal" or "dual" distribution of land in Colombia. In this case the two "modes" are created by the

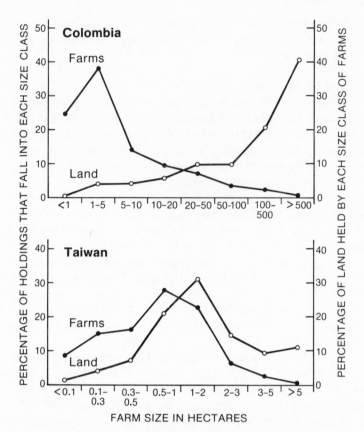

Figure 6-2 Land distribution in Colombia (bimodal) and Taiwan (unimodal) in 1960

Source: Food and Agriculture Organization, Report on the World Census of Agriculture, vol. 1, part A (Rome: FAO, 1966).
Note: In Colombia most farmers live on small farms that comprise a small fraction of the land, while most land is owned by a few large farms. In Taiwan the people and land are both found mainly on middle-sized farms. (The figures for Taiwan are for cultivated land.)

crowding of most farmers onto small farms and the aggregation of most of the land into a few large farms. In bimodal agriculture, most of the production of food for the market, i.e., food in excess of the farm family's needs, is done on the larger, commercial farms. The smaller farms are subsistence plots, producing only enough, or less than enough, for the family's immediate needs.

It is not clear if the quality of land is on average better on small or on large farms. The price of land is artificially high on small farms, since they are small lots and since credit for buying land is more costly for small farmers, so the price of land is not a good indication of its quality. Certainly in some countries, such as Malaysia, Guatemala, and Brazil, there is clear evidence that smaller farmers have worse land; on the other hand, some portion of the land in the larger estates in Latin America is likely to be relatively poor.[9]

In most LDCs there is also a large class of rural people who neither own nor rent land. The percentage of the agricultural work force without land is somewhere between 30 and 40 percent for Asia, Africa, and Latin America, although in some areas it may reach 60 percent.[10] These families, together with the large fraction of farmers whose farms are too small or too poor to support them, depend for their existence upon employment on the larger farms. Except at peak seasons, they are typically unemployed or underemployed.

The unequal distribution of land is the basic distortion within agrarian societies. From this distortion flows the extremely uneven distribution of economic and political power, and hence the other distortions discussed below.

2. Landowner/Tenant Relationships

Much of the land owned by large landowners is not cultivated by them. The landowner may hire laborers to do the work or may act as a landlord and rent parcels of land to the cultivator in return for cash, labor, or a share of the crop. There is an extremely varied and complex set of landlord-tenant arrangements. In almost all cases, however, the cultivators receive a relatively low return for their labor, since there is generally an excess of available renters or laborers and wage and income rates are thus determined in large part by the landlord. As a striking example, about 90 percent of the villagers in central and southern Java do not own the land they cultivate and they keep only 33 to 40 percent of the harvest,[11] although typically in the LDCs the sharecropper would keep about half the harvest. In addition, the tenants' tenure to the land may be very insecure, so that they have no guarantee that they will be able to farm it in the future. In India and Pakistan the Green Revolution has accentuated this problem by enabling richer farmers to buy tractors to replace tenants whose families had worked the land for generations. While production has been increasing in India, more and more landless peasants have been thrown out of work. This has led in some places to violent confrontations; in one incident a Brahman who owned 500 acres led sixty armed men into a village of "untouchables" in Bijar and gunned down four tenant farmers who refused to quit their jobs when the Brahman bought a tractor.[12]

The unequal distribution of land and the inequities of land tenure are perhaps most clearly seen in the *latifundio-minifundio* system in Latin America (see Chapter 8). The *latifundio* constitutes the large estates and haciendas, which in recent years have often become modern commercial farms producing for national and international markets. The *minifundio* is the system of small peasants—subsistence farmers who produce for their own family on tiny plots of land and who labor on the *latifundio* to provide extra income for their families. The system yields enormous power to the large landowner who rents a small piece of land to the peasant—too small to support the worker's family—and then makes sure that the peasant has no employment available other than that on the estate.[13] Similar tactics have been employed wherever plantation crops have been important.

There is disagreement over the depressing effect of sharecropping and other tenancy arrangements upon agricultural production. It seems likely that under many arrangements tenants have a relatively low incentive to invest capital in the land to improve yields, since they take the risk of investment but the landlord will reap much of the gain at harvest time. In some areas, for example in Latin America, this results in the deterioration of already marginal soil and a decline in its productive capacity. As we will see below, the landlord may also have little incentive to improve the land or its yields because of the relative costs of land, capital, and labor. Kocher notes that in a UN study of all regions in India in the early 1960s, there was clear evidence of the depressing effect of the land tenure systems upon investment. Landowners cultivating their own land spent ten times as much per hectare on land improvement as did landowners who leased their land, and four times as much as tenants who did not own the land they cultivated. However, although sharecropping in particular has been singled out as an arrangment that should lead to lower productivity, Berry and Cline contend that there is neither convincing theoretical nor good empirical evidence that this is the case.[14]

From the point of view of our future discussion, the crucial aspect of the landlord-tenant relationship is the power that flows to the landlord. Perhaps the most obvious result of this power is the almost universal failure of LDC governments to implement real land reform, even though land reform legislation has been passed in many countries.[15]

3. Access to and Cost of Credit

High yields result from investing money and labor in the land and in better drainage, irrigation, fertilizer, seeds, etc. Since the investment must be made before income becomes available from the harvest, access to and cost of credit are crucial determinants of the amount and type of investment. Unfortunately, the effects of the skew in land distribution are exacerbated by distortions in the credit system: small farmers have poor access to credit, and that credit is expensive; larger farmers and landowners have easy access to credit, and that credit is cheap.[16]

On the formal credit market, the political and personal network of power ensures that the large farmer has easy access to cheap credit. In India, for example, large farmers typically control credit cooperatives.[17]

These richer farmers are reputedly low-risk borrowers and are given rapid preferential treatment by commercial banks.

The small peasants, by contrast, are high-risk debtors (crop failures can ruin them) and often may not even be eligible for credit. They generally borrow in the informal credit market—from a landlord (who may well obtain the money at low interest from lending institutions) or a moneylender. In these situations the interest rate is higher. Such high interest rates frequently result in the peasant's being in virtual and perpetual bondage to the creditor: to the large fraction of harvest turned over to the landlord as rent is added the repayment of debt, either as produce or labor, or both. Yet the rationale for skewed interest rates, namely that richer farmers are better risks, is often invalid. In India, for example, richer farmers are less likely to repay loans than are the few poor farmers who do manage to get them. This pattern is common throughout the developing world:[18]

> In a traditional agriculture, credit is basically repressive, no matter who provides it.... The private moneylender guards against failure to pay by imposing high interest rates and exercising well-nigh ironbound supervision...the repayment problem is exacerbated by politically influential, wealthier cultivators, who control the cooperatives and use their influence to obtain loans for themselves and to evade repayment...repayment rates for cooperatives are lowest among the high-income cultivators.[19]

Government credit, which is generally low cost, is similarly biased towards the large landowner. Sometimes a criterion for credit is a minimum size of land holding—a policy that in Pakistan excludes 80 percent of the farmers from receiving government credit for a tubewell.[20] The overall result of such institutional distortions is that very few farmers are able to acquire credit (table 6-1).

Hossain provides an example of the distribution of credit among farm-

Table 6-1. Percentage of farm families receiving credit from institutional sources

Country	Percentage	Country	Percentage	Country	Percentage
ica		*Asia*		*Latin America*	
iopia	1	Bangladesh	15	Bolivia	5
ana	1	India	20	Brazil	15
nya	12	Jordan	8	Chile	15
rocco	10	Korea, Rep. of	40	Colombia	30
dan	1	Malaysia	2	Ecuador	18
isia	5	Pakistan	5	Guatemala	2
anda	3	Philippines	28	Honduras	10
stern Nigeria	1	Sri Lanka	14	Mexico	15
		Taiwan	95	Nicaragua	20
		Thailand	7	Panama	4
		Turkey	23	Paraguay	6
		S. Vietnam	21	Peru	17

Source: World Bank, *Agricultural Credit,* Sector Policy Paper (Washington, D.C.: World Bank, 1975), p. 71.

ers from the Phulphur area in Bangladesh.[21] Only 2 percent of the farmers who owned two acres or less received credit from lending institutions, compared with 17 to 24 percent for farmers owning more than two acres. The former, on average, paid twice as much annual interest as the latter. The trends were similar in a second area, where farmers with the smallest plots paid 37 percent interest per year while those with the largest plots paid 8 percent.

These policies are hardly mere accident. Land ownership and other forms of wealth and status bring political power and influence over government policy:[22]

> When the land resources are owned by a small group in the community, this group will control the majority of the Government's activities and exert a great influence over important decisions regarding the allocation and exploitation of resources. Gradually the group builds up its power into a formidable institution dictating the structure of the community.... The situation is aggravated when this controlling force integrates with other commerical and industrial groups inside or outside the countries. Invariably, the concentration of resources in the hands of the minority eventually leads to the exploitation and marginalization of the rest of the population.[23]

Whenever the nation depends on export crops to earn foreign currency, the land-holding class gains additional power to prevent changes in rural society.[24]

The distribution of rural credit reinforces in turn the traditional power structure. Bhaduri has pointed out that the combination of owning land and lending money gives landowners essentially feudal power over their tenants, who are perpetually indebted to them, even for basic needs. Such "semi-feudalism" can actually operate to dissuade landlords from adopting technological improvements that could provide such a jump in yield that tenants might escape their bondage. On the other hand, in the Indian Punjab the gains to the landlord from adopting the new strains of wheat have been so great that owners of middle-sized farms have shared with their tenants the cost of adopting them.[25]

Finally, skewed access to credit has caused even greater unevenness in land distribution in many parts of the developing world. Indebtedness becomes a way of life for small peasants and increases the chances that eventually they will have to sell their land to their creditors. This has been a common cause of further land concentration both in Asia and in Africa, and it has been accentuated by the Green Revolution.[26]

4. Bias in Technology

The bias against the peasant and toward the large landowner has also pervaded research and technological innovation in the developing world's agriculture. Griffin knows of "no recent case of a peasant-biased technical change,"[27] although some innovations may be usable by both large farmer and peasant. For example, most farmers in Asia grow rainfed crops, which remain virtually untouched by the Green Revolution. Very little research has been done on symbiotic and mixed cropping (such as the combination of beans or other legumes with grain, grown by peasants in Latin America and Africa); on disease- and pest-resistant strains; or on ways of reducing fallow periods and erosion while increasing soil fertility. Yet the potential for increasing yields in subsistence agriculture is huge.[28] Fortunately, several of the International Agricultural Centers in the tropics have begun research in these areas.

The advantage that accrues to large farmers in the use of high-yielding varieties results not from the strains themselves but from their need for greater capital inputs—good water control and more fertilizer. That is, their benefits have been biased toward larger farmers because of the unequal access to credit, as discussed above. Indeed, the limits on the spread of the new grain varieties and the low use of fertilizers on them can be traced in large part to inadequate credit for small farmers.[29] This is crucial, for it is clear that much of the yield-increasing agricultural technology (fertilizers, new grains, intensive farming techniques) and the new strains in particular *provide no advantages to scale* in developing countries. That is, in labor-rich and capital-poor agriculture, *yield-increasing technology can be used at least as efficiently on small as on large farms.* Furthermore, given equal access to credit, small farmers adopt high-yielding technology as rapidly as large farmers. In fact, even with the credit system operating against them, Asian peasants adopt the new technology only about one year later than do the richer farmers.[30]

Agricultural research need not be landlord biased. The fact that this is so is again the result of government and international policies that reflect the distribution of political power. Research could focus on the farming systems used by the vast majority of peasants.

CONSEQUENCES OF STRUCTURAL DISTORTIONS WITHIN AGRICULTURE

Of the distortions discussed above, two are most important: unevenness in land distribution and unequal access to credit. Together these have disastrous consequences upon food production in the developing nations. They have these effects by influencing the incentives to farmers and the way in which labor, capital, and land are used by different types of farmers.

Effects on Incentives

The case of the small farmers is quite straightforward.[31] They have very little land, find credit extremely difficult and expensive to get, and have one resource in abundance—their labor and that of their families. Land and capital are scarce and therefore expensive; labor is abundant and therefore cheap. The incentive for small farmers is clear: they can strive only to *maximize their output per unit of land and capital. That is, they must aim for the highest yield they can afford.* (We will see later in this chapter that the yields a farmer can afford to produce are in general kept low by distortions outside the agricultural sector.) Whatever capital they get will be devoted to this aim; it would make no sense to buy labor-saving machinery, for example, since that would replace a resource that is already in excess much of the time. Once immediate and basic needs are met,[32] credit will therefore go for water control, fertilizer, and better seeds. Only the need to avoid calamitous risks will temper a small farmer's efforts to achieve high yields. For example, the threat of crop failure explains in part why small farmers generally do not adopt new practices before they have been shown to be successful locally.

The larger and richer farmers are in a very different position, even in nations where land in general is scarce. For the larger landowner, land is relatively cheap. This is of course particularly true in Latin America but is also the case even in Asia. Credit is also cheap, and government policies usually cause labor-saving equipment to be cheap (see below). By contrast, hired labor is expensive relative to land and capital.[33] Most important, *the more labor that is hired, the higher is each laborer's wage*; conversely, a large pool of unemployed labor keeps the wage rate low. These relationships result from the fact that large landowners hire most of the labor in the area and they therefore determine the demand and hence the wage rate of labor. There is thus a strong incentive for the large farmer to minimize the amount of hired labor. Labor is also "expensive" because it can potentially give trouble and is less manageable and predictable than machinery.

In deciding how to farm their land, large farmers therefore have more options than small farmers do. In particular, they can give up some of the yield that comes from intensive farming in exchange for the reduced labor costs that arise from less intensive farming. This will be particularly attractive when, as is usually the situation, they are paid low prices for their products (see below). The incentive to maximize yields therefore decreases as farm size grows, and there is a clear incentive to substitute land and capital (machinery) for labor.

Effects on Use of Labor and Capital

We can thus see that as farm size increases, the amount of labor used per unit area should decrease (being replaced by machinery and less intensive

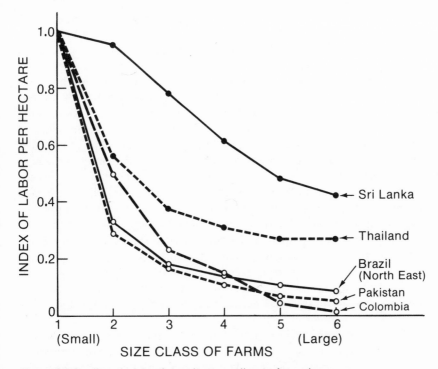

Figure 6-3 Declines in labor intensity according to farm size

Sources: R. Albert Berry and William R. Cline, *Agrarian Structure and Productivity in Developing Countries* (Baltimore: Johns Hopkins University Press, 1979), pp. 55, 59, 87; Keith Griffin, *The Political Economy of Agrarian Change* (Cambridge, Mass.: Harvard University Press, 1974), pp. 39, 42.

Note: In each country the number of hours spent per hectare on the smallest farms has been set equal to one, and the amount of labor per hectare on all larger farms is expressed as a fraction of that on the smallest farms. The size class of farms is relative. For example, large farms in Colombia are much larger than those in Taiwan.

agriculture) and the amount of capital per worker should increase. Such relationships are indeed almost universal in the developing countries. Figure 6-3 shows a few examples of how labor intensity declines with farm size. By contrast, the amount spent per hectare on purchased inputs increases with farm size. Even in Sri Lanka, where credit and material inputs are widely available, the largest farms spend more than three times as much *per acre* on tractors than do the smallest farms.[34]

As a consequence, in the developing countries as a whole small farmers (i.e., those with fewer than five hectares of rainfed land or three hectares of irrigated land) *occupy 30 to 40 percent of the available land, grow 40 to 50 percent of farm output by value, but receive only about 10 percent of the purchased farm inputs* (e.g., machinery, fertilizers). This means that, on average, the large farmer spends on inputs four or five times as much per hectare as does the small farmer, and produces less. On large Latin American farms it is common for the ratio of capital investment to output to be even higher than in the capital-rich United States![35]

The tendency for large farmers to invest in labor-saving machinery in the midst of enormous rural unemployment is strengthened by various government policies that further misallocate scarce capital. Developing governments frequently give low-cost loans specifically for the purchase of tractors and other farm machinery. For example, in Brazil long-term government loans for purchasing tractors have been given to large farmers at interest rates below the inflation rate—that is, the farmers have in essence been paid to borrow the money to buy the tractors. (This policy was aimed at encouraging Brazil's tractor manufacturing, as well as giving support to the politically powerful large farmers in the South.) The results: the number of tractors in Brazil increased twentyfold from 1950 to 1970 (two-thirds of them being concentrated in two southern states), investment was diverted from yield-increasing technology, labor was displaced by subsidized machinery, and the inequalities in income between groups of farmers in a given area and between the poor Northeast and the richer South were increased.[36]

Such policies can result in quite startling situations: in units of wheat, a tractor cost twice as much in Iowa as it did in Pakistan, and in Germany it was twice as expensive to get a loan for farm equipment as it was in the Ivory Coast.[37] Through distortions like these, large farmers are loaned money at interest rates below its "social" or "opportunity" cost (i.e., what it could earn if invested elsewhere), and they use it to buy labor-saving machinery. The nation thus loses both economic growth and employment through the squandering of scarce capital.

Effects on Food Production

These relationships among land, labor, and capital have exactly the effect upon production that one would predict. It is an effect with profound consequences for the world food supply problem: *the yield per unit of land decreases as farm size increases and total food production is suppressed because of this relationship.* This negative relationship between output and farm size has been found throughout the developing world—in Sri Lanka, Thailand, Indonesia, Taiwan, Bangladesh, India, throughout Latin America, and most recently in a broad analysis of more than twenty developing countries in Asia, Africa, and Latin America and in detailed studies of Brazil, Colombia, Philippines, Pakistan, India, and Malaysia.[38]

The relationship is shown for a few countries in figure 6-4. It holds true

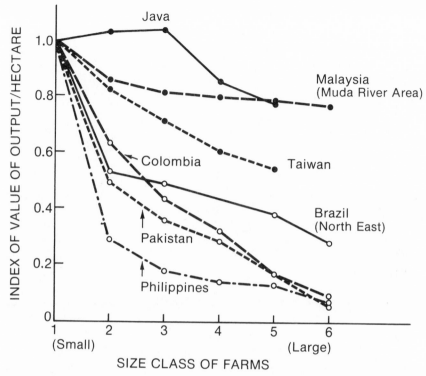

Figure 6-4 Decreases in yield per hectare according to farm size

Sources: Berry and Cline, *Agrarian Structure,* pp. 46, 59, 70, 89, 122, 195; Griffin, *Political Economy,* p. 44.

Note: Yield is measured as value per hectare. For each country the value on the smallest farms is set equal to one, and yield on all larger farms is expressed as a fraction of that on the smallest farms. For Taiwan the values are income per hectare. Again, the size class of farms is relative. For example, large farms in Colombia are much larger than those in Taiwan.

whether all output is lumped by value or single crops are examined, and it is usually true whether yield is expressed per hectare or per cultivated hectare. Berry and Cline show that this powerful trend is not explained by such extraneous features as regional differences in farm type or in land quality. Indeed in Latin America, "lands unsuitable for agriculture—frequently on hillsides, in gullies, or deserts—are cultivated so intensely that output per hectare is high even by the standards of modern agriculture. Yields appear even more remarkable when account is taken of the poor quality of the land, seed, and other inputs."[39]

The single major cause of the universally higher yields on small farms is that smaller farmers make better use of the land by farming it more intensively; as farm size increases land becomes more and more underused.

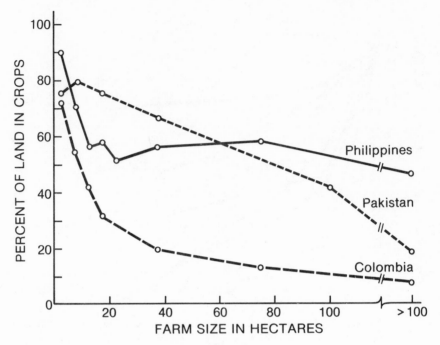

Figure 6-5 Decreases in intensity of farming according to farm size
Source: Berry and Cline, *Agrarian Structure,* pp. 68, 71, 88.

This is most marked in Latin America, where only about one-sixth of the land in large estates is actually cultivated, but it is also true in land-poor Asia, where on larger farms a smaller fraction of the land is cultivated and cropping is less intensive. Berry and Cline show that in all developing countries examined (except Taiwan and Korea—see Chapter 7), land utilization is less on larger farms. Figure 6-5 presents a few of these results. Furthermore, the underutilization is more severe the more unequal the distribution of land is among farmers.

In Latin America the general reason for the drop in output per acre as farm size increases is that crops are replaced by cattle on larger farms. Notice that not only does this result in a product that is less valuable per acre, but the meat produced is too expensive for most of the local population. (By contrast, in Latin America there is no fixed relationship between farm size and yield per *cultivated* acre—the large farmers generally grow crops only on the best of their land and can therefore achieve reasonably high yields per cultivated acre.)

In Asia the main cause of decreasing yields as farm size increases is similarly a greater intensity in the use of the land by small farmers, though again small farmers also concentrate on more valuable or higher yielding crops that generally need more attention. Small farmers do more multiple cropping, more intercropping, and more relay planting (sowing a second crop before the first is harvested). As would be expected, smaller farmers also spend proportionately more capital on yield-increasing inputs than do large farmers.[40]

The Green Revolution has not reversed the superiority of the small farmer. Small farmers still do better than large farmers with the new grains. True, it is easier for large farmers to adopt the new strains because of better credit facilities and so on. Nonetheless, small farmers do not lag behind in their acceptance of these strains by more than a year, and in some countries and some crops small and large farmers adopt the new strains at the same time. The pressure on small farmers to increase yields is so great that they overcome their disadvantaged position to adopt new strains when these are available. In fact, Berry and Cline have been able to show that in general size of farm per se has no effect on the propensity to adopt new technology.

The analysis above leads to an important conclusion about food supply and agricultural productivity in the developing countries. *The distortions in land distribution and credit cause food production to be much lower than it could be.* Labor is potentially a highly productive resource, but it is in excess on small farms and too scarce on large farms. Total production would increase if labor were spread evenly over the land, and in principle the highest production would result from land redistribution that made all farms (corrected for land quality) the same size.[41] Of course, land redistribution with radical reform of access to credit would be much more successful in raising productivity than would land redistribution alone.

Berry and Cline, using detailed data from six countries and assuming that the available land is divided equally among farmers, have calculated that with complete land redistribution, total output would increase by 10 to 80 percent because the overall intensity of land use would increase (table 6-2). Notice that increased production in the land-scarce Asian

Table 6-2. Increases in agricultural production that would arise from land redistribution

Country	Calculated increase (%)	Year data collected
Brazil	25	1962–63
Brazil (N.E.)	79.5	1973
Colombia	28	1960
India	19	1970–71
Pakistan	10	1960
Philippines	23	1960
Malaysia	28	1972–73

Source: R. Albert Berry and William R. Cline, *Agrarian Structure and Productivity in Developing Countries* (Baltimore: Johns Hopkins University Press, 1979), p. 132.

countries would be about as great as those in land-rich Colombia. This is a purely speculative exercise, but it strongly suggests that significant gains in output can be gained by land redistribution.

These analyses show that, without doubt, the small farmer is more productive than the large farmer and makes more efficient use of scarce resources. It is this sort of evidence, among other factors, that stimulated the appearance of a new strategy for development in the 1970s, championed particularly by the World Bank. Increased production by millions of small farmers is viewed as the central element of the new rural development schemes that are expected to play a critical role in overall development (Chapters 7 and 9). It must be stressed, however, that *there is no evidence that it is small size per se* that makes these farms relatively productive. Rather, it is the amount of labor and yield-increasing inputs applied to each hectare that produces larger yields. There is no reason to suppose that larger units that received the same intensity of care and input *per hectare* would produce lower yields. Indeed, there would then accrue organizational advantages of scale in such matters as wells, irrigation construction, and the efficient use of machinery.

Larger farming units can be obtained by cooperative pooling of land or by communal ownership. The latter has the great advantage that it can incorporate the previously landless into the production system. An additional advantage that accrues to communal ownership is that labor can be mobilized during "off" seasons to create improvements to the land such as leveling, terracing, irrigation, and road building. This has been the case in China's communes (Chapter 7). The difficulty with communal farming is in maintaining individual incentives and motivation. Again, China appears largely to have solved this problem by keeping communal units relatively small (around thirty families), by allowing small private plots, and by the general motivation of the population to socialist ideals.

Effects on Poverty

The bimodal farming systems described above depress the incomes of a large segment of the rural population through unemployment, underemployment, suppressed wages, and low aggregate productivity. In addition, over the past two or three decades the degree of income inequality within such bimodal rural societies has become even worse. This has occurred especially where there has been a Green Revolution. Thus Mellor has shown that when the changeover is made to the new high-yielding varieties, the owners of land and capital gain six or seven times as much additional income as do the wage earners (it is this extra income that enables the landowner to replace the laborer with machinery).[42]

There are two major groups of poor in the countryside who are exploited by the bimodal system. The first, and generally the worst off, are the landless laborers. The system exploits them by reducing opportunities for employment and by suppressing wages. One way in which rural inequality has increased is that the ranks of the laborers have grown. For example, Rudra has shown that in India the proportion of landless laborers in the rural work force almost doubled between 1961 and 1971 as the larger landowners bought more land and tenants were evicted.[43]

The second exploited group is made up of subsistence peasants—families living on small farms and producing mainly for their own consumption. Typically, and ironically in view of the relatively high yields it produces, the labor of these families on their farms is grossly under-rewarded because of inadequate resources; these resources in the meantime lie underutilized on the larger farms. In addition, since the farms are in general too small or too poor in resources, the family is forced into the general pool of rural labor, where it has to try to find work on larger farms, once again for suppressed wages.

LAND REFORM AND THE SMALL FARMER

Throughout the LDCs, the inequities and inefficiencies of distorted agrarian systems have given rise to movements for land reform. These movements have aimed, at a minimum, to redistribute land from large to small landowners and to the landless. They have also generally aimed to reform those landowner/tenant and landowner/worker relationships that result in what we might designate as "bonded" labor. The ultimate goal of land reform movements is generally the great expansion of the class of landowning peasants who, by necessity, would usually be small farmers. (This description of course excludes socialist movements that seek the abolition of private ownership and the substitution of communal land ownership.)

Land reform programs have generally led to an increase in production and the efficient use of resources. Examples can be found in Europe, Asia (especially Japan, Taiwan, and South Korea), Latin America, and Egypt. Some programs, for example in Bolivia and Iraq, have resulted in lower production in the short term, but this occurred because they were badly implemented.[44]

Unfortunately, little land reform has actually been carried out. In spite of much legislation on the books in various LDCs, progress has been very slow and in some cases, such as Chile and Guatemala, previous reform has even been undone. Even where land reform has occurred, modern programs have rarely led to a major redistribution of land. Thus, although Mexico's land reform has been the most extensive in Latin America, less than half the land and only half the peasants are in the reform sector. Figures for other Latin American countries are in table 6-3. There has been little land reform in Africa or in Asia outside of Japan, Taiwan, and South Korea.[45]

If there has been very little redistribution of land, there has been even less redistribution of other productive resources. De Janvry and Ground note that in Latin America the land that has been redistributed has been the poorer land on the estates; furthermore, it has carried with it almost none of the capital, such as equipment and improvements like irrigation. In addition, access to credit, markets, extension services, and so on is much poorer on the "reform" farms. As a result, increased production for the market tends to come almost entirely from the larger "nonreform" sector.[46]

In a few special cases (Japan, Taiwan, South Korea), land reform has broadly increased rural welfare because it was carried out along with other policies aimed at the same goal (Chapter 7). Land reform can also provide a one-time increase in the evenness of income distribution as the lower income groups gain and the high income groups lose. This occurred in Mexico and Bolivia, and to some extent in Chile, Venezuela, and Peru. However, the distributional effects tend to erode through time both because of population growth within a skewed economic system, and because the small reform farmers have not been given access to other necessary resources such as credit.[47]

Land reform also carries with it the danger of *increasing* inequality in the rural population. This will be the case particularly when the reform is only partial, and in practice partial reform has been the rule. De Janvry and Ground argue that land reform in Latin America has actually worsened

Table 6-3. Results of land reform in Latin America

Country	Percentages of land and peasants in reform sector following land reform	
	Land	Peasants
Mexico	43	50
Guatemala	5	3
Bolivia	18	39
Venezuela	16	15
Colombia	10	4
Chile	9	4
Peru	42	32
Ecuador	1	4
Dominican Republic	2	2

Source: Alain de Janvry and Lynn Ground, "Types and Consequences of Land Reform in Latin America," *Latin American Perspectives* 19 (1978): 96.

the condition of the poorest rural groups, particularly by increasing the large and growing pool of landless and semi-landless peasants who glut the labor market and are forced to work for extremely low wages. The majority of the peasantry has not been included in the reforms. True, bonded labor in the form of labor-for-rent has been greatly reduced in most of Latin America. But in many cases, as a consequence, peasants have been expelled from the large estates and the amount of employment there has actually decreased. Even where the tenant has received title to some land, his problems are by no means resolved and may be worse. Frequently (as in Venezuela) the plot of land received by the peasant is too small and the peasant and his family are added to the labor pool:

> Receiving title to an acre of land in the middle of a large estate . . . makes little difference where the recipient has no other alternatives for employment, for credit, or for markets than through the patron. In fact, he may be worse off because the patron no longer has the same obligations to support him during hard times.[48]

Thus, while land reform in Latin America has reduced the size of some of the larger estates and created some commercial farms that are productive, it has not removed, and has in places expanded, the *minifundio*—the system of small plots owned or rented by peasants that in general are not adequate to support the family. Such plots tie the family to the land but also force them into the cheap labor pool.

On the other hand, the small fraction of the rural population that does receive commercially viable farms through land reform is able to increase its income greatly relative to the mass of the rural population. This deepens rural class distinctions and may well make further reform more difficult. Limited land reform in India has similarly created a relatively small class of "middle farmers" who now own land and are fighting fiercely against further land reform that would make it easier for small tenant farmers and the landless to own land.[49]

Thus land reform, while it has various beneficial effects, including increased productivity, is unlikely to lead to a resolution of the problem of persistent rural poverty unless the reform is sufficiently radical to cause profound changes in the structure of the rural economy—that is, in the distribution of productive assets and of political power.

It must also be emphasized that even if there were effective and radical redistribution of land, credit, and other resources within agriculture, land reform alone has a strictly limited capacity for increasing food production and solving other rural problems. This is because land reform does not attack directly the biases in the larger economic structure of which agriculture is but one part. Also needed are concomitant changes in the structure of the rest of the economy, particularly in the relationship between agriculture and industry, which will ensure that the farmer has the incentive and the means to produce more food. We turn next to these issues.

STRUCTURAL DISTORTIONS BETWEEN SECTORS OF THE ECONOMY: URBAN BIAS

Government policies in the developing nations have consistently promoted the growth and development of the urban industrial sector to the detriment of the agricultural sector (Chapters 7 and 9). This has had two results. First, the prices of inputs such as fertilizer, which farmers need to increase production, have been high relative to the price paid to farmers for their produce, i.e., the "terms of trade" are highly unfavorable to agriculture. This constitutes a direct disincentive to farmers. Second, investment has gone into industry, and into export crops, rather than into food production and rural institutions.

Disincentives to Food Production

Perhaps foremost among government policies that operate to reduce the farmer's incentive to produce for the market are *cheap food policies*. For a number of economic and political reasons, cheap food for the urban population is important to ruling elites in the LDCs. It helps check inflation, and because workers spend a large fraction of their income on food, it helps restrain industrial wages—that is, cheap food helps ensure cheap labor. Finally, cheap food helps keep the lid on urban unrest.

A number of mechanisms contribute to cheap food policies, which are almost universal in the poor countries:[50]

1. The government may impose price controls on food, keeping the price below its market "equilibrium level" so that the price does not increase as the demand increases. The demand is likely to be met by importing food.
2. The government may buy the produce at a controlled price, then resell it at a profit. Thus the consumer has paid more without this being translated into higher prices to farmers, which would stimulate them to produce more. As an example, in Thailand recently farmers were receiving one-fifth of the world price for rice! In Bangladesh there is a massive black market in rice exports to India, where prices are generally higher.[51]
3. The government may subsidize in various ways the importation of food, thus lowering the domestic market price. One mechanism by

which this is done is by overvaluing the exchange rate, which acts as a subsidy to imports (the currency can buy more imports than its real domestic value warrants). The dumping of surplus food from the developed countries càn further reduce the local market price.

4. At the same time as imports in general are subsidized, certain domestic industries are protected from external competition by tariffs and quotas on imports. These devices protect industries that are in general not efficient (for example, they operate well below capacity) and normally would not persist in the face of more efficient foreign competitors. Unfortunately the fertilizer industry is a prime example, so that farmers are forced to pay high prices for inefficiently produced domestic fertilizer.

A recent study of fifty-three developed and developing countries has established just how strong the disincentives to LDC farmers are. Peterson calculated the amount of standard quality fertilizer that could be bought in each country with the cash obtained by selling 100 kilograms of wheat (or rice, corn, etc. of the same value) *in the same country.* The prices paid and received by farmers in the different countries are therefore corrected for differences among countries in exchange rates and in the standard of living. The results for the period 1968 to 1970 are shown in table 6-4.

Obviously, farmers in the LDCs are paid less in real terms for the food they produce than are farmers in the developed countries. Of the LDCs, only South Korea appears among the top fifteen countries on the list; among the developed countries only Greece and Portugal, until recently often classified as LDCs, appear in the bottom half of the list. Two of the largest LDCs, India and Brazil, are not in the table. There also, farmers generally have been paid very low real prices for the food they produce relative to the fertilizer they buy. By contrast, in Taiwan, which is not in the table but is an LDC with exceptionally high yields, farmers receive high real prices.[52]

The absolute difference in prices is quite large. The real price paid to Japanese farmers was more than seven times greater than that paid to farmers in Niger. The average real price received by farmers in the top ten countries was almost four times higher than the average of those received by farmers in the bottom ten countries. The real cost of fertilizer to farmers in some of the LDCs is so high that, even if they could find the credit, and even if they were willing to risk paying out so much cash against a future crop, they would quickly reach levels of fertilizer use at which the additional yields obtained would not pay for the additional fertilizer required to produce them.

Peterson's study also demonstrates an important relationship: *the yield per acre increases sharply as the price paid to the farmer, relative to the price of fertilizer, increases.* This relationship persists when the effect of differences in climate and level of technology among countries has been factored out. It also occurs within the LDC group of countries, as well as in the fifty-three countries as a whole. This relationship suggests that if the real price paid to farmers in the bottom twenty-seven countries in table 6-4 had been the average real price paid in the top twenty-six countries, *food production in those twenty-seven countries from 1968 to 1970 would have been, in aggregate, 63 percent higher than actual production.* Notice that this estimated potential increase arises only from increases in yields per hectare; no account is taken of possible increase in arable land. This

Table 6-4. Real prices paid to farmers in developed and developing countries, 1968–1970

Kilograms of fertilizer that could be bought with cash from 100 kilograms of wheat or its equivalent			
Developed Countries		*Developing Countries*	
Japan	52.5	S. Korea	43.8
Hungary	51.9	Pakistan	32.2
Switzerland	45.5	Turkey	29.8
Finland	44.5	Sri Lanka	27.9
United States	44.0	Mexico	25.8
Norway	43.3	Chile	25.4
France	41.2	Colombia	25.4
Sweden	40.4	Morocco	25.2
W. Germany	38.0	Tunisia	23.0
Belgium	37.6	Kenya	20.8
United Kingdom	36.7	Ghana	20.7
Poland	36.3	Panama	19.9
Denmark	35.9	Jordan	19.7
Ireland	35.9	Senegal	19.1
Austria	35.5	Guatemala	18.2
Yugoslavia	32.4	Iraq	18.0
Spain	31.2	Cameroon	16.1
Netherlands	29.4	Ivory Coast	15.9
Italy	29.2	Peru	15.8
Israel	28.5	Uruguay	15.5
Canada	27.8	Philippines	15.0
Cyprus	27.8	Upper Volta	14.3
Greece	23.1	Argentina	13.4
Portugal	22.0	Dahomey	13.0
		Burma	12.2
		Guyana	10.8
		Khmer Republic	10.2
		Paraguay	8.4
		Niger	7.1

Source: W. L. Peterson, "International Farm Prices and the Social Cost of Cheap Food Policies," *American Journal of Agricultural Economics* 61 (1979): 14.

additional 220 million tons is *almost twice as large as the most pessimistic projection of the total food deficit in all the LDCs in 1990* (Chapter 5):

> On the basis of this evidence, one strongly suspects that if farmers in the LDCs had enjoyed the level of prices that prevailed in developed nations, or even in the world market, there would be no such thing as a world food shortage.... Indeed, one might go so far as to say that if farm prices in the LDCs were to approach world market levels these countries would likely become substantial exporters of agricultural products.[53]

Exceptions to the LDC pattern of cheap food policies illustrate the power of high prices to raise production.[54] The most obvious examples are South Korea and Taiwan, which have the world's smallest amounts of arable land per capita, barring only Japan. South Korea, where rice yields per hectare (almost seven tons) are even higher than Japan's, has even managed to export some rice in spite of greatly increased domestic consumption. Taiwan actually has been having trouble with excess rice production (as has Japan). In India, prices paid to farmers for rice have been consistently below world prices, rice yields have remained very low (under two tons per hectare), and rice production increased only about 35 percent between 1968 and 1978. By contrast, during most of this period wheat prices in India have been above the U.S. price and production has almost doubled in this same period. India has recently been an exporter of wheat.

Cheap food policies thus act as disincentives to increased production by the farmer. They discourage farmers from planning future expansion and from using more productive inputs (fertilizer, new seeds, etc.), and they may drive marginal farmers out of business. They are precisely the opposite of the policies developed to protect farmers' incomes in rich nations, as discussed above for the United States, and they have the obvious result of decreasing food supplies and suppressing rural incomes. They thus not only contribute to the food problem but are a major source of urban/rural economic inequality, the demographic consequences of which were discussed at length in Chapter 3.

At first it might seem that, in the presence of malnutrition, cheap food policies are humanitarian. But this is generally not the case. By creating disincentives to increased production, cheap food policies lower the supply of food available. They are also a technique for transferring poverty from the cities (where unrest is politically dangerous) to the more diffuse rural population which, one must recall, is the majority. The welfare of the rural population rests squarely upon the productivity of agriculture, and by suppressing that productivity cheap food policies perpetuate rural poverty. In brief, there is an unequal exchange of food for industrial goods, to keep urban wages low and urban profits high, and the rural population is squeezed to promote urban manufacturing.[55]

Low Investment in Food Production

An investment of capital, unless it comes from outside the system, requires savings. That is, to increase production, agriculture must produce enough for its own needs, plus a marketable surplus, and it must consume less than the total income gained. In essence, given the present maldistribution of productive resources in bimodal agriculture, this puts the burden of saving mainly on the large landowner. Landless laborers cannot invest savings in the land, and saving is also extremely difficult for tenant farmers—typically half of their gross output goes to landowners as rent, and a large fraction of the remainder is likely to be turned over either to moneylenders or landlords in payment of debts.

The surplus for the market is thus almost all in the hands of the large landowner. In India, for example, only 7 percent of the rural population, each person holding twenty acres or more, produces almost half of the marketable surplus, even though their output per acre is less than that of the small farmer. Their control over most of the land allows the small land-owning class to appropriate the agricultural surplus, sell it, and accumulate income. Griffin provides detailed evidence of this for a number of Asian and Latin American nations.[56] In parts of India the income of the large landowner from the farm alone is typically 100 times that of the farmworker and family farmer.

Some of the income of large landowners is reinvested in agriculture, but frequently it moves out of the countryside where it is produced, either to the cities or, quite commonly, abroad. A large fraction is not invested but merely spent in the city, often on imported luxury goods, i.e., it serves to transfer capital abroad and to raise the urban standard of living rather than the rate of investment (see Chapters 7 and 9). Barraclough notes that in Latin America large landowners invest a very small fraction of their income, spending 84 percent of their disposable income on consumption, a much higher fraction than is spent by people in the developed nations who have comparable incomes.[57]

Of the income that is invested, most goes to urban industry. The landlord is often absentee and lives in the city, and in any case government policies and the structure of costs and prices ensure that rates of return are higher in urban industry than in agriculture. Since urban industry is generally highly protected and inefficient (Chapter 9), the investment of resources transferred from agriculture is relatively unproductive.[58]

Mechanisms other than the market and private investment also operate to transfer resources out of agriculture. Government taxes often serve this purpose, and so do all of the mechanisms discussed in the previous section that turn the internal terms of trade against agriculture; reducing the price of farm products relative to farm inputs is simply an indirect way of getting resources out of the rural population and into the city in the form of higher profits in industry.

The bias against agriculture is most clearly seen in national investment policies. In twenty-two LDCs for which data were available, agriculture received an average of only 20 percent of the total investment made during the period 1950 to 1965, yet it contributed about half the gross national product and, even before the Green Revolution, it yielded about three times as much extra output, per unit of input, as investment elsewhere. This state of affairs has persisted in the intervening years throughout the LDCs. For example, in India in the mid-1970s only 16 percent of investment went to agriculture, which employed 70 percent of the workers and produced 45 percent of total output.[59]

The transfer of resources to the city is combined with a failure to invest not only in farming itself but in the basic institutions that ultimately generate agricultural growth—agricultural research, an extension system for spreading new technology, rural roads and other "infrastructure" elements, and rural schools to develop "human capital." Indeed, one cause of the landlord's migration to the cities is that only there can the children obtain a decent education.[60]

It is important to remember, amidst these impersonal notions of investment, the transfer of resources, and the like, that the major consequence of this "urban bias" is the continued impoverishment of the rural majority, whose average per capita income is only one-fifth to half of the urban minority's.[61]

Cash Crops versus Food Production

As we shall see in more detail in Chapter 9, earning foreign currency from expanding exports is a key element in the strategy for industrialization throughout the developing world, and agricultural products are the main export commodity for most developing countries. These crops are generally not staple foods. They include coffee, tea, cocoa, sugar, palm oil, spices, tropical fruits, jute, cotton, rubber, tobacco, and sometimes meat. One or a few of these products earn 60 to 80 percent of the total foreign exchange earnings of many LDCs.[62] These cash crops are typically produced on estates, plantations, or commercial farms, though some production in peasant agriculture also occurs.

The existence of a large agricultural export sector has almost always led to the suppression of food-producing agriculture; indeed, Bairoch has shown that productivity in food agriculture is inversely proportional to the importance of export crops. In particular, export crops have received most of the investment in agriculture and have produced distortions in rural institutions and infrastructure. They also generally use the most productive land.[63]

The export sector is typically modern and well-capitalized. Until very recently, essentially all of the money spent on tropical agricultural research was on cash crops. In India even as recently as 1968, three to six times more money per unit of output was spent on research on commercial crops (e.g., sugar, jute, and cotton) than on rice. In some LDCs over half of the fertilizer used is applied to cash crops, while in Latin America only about 10 percent of the total is applied to basic food crops. The distortion in infrastructure is equally serious. Roads, markets, storage facilities, and research institutions are developed for the production and sale of cash crops rather than for the complex needs of food production and marketing. This has been aggravated by the developed countries, where agricultural training programs for students from developing countries have been geared to export crops.[64]

The concentration of resources on export crops has quite naturally resulted in huge differences in the rate at which yields of food and cash crops have increased. Brazil provides a good example.[65] The three main domestic food crops are rice, beans, and corn. Brazil's rice yields are among the lowest in the world and have actually declined about 12 percent since 1940. Yields of beans are extremely low compared with the United States, Japan, or Mexico and have declined 27 percent in forty years. Corn yields are one-quarter of those in the United States or France and have stayed about the same, on average, over the past few decades. By contrast, the yields of the three major exports have grown dramatically. Cotton yields have increased fourfold in thirty years, coffee yields doubled between 1952 and 1968, and sugar cane yields have increased almost sevenfold in thirty years.

U.S. and European international agribusiness firms are extensively involved in the production of export crops in the LDCs. In particular, the production of livestock and feed for livestock, and of vegetables for the off-season market in the United States and Europe, has been expanding in Latin America and Africa. This has been accompanied by a reduction of land devoted to staple food crops, a diversion of scarce government investment, and even deterioration of the land—as in Mexico, Central America, Colombia, the Dominican Republic, and in the Sahel and Ethiopia (Chapter 10).[66]

The power of these distortions to suppress food production is most starkly illustrated by Africa.[67] Most of us are perhaps inclined to associate African food problems with the recent droughts in the Sub-Sahara, but Lofchie has pointed out that Africa's food problem is virtually continent-wide and has been chronic for more than twenty years:

To the extent that there is a connection between drought and famine, it is mediated by the political and economic arrangements of a society. These can either
minimize the human consequences of drought or accentuate its effects. *In
Africa, political and economic arrangements have converted a problem of climatic unpredictability into an immense human catastrophe.*[68]

Food production in most African countries has been inadequate and
virtually stagnant since the 1950s (figure 5-3). Indeed, per capita food
production has probably declined recently. Yet in the midst of this tragedy
is an amazing paradox: *"a continent unable to produce sufficient food to
provide the majority of its citizens with even a barely minimal diet has
been able to record sharp increases in its annual production of agricultural goods destined for external markets."*[69]

In the latter half of the 1960s the annual increase in export crops in
Africa (4 percent per year) was almost twice as great as the increase in
food production. In the Sahel, Mali's corn production fell by more than a
third between 1969 and 1971, and millet showed no increase. At the same
time export crops reached record heights: cotton seed production increased
more than 400 percent between 1966 and 1972, groundnut production increased 70 percent in four years, and rice production (mainly for export)
was a record 174,000 tons in 1972. Mali's figures are striking, but the
same pattern holds for much of Africa. One must ask: if drought explains
low food production, why are export crops immune? The answer is that
Africa's failure in food production has deep economic and political roots
and that adverse short-term climatic conditions merely make the failure
temporarily more evident (see also Chapter 10).

The failure of Africa's food production stems from the dual nature of its
agriculture—the division between large-scale, capital-intensive production of cash crops and the small-scale, labor-intensive, food-producing
peasant sector. Cash crops are crucial earners of foreign currency in countries such as Ghana, Senegal, and the Ivory Coast in West Africa, through
the Sahel to East African countries such as Uganda, Kenya, Tanzania,
and Malawi. The export sector in these countries has soaked up investment for decades, leaving the food-producing sector starved of capital, infrastructure, and government services.[70]

Roads and railway systems are designed to help export crops rather
than to distribute food internally; indeed, transport and storage facilities
are so bad that food crops spoil in rural markets while urban demand goes
unfulfilled. The agricultural extension services are directed toward export
crops, as are research and lending institutions. Government irrigation
schemes are designed for cotton, rice (for export), and groundnut crops.
While the most common farm implement among peasants is the hand-
held hoe, diesel tractors work the estate crops. While cash crop farmers

are assisted by government marketing boards, "the establishment of a state-supervised marketing system for basic food items is not even a remote possibility in most nations."[71]

The sacrifice of African peasant food production to the production of export crops is facilitated by pricing policies. Government prices for export crops are high, which has caused a shift in land use from food to cash crops and is producing a small wealthy rural class and urban groups with rural investments. The price for food, however, is kept low by several of the mechanisms discussed earlier. Rapidly increasing food production in Africa, as elsewhere, requires basic structural changes both within agriculture and in the larger economy.

SUMMARY OF CONSEQUENCES OF STRUCTURAL DISTORTIONS

In Chapter 5, I concluded that low food production in the LDCs was not the result of natural agricultural or technical disadvantages. The message of this chapter is that the immediate causes of the world food supply problem, and consequent malnutrition, are structural (i.e., economic, social, and political) rather than biological or physical. There is argument in the economic literature over whether "inefficient pricing," disincentives, or skewed land distribution and land tenure systems are the cause of the problem, but it seems clear that all of these features operate together to produce agricultural stagnation. The distortions external to agriculture, embodied in urban bias, lead to low aggregate food production and overall rural poverty. The distortions within the agrarian system further reduce food production and create gross inequality among different groups of the rural population. Together they also ensure that scarce capital is wasted and abundant labor underused. Radical change is thus needed not only in the structure of agrarian society but in the relationships between different sectors of the economy, particularly between the urban and rural sectors.

There is no estimate of the amount by which food production in the LDCs could be increased if all the necessary structural changes were made. However, in the light of estimates of potential increases presented above, and recalling from Chapter 5 that production on existing available land in the LDCs could be increased considerably with existing technology, it is clear that the food problem could be handily solved for the foreseeable future by structural changes alone. Note also that this solution would in general require no extra available land, a matter of considerable importance where the use of marginal farmland leads to environmental degradation (Chapter 10).

Clearly, we need to pursue further the question of causes. How did the structural distortions discussed in this chapter arise, and why do they persist if they are so manifestly inequitable and inefficient? To answer these questions we need to look at the history of the developing nations (see Chapter 8), and at their current political and economic structure (see Chapter 9). Before we do so, it is important to examine the role that agriculture can and must play in the broad process of economic development. This is the topic of the next chapter.

DEVELOPMENT

7

THE ROLE OF AGRICULTURE IN ECONOMIC DEVELOPMENT

Chapter 6 examined how structural distortions affect agrarian societies. But this is only a partial view of poverty and development. Town and country, industry and agriculture, interact; we now need to ask how the suppression of agriculture and the distortions in agrarian society affect industrial growth and development, and how the interaction between agriculture and industry affects overall development. It turns out that the nature of this interaction is the key to development, including the alleviation of poverty.

Agriculture has played a key role in the development of the now-rich nations and will be crucial to the development of those now poor. Some exceptions are possible: a few very small countries, like Hong Kong, may achieve development mainly by expanding exports to world markets that are enormous relative to their own small economy. Some others—for example, in the Middle East, and Venezuela—may gain most of their needed capital from exporting oil. However, the mere accumulation of capital is not synonymous with development; even the oil-rich countries eventually will need a sound internal structure for sustained development, and agriculture must be an important part of that structure. For the great majority of the developing nations, a dynamic agriculture will be necessary for the process of economic development from its early stages.

THE NATURE OF ECONOMIC GROWTH AND DEVELOPMENT

Economies produce two kinds of goods: consumption goods (such as food, clothing, and symphony concerts) and capital goods. The latter are goods that can be used in the production of other goods—either consumer items or more capital goods. Capital goods can be directly productive equipment such as factories, industrial machinery, tractors, power plants, diesel pumps for irrigation, and hand-operated threshing equipment. Also included in this category are "intermediate goods," such as oil and fertilizer used to produce consumer goods. Capital goods may also take the form of roads, railways, communication systems, and so on. This is the "infrastructure" that facilitates the use of other capital goods. The creation of new capital goods is called investment or capital accumulation. Investment can also take the form of maintaining or improving existing capital goods or resources—for example, draining, leveling, or irrigating farmland. Finally, investment can also be in human capital—that is, in educating and improving the skills and abilities of people. Investment, or capital accumulation, is thus the process whereby current consumption is forgone so that the future rate of production and consumption can be increased.

Economic growth is an increase in the capacity to produce goods and services. It results from increases in productive resources, namely labor, capital, and land,* *and from using these resources more efficiently*—that is, by gaining more production from each unit of resource, such as a dollar of capital, a ton of coal, or an hour of work. The accumulation of savings that can be used for investment to expand and improve resources is thus a fundamental and necessary element in the process of development. However, of equal or perhaps greater importance is the continual improvement in the efficiency with which resources, particularly scarce resources, are used. Such increasing efficiency has played a truly remarkable role in the development of the rich nations. Kuznets, reviewing the development of the industrial nations, states that for Europe:

> ...the inescapable conclusion is that the direct contribution of man-hours and capital accumulation would hardly account for more than one-tenth of the rate of growth in per capita product. The large remainder must be assigned to an increase in efficiency in the productive resources—a rise in output per unit of input, due either to the improved quality of the resources (including human labor), or to the effects of changing arrangements, or to the impact of technological change, or to all three.[1]

The case for the United States has been similar: "increased output per unit of input, due largely to economies of scale and the spread of technical knowledge, contributed together over 85%" of the increase in real national income.[2]

In essence, then, the major driving force of economic growth is human ingenuity, skill, and enterprise. The rise in per capita product has been achieved mainly through investment in human training and other arrangements that increase knowledge and lead to the more efficient use of resources.[3]

Three conditions are therefore crucial to economic growth: the accumulation of capital; the care, education, and training of the population so that it can develop and apply its skills, abilities, and imagination; and the presence of appropriate social, economic, and political institutions that

*Land includes minerals and other useful materials that can be obtained from the land.

allow those skills and abilities to increase productivity. We will see in this chapter that this last condition, the nation's overall economic structure, is a crucial determinant of the efficient use of resources. In particular, it is important that the different parts of the economy are integrated with one another so that the needs of each are supplied and so that each part stimulates appropriate production in the other. As an example, connections are important between food-producing agriculture and those parts of industry that supply its needs, including farm equipment, machinery, and fertilizer.

The relationships of reciprocal stimulus (demand) and response (supply) between parts of the economy are called "linkages." Agriculture requires goods, such as diesel pumps and plows, that allow it to produce food and other goods; these requirements for producer goods create "backward linkages." Agriculture also produces goods such as cotton that are used to produce other goods, and these create "forward linkages."

From the foregoing it is clear that institutional as well as technological innovation is important in development. Through technical innovation we now need only one ton or less of coal to produce one ton of cast iron, instead of the six tons of coal required in the late nineteenth century. An example of social and political innovation is provided by the Chinese Revolution, discussed below, which has transformed an unemployed and underemployed population into an essentially fully employed and productive one.[4]

Finally, we are concerned not merely with economic growth but with development. Development implies not only aggregate growth but also the improved welfare of the mass of the people, their participation in an economy that becomes structurally and technologically richer, and the creation of an economy structured to sustain future growth and development. We need to be concerned, therefore, with what is produced, how it is produced, and how it is distributed.

An economic system always has a choice of what to produce and how to produce it. Both the product and the means of production have changed greatly during the development of the rich nations. First, as basic physical needs have been met, more technically elaborate and sophisticated goods and services have been produced to supply both these needs and other additional wants. Many of these goods and services, in terms of needs in LDCs, are luxuries. Second, as capital has accumulated, it has become less expensive relative to labor, and the trend has been to develop production techniques that require more and more capital relative to labor—i.e., production has become capital intensive and labor saving. Large-scale factories using relatively little labor produce other factories that produce large-scale machines. With relatively little labor, those machines produce large-scale farming equipment which, with little labor, harvests, threshes, bags, and bales a wheat crop. The wheat is transported in large trucks, built with great investment of capital, on huge freeways built by large machines and little labor, to large-scale, capital-intensive bakeries. And so on.

In the poor countries, by contrast, the basic needs of a large fraction of the population have not yet been met. By definition these countries also have very little capital, and most have abundant labor. As a general rule, it will therefore not be appropriate to produce or import luxury goods* and, while there may be some instances where capital-intensive production is appropriate, it will in general be more appropriate to use labor-intensive means of production.

POTENTIAL CONTRIBUTIONS OF AGRICULTURE TO DEVELOPMENT

There are five contributions to overall economic development that agriculture has made in the past and can and must make in the future. The first is its direct contribution to economic welfare. Of the billion or so people who live in absolute poverty in the LDCs, perhaps 800 million are rural and their livelihood is based in agriculture. Agriculture's first potential contribution is therefore to raise the general level of welfare of the rural population. The poor participate in development actively and directly through increasing employment, i.e., through an increasing demand for their labor, which agriculture in large part must provide. That labor, of course, must be *productively* employed and, since capital is scarce, it must be used in activities that do not require a large capital investment per worker.

Secondly, agriculture must be increasingly productive to meet the needs of the expanding urban labor force, which spends more than half of its income, and half or more of its increases in income, on food. If food production lags, food prices rise, and this leads to demands for higher urban wages and to reduced growth of manufacturing. Agriculture must therefore supply the physical goods to support increased employment and incomes. As Mellor notes, "It is thus the dominance of agricultural com-

---

*"Luxury" is a relative term. Goods that are luxuries in the context of an LDC often might not be considered luxury goods in developed countries. In a very poor country automobiles, televisions, and air conditioners are clearly luxury items. But for many such countries so are, say, commercial soft drinks, bottled milk for infants, and a wide range of "modern" consumer goods sold to urban workers.

Luxury goods also include much of the building and infrastructure—apartment buildings, offices, modern hospitals, administration buildings, freeways, etc.—associated with LDC cities. Inappropriate capital goods include the factories for the production or assembly of inappropriate consumer goods, large "showcase" projects such as capital-intensive irrigation schemes built where smaller or cheaper technology is more appropriate, and much of the labor-saving machinery used in farming.

modities as wage goods and the large supply of labor available for mobilization which combine to make creation of a modern, technologically dynamic agriculture so important to economic growth and to the participation of the poor in that growth."[5]

Third, agriculture can make a direct financial contribution to industrial development in the form of a transfer of surplus capital. This can happen through savings, taxation, or other means. However, agriculture cannot provide excess capital unless it also first receives adequate investment and is so structured as to become a dynamic sector.

Fourth, agriculture can make another financial contribution by helping the foreign exchange situation. This can be direct, through exports that earn foreign currency, which can be used in turn to import key items for development. Or the contribution can be indirect, by providing food that otherwise would need to be imported.

Finally, agriculture can make a *structural* contribution by generating a growing demand for consumer goods and producer goods—a demand that stimulates the development of indigenous industry in a labor-intensive and capital-saving way. The type and pattern of the demand are crucial in determining the structure of expanding industry. It is here that agriculture has the key role to play in creating an integrated and balanced developing economy.

THE MODERN FAILURE OF AGRICULTURE IN DEVELOPMENT

There are two aspects to the failure of agriculture in the LDCs. The first is a failure of production: for the majority of developing nations, food production simply has not grown fast enough. The second is the failure to bring about the structural integration of agriculture with the rest of the economy. A few nations, such as Mexico, have solved the productivity problem in agriculture for quite long periods, but very few have solved the structural problem.

The Failure of Production

Chapter 5 dealt with food-agriculture's poor performance relative to needs and potential. The immediate causes of this failure (Chapter 6) are internal distortions that divorce labor from the land and from capital and credit; scarce capital that goes to labor-saving rather than yield-increasing technology; cheap food policies and distortions in urban/rural prices that remove farmers' incentives to produce; lack of investment in food production; and an emphasis on the export of cash crops that receive the investment, fertilizer, technology, roads, and markets.

The more basic cause of this failure has been the virtually universal emphasis on industrialization as the agent of development, and the corollary suppression of food-producing agriculture. This strategy has conformed to the self-interests of the rich in the LDCs, as we will see in Chapter 9, but it also arose from the failure to appreciate the potential, and essential, contributions that agriculture must make to development.

To appreciate agriculture's role, we need to spend a few moments on the industrial strategy that has been pursued by the LDCs. The pattern is well illustrated by India, which provides a particularly instructive example because from the 1950s it was a paradigm of industrially oriented, western-inspired capitalist development. An excellent analysis of India's development history is provided by Mellor.

Soon after independence, with the Second Five-Year Plan (1955–1960), India began a determinedly capital-intensive approach to development, based on the explicit assumption that growth in agriculture was unlikely. Economic growth was to come from investing admittedly scarce resources in a "modern" large-scale capital goods industry, especially steel works and machine-building factories. These industries required large amounts of investment per worker (they are capital-intensive), they employed few workers, and much of the equipment had to be purchased from the industrial nations. The plan assumed that the increasing productivity of these industries would allow a high savings rate and hence investment in still more capital goods. Consumption and a growing wage bill would detract from such savings; hence low consumption and low employment were explicitly part of the Plan.[6] There was no intent to alleviate poverty by harnessing the great resources of unemployed labor.

Existing consumption of imported luxury and semi-luxury goods by the urban elite and the large landowners was to be replaced by domestically produced goods through the process of "import-substitution"—i.e., by another type of urban industrialization. (Import substitution is the process whereby a range of previously imported goods is now produced or assembled domestically.) This process was to serve two purposes: saving foreign exchange and furthering the growth of urban industry. (In most developing nations industrial development was largely confined to such import substitution and did not encompass the creation of industry to produce capital goods such as steel.) Much of the needed capital for purchasing the initial industrial plant was to come as aid from the western nations.

To some extent the strategy was implemented as planned.[7] Between 1951 and 1965 the capital goods industry grew faster than consumer goods activity (e.g., clothing, furniture, and food), and large-scale industry grew faster than its small-scale counterpart. Industry became more capital intensive; metal production increased its share of Indian capital from 3.5 to

19 percent, and investment in power, petroleum, coal, and machine building grew very rapidly. At the same time, investment in labor-intensive industries grew very little and the fraction they received became progressively smaller. Two areas—basic metals and power (electricity and steam) —absorbed most of the investment in this period. Investment in metals increased thirtyfold and in power fifteenfold.

Unfortunately, increase in production by these industries was not commensurate with investment, especially in the metals industry.[8] Efficient operation is absolutely essential in such capital-intensive industries, but in India and other LDCs they typically operate well below capacity because these nations have limited technical and managerial skills, their infrastructure is underdeveloped, sophisticated economic planning is not well implemented, and the local market is not large enough. In India delays associated with foreign financing also occurred. In short, a highly sophisticated technology was transplanted into a system that had not yet evolved enough to cope with it efficiently.

The strategy also greatly worsened the urban unemployment problem, and hence the problem of raising the general level of economic well-being. If all investment in this period had instead followed the pattern existing in 1951, total employment in manufacturing by 1965 would have been at least 2.3 times greater.[9] Again, the failure of industry to absorb the growing urban labor force is a general problem in the LDCs, where urban unemployment is in the range of 15 to 30 percent.

The industry-first policy meant that agriculture was starved of investment. The agricultural strategy, which took final shape only in the late 1960s, was analogous to that pursued in industry. It aimed for overall growth by concentrating on larger farmers who were already modernized (and therefore rich). It hinged on the introduction of new technology and explicitly assumed that institutional reform—the creation of employment and redistribution of resources and income—was not appropriate; indeed, the policy assumed that it would be wasteful to spread resources to the poorer smaller farms.[10]*

This strategy failed to create adequate increase in agricultural production, even though Indian agriculture has immense potential for growth. During the 1950s, following some land reform and investment in irrigation, and helped by good weather, agricultural production grew quite rapidly. However, this momentum was then lost. From 1950 to 1977 food

*With the benefit of hindsight it is easy to be critical of earlier development strategies. However, the ideas and advice of planners and development experts made good sense within the political framework in which they worked, and in light of the existing theory in economic development. The decision to concentrate resources on progressive farmers mainly reflected the fact that the problem was viewed as one of production and of a need for technological innovation. In the complex area of development progress will inevitably be accompanied by much trial and error.

production grew at only 2.4 percent, barely keeping pace with population, and there is evidence that the rate of increase has been falling in the last two decades.[11]

Growth of agricultural production has also consistently failed to keep up with demand from the nonagricultural sector, and low agricultural production has constrained both industrial and overall economic growth.[12] The significance of agricultural output to industrial growth is illustrated by the fact that fluctuations in agricultural output (caused partly by the weather) accounted in large part for the variation in the rate of expansion of industrial output. These fluctuations caused large changes in national income and therefore in saving and investment, and they affected the national wage bill through the price of food: changes in agricultural production affect agricultural prices, which affect wages and therefore the demand for nonagricultural consumer goods, all of which affect production, profits, savings, and investments in industry. As average agricultural productivity was suppressed, so therefore was its contribution to overall growth through these mechanisms. India's agriculture thus failed, through low productivity, to make any of the first four contributions to development described earlier in this chapter.

The strong connection between agricultural productivity and industrial growth is not confined to India, but rather is a general phenomenon in the developing world. For example, China's harvests were drastically reduced during the Great Leap Forward in 1959, 1960, and 1961, a time of bad weather that also followed a period of inadequate investment in agriculture. The result was not only near-famine and urban food shortages but, especially in 1960–1962, a sharp reduction in industrial output. There was a shortage of raw material from farms, a reduced demand for agricultural equipment and other producer goods and for consumer goods, which in turn led to urban unemployment and further economic depression. Bairoch has shown that for forty developing countries over the period 1950 to 1970 there is an extremely close relationship between variation in agricultural production and variation in industrial production *in the following year*. Each decline in agricultural production is followed a year later by a decline in industrial production, and the same holds true for increases. He was also able to show this pattern in the early development history of the now-rich nations.[13]

Although predicated on the notion that economic growth was both necessary and sufficient for an eventual increase in general welfare, the Indian strategy did not succeed in generating rapid economic growth, as it has similarly failed to do in other developing countries. Between 1951 and 1971 total economic output in India grew by an average of about 3.5 percent per year, a per capita annual increase of about 1.4 percent. (This should be compared with a 2.1 percent average annual rate of increase of per capita GNP for all non-Communist poor countries. Over roughly the same period China's growth rate was 6 percent, with a per capita growth rate of over 3 percent.) Furthermore, in India the growth achieved was heavily dependent on foreign aid, as became distressingly apparent when aid began to decline in the mid 1960s and the growth rate of the economy also began to decline. Indeed, the economy virtually stagnated from 1965 to the mid-1970s.

Not only was growth inadequate, but the strategy failed to develop the basic structure for future sustained economic development. Industry continually needed more imported raw materials and more imported machinery but could not earn enough foreign exchange through exports to buy them. The capital-intensive strategy required ever more capital investment to keep expanding, but capital on this scale was not available, especially as foreign aid declined. The strategy could not be sustained without forcing ever higher savings through reduced consumption, a process that could not long persist, as consumption was already at an extremely low level.

The rural and farming population, having been intentionally excluded from the growth strategy, was prevented from contributing to the overall development of the nation's economy. The strategy also failed disastrously to bring real development or increased economic welfare to the bulk of the Indian population. Labor-intensive industry grew very slowly, since it was largely neglected, and agricultural employment also increased slowly. Employment has grown only about as fast as the population has increased, so that the number of unemployed has grown enormously; in the past decade while the population grew by about one-fifth, the registered unemployed alone increased fourfold.[14] The poor have thus been shut off from the growth that did occur, and the numbers in absolute poverty have grown relentlessly.

It is important not to oversimplify the lesson to be learned from the Indian example. In some cases, at some times, and for some purposes, it will be appropriate for LDCs to invest in large-scale, capital-intensive industry. For example, when electrical power is required to run machinery that produces appropriate goods and employs many people, it will usually be necessary to build large-scale generating stations.[15] However, investment in such "modern" industry should not be the goal in itself. The goal should be improvement of economic well-being and creation of the ability to continue improving it.

The following are two critical arguments against devoting to large-scale industry a large fraction of the nation's savings:

1. To begin with, such industry will likely have a low rate of growth relative to investment, and thus it will slow the rate of savings without

increasing employment or living standards. While such industry increases the productivity of labor (the output per hour worked), and while this in itself is desirable, it will often reduce the productivity of all resources, including labor, taken together. This is because it substitutes expensive capital for cheap labor (which is left idle) and thereby increases the total cost of production while saving on labor costs. This is more serious the more foreign exchange is needed to buy the capital equipment.

2. Capital-intensive investment diverts money from capital-saving and labor-intensive operations that can contribute directly to economic growth, savings, and increased living standards; in so doing, such investment tends to magnify the future problem of increasing economic well-being.

India's investment in a modern steel-producing industry was an example of overcommitment to large-scale imported technology. Steel can be produced in smaller and less capital-intensive mills that use a higher fraction of local materials. It may also be better to import it for some time, and it is crucial to determine in the first place that the steel is being used for purposes appropriate to the population's needs. These needs will, in general, not be met by automobiles, electrical appliances, modern city buildings, most large farm machinery, armaments, and yet more "modern" industry.

The other Indian industry that soaked up investment was large-scale power generation. While it can be argued that electrification can greatly increase employment,[16] it is also the case that much agricultural and other machinery can be run by other types of power. Chapter 5 discussed the use of methane gas, which can be produced through biogasification, as an example. Thus, even in power generation there are opportunities for saving capital (and scarce materials like steel) and for using small-scale labor-intensive techniques.

Structural Failure: The Bimodal Strategy in Agriculture

Whether agricultural productivity has grown slowly, as in most LDCs, or rapidly, as in Mexico, virtually everywhere the growth has been achieved through increasing distortions in agrarian society (Chapter 6). Development strategy has concentrated investment, research, infrastructure, and hence benefits, upon a relatively few already semi-modernized and prosperous farmers and has largely excluded small farmers, thus accentuating existing differences in income. This has occurred throughout the developing world. It can be seen clearly in Mexico, where investment and research were concentrated on the richer wheat farmers of the north, and in Pakistan and India where (since no breakthrough occurred in rice) they were similarly concentrated on richer wheat farmers of the Punjab.[17]

This bimodal strategy exacerbates the "dual economy" within agriculture.[18] It accentuates the imbalance between a relatively few large capital-intensive commercial farmers (who sell a large fraction of their product on the market) and the remainder, who work either very small farms or have no land at all, produce crops mainly for their own subsistence, have virtually no capital, and depend upon primitive technology and human labor.

There is a certain logic to bimodal policies. Given proper incentives, it will likely be easier to spread technological innovations to richer farmers who are already semi-modernized, better educated, and have better control over their production through such techniques as irrigation. This last feature is important. Wherever rainfall is unreliable, the output of the farmer who can make little investment in irrigation fluctuates widely from year to year. He therefore runs the risk of, and is familiar with, frequent crop failures. Such a farmer therefore cannot easily commit whatever capital he has to an innovation which, for all he can tell, may well result in disaster. In addition, the larger farmers sell food to the cities, where food shortages are politically most aggravating, and increasing their production might seem the most astute procedure politically.[19] But as we have seen in Chapter 6, even without such an external logic, the internal economic social and political structure of agricultural society is bound to result in innovations first reaching the richer farmer.

In practice the bimodal strategy seriously disrupts the process of development by preventing agriculture from making the fifth contribution listed earlier: stimulating the development of *appropriate* industry. This structural failure affects the development of industry, the integration between different parts of the economy, and overall development, through its effects on both producer and consumer industries. We deal with these two types of connections separately. In each case the crucial factor is the range of goods that the rural population wishes to buy, which is determined by the distribution of income and wealth within the rural population.

Structural Distortions in Agriculture and Links to Producer Industries

Bimodal agriculture's effects on industry are nicely illustrated in a comparison, drawn by Johnston and Kilby, between the effects of alternative types of agricultural technology in Pakistan.[20] The first type of technology centers around capital-intensive machinery, exemplified by the four-wheel tractor and its associated equipment. The second type is a "bullock package" in which the implements represent an intermediate technology. They are simpler, easier to make and require less fossil energy and more human labor to operate. However, they are more complex and efficient than the generally used but persistently primitive tools such as the spade, hoe, hand sickle, and stick plow.

The two types of technology in Pakistan have effects both on the farm and in industry. On the farm, the effects are straightforward. The tractor package requires more capital and less labor and, the former being very scarce, causes a severe misallocation of a scarce resource. The tractor package ties up capital that could be used productively elsewhere, raises yields much less than is possible, and generates less employment on the farm than the alternative package.

Off the farm, the effects ramify throughout the economy. First, manufacturing the tractor package requires a more sophisticated technology. It is manufactured in a relatively few large-scale enterprises, generally in partnership with a large international company. These enterprises are capital intensive, once more using scarce capital, and they generate relatively little employment. They require a large component of imported goods, which means that hard-earned foreign exchange must be spent to manufacture agricultural equipment that is less beneficial to the economy than is the alternative package.

In these respects the bullock package is clearly superior. The implements can be manufactured on a relatively small scale, require quite modest capital investment, and use abundant labor. Even the light engineering workshops making irrigation pumps and motors and similar equipment are usually small concerns located in towns near or actually in the farming area. The needed skills, such as metal working, can be learned on the job, and expensive imported machinery and technology are not required. The requirement for foreign exchange is only about half that of the tractor package. The bullock package simply makes better use of available and abundant domestic resources of material and labor.

A second and crucial difference between the packages concerns the degree to which each technology yields backward linkages to the manufacturing sector and therefore creates more jobs and income. This is really the heart of the matter. Economies develop by becoming structurally richer. Each productive part of the economy, if it uses resources well, not only produces goods needed elsewhere in the economy but itself creates a demand for products that it can use and for those that can be supplied efficiently by people elsewhere in the economy. It thus creates productive jobs and incomes. Various parts of the economy are integrated when they meet each other's mutual needs and create reciprocal opportunities for employment. In this respect the bullock package is again clearly superior in involving a larger variety of secondary activities that go to complete the final product and the delivery and subsequent servicing of the implements.

Third, the bullock package leads to a greater total manufacturing output than the tractor package does. Indeed, the tractor technology has a suppressing effect on manufacturing and on developing technology: because it sucks up so much of the available capital, farmers cannot in general afford the intermediate technology represented by the bullock package; they are therefore forced to persist with the primitive implements they have used for centuries. These primitive tools are not only unproductive in farming, but their manufacture requires little labor and does not generate secondary employment in producing parts or servicing them.

Finally, the emphasis on tractor technology also has a profound effect on the development of indigenous skills and technology that are crucial to further development. Its manufacture requires engineers and scientists with a high degree of training; innovations are generally made by foreign engineers, and the advanced technological skills simply do not diffuse through the labor force. But the mainspring of economic development is the more productive use of resources—i.e., better designed equipment, technical innovations, and improved skills. These improvements and innovations, if they are to succeed, must be appropriate to local conditions, and eventually the ability to create such improvements must become internalized in the population of the developing country. The direct importation of tractor technology has failed to produce this development of local skills.

Structural Distortions in Agriculture and Links to Consumer Industries

Equally important for development is the type of demand for consumer goods generated by the massive agricultural population. The shape of this demand greatly affects employment, incomes, and the degree to which the economy is integrated.

The shape of the demand for consumer goods is also determined by the distribution of income. In bimodal agriculture income is distributed extremely unevenly and this distortion has worsened, so that the relative and absolute gap between the rural rich and the rural poor has become progressively wider. The consequent distortion in the shape of consumer demand has effects that are quite analogous to those that flow from the skewed demand for producer goods. A small rural elite demands luxury and semi-luxury goods: motor vehicles, air conditioners, electrical appliances, and so on. These are typically produced in large-scale, centralized, capital-intensive, urban industry; they generally involve a high fraction of imported material or components and thus require scarce foreign exchange. Suppressing the incomes of the majority, on the other hand, reduces the demand for items such as nongrain food, bicycles, simple metal utensils, and wooden furniture, all of which can be made in small, decentralized, semi-rural or urban workshops with low capital investment, largely local resources, intensive use of labor and a low fraction of imports. Once again, the multiplier and employment effects, and the linkages with manufacturing, are stronger and richer in the unimodal system.[21]

Structural Distortions in Agriculture and Savings for Industry

One of agriculture's potential contributions to development is the transfer of some of its savings for investment in industry. I noted above that low food production prevents this. But a bimodal agricultural strategy also prevents it, even when food production increases rapidly.

The point is well illustrated by Mexico which, since 1940, has experienced a rapid increase in agricultural production in response to innovative research and government investment.[22] Farm output grew at 4.7 percent per year from 1940 to 1953 and at 3.7 percent per year from 1954 to 1965. Between 1965 and 1970 wheat production increased sevenfold and corn production fourfold. This increase eliminated or reduced the need to import wheat, thereby saving foreign exchange. Moreover, increased exports of items like cotton, coffee, sugar, and vegetables have earned more foreign exchange. The increasing demand for food by the industrial sector was met; however, the flow of savings from agriculture for investment in industry has been negligible, and indeed the net flow of funds (mainly government subsidies to large farmers) has on balance been *into* agriculture. Thus, because commercial farming is itself so capital intensive, it has not been able to produce capital for investment in industry.

SUCCESSFUL AGRICULTURE

Agriculture has by no means always failed to contribute to economic development. On the contrary, it has played a crucial role in the historical development of the now-rich nations and in a few modern developing nations. We will examine both of these experiences next.

The Historical Contribution of Agriculture in the Developed Nations

A cursory glance at the history of the developed nations would suggest that agriculture has been of minor importance compared with industry. For much of their recent history this has been true, and it has become increasingly true as agricultural output has gradually contributed a smaller and smaller fraction of national output and has employed an ever-decreasing fraction of the work force—even though its total output has increased. But hidden behind the current preponderance of industry is the key role that agriculture played universally in providing the initial impetus for economic development.[23] This initial impetus was essential in Europe and the United States in the eighteenth and nineteenth centuries and in Japan in the late nineteenth and early twentieth centuries.

When the process of development in the now-rich nations began, their agriculture contributed half or more of the Gross Domestic Product (GDP) and employed 70 to 80 percent of the labor force. It was the major single sector of the economy, much larger than the tiny manufacturing sector. Much of the savings and capital that were needed had to come from agriculture. But agriculture could be a source of savings only if it could become more productive itself—that is, a dynamic agriculture was essential for overall economic development.

Europe

The events that set in motion the process of development in Europe constituted the agricultural revolution of the eighteenth century.[24] Before that time, agricultural productivity had remained constant for many centuries and famines were frequent events throughout Europe, occurring on an average of every eight years in England up to the seventeenth century. But by 1750 British agriculture was producing an agricultural surplus that was exported to the rest of Europe, even though the British population and its food intake per person had increased in the first part of that century. The revolution that created this surplus then spread slowly in the late eighteenth century to France, the United States, Switzerland, Germany, and Denmark; in the early nineteenth century to Austria, Italy, and Sweden; and in the late nineteenth century to Spain, Russia, and finally Japan.

The early revolutionary innovations that led to increases in productivity included crop rotation (which reduced the need for fallow land), the introduction of new crops (e.g., turnips, clover, potatoes), improvements in the plow, the invention of the scythe, the beginning of crop and animal breeding, land clearance, and the increased use of horses instead of oxen. These improvements led to annual increases in agricultural output per man of around 1 percent per year from 1800 onwards. Occasionally this rate fell somewhat lower than 1 percent, and sometimes it went as high as 2 percent. In the United States at the end of the nineteenth century, because of the opening up of new land, the rate reached 2.5 percent, astonishing for that era.

The agricultural revolution preceded and made possible the industrial revolution with which we normally associate the beginning of "development." In Britain, where both began, the lag between these two revolutions was roughly fifty to sixty years, the beginning of the industrial revolution being marked by the introduction of the flying shuttle and the spinning jenny to the cottage textile "industry" around 1760 to 1770. As these revolutions spread to other countries, the lag time shortened to perhaps thirty to fifty years.

Bairoch has been able to show that the level of industrial development in different parts of Europe at different times was very highly correlated with the level of agricultural productivity, and even more highly correlated if a lag of several decades is introduced. Indeed, it is easy to see that the industrial revolution, which was initially one within cottage industry, could not proceed unless it was itself preceded or at least accompanied by an agricultural revolution. Industrial development required new labor, which could come from the agricultural population only if agricultural productivity per worker increased; the then-poor countries had no excess labor pool. Furthermore, industrialization needed capital, which at the time had to come mainly from an increasingly productive agriculture. And an expanding industry needed somewhere to sell its products, at first particularly clothes and farm implements, which could be bought only by a surplus of income held by the large agricultural population.

Some of these problems could have been solved by trade—food imported from elsewhere, industrial products sold elsewhere—and indeed trade accounted for much of the accumulation of capital in Britain before the agricultural revolution.[25] But a radical change in transportation, and hence a great reduction in transport costs, did not occur until the mid-nineteenth century. Until then, economic development had to depend largely on a mutual enhancement between industry and agriculture, with industry gradually drawing both labor and capital from agriculture during the period that industry was small relative to agriculture. Only when transport costs began to fall did foreign trade become important. Britain's factories were then supplied in part with raw materials from the United States and the colonies. By 1850 Britain was importing 13 percent of her wheat consumption; this rose to 30 percent by 1860 and to 79 percent by 1895. (By contrast, food imports in the rest of Europe were minor throughout the nineteenth century, and even in Japan rice imports became important only after 1925.) But until as late as 1830 (sixty to seventy years after "development" was underway), Britain imported only 3 percent or less of her wheat consumption.

The textile industry was the first to be stimulated by the growth of agriculture. On average, agricultural productivity per man doubled in about the first seventy years of the agricultural revolution. Some of the extra income was used to improve diets, but much of the rest went to purchase clothes and thus to stimulate the textile industry and the production of small-scale machinery used in manufacturing textiles. A huge surge occurred in the demand for cotton and hence for cotton imports, which more than doubled in the first fifty years of agricultural development. Even as late as 1840 in Britain, textiles contributed up to 75 percent of industrial employment, with cotton contributing half.

This initial industrial development constituted a long process of change from small-scale cottage industry to urban factories. For decades industry was small scale and very closely tied to the agricultural population that demanded its products. From the beginning, agriculture and industry were not only integrated through reciprocal production and demand, they were *spatially* close together, industry being scattered in towns and villages throughout the country. In Britain by 1820, although only 30 percent of the labor force was still employed in agriculture and much of the "structural transformation" to an industrial society had occurred, there was still no development of the massive, urban, capital-intensive industrial conglomeration that today is equated with development. In fact, as late as the 1890s in the village in Scotland where I was born, a mere twenty miles from Glasgow, weavers still worked at hand-operated looms in their homes. In nineteenth-century Western Europe in general, industrialization proceeded much faster than urbanization.[26] In France in the 1850s, although 29 percent of the work force was in industry, only 10 percent of the population lived in cities; in Germany in 1870, although 30 percent of the work force was in manufacturing, only 12 percent of the population lived in cities.

Iron and steel production was the other major activity in the developing industries of Europe in the eighteenth and early nineteenth centuries. Once again its development was driven by widespread demand from agriculture. In Britain changes in agriculture between 1720 and 1760 accounted for virtually all of the 50 percent increase in iron consumption, which was used for plows, horseshoes, and other implements. Bairoch shows that even the metallurgists and industrial entrepreneurs came out of the small rural workshops and farming communities. Moreover, the capital needed to finance industrial development was generally local, i.e., agricultural. Industrialization could proceed from quite modest investment of capital because early industry, being small scale and labor intensive, did not require much capital—the equivalent of four to six months' wages set up a new worker in British and French industry around 1800 to 1820.

This stress upon agriculture is not meant to imply that industry was an unimportant or a passive agent in development. Benefits also flowed from industry to agriculture. In fact, the essence of the early process of development was a reciprocal and positive feedback between the two. Industry produced the improved implements that helped create increased agricultural productivity, and agriculture's increasing demand for iron, coupled with innovation and additional capital in industry, led to cheaper iron that gradually replaced wood in farm implements and hence raised farm productivity. Industrial growth, resulting in larger nonagricultural incomes, also increased the demand for agricultural goods, thus stimulating agricultural production.

As the industrial sector has grown ever larger, the subsequent history of development has seen a decline in the relative importance of agriculture— a process known as the "structural transformation." However, even up to the end of the nineteenth century European industrial production was strongly influenced, and to a large extent driven, by agricultural production and demand. Today, by contrast, in most developed nations less than 10 percent of the population is employed in agriculture and it contributes less than 10 percent of the GNP.

Japan

The early process of development in Europe and the United States was repeated later in Japan. Japan's experience is worth recounting briefly, since it is recent and good data are available for the entire period of agricultural and industrial development (1875 to the present). It shows again the fundamental role played by agriculture and the strong synergy that occurred between farming and fledgling industry. It is often overlooked that behind Japan's phenomenal postwar industrial growth was an earlier phase of agricultural and industrial development that gave impetus to the entire process.

Japan's experience is also relevant in many respects to the underdeveloped Asia of today. Its period of agricultural development began when the amount of land per person was already low (table 7-1). Most farmers cultivated tiny plots of land, and more than half were tenants.[27] Until 1954, which marks a turn towards labor-replacing machinery, *agricultural development and increasing productivity came through labor-intensive innovation*. Japan's average farm size remained very small—indeed, it hardly changed over this period. Unlike Europe and the United States, the number of people employed in agriculture remained virtually unchanged between 1875 and 1954, although the increments from rural population increase did move to the cities.

The restoration of the Meiji dynasty in 1868 marked the end of feudal Japan and began the changes that created the modern nation. At this time there were strong incentives to farmers, since the price paid for rice generally rose in relation to the price of external inputs (cf. Chapter 6).[28]

Tenants initially paid well over half of their produce in rent, but this fraction declined to about half by 1900. In 1873 government taxes were leveled on the land as a function of its previous yields, thus forcing the peasants to produce as much as possible to avoid falling into arrears. There were also strong incentives to the landlords, who not only invested in agriculture but generally farmed their own land and, in response to pressure and exhortation from the government, devoted themselves to improving agriculture—introducing water drainage and better water control for double cropping, and sponsoring superior rice strains and other new agricultural techniques. The spread of improved traditional crop varieties and of better methods of cultivation were the technological innovations that generated greatly increased productivity at this time.[29] This was therefore a period of investment and improvement in agriculture.

The development of Japanese agriculture did not occur by mere chance. The Meiji leaders decided early to develop agriculture and created agricultural colleges and research stations. They aimed for universal primary education in the rural areas. With remarkable foresight, they recognized the great value in an educated and technically adept rural population. The preamble to the 1872 Education Code stated that: "Every man only after learning diligently according to his capacity will be able to increase his property and prosper in his business. Hence knowledge may be regarded as the capital for raising one's self; who then can do without learning?"[30]

As early as 1880, peasants in Japan were showing their capacity to respond to opportunity by adopting innovative techniques, and the leaders

Table 7-1. Arable land per capita in various countries

Country	Period	Hectares of arable land per capita
Japan	1884	.12
Japan	early 1970s	.05
Taiwan	early 1970s	.06
South Korea	early 1970s	.07
China	early 1970s	.13
Bangladesh	early 1970s	.13
United Kingdom	early 1970s	.13
Indonesia	early 1970s	.15
Philippines	early 1970s	.23
India	early 1970s	.30
Thailand	early 1970s	.32
Pakistan	early 1970s	.40
United States	early 1970s	.86

Sources: International Bank for Reconstruction and Development, *Land Reform,* World Bank Paper-Rural Development Series (Washington, D.C.: World Bank, 1974), p. 51; V. D. Lippit, "Economic Development in Meiji Japan and Contemporary China: A Comparative Study," *Cambridge Journal of Economics* 2 (1978): 55–81.

among them, significantly, were landowners who cultivated their own land. Indeed, several of the most innovative farmers became instructors at the new agricultural colleges and others became itinerant "extension workers." There was also some very selective borrowing of agricultural technology from the West but, after a failed experiment, western large-scale farming was rejected in favor of labor-intensive, small-scale farming and technology. (The shortcomings of modern LDC governments and their advisers in this respect make the Meiji Japanese seem all the more prescient.)

Industrial development in Japan has been unusual among the developed countries in that it occurred essentially concurrently with agricultural development.[31] Because it developed later and faster than in Europe, industrial growth required rapid accumulation of capital and, initially, increasing agricultural productivity supplied virtually all of this capital. Japan's agriculture was able to do this by being productive, capital saving, and labor intensive; the ratio of output to investment increased steadily throughout the early period of agricultural growth.

A growing surplus in agriculture was thus available for investment in industry, provided it could be captured. This capture was effected by the simple procedure of heavy government taxes, especially on land. Throughout the process of Japanese development, until World War II, government investment was a large fraction of total investment; until the 1890s agriculture supplied 85 percent of the government tax revenues, and by 1920 still accounted for 40 percent.[32] Landlords were also able to invest some of their rent in industry, though reinvestment in agriculture, favorable rice prices, government research, and rural education all ensured that agriculture also received enough investment to continue increasing its productivity.

The transfer of agricultural surplus was by no means a wholly efficient process. Much of the landlords' rents and the rural merchants' profits was squandered on luxuries, while the government used tax money to put down a multitude of rebellions by peasants and the poorer samurai.[33] Japan could have done even better than it did.

The interaction between agriculture and industry was much more symbiotic and profound, however, than a mere flow of capital from agriculture to industry.[34] As the nonfarm population increased, the growing demand for food provided a stimulus to agriculture. These purchases were made possible by growing nonfarm incomes that arose largely from the sale of new and improved inputs to farmers. As at the beginning of development in Europe, industrialization was originally rural and small scale; it developed in response to the needs of the agricultural population, in thousands of small workshops and factories. The typical origin of this rural industry was the increased profits of the rural landlords; indeed, many individuals were simultaneously rich peasants, landlords, traders, and small-scale manufacturers.

Several crucial features attended Japan's agricultural dynamism and consequent industrial growth. A backlog of technological innovation had built up among "veteran farmers." The great achievements of Meiji government leaders were to remove feudal social constraints and so bring about the spread of these techniques throughout the nation, to encourage further innovation through rural education and research (which together largely account for Japan's increasing agricultural productivity over almost a century),[35] and to create economic incentives for farmers. That is, they encouraged the productive development of human and technological resources. They did this without plowing much additional capital into agriculture, by concentrating on labor-intensive, small-scale, and capital-saving technology that enabled agriculture to pay for industrial development. Yet they invested enough in agriculture and its surrounding institutions that it was able to increase its productivity. They achieved all of this by carefully preserving and developing indigenous and local skills and by adapting new technology to local conditions.

A final comment is needed on the Japanese experience. The development revolution was carried out by a large middle and upper class of rural peasants, landlords, and entrepreneurs who, initially, were also its main beneficiaries. Particularly in the early years of the Meiji dynasty, the lot of the poorer peasant probably worsened, and there was a temporary increase in the concentration of land. During the first thirty years or so of industrialization (from the mid-1880s) factory workers, who were mainly women and children, were badly exploited.[36] Early Japanese development, like early European development, was by no means a painless process for the poor.

The implications of the historical development of the now-rich nations for the currently poor countries seem clear, and Japan's early experience seems especially relevant to the rest of Asia. There are of course differences in the situation then and now. Economic development in the rich nations was marked by a flow of population from agriculture to industry. In most nations this flow resulted in a gradual decrease in the total agricultural population, although in Japan the labor force in agriculture actually increased somewhat between 1880 and the mid-1950s. The developing countries today face much higher population growth rates, and developing industry is not likely to be able to absorb much of that increase initially. Agriculture in the LDCs therefore has to do better at absorbing labor than did the agriculture of the rich nations, and it must as a consequence be strongly labor intensive.

On the other hand, the modern poor nations have potentially powerful advantages. There is now a great backlog of technology that has been developed in the rich nations which, with appropriate modifications, could produce much greater rates of increasing productivity than Japan achieved.[37]

Successful Agriculture in Development: Modern Experiences

The developing countries today are in many respects similar to the rich nations at the time the latter began developing. The population typically is about 70 percent agricultural; half or more of the GDP is based in agriculture; they are capital poor; they have poorly developed institutions, and the people are relatively unskilled. They also suffer from additional disadvantages: they have very rapidly increasing populations and are generally tied to an international trading system that is to their disadvantage. (Nations in Europe, such as Germany, suffered from a similar disadvantage in the late eighteenth century when Britain got ahead of them in the process of industrialization.) But poverty, a largely agrarian society, and rapidly expanding populations are not insurmountable obstacles to rapid economic development today, as several successful developing nations are demonstrating.

Taiwan

In direct contrast with the European colonial nations, the Japanese regarded their colonies, Taiwan and Korea, as sources of staple food. The results of policies designed to encourage food production have allowed these countries to develop successfully since decolonization. In the first place, in the early twentieth century Japan transferred to the colonies the land- and capital-saving technology she had developed at home. The Japanese also paid great attention to the development of irrigation in the two colonies (although Korea's agricultural development was allowed to lag behind that of Taiwan) and to education as a means of fostering innovation.[38] Their agricultural productivity increased rapidly as a result.

The Japanese strategy was highly successful from Japan's point of view, in that large amounts of excess food were produced for export to Japan from the 1920s onward. In the period 1911/15 to 1934/40, Taiwan's crop output increased at an amazing 3.5 percent per year.[39] This great productivity allowed an enormous transfer of capital out of agriculture over the entire period 1911 to 1955. Much of this excess capital was siphoned off by the Japanese, thus preventing any substantial increase in the standard of living in Taiwan before World War II. But the remainder paid for the development of Taiwanese industry (table 7-2).

The end of World War II marked the beginning of a period of rapid overall economic development for Taiwan, even though its population in the two decades following World War II increased at 3 percent per year. Taiwan began that period as a largely agricultural economy (62 percent of the work force was in agriculture in 1951) with a per capita income only 75 percent of India's. What then occurred was a period of rapid economic

Table 7-2. Transfer of Taiwan resources from agriculture to nonagricultural segments of the economy in representative periods between 1911 and 1969

	1911–1915	1921–1925	1931–1935	1936–1940	1950–1955	1961–1965	1966–1969
Agricultural output (dollars)[a]	162.9	238.0	361.4	422.5	513.3	801.6	1,044.9
Percentage sold in market	56.3	63.8	71.7	71.4	58.0	60.6	61.9
Percentage transferred	30.5	26.1	24.8	21.1	22.0	13.4	13.8
Amount transferred (dollars)[a]	71.3	87.3	102.1	120.7	215.5	315.8	398.1

Source: Bruce F. Johnston and Peter Kilby, *Agricultural and Structural Transformation: Economic Strategies in Late-Developing Countries* (London: Oxford University Press, 1975), p. 318.

[a]Numbers are millions of Taiwan dollars at 1935–1937 prices.

growth and development that was led by agricultural productivity. Exports did not become a dominant source of capital until this process was well underway. Foreign aid, which was important, was used to pay for raw materials rather than for sophisticated, imported capital-intensive machinery, and so foreign aid was also used to implement the labor-intensive strategy. Taiwan is thus a rare example among the developing countries of agriculture-led development.[40]

The equitable structure of Taiwanese agriculture (figure 6-2) has been especially important in stimulating highly diverse and appropriate industry that is integrated with agriculture and is also labor intensive and capital saving. This unimodal structure was in part a holdover from colonial days and in part was created by intensive land reform carried out between 1949 and 1953. The reform greatly increased the proportion of farmers who owned their land, lowered the average farm size, increased the number of farms, and encouraged intensive farming. (A major result, in addition to rapidly increasing agricultural productivity, was to slow down the migration of people to the cities and hence alleviate social and economic pressures there.) Farm incomes are even and most farms are modernized to a similar degree. Increases in production have been spread across the entire range of farm sizes.[41]

The efficacy of the unimodal strategy in setting up a positive feedback between agriculture and the manufacturing industry is shown in an illuminating comparison between Taiwan, and India and Pakistan, as drawn by Johnston and Kilby.[42] In Taiwan there is an amazing diversity of well-adapted, cheap, small-scale, efficient agricultural equipment, the demand for which has generated a great diversity of manufacturing activity. The manufacture of this equipment is labor intensive, decentralized, capital saving, and low in its need for imports. An outstanding feature is that the tools have become highly adapted to local needs and specific tasks, and a large class of engineers and skilled workers has grown up that is capable of appropriate innovation.

There are, for example, eleven different types of harrows, each serving a different purpose. There are six different basic types of hoes, adapted to the soil conditions and crops grown in the six different farming zones. Of forty new implements introduced between 1922 and 1952, twelve performed completely new yield-increasing tasks, sixteen greatly increased the speed of performing previous tasks, and the remainder did a superior yield-increasing job. Farm tools in 1952 were mainly small implements weighing less than ten pounds, and half of them cost only $10 to $40.

Since 1952 there has been a large increase in locally made, portable irrigation pumps using small diesel engines. Other new equipment, adapted and produced locally, includes dusters and grain dryers. Small motors have been added to the threshing and winnowing processes, improving speed and efficiency while using labor and locally manufactured goods. Most recently a small power tiller adapted from a Japanese model has been gradually spreading to many farms.

The contrast with India and Pakistan is dramatic. There the vast majority of farmers are constrained to farm with a small number of implements unchanged in their design for centuries: the spade, hoe, leveling plank, hand sickle, oxcart, stick plow. Only three twentieth century innovations are widespread (hand-operated fodder chopper, bullock-powered sugar cane crusher, motorized pumpsets), compared with forty in Taiwan by 1952. Even the richer farmers in India and Pakistan have few recent innovative implements. Four-wheel tractors are common on large wheat-growing farms, but since tractor technology has been poorly internalized, the lack of trained mechanics and spare parts greatly lowers their efficiency. The technology is inefficient, poorly suited to the resources of the area, and has a very limited stimulatory effect on manufacturing.

Taiwan's experience also emphasizes the importance of the *spatial* integration of agriculture and industry:

> In Taiwan...the categories "rural" and "urban" do not correspond very closely to "agriculture" and "industry." For many years the policy has been to disperse industry throughout the countryside....
>
> The effect of this policy...has been to increase further the linkages between the various sectors of the economy.... This is of immense potential significance, because it enables members of a farm family...to combine employment in industrial activities with agricultural pursuits. This in turn enables a family to diversify its sources of income (and thereby reduce risks of income failure), to obtain employment for a larger number of days per year (and thereby reduce unemployment and raise income), and to acquire several types of skills (and thereby increase the mobility and adaptability of the family).[43]

Finally, Taiwanese industry in general, not only that associated with agriculture, is remarkably labor intensive.[44] Even those industries that almost everywhere else are capital intensive, such as the metal and chemical industries, are labor intensive in Taiwan. This is critical in the context of our earlier discussion of the Indian strategy because it shows that even the basic capital-goods industry can be developed in a way that is appropriate to the resources of the LDCs.

China

China, the most recent example of successful development, has performed astoundingly well by any standards.[45] Between 1952 and 1974 economic growth averaged 6 percent a year, or almost 4 percent per capita; industrial production, growing at over 10 percent a year, doubled about every six years. Per capita economic growth has been more than three times faster than India's and twice as fast as Pakistan's, although it has been slower than Japan's and Taiwan's. The rate of savings and investment has been very high, again about twice as high as in India and Pakistan. All of this has been achieved with minimum foreign aid, and indeed in the face of economic exclusion by much of the western world. Loans from the U.S.S.R. in the 1950s totaled only $2 billion over ten years and represented only 3 percent of investment in the mid-1950s. By 1955 repayments to Russia exceeded new loans, and by 1965 the loans had been repaid. Since 1955 China has given $7 billion in foreign aid and is the only developing country to have such a program.[46]

Economic growth has been accompanied by great increases in the welfare of the population. This has been achieved mainly by redistribution of land and income and by the provision of social services (public housing, health care, education, old-age security, etc.), rather than by emphasizing a great expansion of consumer goods.[47]

Before evaluating agriculture's role in China's development, it is important to stress the severe constraints Chinese agriculture faces.[48] Usable land in China is extremely scarce: the Chinese feed a quarter of the world's population on about 7 percent of the world's usable land. Even in 1952, with a population of about 630 million, the area of usable land per head was only 0.19 hectares, and it is now probably close to 0.12 hectares. Japan in 1884 also had only 0.12 hectares per head, but the soil is and was much more fertile than China's. In particular, the soils of China's rice-growing area in the south are quite poor. There was also a great deal of good and easily reclaimed additional land available in Japan, whereas by 1950 China had cultivated almost all of the land available—the land not cultivated is not very fertile and is difficult to reclaim. Some feeling for China's problem can be gained by noting that China has only half as much arable land as the United States, but its population is four and a half times larger.

By 1950 much of China's farmland had been ravaged by centuries of neglect, flooding from uncontrolled rivers, and recent wars, both civil and against the Japanese. Its agricultural potential contrasts poorly with India's, for example, not only because there is less land per person (table 7-1), but because the growing season is shorter and there is therefore less opportunity for multiple cropping, and because the quality of the land is lower. Unlike Meiji Japan, China in 1949 had no backlog of agricultural improvements waiting to be applied.

The Chinese responded to these formidable difficulties in the 1950s by relying upon the redistribution of land and the reorganization of farm ownership to release the energies of the rural population.[49] First, the Revolution distributed to 300 million poor and landless peasants the land

and implements previously held by 10 million landowners.* Then in the mid-1950s private ownership was gradually replaced by collective ownership, apparently with no large-scale resistance from the peasants,[50] and by 1958 collectivization was largely complete. Since 1962 units of land and implements have been owned by the production team (thirty to sixty households), which also allocates resources and shares the income. Some 5 percent of the land is in private plots that produce vegetables, pigs, and poultry.

These policies were certainly successful in improving the lot of the peasants and they also resulted in increases in food production in the 1950s, although some of the increase was caused by good weather. Since 90 percent of the population was rural in 1950, these improvements constituted major progress in development. However, the Chinese invested very little in modernizing agriculture, relying instead upon traditional farming methods.[51] The inadequacy of this investment was starkly demonstrated in the three disastrous harvests of 1959 to 1961, brought on by a combination of poor weather and political and economic disruption.

These disastrous years marked a major turning point in Chinese agriculture. From 1962 onward there has been an agriculture-first policy. This policy has redirected investment toward agriculture to supply modern inputs—fertilizers, labor-enhancing machinery, and new seeds. It has also changed the internal terms of trade in favor of rural areas; the prices received by farmers have risen faster than the prices they pay for industrial inputs such as fertilizer. By 1970, a given amount of agricultural produce could buy 67 percent more industrial goods than it could buy in 1950.[52] The policy has created rural industry to supply agriculture's needs and has encouraged great improvements in irrigation, drainage, storage, and other rural infrastructure elements. These last two points are worth pursuing in detail.

A crucial feature in Chinese agricultural development since the early 1960s has been the development of decentralized, small-scale, capital-saving, labor-intensive, rural industry designed to produce the goods needed by agriculture and to process its products.[53] Very often this industrial development is based on the scaling up of traditional cottage industry, which is converted into modern small-scale industry by collectivization, electrification, and the introduction of low-cost machinery. Such industries use local resources and meet local demand for producer goods, emphasizing once again the importance during early development of close spatial ties between agriculture and its related industry. These industries,

---

*China's initial land reform was quite moderate. Only 44 percent of the land was distributed, and the land and rights of the rich peasants were actually protected.

which are owned by the communes, brigades, and counties, produce fertilizers, cement for construction, bricks, iron and steel, power pumps, tractors, and other farm implements, and machinery. The supply of fertilizers, tractors, and irrigation equipment has increased several hundred-fold since 1950. Such machinery does not displace labor but enhances it; indeed, rural labor is actually sometimes in short supply. This integration of agriculture and rural industry is of course relatively easier to achieve in China than elsewhere, since both activities are carried out within the same collective unit—for example, the commune.[54] Rural industry is still expanding very rapidly.

Notice that the integrated development of agriculture and rural industry achieves the aims discussed earlier in this chapter. It increases agricultural production, creates rural employment (half of China's industrial labor force is employed in rural industry), raises rural incomes, uses dispersed local resources, reduces migration to the cities, and uses scarce capital very sparingly.[55]

Turning to the second point, one of the remarkable achievements of the Revolution has been to turn the "problem" of a vast underemployed rural population into a powerfully productive asset. This has been done through the collective units—the production teams, brigades, and communes.[56] The collective decides what needs to be done in the way of irrigation, drainage, building of reservoirs, leveling or squaring fields, building of roads, etc. It then plans and organizes the work, which in each case is done by the unit that will benefit and by the smallest unit possible. Individuals are rewarded by work points that determine their share of the collective's income. Most of the work is done in the winter, and probably about 20 percent of annual rural labor is devoted to these tasks. The Chinese have thus been able to convert otherwise unemployed labor into investment in land and infrastructure.

This revolutionary political and social innovation has had tremendous effects. Without it China could hardly have succeeded in increasing per capita food production. The area irrigated has increased threefold since 1950 so that now about half of the cultivated area is irrigated. Two-thirds of low-lying farmland is now provided with drainage systems. These improvements have been crucial in providing the conditions for efficient use of improved seeds and fertilizer. Lardy notes that because of these activities China in the late 1970s was well prepared to take advantage of the great increases in fertilizer supplies that they will be producing, and rapid increases in food production can be expected.[57]

Given the constraints noted earlier, Chinese agriculture has performed well. Grain production increased at more than 3 percent a year from the early 1960s, when agriculture-first policies were adopted, until the mid-1970s. Production per head about 1975 was roughly one-quarter higher than it was around 1960.[58] It must be stressed that these modest gains have been made in spite of the fact that China's per capita grain consumption was already quite high by LDC standards. By the mid-1970s production was about 290 kg. of grain per head, more than 70 percent higher than India's 170 kg. In spite of poor soils, rice yields average 3.5 tons per hectare, greater than in any developing country except Taiwan and Korea (figure 5-5). Bad weather and political and industrial disruption caused grain production to remain almost constant from 1975 to 1977; however, two decades before, such weather would have caused disastrously reduced harvests, and a major feature of China's agriculture is that it is now much less vulnerable to fluctuations in the weather. In 1978 grain production increased 6 to 9 percent, to about 300 million tons, in spite of one of the worst droughts of the century.[59]

Agriculture has also played an important part in overall development. As in Meiji Japan, it provided much of the surplus to finance development, but it did so more efficiently (i.e., with less loss to luxury consumption) and with a concomittant increase, rather than a decrease, in economic equality. In the early years of development the surplus in agriculture was first distributed to the rural population, which retained roughly half of it, the other half being extracted by the government to develop socialized industry. Industry has developed so rapidly, however, that it has quickly been able to generate its own savings for future development. In fact, agriculture now constitutes only 20 percent of the GDP, while industry constitutes over half, the same share as in developed nations.[60]

In spite of its creditable performance, China's agriculture has not contributed as fully as it could have to development because investment has been less than adequate. Dernberger and Fasenfast note that if agricultural production could be increased more rapidly, the consumer-goods industry could expand faster in response to higher farm incomes, thus adding to employment in manufacturing and hence economic well-being[61] (although Chinese policy has been to stress social services rather than consumer goods). Even so, agriculture has done impressively well in fulfilling its role in development.

AGRICULTURE, BIRTH RATES, FOOD SUPPLY, AND POVERTY

At this point it is worth stepping back to look at the relationships among the problems we have discussed in these first seven chapters and at how the various apparently disparate problems in the underdeveloped countries focus around the need for a dynamic and egalitarian agriculture.

Chapters 2 to 4 showed how birth rates and hence the rates of popula-

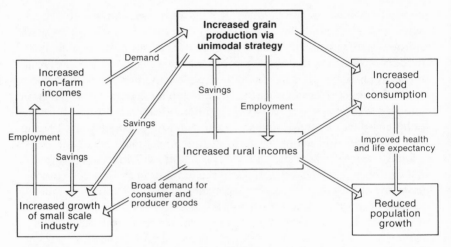

Figure 7-1 Flow of benefits from increased foodgrain production under a unimodal strategy

tion growth can be reduced rapidly only by improving the lot of the poorest segments of the population, particularly the rural poor. They stressed how increased economic equality could greatly accelerate this process and how in rural societies this means both radical reform and the vast expansion of productive employment in agriculture and agriculture-related activities.

Chapters 5 and 6 made the obvious point that the food problem is one of unproductive agriculture, but they also elaborated the less obvious point that the food problem arises directly from the structural poverty of the rural population. This in turn can be solved only by an egalitarian, or unimodal, strategy of agricultural development. In the present chapter we have seen that the process of economic development itself equally depends not only upon creating a dynamic agriculture, but upon an agricultural system that is based on broad participation by the rural population. Thus the need for a productive agriculture is the core of the problem, but the egalitarian pattern of agricultural development is as important as its aggregate growth.

These relationships are outlined in figure 7-1.

AGRICULTURE AND INDUSTRIALIZATION

This and earlier chapters stress the central role of agriculture in development. This emphasis should not be taken to mean that industry is any less crucial than agriculture, or that industrialization is undesirable in development. To the contrary, development cannot and should not proceed without industrialization; indeed, agricultural development itself depends upon the flow of ever more productive inputs from industry. Industrialization is essential because increased productivity, and hence higher living standards, require that equipment and machines enhance labor. Furthermore, over the longer run, the LDCs will need to create a structural transformation to a more industrialized society in which, as economic well-being increases, relatively less effort need be directed toward agriculture.

Even in the earlier stages of development, when agriculture bulks large in the economy, industry that is not geared to agriculture also needs to be developed. In an agriculture-first strategy, LDCs still need appropriate nonagricultural consumer goods and therefore the industry to manufacture them, the industry to produce the capital goods that this manufacturing requires, and, finally, an appropriate infrastructure and the industry needed to create it.

The critical issues concern the goal at which this industrialization is aimed and the means by which it is created. The thesis of this chapter is that the goal should be satisfaction of the present and future needs of the mass of the population by means that are appropriate to the resources of the LDCs. This means that the economy should be driven and shaped by the demands of the bulk of the population, which usually is agricultural. As I have shown, when this strategy is followed, the consequence is industrialization that in general uses sparingly the scarce resources of capital and foreign exchange and depends heavily upon labor and other local resources. The technology can certainly be modern, but it will usually not be the large-scale, capital-intensive type predominant in the industrial nations, a technology that has itself tended to be the goal of development in the LDCs.

CONCLUSION: AN APPROPRIATE AGRICULTURAL STRATEGY

Recall that agriculture has five roles to play in development. It must increase the general level of welfare of the rural population through increasing employment and through increasingly productive employment. It must keep up with the demand from the growing industrial sector. It must create savings that can be used to fuel industrialization. It must save foreign exchange by producing enough food, so that food imports are reduced to a minimum, and it often will need to produce crops for export, at least in the early stages of development. It must be so structured that its demand for producer and consumer goods generates a pattern of industrialization that is appropriate to the nation's resources, integrates agriculture and industry, is based mainly on indigenous skills and materials, and expands employment. Implied in this list, of course, is the requirement that food production should expand rapidly to improve the diets of the population.

The outline of an appropriate agricultural strategy to fulfill these goals emerges logically from the above analyses. For most developing nations it must be a unimodal strategy, broadly egalitarian, labor intensive, capital saving, and technologically innovative. I have already made the straightforward point that only such a strategy can solve the problem of rural employment and economic well-being; in addition, a unimodal strategy increases production and therefore the total income from which savings can be made, and it uses each unit of saving invested much more efficiently.[62] Finally, it stimulates the production of industry that is integrated with agriculture and is appropriate to the needs and resources of the nation.

In modern LDCs such a situation has been achieved within a capitalist framework in Taiwan.* However, Taiwan's colonial legacy of a relatively egalitarian agriculture was virtually unique and facilitated further changes toward a unimodal system. By contrast, it will be politically very difficult to make the required drastic changes when there are strong structural distortions, as in most LDCs. Alternatively, a unimodal strategy can be pursued in a socialist setting involving communal land ownership, as in China.[63]

The elements of an appropriate agricultural strategy are clear:

1. Radical reform of land distribution, tenure, and credit institutions—so that the potentially productive pool of rural labor can gain access to the land and to appropriate yield-increasing technology;
2. Appropriate pricing and other government policies controlling imports, taxes, exchange rates, etc.—so that agriculture as a whole is not suppressed through cheap food policies, and so that farmers demand appropriately-scaled technology that can be produced by, and will encourage the development of, small-scale, labor-intensive domestic manufacturing;
3. Appropriate research by both government and international institutions—so that the abundant new agricultural technology that exists is adapted to local needs and helps develop local technical skills;
4. Appropriate aid policies by donor nations and agencies—so that these aims are supported;
5. The provision of a suitable infrastructure from government taxes on agriculture, and a commitment to rural development, including primary and secondary education.

*South Korea provides another example, for very similar reasons.

So far, it all seems quite clear; indeed, there are now many development experts who would agree with the broad outlines of such a strategy. As Barraclough has said, "in poor countries profound structural changes are not only a prerequisite for real development but, by definition, they are a necessary part of the development process." It is now recognized that development planners and experts in the 1950s and 1960s sometimes gave mistaken advice, and they are generally now prepared to give better advice. Unfortunately, the new advice is hardly likely to be as welcome as the old, and the mere formulation of the new strategy is unlikely to lead to its rapid implementation. The radical changes required directly confront the existing power structures in the LDCs.[64] The fundamental fact is that the distortions which for thirty years have crippled agriculture and development in general in the LDCs are not the result mainly of mistaken advice. Instead, they spring directly from the nature of the developing countries themselves; from their history, their relationships with the developed nations, and above all from the distribution of political and economic power within them. To bring about changes in agriculture and the course of development in general is a deeply political problem. Unfortunately, there is no evidence that the changes needed in the political-economic structure of developing countries are likely to come easily or rapidly.

The remaining chapters analyze this broad political and economic framework—the dual economy—that must be understood before agriculture, food supply, and population growth can be seen in proper perspective.

8

THE DUAL ECONOMY: HISTORICAL ORIGINS

The development strategy pursued by the less developed countries over the past three decades has emphasized urban industrialization. It has relied upon exports to the developed world to finance this process. This strategy has been broadly unsuccessful. A few economies have expanded rapidly, and some segments of the population in most LDCs have become significantly richer. But the strategy has failed to improve markedly the welfare of the general population in most LDCs; it has generally failed to create a sound economic structure for sustained growth in the future; and in most instances it has failed even to attain satisfactory rates of aggregate economic growth. It has failed because it is not appropriate to the needs and resources of most of the developing nations.

The distortions in the policies that make up this strategy result from the structural distortions in the economic, social, and political fabric of the LDCs. We examined these issues in the case of agriculture in the last two chapters and look at them in a broader context in Chapter 9. Briefly, economic wealth and political power are concentrated in the hands of a small, largely urban, elite, and distorted policies are pursued because they benefit that elite, to the enormous detriment of the majority of the population. It is this dichotomy between the interests of a rich minority and those of the poor majority that characterizes the developing world.

To understand the persistence and pervasiveness of this dualism, we must examine its origins in colonial history. But first we need to look briefly at the structure of modern, integrated economies to provide a basis for comparison.*

THE MODERN INTEGRATED ECONOMY

The economic history of the rich nations stands in illuminating contrast to that of the LDCs. Once development in the now-rich nations was under-

---

*This comparison is not meant to suggest that the modern capitalist economy is in any sense the optimal end result of economic evolution. However, in spite of their warts, such economies are able to provide a decent standard of living for the great majority of their people. Marxists would of course argue that development in these economies is sustained only by exporting to the LDCs the problems arising from the "contradictions" of capitalism (see, for example, Alain de Janvry and Carlos Garramón, "Laws of Motion of Capital in the Center-Periphery Structure," *Review of Radical Political Economics* 9, no. 2 [1977]: 29–37).

way, it proceeded through the process of "structural transformation"—by which industrial rather than agricultural production bulked ever larger in the nation's output. Although this process was by no means always smooth, it has been characterized by a strong internal structure of linkages based on reciprocal supply and demand among the different parts of the economy.

For most of these countries, for most of the time since development began, their focus has been *internal*. Though they have traded with other nations, the market for their products has been mainly within the nation itself and the economy has been structured to produce mainly for the internal market. This has been fundamental: the expansion of industrial production has required the expansion of internal markets, and *such expansion could be achieved only through the ever-increasing pruchasing power of the workers*. This required that workers receive increasingly higher wages in return for their increasingly productive labor. Indeed, in spite of the social horrors of mid-nineteenth century industrialization, the general trend in the development of the rich nations has been toward greater equality of income distribution.[1] The reason is simple: since the products of industry have to be sold mainly in the producing country, it has been essential to ensure that the population at large is able to purchase them—there is no point in a Henry Ford mass producing automobiles if the workers in his factories can only afford to come to work on bicycles. Thus the need for expanding internal markets inexorably leads to an integrated economy.

In the modern balanced economy there is strong integration between the major sectors of the economy—the one producing consumer goods and the one producing capital goods. (Consumer goods include food, clothes, furniture, appliances, and automobiles. Producer or capital goods include steel, factories, machines for making appliances and automobiles, mining machinery, and tractors.) Consumer goods are bought by wages and other income, which are a return to labor; capital goods are bought by profits, which are a return to investment or capital. Rising wages, in providing a demand for consumer goods, also create indirectly an increasing demand for the capital goods needed to produce the consumer goods. Increasing productivity provides both the rising wages and the rising profits, and both capitalists and workers gain from the increased production. As we will see, no such logic derives from the economic forces that operate in the LDCs.

COLONIAL HISTORY OF THE LDCs

Let us turn now to the colonial history of the LDCs to see how they arrived at an economic structure very different from that of the rich nations. Almost without exception, the poor countries were at one time colonies of the European imperial powers—Britain, France, Spain, Holland, and Portugal. Their economic history has been discussed by many authors.[2] Among the major LDCs, only China has not been a colony. However, in the nineteenth century China was subjected to an economic domination by the European powers that was in many ways analogous to colonialism, as were Egypt and Thailand—which were economic colonies in fact, if not in name.[3]

The European nations established two types of colonies. Those in the north and south temperate zones (e.g., North America, Australia, New Zealand) were settled by Europeans who quickly outnumbered and became independent of the native populations. These colonies became essentially buds of the mother country, complete with all the organs necessary for sustained economic and political life. Capital was invested in them, food production was emphasized, industry was developed. They were settled and developed in the expectation that eventually they would be fit environments for Europeans.

By contrast, the tropical colonies were not regarded as permanent homes for Europeans—except for a few such as Kenya, where whites were always a tiny minority ultimately dependent on the labor of the native population. These colonies were developed mainly for the evacuation of raw materials and they received capital and technical and managerial expertise sufficient only to expedite this evacuation: no attempt was made to develop them as replicas of the mother template. Indeed, their economies were designed specifically to *complement* the central colonial industrial power. The distinguishing feature in the history of the LDCs, therefore, is not that they were colonies, but that they were a particular type of colony. In the ensuing discussion it is this second type of country that will concern us.

Colonialism in the tropics did not begin as a search for land but as a means of facilitating trade. Europe's trade historically had been with the East, although Oriental spices and manufactured textiles were paid for with African gold. This gold was obtained from Arab traders until the late fifteenth century, when Europeans first reached the Gold Coast (now Ghana).[4] However, much greater deposits of precious metals were discovered in the New World in the sixteenth century, and soon Latin American gold and silver were being used to pay for Oriental goods. Slaves replaced gold as Africa's contribution to colonial trade.

Trade continued to be the major purpose of colonialism from 1500 till the late 1700s;[5] only in Latin America was there significant European settlement to obtain the goods for trade. This trade tied together the economies of the three colonial continents. Manufactured goods (for example, rum, guns, and, later, textiles) from Europe were transported to West

Africa and traded for slaves. The slaves were shipped to the New World plantations (at first in Brazil and later in the Caribbean and the southern United States), and raw materials, including precious metals, were shipped back to Europe. The precious metals paid for Oriental tea, spices, silk, cotton, and other agricultural products.

At each stage in the proceedings the European colonial or merchant power made a profit. Tropical goods were often reexported rather than being consumed at home, again at a profit. Indeed, goods were frequently reexported without ever reaching the colonial nation. These mercantilist profits were a major source of the capital that was invested in agriculture in Britain before the agricultural revolution.[6]

Really massive evacuation of raw materials from the colonies was not possible, however, until the nineteenth-century revolution in transportation and the consequent reduction in transport costs. On land the agent was the railroad and on the seas it was the iron-hulled, propeller-driven steamship. In the course of the nineteenth century, these inventions reduced the cost of long distance transport by 90 percent. As a result, the importation of raw materials grew at enormous rates, especially from 1840 onward. For example, in 1700 only 42 tons of tea reached Great Britain; by 1850, 25,000 tons were imported, and by 1950 the figure was a quarter of a million tons.[7]

The two major raw materials produced by the colonies were mining products and agricultural crops such as coffee, tea, cocoa, sisal, palm oil, rubber, jute, spices, cotton, and sugar. This agricultural and mining activity had not, of course, been large before colonialism; in fact, the cash crop was often introduced into the colony.

We now review in turn the colonial histories of Latin America, Asia, and Africa. Colonial history has of course been extremely complex and varied, and it is impossible to do justice to this complexity in such a brief space. Nevertheless, we will see that "common political and economic forces were in operation which tended to transcend historical differences... and which transformed much of the developing world in a similar pattern."[8]

Latin America

The earliest colonies were in Latin America, although minor footholds were gained in Asia at about the same time. The colonization of Latin America was also the most pervasive and the most radical in the changes it caused. Spanish America (most of Central and South America except Brazil) was not only colonized but conquered in the early sixteenth century in a process that extirpated up to 90 percent of the indigenous population and established the tremendous political and economic power of a small class of individuals, the Spanish *conquistadores*. The primary purpose of the conquerors was the export of precious metals that would provide fortune and status in Spain, an outward orientation towards the "central" imperial powers that has characterized colonial history.

The early conquerors wrought havoc upon the continent. Before colonization there were perhaps 30 to 50 million Indians in Spanish America, living in complex societies based on well-developed agriculture and handicraft industries. The Spaniards set up a mining economy for precious metals which, together with the conquest itself, killed most of the population through warfare, enforced long marches, forced labor, the disruption of food production, and the spread of epidemic diseases. By the mid-seventeenth century the population of Spanish America began to grow again as subsistence agriculture, tied to large estates, replaced mining. But by 1800 it had still reached only about 16 million.[9]

The *conquistador* who subdued the native population was the driving force of the conquest. Starting in 1503, each *conquistador* was ceded certain rights and privileges via the institution of the *encomienda* (meaning the "right to collect tribute from Indians"). The core of this arrangement was that a section of the Indian population was allocated to his "care." Each *conquistador* was obliged to pay the Spanish Crown what amounted to a tax in return for his grant of Indians,* and, in return, he had the right to use them as a labor force. Thus some Indians were forced to work in the mines while others were forced to produce additional food for the mine workers. Labor was obtained basically by coercion, and in some cases through outright slavery, although sometimes it was done by concentrating the native population into certain areas and obtaining labor through the local chieftans.

It is worth dwelling for a moment on this early example of colonialism, for it portrays in starkly simple terms the basic structure of colonial economies elsewhere. The *conquistador* exported a surplus of goods to the colonial power. In addition to establishing his fortune in Spain and adding to Spain's capital, he imported from Spain goods that could not be had in America. The sole function of the indigenous population in this transaction was to provide cheap labor to extract the transferable surplus. To ensure that the labor was forthcoming, the indigenous population and economy were reordered to bind them to the "export enclave."

As the colonies expanded, the mines generated a demand for food and other goods. To supply this demand, grants of land (*mercedes*) were made as follows:

*There was tension between the Spanish Crown, which wanted to have strong political control over the colonies, and the *encomenderos*. In fact, in 1542 the Crown tried to end the *encomienda* system but succeeded only in stirring revolts in Mexico and Peru. These revolts were the last efforts at gaining independence from Spain for 200 years.

...in the same spirit as grants of Indians; as an incentive to private action so as to pave the way for the Conquest and produce a surplus for the benefit of the Crown. Land, in itself, was not an attraction. However, given the demand for agricultural products, it could become the source of a surplus to be extracted from the population ceded to the encomendero.[10]

These grants of land laid the basis for the fundamental economic structure that survives today in the form of great estates (*haciendas*)—the *latifundio*.

Over a period of 200 years, starting in the mid-sixteenth century, the Spaniards gradually took over most of the remaining Indian land. Some was ceded by the Crown directly to Spaniards as grants, but frequently Indian land was bought at low prices, or seized by violence or by resettling the Indians elsewhere. Only after the fact and in return for payments to the Crown did the state give legal ownership to these illegally procured lands.[11] The great *haciendas* were built up by the buying and selling and coalescing of these variously obtained tracts of land.

In Frank's view, the *haciendas* were commercial enterprises from the beginning and were not estates held merely for reasons of status. Their owners were entrepreneurs, often owners of mines or other commercial enterprises. From the beginning many of them were absentee, preferring to live in the cities near their other enterprises, foreshadowing again a general characteristic of the colonial economy. The *haciendas* produced wheat, cattle, sugar, and indigo, some of which was for export. However, the Spanish urban population was increasing rapidly. For example, by 1646 there were 125,000 Spaniards in Mexico, mainly in cities, and the main demand for wheat, meat, and hides came from the cities and mines.[12]

The *latifundio* quickly replaced the *encomiendas* as the means of controlling the Indian population; in fact, although not formally abolished until the eighteenth century, the *encomiendas* essentially died out by the end of the sixteenth century. By this time successive epidemics had brought the Indian population to a very low level, the system of forced labor had been abolished, and labor was very scarce. In these circumstances a major reason for the growth of the *haciendas* was to obtain Indian labor. This was done by displacing Indians from their land, and hence from their means of support. (Frequently much more land was obtained than the Spaniards could possibly use, simply for the purpose of denying the Indians access to an alternative means of supporting themselves.) The labor force was controlled in two ways. Indian families were settled on the *hacienda* and were advanced money and goods, thus creating "debt peonage labor." Alternatively, families were allowed to rent small plots of land in return for their labor.[13]

Mining for precious metals, which had first brought the Spanish to Latin America and had set in motion the seizure of Indian land, virtually disappeared by the middle of the seventeenth century. But left behind was

a feudal system in which enormous power was invested in the owners of
huge tracts of land, which now produced a surplus not for Spain, but for
the landowners:

> These vast rural domains, essentially based on a subsistence economy and al-
> most entirely cut off from the authority of the State, were to become one of the
> most characteristic features of Latin American society. The ownership of land
> became the basis of a system of social domination of the mass of the people by a
> small ethnically and culturally differentiated minority.[14]

This, then, is the system of *latifundio-minifundio* in which the rural mass
is tied to the estate owner through the latter's political, economic, legal,
and social power.

During the eighteenth century, trade with Spain was reduced. The demand in Europe for tropical agricultural goods such as cocoa, cotton, and
hides began to grow, and the region moved from a mining to an agricultural economy. Even so, trade was not extensive. Until independence,
Spain strictly limited the colonies' trade with other nations. For example,
Mexico was allowed to have only one ship a year sail to Asia (Manila in
this case). In the last century of colonial rule, the opportunities for international trade were therefore limited, and the landowners were concerned
mainly with extracting a surplus for their own local use.

Brazil's colonial history followed a different course, indeed almost the
reverse of Spanish America's, yet one that has had similar final results.
When Portugal colonized it, Brazil had a sparse population and no evidence of precious metals. Africans were imported as slaves to work in
large sugar plantations producing for export. But in the late seventeenth
century sugar production elsewhere drove down prices, Brazil's export
activities declined, and its agriculture became mainly a subsistence economy, again developing into a *latifundio-minifundio* system. The introduction of coffee production in the 1840s acted to extend this system through
the development of large estates.

Gold was discovered in Brazil in the early eighteenth century, just as the
mining of precious metals had declined elsewhere in Latin America. The
British controlled this trade and most of the gold ended up in Britain in
exchange for British manufactured goods.

The beginning of the nineteenth century marked a crucial turning point in
Latin American history. The colonial period ended. That period determined much of the area's present internal social structure, but it was during the ensuing century that Latin America's economies became dominated
by exports to the rich nations. The continent was gradually made a part of
the international trading system, which thereafter determined the pattern
of its economic development. It is also during this postcolonial period that

we can see clearly in Latin America how developing countries could be maintained in the colonial mold, even when they were not colonies, through the force of the economic and political hegemony wielded by the developed nations.[15]

The Spanish and Portugese empires began to decay increasingly at the end of the eighteenth century, and the first part of the nineteenth century saw the struggle for political independence in Latin America and the creation of the nation-states that exist today. This process was accompanied by the replacement of Spain and Portugal by Britain as the dominant trading nation in the hemisphere—it must be recalled that in the early nineteenth century the industrial revolution was almost confined to Britain, which also controlled the world's investment capital and its shipping.

There were two main classes in Latin America that developed economic and political power during this period. The first were the landowners (including the church), whose power derived from centuries of Spanish colonialism. The second was a new class of traders and mercantilists, a new urban bourgeoisie (which included the army), whose aim was to expand trade with Europe wherever possible. The traders were interested in importing British manufactured goods and necessarily had to turn to the landowners for goods for export in exchange. Thus the interests of these two classes soon coalesced. (Mexico, Peru, and Bolivia were rather different in that here economic and political power still resided in mining, which already was a part of the international trading system.)

The essential economic and social structure of modern Latin America was thus clearly defined by the mid-nineteenth century. A small group of landowners, who developed urban economic interests, together with urban mercantilists, often of European origin, held the economic and political power. The mass of peasants, bound in a virtually feudal system, contributed cheap labor to produce a largely agricultural surplus that was consumed by the elite or was exported in exchange for European manufactured goods, which in turn were imported for the elite. In economies dominated by mining, the indigenous population served as cheap labor in the mines or indirectly by producing food for those employed in mining. Local cottage industry and internal trade had atrophied and there was little trade among the different Latin American nations. European colonialism had been replaced by European, and largely British, economic hegemony, exercised increasingly in the nineteenth century through British control of investment capital, manufacturing technology and capacity, free trade, and Britain's ability to obtain and transport raw materials from all over the world.

In Latin America the events of the second half of the nineteenth century were caused by the expansionary processes that flowed from the national and international structures set up by mid-century. World trade expanded enormously as Europe and the United States underwent massive industrial economic growth. The value of world trade in the 1820s was about $1.5 billion but reached $40 billion by 1914. And in this vast expansion Britain was dominant: for most of the second half of the century, two-thirds of the manufactured goods in world trade were made in Britain.[16]

The transport revolution of the mid-century meant that now Latin America could export increasing quantities of raw materials. One large group of nations (Brazil, Colombia, Ecuador, Central America and the Caribbean, parts of Mexico and Venezuela) exported tropical agricultural products (e.g., tobacco, sugar, coffee, cocoa). Another group (Mexico, Chile, Peru, and Bolivia) exported industrial minerals. The mining was carried out on a large scale, was controlled by foreign (often U.S.) capital, and was administered from abroad. Argentina and Uruguay were different. They exported *temperate* agricultural food products based on extensive farming and introduced European technology. Significantly, these two nations became relatively wealthy and are the two countries in Latin America that are now often considered to be among the developed nations.

By the early 1900s Latin America had thus become an important source of raw materials for the industrialized countries. In 1913 its share of world exports ranged from a low of about 10 percent for livestock products and vegetable fibers to over 60 percent of the world's coffee and cocoa.

It is important to stress that Latin America was part of an *integrated* international *system*. This system was not merely countries trading with each other. To the contrary, although colonialism had disappeared in Latin America, the process of trade and development was still controlled by "the center" (mainly Britain) through its control of capital, technology, equipment, manufacturing, and transport.

European capital continued to dominate the economies of Latin America until the twentieth century. However, in the first half of this century, U.S. companies gained control of much of the region's sources of raw materials, public services, and trading and manufacturing activity. Thus, in this century the United States has replaced Europe as the dominant external economic force, and most Latin American countries have become dependent upon U.S. capital and trade.[17]

One example, Chile, will suffice to illustrate how these developing economies were controlled by foreign capital. Throughout the nineteenth century Chile was a British economic dependency, exporting raw materials and importing British manufactured goods. However, following explicitly stated government policy, U.S. private capital in the first two decades of the twentieth century quickly replaced British capital, during a period when Britain's economic power was fading rapidly. America simply replaced Britain in the role of *de facto* colonial power.[18] Chile's main export was copper, and by 1924 private U.S. capital owned over 90 percent of the

Chilean copper industry. Chile's second major export, nitrates, was similarly U.S. owned. Since this country also controlled the sale of copper abroad, it had a monopolistic control over price. The dependency was further increased as the United States became the main buyer of these exports. These capital investments gave America indirect control over Chilean government revenues, which depended mainly on exports, and therefore over the way the government spent and invested those revenues.

Asia

The colonization of Asia was a much more complex and drawn-out affair than the conquest of Latin America. I will mention merely a few of the major features.

Trade flourished in Asia long before the appearance of the Europeans in the sixteenth century. The Arabs, for example, were involved throughout Southeast Asia trading in spices and teak, and there was very active trade among India, China, and the rest of Asia in silk, cotton, spices, tea, and other goods. European intervention was driven by the desire to capture this trade and its attendant revenues. The Dutch and English by the end of the sixteenth century were trading on a small scale in spices, silk, and cotton, and later in tea from China and Japan. In the seventeenth century both nations set up private East India trading companies, the British concentrating mainly in India and the Dutch in the Malayan peninsula and Indonesia.

Until the late eighteenth century, Europe's relationship with Asia was quite different from its relationships with Latin America and Africa. Since Asia was industrially more advanced than Europe during this period, there was little the Europeans produced that the Asians wanted. The Europeans, however, wanted not only Asia's natural products but her manufactured goods, especially her cottons and silks. Since Europe had little to offer in return, it had to pay in gold and silver. The Europeans were thus mainly purchasers of goods in Asia in this period, and for this reason they had little effect on the structure of Asia's economy.[19]

The East India Companies were the real founders of empire on the Asian continent.[20] In India in the late eighteenth and early nineteenth century the employees of the Company inserted themselves into local trade as private individuals. However, the main attraction of India to the Company was the fact that the indigenous system of revenue collection yielded huge sums of cash that arose from the surplus of the villages. The Company in many cases eliminated by force the local intermediaries and collected the revenues directly through its own official bureaucracy. It used these revenues to obtain Indian goods for export and, through the sale of opium, to buy tea from China for export to Britain. Not only was the "surplus of Indian revenues thus sent home in teas from China, but it was through this payments link with China that India was enabled to purchase the new textile manufactures of Lancashire and become one of the industry's major markets." It was this need to collect revenues, to maintain local control and to maintain Britain's "presence" in the East that led the British to take over much of the administration of India. In Indonesia, by contrast, the Dutch interfered very little in local administration and were content to redirect traditional tribute into the production of export crops (including opium).[21]

Large-scale colonial activity in Asia did not begin until the nineteenth century. The British Indian empire grew very slowly and piecemeal as soldiers were sent to provide "law and order" so that the East India Company could get on with its business. Only in 1857 did Britain finally exercise direct colonial rule. The massive commercial exploitation of India was similarly delayed until the mid- to late nineteenth century. Tea growing on a commerical scale began only in 1870. Coffee was introduced into India (and Java) in the seventeenth century, but the British did not begin to plant coffee estates in India until about 1825. Rubber plantations in Asia are a twentieth-century phenomenon. The Dutch empire in Indonesia similarly expanded gradually over a period of 300 years and was finally complete only in 1908. However, evacuation of raw materials got well under way in the nineteenth century. For example, between 1840 and 1886, India's foreign trade increased eightfold and played a crucial role in helping to pay for Britain's imports from her other trading partners.[22]

Throughout Asia in the nineteenth century, under the increasing pressure of the colonial powers, the new plantation crops came to replace the traditional trading goods. In India, tea, coffee, and rubber predominated; oil palm and rubber were dominant in Indonesia and Malaya; hemp, sugar, tobacco, and coconuts were the main crops in the Philippines. In Ceylon in 1815 the British colonial government assumed ownership of all uncultivated land and introduced coffee, the main export until it was devastated by disease in 1880, when tea and rubber replaced it.[23] By the early twentieth century the Asian colonies had thus become dominated by export enclaves set up to produce mainly agricultural raw materials for Europe.

The other side of the colonial coin was the development of colonies as markets for European manufactured goods. In Asia, again, the pattern was the replacement of indigenous by foreign goods. The British, in particular, specifically developed their colonies for this purpose, being careful that no indigenous development should occur that would compete with British goods. India under East India Company rule, for example, had been an exporter of manufactured textiles, but after colonial rule it became an importer of British textiles and an exporter of raw cotton.[24]

The suppression of indigenous manufacturing was general in the Asian colonies. As an example, Resnick provides details of the decline in rural industry from 1870 to 1938 in Burma, the Philippines, and Thailand.[25] (Thailand was not a formal colony but, as shown below, it was a colony in fact.) Among the reasons for the decline was that the labor requirements of the export crops took time away from spinning, weaving, making farm implements, building houses, and so on. In addition, local goods were gradually replaced by imported manufactured goods. This set up a cycle in which, as local goods became less abundant, it became more necessary to labor on export crops to make cash to pay for imported goods. As a consequence of these changes in the Philippines, for example, the output of rural industry declined from 19 percent of agricultural output in 1902 to only 6 percent in 1938, while agricultural exports rose by 4.2 percent a year.

Control of taxation, government expenditure, investment, banking, and trade allowed the colonial powers to tailor the colonial economies. In Asia, those nations escaping direct colonial authority were nonetheless cast in the colonial mold. Thailand serves as a good example.[26] Britain gained virtually total control of Thailand's economy by an 1855 treaty. Taxes, and therefore government revenue, depended on trade, and these levies and taxes were controlled under the treaty. Government expenditures could not be made without the approval of the British Financial Advisor, who in fact had great influence in Thailand until World War II. Britain controlled most of Thailand's trade, providing most of its imports and buying most of its exports (at prices determined largely by Britain). Britain encouraged Thailand to export rice, caused it to import other foods that it had once produced, and ensured that it had to purchase British manufactured goods.

The most dramatic example of the effect of colonial policies in Asia is possibly that part of colonial India that is now Bangladesh.[27] Bangladesh (then part of Bengal) was a prosperous region right up until the late eighteenth century. It had a productive and diverse agriculture and a silk and cotton industry that produced manufactured exports. With the coming of the British East India Company, East Bengal's balanced agriculture was converted to producing raw materials for export (indigo and safflower and later jute and tea). The local textile industry essentially disappeared in the face of the influx of British textiles, and the population of the main commercial centers declined. Over almost two centuries of colonial control, the region's large surplus of agricultural production was captured and extracted by the British, leaving behind very little for investment. Out of this background the tragedy of modern Bangladesh has emerged.

Perhaps the most profound internal changes wrought in the colonies, wherever they were, was in land ownership and distribution. These changes had far-reaching effects that persist today, as we saw in Chapter 6. In Latin America the change was achieved in a straightforward way, mainly through the Spanish land grants and the formation of estates. In Asia (and the Caribbean islands) the change was also straightforward in the case of plantations set aside for estate crops: vast areas of land were simply appropriated and placed under foreign ownership. But outside the plantations the process was piecemeal and often complex. This is nowhere better demonstrated than in the complicated and sometimes bizarre history of the British influence on Indian land ownership. It is worth looking at this history in some detail, since India had proportionately less land in plantations than the other Asian colonies, yet colonization greatly affected land ownership and distribution. The following account relies mainly upon Frykenberg.[28]

Before the British presence became important in India in the late eighteenth century, there was no concept of absolute private ownership of land in the sense that someone could sell a plot of land, with exclusive and inalienable right of use, to someone else. In the first place, *rights* to land, but not the land itself, were likely to be owned by groups—the village, extended family, or lineage group. In the second place, there was usually an extremely complex web of "customary rights," which might well be absolute. These rights referred to the *use* of the land or its produce, and no one owned title to the land as owner.

In Northern India the cultivator had a hereditary right to farm the land and retain perhaps half of its harvest. In return for this right, the cultivator could often be forced to farm the land—a critical obligation in a time when there was surplus land. However, if taxes became too heavy, cultivators would sometimes migrate from the area. The remaining 50 percent or so of the harvest was the agricultural surplus that was extracted as revenue. The immediate revenue collector, or zamindar, had a right to a percentage of the revenue from a village, part of a village, or group of villages; in turn the zamindar had the obligation of collecting and passing on the remaining revenue to one or more hierarchical levels of "owners"—talukdars, rajas, etc. The upper levels of this pyramid had a "right-to-rule" rather than a "right-to-own," and this right was more directed to the labor of the people on the land than to the land itself.

In Southern India, before the British came, the prevailing mode of land control was the village system: individual identities were secondary to the general welfare of the village, as determined by its leaders or rulers. At a higher administrative level, Southern India had been ruled for four centuries by many disparate warrior groups for whom, as in Northern India, land was not a commodity to be owned but a territory to rule and from which to extract an agricultural surplus.

The British came into this alien system with firm eighteenth-century ideas not only of absolute private property but of the prime importance of a land-owning gentry or aristocracy as the backbone of the nation. They therefore looked around in India for the "rightful" proprietors of the land and, finding none, they created them or "recognized" them from among the upper levels of those with rights to the land. The British, therefore, while they diluted much of the power-to-rule concept, created, codified, and legalized the private right to absolute land ownership. They did this in different ways in different areas of the country, but virtually always with the consequence that those lowest in the hierarchy had their customary rights weakened, while most of the land owning tended to concentrate in fewer and fewer hands in the upper classes. The central reason for this re-ordering was the need to assign to *someone* the legal responsiblity to collect revenue from the land; however, an additional hoped-for benefit was the creation of a landed class that would provide leadership—an Indian yeomanry.

In Southern India the British East India Company replaced the warrior groups with more peaceful and literate Brahmans and Sudras, who formed the tax-collecting link between the British and the peasants. Since the British did not always understand the complexities of customary rights, these already wealthy Indian classes used their new powers to gain even more influence, power, and land. The other major change made by the British in Southern India was to strengthen greatly the land-holding rights of the village elite classes.

Tax collection and land-owning arrangements were more varied in Northern India, but again led to land concentration. In one area (Oudh) this came about by the simple process of the British arbitrarily giving legal ownership to a specific list of large landowners in 1858. But land concentration also came indirectly. For example, one consequence of introducing land ownership was that land could now, for the first time, be bought and sold. Under the Bengal Regulations of 1795, "estates" that were in arrears in taxes or, later, whose owners were in debt, could be sold to the highest bidder. (Of course these "estates" were bureaucratic figments invented for tax collection purposes.)

The British designated zamindars (revenue collectors) as owners but then created arrears by misassessment, or by setting up powerful tax collectors who were able to juggle records so as to cause other landowners to be in arrears. The consequence was a huge turnover of land that fell into new, and fewer, hands. By 1850 in the Banaras area, for example, most of the new owners were urban and not local; they were not in agriculture but were moneylenders, or in law. By 1885 in that area, 134 large landowners owned about a third of the land while over 100,000 small farmers divided the rest among them.

The distortions in land ownership and distribution were closely linked to widespread rural indebtedness, especially of the peasant to the money-lender or the landowner. Such indebtedness amounted to bondage, since the peasant was then tied to working land for the landowner not only to survive but to pay off a debt that seemed everlasting. Here again, British legislation was passed in favor of the creditor, which added to the bonds of the indebted peasant.[29] Thus, quite often by mistake and through ignorance of existing customs, the British in India created a fundamental distortion in rural society that has helped keep the rural masses in poverty and has made agricultural development extremely difficult.

Africa

Before the colonial era began in Africa at the end of the nineteenth century, Europeans traded there for exotic goods—for example, gold, ivory, palm oil, and spices. This trade, however, was greatly overshadowed by the traffic in slaves, and both East and West Africa suffered centuries of depradation by slavers—Arabs in the east and Europeans in the west. These activities reached a crescendo in the nineteenth century, when millions of Africans were taken as slaves, although it is difficult to know even roughly how many people were affected. European explorers in East Africa pointed out that many of those captured never reached port and that there was terrible devastation of villages in the fighting that occurred during slave raids.[30]

Slaves from East Africa were taken through Zanzibar and Cairo, and one estimate is that over 2 million slaves passed through Zanzibar alone in the period 1830 to 1873. Using high estimates of attrition rate, this suggests that up to 20 million people were killed in East Africa in this period. On the other hand, Kjekshus thinks that both the numbers at the markets and the attrition rates were much lower than this. In West Africa from the sixteenth to the nineteenth century, millions of people were shipped out to provide slave labor in the western hemisphere. Wholly new military states were created—for example the Dahomey and Yoruba kingdoms—to raid, capture, and sell neighboring people.[31]

It is not known to what extent slave raiding disrupted the basic economic activities of the exploited peoples and states. Nevertheless it is clear that in the mid-nineteenth century, in spite of slave raiding, there was widespread development of agriculture, handicrafts, and trade—the precursors of modern economic development. In both Central and West Africa, complex, centrally administered city-states, kingdoms, and extensive empires had existed for several centuries, based on agriculture that could produce a surplus over subsistence needs. These states and empires traded in a variety of goods, sometimes over enormous distances. Trade from

Central Africa reached to Arabia, India, and China, while the trading links of the kingdoms of Mali and Ghana, and of the city-states in present northern Nigeria, reached into southern Europe.[32]

In East Africa evidence has accumulated recently against the notion that before the advent of the Europeans, the area was essentially undeveloped. The real condition of precolonial agriculture was that large areas were settled permanently by a population that frequently produced a surplus, while slash-and-burn practices were followed only by a small minority. The flood plains were fertile: they grew maize, rice, and millet, and they supported dense populations. Away from the flood plains there was a variety of complex agricultural systems spread throughout the country. Excellent irrigation systems were present in some areas (for example, around Kilimanjaro) and were associated with high productivity and multiple cropping, although elsewhere they were unnecessary since land was abundant. In the Tanganyika highlands there was crop selection, crop rotation, soil conservation, ridging, and the use of legumes in rotation to restore soil fertility. Elsewhere, in areas of low fertility, methods were developed for deepening the layer of fertile soil by using decaying vegetation. Terracing was carried out on hillsides to prevent erosion, and the use of cattle manure to increase fertility was known.[33]

Perhaps most remarkable in light of the present vast game reserves and the prevalence of the tsetse fly is that domestic cattle (which are vulnerable to sleeping sickness carried by that fly) were extremely numerous and widespread in East Africa in the mid-nineteenth century. Indeed, at that time much of what is now wildlife reserve and tsetse fly habitat supported extensive cattle herds. The Africans appear to have understood the relationships among cattle, tsetse fly, and wildlife. They cleared the woodland (leaving strips between neighboring villages) thus isolating the wild mammals and their associated tsetse flies. Herds were kept away from areas known to be infested with tsetse and these areas were controlled by burning. When cattle had to be driven through such areas, this was done at night, which is safer, and the cattle were smeared with repellants that seemed to work. Infected cattle were killed immediately to stop transmission.

Iron smelting, tool making, salt making and cotton manufacturing occurred widely in East Africa. Cotton spinning and weaving were very common, cotton clothes were abundant, and looms could be found in every village. There was a fairly high degree of sophistication and versatility in smelting and forging techniques. There was extensive marketing and trading at local markets, and some goods such as pottery, salt, cattle, donkeys, tobacco, bananas, coffee (for chewing), and grain moved over trading routes several hundred miles long.[34]

It must be remembered that it is precisely from such activities, and from their interaction, that real development proceeds (Chapter 7). However, colonialism disrupted and at times destroyed these activities in Africa. The disruption in West Africa is treated in some detail in Chapter 10. In East Africa a sequence of calamities associated with European intrusion and colonization had a devastating effect on economic life.

The first of these calamities, and one that destroyed much of the basis of life in East Africa, was the rinderpest epidemic of 1890. The rinderpest is a disease that attacks cattle and other ruminants and swine. It was introduced in the 1880s, probably in the livestock of invading European armies. It reduced cattle herds to a few head, in one area from 30,000 to 40,000 down to 100 cattle. The Masai, wholly dependent upon cattle, were almost wiped out. It is estimated that 95 percent of their cattle were killed and that two-thirds of the tribe died in the resulting famine. Entire villages were abandoned and in 1891 travelers encountered the tribe as starving skeletons begging for food. Lord Lugard, the military adventurer who opened up much of East Africa for the British, could see benefits in such a holocaust: "Powerful and warlike as the pastoral tribes are, their pride has been humbled and our progress facilitated by this awful visitation. The advent of the white man had else not been so peaceful."[35]

The dislocation no doubt greatly worsened the effect of a sequence of subsequent disasters over the next two decades—smallpox epidemics, plagues of disease-carrying fleas introduced to the area, a great extension of the tsetse fly and of sleeping sickness, and famines. The famines were certainly in part man made. In the 1890s the Germans were carving out an East African colony. They took food from the population for the army and for their railway building and other projects. In addition, they used a scorched-earth policy against resistant tribes and stationed troops at strategic areas to prevent crop production. Indeed, "the military command found that (induced) famine was its most useful weapon."[36]

Following the spectacular (and bloody) military conquest and devastation in Africa, the relentless progress of more peaceful colonization proceeded to undermine the African's remaining economic base. As elsewhere, this was done in the process of converting subsistence agriculture into a system for producing export crops, and by the replacement of indigenous manufactured goods with those imported from the colonial power.

The transformation of agriculture was achieved by the use of one of two main strategies.[37] South Africa, Southern Rhodesia, the pleasant highland areas of East Africa, and parts of North Africa were dominated by a white settler economy in which the African served as cheap labor on settler farms. In the rest of Africa, including Uganda in the east, export crops were produced by African peasants. A third strategy—large-scale, white-run plantations—that was so common in the Caribbean and Asia, was general only in parts of West Africa such as the Belgian Congo, Liberia, and the Ivory Coast.

In South Africa, the process of colonization was simple and somewhat different from elsewhere. The settlers, not the colonial troops, "opened up" the land: "the greater part of the African land was confiscated by the settlers, the economically unproductive members of the population were herded into small reserves set aside for them, and the able-bodied males were thus forced by economic necessity to sell their labour to the settlers who had dispossessed them."[38]

In other settler-dominated colonies the settlers came into areas "pacified" for them by the colonial power. For example, in Kenya by the end of World War I, Europeans were given exclusive rights to the roughly 13,000 square miles of prime agricultural land in the highlands, while the African population was largely confined to 52,000 square miles of "reserves." Even by 1963 this highland area (about 20 percent of Kenya's good farmland) was divided among only 3,000 European farms, while almost 10 million Africans lived on the remainder. In colonial North Africa Europeans seized a third of the best land.[39]

The settler-dominated colonies depended wholly on African labor to produce the export crops. Outright coercion of the Africans occurred sometimes but in general was not necessary. While his livelihood was reduced by land alienation on the one hand, the African was forced on the other hand to produce a cash income to feed himself and meet the hut and poll taxes imposed by the colonial administration. However, no source of cash income other than laboring for white farms, plantations, or mines was available because the African was generally prohibited from producing the cash crop himself. (In the white highlands of Kenya, Africans remained on some of the land on sufferance as "squatters" but were allowed to pay for this privilege only with their labor and not in cash.) In peasant-dominated colonies, taxation was the initial method of forcing the African into the cash economy and hence into the production of cash crops.

The colonists also needed African labor to build railways, roads, and buildings and this labor was also obtained as payment of the taxes imposed by the colonial government. By way of example, in the German colony of Tanganyika by World War I there were 170,000 such laborers. These men lived mainly in labor camps, where the mortality rate was 50 percent.[40]

African agriculture quite naturally deteriorated under these pressures.[41] In the settler-dominated colonies conditions in the African reserve areas steadily worsened as the density of people in them was greatly increased (see Chapter 10), while at the same time many of the able-bodied men were off working for the settlers and were unable to maintain the land. Whatever resources were available for development were funneled into settler cash cropping and away from African agriculture.

In East Africa, in particular, the deterioration was accelerated by the development of big game hunting, beginning around 1890. The Germans in Tanganyika set aside reserves, at first to protect rare species and then for hunting exclusively by Europeans. The British continued this policy in Tanganyika and throughout East Africa. For example, they moved 40,000 agrarian Africans to create the Selous Game Reserve, which in the mid-nineteenth century had relatively little game. In the nineteenth century the cattle-herding Masai were abundant in the Ngorongoro crater and what is now Serengeti National Park. (One-quarter of Tanzania is now given over to game reserves.) Since the tsetse fly is strongly associated with wild game, the spread of the reserves has been accompanied by the spread of the fly, which has covered vast new areas since the nineteenth century. In fact, before 1900 sleeping sickness was not recorded from East Africa and probably did not occur there; by 1906, 200,000 people had died of the disease. New laws expanded these already enormous incursions into the cattle-raising lands by prohibiting grass burning, hunting, and clearing, which allowed the brush to encroach still further.[42]

Environmentalists are concerned now with soil erosion and other environmental degradation in East Africa. However, the process of colonization had already ruined much of the area's agriculture in the early part of this century. And by the time the British were well established in East Africa, the rural population had been so disrupted that the knowledge of much of the agricultural technology of the nineteenth century, described above, had been lost.

The nomads of the semi-arid areas of Africa fared no better than the sedentary peasants. Although nomadism is probably the optimal way to exploit such regions (Chapter 10), this way of life made more difficult the colonial task of imposing "law and order," not to mention collecting taxes. As a consequence, the colonial powers in both East and West Africa restricted those large-scale movements of the nomads that were so crucial to their existence. They also were starved of resources. For example in Kenya, where some 75 percent of the land is naturally suited to nomadism, up to the present the nomad economy has received no government investment. In the early twentieth century the colonial government "pacified" the nomads, killing large numbers, burning their villages, and taking their livestock. In an attempt to prevent pastoralism, nomad movements were restricted, the best grazing lands were seized, access to crucial breeding stock was prevented, and, when it was clear in the 1930s that the pastoralists were still able to compete with white settlers in the production of beef, a quarantine was placed on nomad cattle with the explicit purpose of removing this competition.[43]

Africans living in colonies where the peasants themselves produced the export crop were probably least affected by colonialism. However, they were still forced, through taxation, to labor for the colonial power, and their absorption into the cash-cropping economy led similarly to the disruption of food-producing agriculture and the deterioration of their land. Cash crops were needed to pay taxes and, as more and more effort was devoted to the production of cotton, groundnuts, palm oil, etc., subsistence food production suffered. Furthermore, with the loss of indigenous handicrafts and industry, the cash crop became even more essential for buying imported clothes and other manufactured goods.[44]

The cash-cropping peasant, moreover, was now caught hopelessly in an economic system in which he could never hope to prosper. Except to a minor extent in West Africa, Africans were excluded from any part of the export process except the production of the crop. The lucrative activities of buying the crop, transporting, processing, and marketing it abroad were all in the hands of a few large foreign firms (mainly British and French). Furthermore, since a few firms controlled these activities, the price paid to the producer was determined by the buyer and was kept extremely low.[45] Thus, while the African elsewhere produced a surplus for the colonial powers through cheap labor, the peasant producer did the same through the production of cheap crops.

As elsewhere, colonialism in Africa had a profound effect on systems of land tenure and therefore on the peasant's livelihood. In settler colonies and where plantations occurred, a huge class of landless Africans was created. Where the peasants themselves were induced to produce cash crops, especially in West Africa, customary land rights were gradually replaced by private land ownership, in ways quite similar to those that operated in India, and often for the same reasons. In some areas, such as Ethiopia, Nigeria, and parts of Central Africa, settlers were not an important influence and colonies were ruled locally through the existing ruling classes, which therefore grew more powerful. They achieved new control over the land during the colonial period, and the peasants became mere tenants paying taxes or rent to the landlord.

Local handicrafts and industry decayed in Africa as they did in colonies everywhere. Economically forced labor took men away from handicraft industries, and Europeans brought with them cheap manufactured goods such as textiles and farm implements that supplanted local products. The colonial government suppressed local African markets, gave support to European-run markets, and took capital out of African hands (in the form of taxes) without replacing it. The result was a rapid decline of indigenous industry in the first few decades of the twentieth century, especially iron smelting and the manufacture and production of textiles.[46] On the other hand, the development of modern industry in the colonies was prevented, since this would have created competition with imported European goods.

The consequence of colonial rule was thus the impoverishment of the African by several means. Food-producing agriculture declined and cash cropping was either prohibited or the peasant was paid very low prices. Africans labored for farms, plantations, and mines at wages that were a tiny faction of those paid for the same job in Europe. With very few exceptions, Africans were excluded from the well-paying jobs and entrepreneurial opportunities associated with the new trade and colonial administration. At the same time, the African was taxed to support these activities. The colonial administrations were expected to become self-sufficient as soon as possible, and it was further assumed that the African could be taxed to provide capital for colonial business ventures. In Kenya, for example, Africans contributed to the white settler economy through direct hut and poll taxes and, increasingly, through indirect taxes and duties placed on cheap manufactured goods such as clothes imported from Britain. At the same time, the white settlers paid no direct and few indirect taxes.[47] Thus Africans contributed heavily to government investment in white business.

Only a tiny minority of Africans benefited from colonialism. Those chiefs and other local figures of authority who cooperated with the colonial power gained extra land or other sources of income; a few Africans were given special access to the exporting of crops and became rich; the sons of locally powerful Africans were given advanced educations and so were able to take advantage of new economic opportunities in the modern economy. Such differential access to oportunities was the seed from which sprang the strong inequalities that characterize Africa today.[48]

The role available to the great majority of Africans was foreseen only too well by Lord Lugard, who in 1922 noted what he considered to be the "backward condition of the people, and their preference for agricultural pursuits." These characteristics fitted them admirably to be cheap producers of tropical "raw materials and foodstuffs which . . . are so vital to the needs of civilized man," and to be a growing market for manufactured goods from Britain. Colonial policies, with their emphasis on the African as an inferior being and on the need to maintain his "traditional" and agricultural character, ensured that Lugard's prognosis was closely matched by the ensuing reality:

"As a result of almost a century of British colonial rule, the vast majority of Africans barely earned or produced enough on which to subsist at the time of independence. This was the sum consequence of policies of the British that resulted in the 'fossilization' of the backward peoples in their conventional roles of undifferentiated cheap labor and unspecialized peasant producers."[49]

THE COLONIAL DUAL ECONOMY

In this section we extract from our observations of colonialism on three continents the general structural features of the colonial economy. In Africa and Asia these features persisted from the mid-nineteenth century until independence was gained in the two decades following World War II. In most of Latin America, political colonialism had disappeared by the early nineteenth century. However, as noted above, the essential economic features of a colonial economy persisted after this period: "colonial dependency relationships do not end with the termination of formal legal control, but continue for as long as the situation of substantive inequality persists," a conclusion supported by the quantitative analysis of Birnberg and Resnick.[50] I therefore include nineteenth and early twentieth century Latin America under the rubric of the colonial dual economy.

The colonial experience reached into every aspect of the colonized nations. Land distribution and land tenure, food production, social and legal customs, political power, the national economic structure, regional and international economic relations were all altered, distorted, and set in rigid patterns that severely handicap the development of the ex-colonies to this day, creating what Frank has called "underdevelopment."[51] I will start with the internal economic structure that was the fundamental distortion.

Internal Economic Structure

The precolonial state was overwhelmingly agricultural. Village industry, handicrafts, and trade supplied the nonfood needs of this agricultural population. During the colonial period, however, the colonies became increasingly specialized in the production of export crops and minerals. In the process, resources were moved out of the "traditional" activities. These resources included both labor, which moved out of traditional rural industry and subsistence agriculture into export production, and actual capital in the form of taxes, rent, and profits.

As resources shifted and exports increased, so too did the demand for imported goods. The colonies became importers of capital goods such as agricultural tools and machinery; machinery to process agricultural goods (e.g., cotton gins); and iron, steel, and cement for construction. They also became importers of intermediate goods such as fuel and fertilizer, and of consumer goods, especially those demanded by the white managers and settlers and by the labor in the export enclave. Ironically, food supplies were often among the consumer goods needed for the low-paid labor force in the export enclave, since in many cases indigenous agriculture could no longer feed it.

The colonial governments' policies of taxation, investment, and export promotion were crucial in this process.[52] Government revenue (from taxes on the native population and on exports and imports) was spent on harbors, wharves, roads and railroads, storage facilities, and even scientific research that would facilitate the production and movement of exports. This was also crucial in making private foreign investment profitable. In countries that were colonies in fact, but not in name, government taxes and expenditures played a similar role in encouraging exports and making foreign investment more profitable. Here control was exerted through treaties (e.g., Thailand), through the fact that the "colony" was deeply in debt (e.g., Egypt), or through the foreign-owned companies that controlled the revenue-producing export enclave (as in Latin America). Behind all of this was also the power that derived from controlling the capital needed for building up the enclave.

This recasting of the colonial economy in a highly specialized export-producing mold created a fundamental structural distortion that has continued to thwart development: the divorce between the "modern" industrial sector of the economy (the export enclave) and the "traditional" agricultural sector. Figure 8-1 illustrates this structural distortion. Development was limited to the enclave. That part of it not in the hands of the peasants was adequately capitalized with modern machinery and infrastructure. Managerial and technical expertise was imported from the colonial power. As agricultural science developed, the export crops benefited from intensive scientific research, as the mines did from advances in engineering.

The export enclave needed one main commodity from the traditional sector, namely *cheap labor*, which depended ultimately on subsistence farming. In many cases the laborer was given access to a subsistence plot on which he could feed himself and his family, and his wage could therefore be much below subsistence level. In Latin America the power of the "patron" assured the labor supply or, as in Asia and the slave economies, the labor was imported where necessary. In Africa migrant labor, paid only enough to support the laborer himself, was often used. The laborer's family, and the laborer himself during slack times, were supported by subsistence agriculture. Lord Lugard once again saw Britain's interests quite clearly: "Since...the wants of the African peasant are few and are not necessities...there is...but little incentive to earn wages, and it may often happen that as soon as the small sum he requires has been obtained

THE COLONIAL DUAL ECONOMY

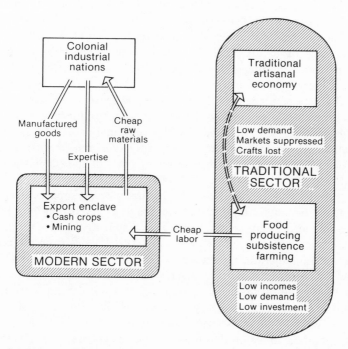

Figure 8-1 Diagram of the colonial dual economy

he will cease to work. The higher the wages in such a case the less the work."[53]

Lord Hailey formulated in the 1950s this simple economic argument in terms unclouded by sentiment:

> In Africa the organization of wage labour has proceeded on the assumption that except where farms are worked by "squatter" labour (resident labourers) the homes of the labourers will continue to be in native areas, and that responsibility toward them will be discharged if they are remunerated at rates suitable to a single man and are adequately fed and housed in their temporary place of employment.[54]

This underpayment of labor constituted a transfer of "surplus value," or profit, from the colony to the central power—it was in essence a source of cheap capital.

The traditional sector, although commercially unimportant, contained the great majority of the population. It remained predominantly agricultural, produced food for subsistence needs rather than the market, was undeveloped, and indeed in many instances grew less developed as it lost land, the most able-bodied men, local markets, and resources. Since it created virtually no commerical demand, it had virtually no influence over the nature of industrial development.

The lack of integration between these two sectors of the economy has had the most profound effect upon development. The initiation of economic development hinges on two complementary forces (Chapter 7). The first is a broadly based demand from a largely agrarian population for goods that can be made from locally available sources. The second is increasing productivity and savings arising from appropriate investment and the efficient use of the labor force in combination with technological innovation. The crucial *structural* development is the creation of many complementary *linkages* between different parts of the economy, based first in a dynamic agriculture. The export enclave suppressed precisely these crucial forces and processes. In the first place, it suppressed the demand from the mainly rural population for those goods that local handicrafts and cottage industry might have provided. In the absence of such demand, and in the face of cheap manufactured goods from the central power, local handicrafts withered and disappeared. In the second place, there was no investment outside the enclave; profits were exported or reinvested there. Improvements in technology did not diffuse outwards to agriculture or to cottage industry, and no schooling was available to improve the skills of the mass of the population.

It is important to realize that uneven allocation of resources sets in motion positive feedback mechanisms that create more inequality.[55] The uneven development of infrastructure, such as railroads and administrative centers, increases the future difference between favored and unfavored areas. The advantaged regions draw off labor, skills, entrepreneurship, markets, investments, and so on from less advantaged regions. The resulting geographic differences are critical, for it is extremely difficult later to reverse this process of differentiation in space. The Chinese, for example, have found this to be true in trying to redress the imbalance in the regional distribution of heavy industry that was left by economic colonialism (Chapters 3 and 7). To choose a very different example, Tanzania continues to suffer from the colonial concentration of East African administrative facilities in Kenya.[56]

The agricultural plantation has played such an important role in the colonial export enclave that it is worth appending to this section a brief account of its general features. Foreign-owned plantations producing tropical agricultural products for export were spread across the colonial map. They were, and still are, important on the Latin American mainland mainly in Brazil's northeast and in Guyana, British Honduras (now Belize), Honduras, Guatemala, Costa Rica, and Panama. They dominated, and still do, the Caribbean islands and much of Asia, especially Southeast Asia (Ceylon, Malaysia, Indonesia, and the Philippines). They were also important in India, where today they cover 10 to 20 percent of the cultivated land. In Africa they were important in some nations in Central and West Africa, in the Sahel, and in Tanganyika. In many of these areas the plantation has been the dominant economic social and political institution and often continues to be so.[57]

The plantations brought foreign capital and management and reordered the entire structure of the colony for the purpose of exporting raw materials. They commonly imported unskilled labor from other colonial areas. Plantations in Brazil and the Caribbean, whose native population was essentially wiped out, were manned by African slaves. Labor from China, India, and Sumatra was spread across the plantations of Asia.

From the beginning, the plantation was not only an economic institution but a "unit of authority with control over all aspects of the lives of people within its territory."[58] In some cases the peasant's plot of land was owned by the plantation and rent was paid either by growing the export crop on some of that land and contributing part of it to the estate, or by laboring on the estate for a fixed number of days. In other cases the peasant could not support a family on his subsistence plot and therefore needed to work on the plantation for a supplementary wage. Most fundamentally, the plantation outcompeted the peasant for land, especially for good land, and for the resources to exploit the land. In the use of that land the plantations thus directly suppressed further development of subsistence agriculture, frequently importing the food they needed. In some places (such as Indonesia) high taxes, the forced delivery of food to the estates, and restrictions on peasant growing of commercial crops "gave peasants neither the incentive nor the opportunity to become progressive modern farmers."[59]

Food Production

The colonial powers both directly and indirectly set back food production in their colonies (the Japanese colonies and Argentina and Uruguay are exceptions we have already noted). The Spanish in Latin America did this early and directly by their disruption of the indigenous population and its agriculture, and later through the *latifundio-minifundio* system. Such direct destruction was less important elsewhere and in later times, but other policies were equally suppressive. A stagnant agriculture was the inevitable consequence of the export enclave economy and its suppression of the "traditional" sector. Without investment, markets, innovation, or the stimulus of demand for its products, agriculture ceased developing. Plantations and estates frequently preempted the best land, and the wholesale movement of labor disrupted traditional agriculture. The infrastructure of roads, storage, and marketing facilities was designed for export crops and not for internal food distribution and marketing. Finally, in the European-settled colonies in America and Oceania, vast food-producing lands were being opened up and it often became easier for the colonial powers to feed the enclave labor with cheap imported food than to do anything for local agriculture. As we saw above, land policies introduced by the colonial powers exacerbated existing inequalities in the rural population and led to the food-suppressing distortions that we noted in Chapter 6.

The result was that food production virtually stagnated while these same colonies increased rapidly their production of export crops. Between 1880 and 1970 the nine major tropical export crops grew at exponential rates varying from 2.6 to 4.2 percent a year, the latter implying a doubling time of seventeen years, while food supply grew at less than 1 percent a year. The British in Ceylon, for example, turned much of the island into a vast tea estate, neglected local food production, and for the century up until independence in 1948 relied upon food imports.[60]

The history of food production in Africa is the worst among the LDCs. Amin has examined the West African experience.[61] As an example, he notes that in Senegal, which is not an extreme case, the colonial economy centered around groundnuts, grown to produce cheap vegetable oil for French consumers. Groundnut production covered ever larger areas of the country and grew extremely rapidly, increasing by eightfold in one thirty-year period alone. It received all of the agricultural research and infrastructure, yet the nation's food-producing potential lies in other parts of the country that were left untouched by agricultural development. As a result, food production barely increased in the colonial period.

Distorted land ownership and distribution have underlain the continuing stagnation of food-producing agriculture in the LDCs, yet is often not appreciated that *exclusive land ownership and its inheritance were largely nonexistent in Latin America, Asia, and Africa before the advent of the European powers.* Only in some areas of Africa have traditional (generally communal) patterns of ownership remained.

Social and Political Consequences: The Creation of an Elite

Grossly inequitable economic systems do not survive unless political power resides in the hands of those who reap the benefits of those systems. The explanation for the persistence of gross economic inequity in modern LDCs is thus to be found in the processes through which the colonial powers established a local economic and political elite in the colony. These elites were sometimes created *de nouveau*, as in Spanish America, or existing elites were given increased wealth and power, as in most of Asia and Africa. In general both processes occurred, particularly as an urban power elite emerged through the development of colonial trade and administration.

The processes that brought about increasing concentration of economic and political power were multifarious. They included changes in land ownership; the organization of export production; the distribution of legal and administrative posts; patterns of education; and the granting of trading, marketing, or other licenses. While the enclave was run by expatriates, there were always a select few of the indigenous people who one way and another became rich in the service of the colonial power: local rulers who helped smooth the governing process, traders, or large landowners.

Myrdal has pointed out that it was inevitable that the colonialists would ally themselves with already existing locally powerful and privileged groups, since these could be relied upon to have an equally deep interest in "law and order," which mainly implied maintaining and enhancing the economic, political, and social status quo.[62] However, in some cases new privileged elites had to be created to help with this task of "stabilizing" the colony.

Among the mechanisms aggravating existing inequalities, the colonial educational system was extremely important. In Asia and Africa only by accident—for example, through missionary teachings—were any of the masses of people exposed to formal education. The colonial era ended by leaving behind virtually universal illiteracy. By contrast, a small rich elite attended elementary schools and then secondary and even tertiary schools, where they learned "academic" subjects but virtually nothing that could be put to direct use in the development of their country. The most privileged of these elites might even finish their education in the universities of the colonial power.[63]

Such an educational system not only created a class with a deep ignorance of and disdain for the practical, it also maintained and widened the social, economic, and cultural chasm between the entrenched elite and the masses of people, and it created a class in which the greatest goal was to emulate the life style of its western masters; this last factor has remained extremely important in keeping the LDCs tied to importing goods from the rich nations. The concept of "development" that was internalized became development's outward manifestations as seen in the West: huge projects, fine administrative buildings, but above all, the development of modern urban industry.

The urban nature of the postcolonial elites has been crucial. It arose quite naturally from the fact that the colonial centers of power and economic wealth were the cities in which the administrative, commercial, and trading activities were carried out. It is true that the source of much of this wealth was rural—the plantations, mines, or rents from the land. But education occurred in the cities and drew there the children of rural landlords, and those families whose incomes did not arise from the cities frequently invested their rents and other rural income in city enterprises.[64]

External Economic Dependence

The atrophy and underdevelopment of the internal organs of industrial growth inevitably made the colonies dependent upon the industrial countries for modern capital goods—mining machinery, vehicles, storage facilities, etc.—as well as for the consumer goods demanded by the elite. Foreign exchange to buy these goods had to come either from exports to the developed countries or from capital loaned by them or invested by foreign companies.

The nature of the colony's exports tied it even more closely to the central power. Each colony was developed to produce a very small range of export goods and was therefore entirely dependent on the narrow market in the central power. One or a few firms controlled the purchase and marketing of these products and could greatly influence the price that the colony received.

These distortions extended also to broad geographic regions. The colonies in a particular region (and even sometimes in different regions) were developed to produce the same or similar exports. Sugar was produced throughout the Caribbean, in Brazil, the Philippines, and some Pacific islands; rubber was grown in Malaysia, Indochina, Indonesia, India, Ceylon, and Brazil; tea and coffee were grown in Latin America, Africa, and India; and so on. This duplication meant that several sources were always available to the central power and the colonies were thus forced to compete with each other to produce cheaply the raw materials needed by the "center." It also meant that the colonies in a region could not cash in on their innate differences to develop complementary products that could lead to trade among themselves. Regional trade languished in areas where it once had flourished, and so therefore did the industry that had made that trade possible and had been stimulated by it. This occurred in Latin America and to some extent in Africa, but the effect was more serious in populous and previously vigorous trading regions such as India and China. The colonialists took over existing regional trade and changed its nature to the export of raw materials and the import of manufactured goods.

The colonies were thus caught up in an international economic system from which they could not escape. Their role in the international division of labor that developed in the nineteenth century was to produce cheap raw materials for the industries of the developed nations while, in turn, the labor in these latter nations moved from agriculture into industry.[65] The other side of this coin was the colonies' purchase of manufactured goods from the developed nations. The result was a stronger integration between the export enclave and the central powers than between the enclave and the rest of the colony (figure 8-1).

Each colony was sent irrevocably down a narrow developmental cul-de-sac. The focus was external, and the colony was without the means to develop appropriate internal economic structures. Even if it had wanted to break the dependence, it was powerless to do so, since it had no control over the important processes in the economic exchange. The colonial nations had a monopoly over capital, and they controlled trade, transportation, and markets as well as production. As a consequence they greatly influenced prices and the terms of trade (i.e., the amount of the colony's exports required to buy a given amount of imports). They even controlled the labor supply and the wage rate in the colony. The colony was bound, through its colonial position and also through the favored position of its dependent elite, to this system of controlled exploitation: "Suspended... between the two poles of plantation and mine, the (colonies) grew both highly vulnerable to outside economic influences and excessively dependent on them."[66]

Two events in the early twentieth century, World War I and the Great Depression, underlined the grave consequences of dependence. The economy of the colony, including its ability to import, depended on export earnings. Demand for colonial exports was determined by government policies in the developed nations and by real incomes and prices there. During World War I those colonies dependent on Great Britain and Germany suffered large export losses and consequently had their imports cut severely. The British, in fact, were able to shift part of the costs of the war onto their colonies by this means.[67]

By contrast, colonies dependent on U.S. markets did not suffer. However, during the Great Depression when real incomes fell the most in the United States, developing countries dependent on trade with this country suffered the most. Between 1929 and 1933 the value of world trade fell by half. This had the most catastrophic effect on Latin America, since that region was the most fully integrated into the world economy.[68] In addition to losing exports, Latin American countries could no longer pay the interest on their debts, and this made it even more difficult for them to get loans to pay for the imports they needed in order to industrialize.

Colonialism is often characterized primarily as a process of exploitation, and indeed it has been, both in the evacuation of natural resources and in the export of cheap goods based on the grossly underpaid labor of the colonial peoples. But what is often not appreciated is the fact that the colonial powers left behind nations whose economic, political, and social structures have been so fundamentally distorted that they tend to be incapable of recovering from their history of exploitation. They are incapable of proceeding with the task of real development without radically altering these structures, and yet the structures themselves render such alteration extremely difficult because power is held by those who gain from the distortions.

A few remarks are needed to offset this wholesale indictment of colonialism. It would be foolish to contend that colonialism was a disaster for the colonies unrelieved by positive or well-intentioned acts. Indeed, although economic (and sometimes political) gain was always the mainspring of colonialism, many of those actively involved had the highest ideals and motives. Particularly among British colonial officers, empire was seen as a moral and civilizing force. The men involved had high standards of honesty, justice, and service; and they were convinced that colonialism was truly mutually beneficial to the ruled and the rulers.[69] Moreover, colonialism also introduced some modern technology to the colonies. For example, it created roads, railways, and irrigation in those parts of the colonies that were concerned with exports.

Nor can it be claimed that before colonialism Africa, Asia, and Latin America were idylls of peace and justice; clearly they were not (nor was Europe for that matter). Colonialism sometimes broke down feudal arangements that would have slowed development and on some occasions it introduced a less arbitrary and fierce system of justice.

On balance, however, colonialism was clearly a negative force in the lives of the colonies. It tended to accentuate and solidify existing inequities and to create new forms of inequality. It also left behind rigid and inappropriate economic and political structures that have not yielded to change without revolution.

9

THE MODERN DUAL ECONOMY

The modern dual economies of the LDCs are best understood as extensions and modifications of the colonial dual economies. For the most part, the basic structural distortions of colonialism remain, and the traditional agricultural economy persists as an economic backwater. The modern sector is still cut off from the traditional economy and is still geared to the provision of goods for an elite—albeit an indigenous rather than an expatriate elite, and one that has in some cases grown quite large. The modern economies have moved varying distances down the road of industrialization, so that some goods that were once imported are made or assembled locally. Nonetheless, economic dependence upon the "central" developed economies remains because the LDCs need markets, capital, and technology. The direct political power of the central nations has declined but has certainly not disappeared, and it has been partially replaced by the more subtle power of economic dependence. The international corporation has come to play a large and growing role as a major conduit of that economic power.

There have been important differences in the postcolonial history of the developing nations. As discussed in Chapter 8, Latin American nations generally have been politically, although not economically, independent for a century and a half or more. The Latin American continent also has the highest per capita income of the developing world and is the most highly urbanized and industrialized. By contrast, Asia's postcolonial period dates from the late 1940s. Asian nations generally are less industrialized than Latin American countries, and Asia is less urban. India is something of an exception in ex-colonial Asia in the degree to which it has developed a capital goods industry (Chapter 7).

African countries are only now emerging from colonial conditions, most of them having been independent for only fifteen to twenty-five years. They are still mainly export-enclave economies, with rather little industry. In addition, in West and Sub-Saharan Africa in particular, they suffer from arbitrary and economically inappropriate political boundaries left by the departed colonial administrators.

A special class of developing countries—those owning large amounts of relatively scarce and expensive commodities—has emerged. Its main representatives are the richest oil-exporting (OPEC) nations. This class of nations is anomalous in that it has become suddenly richer without reaching an equivalent level of development. Although the richer OPEC countries are critically important in world trade and economic growth, their condition is so special that they are excluded from the general discussion of the condition of LDCs in this chapter.

The two main features that characterized the colonial dual economy remain in the modern dual economy. These are: (1) a fundamental schism between the "modern" urban sector of the economy, and the stagnant, mainly rural, "traditional" sector where the majority of the population maintains a marginal existence; (2) a basically outward orientation created by the need to promote exports as a major source of foreign exchange. This foreign exchange is needed to buy the imports required for urban consumption and industrialization and to service debts accumulated for the same purpose. Let us deal with these two main features in turn.

INTERNAL STRUCTURE OF THE MODERN DUAL ECONOMY

The Economic and Power Elite

The crucially important process that has maintained the distortions of the dual economy has been the transfer of economic and political power after independence. With a few notable exceptions, power has been inherited or grasped by the elite group that was entrenched in colonial days. This group includes large landowners (who frequently live in the city or have urban economic interests); other property owners; industrialists and traders; professionals such as bankers, business executives, technocrats, and higher bureaucrats; and military and religious leaders. Where shifts of power within this group have occurred, they have been away from landowners and toward the urban group. Kuznets shows that for the most part the LDCs are governed by such small, urban, western-educated, authoritarian elites, which are almost wholly lacking in public support and generally require police and military support to maintain their position.[1]

The persistence—indeed, the intensification—of the biases and distortions in the LDCs can be attributed largely to policies pursued by this elite. Their consistent aim has been the rapid development of urban industry. Such a strategy is not only in their own immediate economic interests; it has been mistakenly but genuinely thought of as an application of the paradigm of western development.[2] While this strategy is at first sight very different from that pursued by the colonial nations in their colonies, it is based on essentially the same structure, and involves much the same processes as were developed in colonial times.

The West has often played a strong part, not only in creating such elites, but in maintaining them in power. On some occasions (as in Iran, Laos, the Philippines, Vietnam, Zaire, Chile, Guatemala, the Dominican Republic, Bolivia, and Peru) this has amounted to direct military incursions or covert but violent interference. In other places more indirect methods suffice—military aid, economic aid, bribery, and the like. Private support in the form of investment by western enterprises has similarly helped, expanding after rightist takeovers and waning when leftist regimes have come to power.[3] Indeed, support for these elites is a quite natural consequence of the industrial nations' desire to do business:

> When the political stability provided by colonialism had disappeared, it was only natural that the rich Western countries should feel a special sympathy for such a newly independent country where the rule was tightly kept by a conservative regime that preserved the social, economic, and political power situation inherited from colonial times.
> That business interests in the West would be more willing to invest in such a country was equally natural. It was also natural that they preferred to deal with the rich and mighty there. That this, in turn, strengthened those groups at home is highly self-evident.[4]

We turn now to the details of the internal economic structure. As always, we run the risk that in characterizing and classifying a huge array of very different countries, we will oversimplify and blur important differences. Nevertheless we will not go too far wrong in recognizing two basic types of LDCs: export enclave and import substitution economies. (From these two classes we should exclude China, Taiwan, and South Korea, which have in large part avoided the dual economy trap.)

The Modern Export Enclave Economy

Here the major "modern" economic activity is the production of exports to earn foreign exchange. These exports are mainly cash crops and mining products, but in some cases new light industry produces simple manufactured goods for export. There is a negligible amount of manufacturing of modern goods for local needs, so foreign exchange is spent on importing manufactured consumer and capital goods from the industrial nations.[5] As noted in Chapter 7, a large fraction of the goods imported are inappropriate to the needs of the majority of the population. The consumer goods tend to be luxury goods (in the context of a poor country), and the capital goods tend to be large scale, capital intensive, and labor displacing.

This type of economy is typical of Africa and of some Asian countries (e.g., Bangladesh, Burma, Sri Lanka). In the western hemisphere it is epitomized by the Caribbean nations, which are dominated by plantations producing sugar and other tropical crops for export. The majority of the poorest, or "Fourth World," nations are export enclave economies, although there are important exceptions such as India (see appendix C).

The main change from colonial times is that export enclave economies are now run for the benefit of a local elite rather than for the colonial power. Throughout Africa, for example, a small group—government officials, managerial personnel in large international firms, some wealthy cash crop farmers, and traders—comprising 7 to 10 percent of the population has accrued almost all of the increase in income and wealth that has resulted from the narrow expansion of the export enclave.[6]

The increasing skew in incomes, and hence in demand, has aggravated the dualism of these economies (Chapter 7). This process has been reinforced by the continuation of lopsided investment in the export enclave and in the inappropriate, if tiny, manufacturing sector. The internal distortions are familiar. As in colonial times, low wages, low investment, and stagnant technology all suppress agricultural production and therefore the demand for the products of handicraft and other rural industries (figure 8-1). The traditional sector lies largely outside the monetary economy and functions merely as a source of cheap labor, plus perhaps some capital via landlords' rents and profits. The foci of development, the potential nodes of integration between agriculture for food and rural and semi-rural industry, remain underdeveloped (Chapter 7). By contrast, members of the new elite demand expensive housing, automobiles, televisions, electrical appliances etc., so the colonial pattern of importing manufactured goods continues. What modern manufacturing exists is also heavily dependent on imported parts and materials, is capital intensive, and is concentrated in urban areas.[7]

The export economy is largely cut off from the traditional sector except for its need for cheap labor. Economic links are between the enclave, the urban elite, and the developed nations. This is particularly well exemplified by economies dominated by plantations, especially those in the Caribbean. In the Caribbean plantation economies, most arable land is devoted to cash crops, and these plantations yield very few linkages internally—i.e., they do not create ancillary employment and production. Beckford has shown how vertical integration in the foreign corporations that run the plantations accentuates this tendency. Rural workers in these plantation economies cannot even grow enough food to feed themselves and are fed and clothed by imports that, ironically, create employment in the developed nations. This type of problem is growing in Latin America and Sub-Saharan Africa with the rapid expansion there of agribusiness production for export of livestock, feed for livestock, vegetables, and horticulture.[8]

The plantation also remains an important aspect of underdevelopment today in areas beyond the Caribbean. There are 24 million hectares of plantation land in Sri Lanka, India, Indonesia, and Malaysia; there are 14 million hectares in Colombia, Costa Rica, Ecuador, and Peru; in Brazil, Malaysia, Mauritius, Sri Lanka, and the Ivory Coast over half of the cultivated land is in plantations.[9]

The internal structure of the export enclave economy thus remains little changed from colonial days (figure 8-1). Only the cast of characters in the leading roles is different.

Import Substitution Economies

Many export enclave economies have gradually evolved into import substitution economies, and indeed there is no hard-and-fast dividing line along this continuum. Import substitution (I.S.) is the process whereby a range of manufactured goods that previously were imported come to be manufactured locally. They may be manufactured from basic raw materials or, commonly, assembled from imported components, as is the case for automobiles in Malaysia. Typically, I.S. has replaced imports of consumer goods such as radios and electrical appliances. However, there has also been some substitution of previously imported intermediate goods, such as fertilizers, and of producer goods. Brazil's tractor industry, discussed in Chapter 7, is an example of the latter.

The new manufacturing industry may be locally owned or, more commonly, it may be a branch or subsidiary of an international firm, in which case it is likely to be partly or wholly owned by that firm. I.S. requires the growth of an industrial plant, and in general these capital goods must still be imported.

From the 1950s and onward, import substitution was seen by leaders of the LDCs as providing simultaneously the beginnings of industrialization and a way of replacing imported goods with domestic goods, thereby saving foreign exchange and reducing dependence on the developed countries. In recent years, however, many LDCs have become disillusioned with I.S., for reasons that we will discuss. These countries are now looking for alternative and additional routes to industrialization. However, I.S. has been the common strategy until now, and it accounts for the present economic structure of the more industrialized LDCs; thus we will examine it in some detail. It is most prevalent in Latin America, but is also well advanced in Asian countries such as India, Indonesia, Pakistan, and the Philippines.

The broad structural consequences of I.S. can be seen in figure 9-1. Most obviously, there has been an increase in the size of the modern industrial manufacturing sector, which is typified by large capital-intensive family firms, corporations, and state enterprises. This increase has been

THE MODERN DUAL ECONOMY

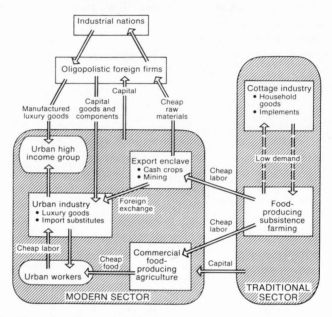

Figure 9-1 Diagram of the modern dual economy

associated with a burgeoning of urban populations and the establishment of a sizable new and relatively privileged socio-economic class, which shares certain broad interests with the elite. The new class (the "urban workers" of figure 9-1) is employed in modern industry, business, and government and is made up of skilled manual laborers, factory workers, and the broad class of white collar workers (table 9-1). These groups tend to have relatively secure employment, they earn relatively high wages compared with the national average (but much lower than in the developed countries), and they have relatively advanced education. (The enlarged privileged class, consisting of the traditional elite plus workers in the modern sector, will be referred to hereafter as the urban high-income group).

The need remains, however, to keep the total urban wage bill as low as possible, and cheap food for the urban work force is still a high priority. In the modern dual economy this cheap food is likely to be produced mainly on large commercial farms, with the "traditional" sector supplying cheap labor on these farms (Chapter 6). Thus, although the mechanisms of exploitation are more complex, the basic suppression of wages, and hence of development, in the traditional sector remains.

Industrialization has also stimulated the enormous growth of a second class of urban dwellers, who make up the "informal" sector (not shown in figure 9-1). People in the informal sector are self-employed, work in small labor-intensive family businesses, carry out various illicit activities, or are simply unemployed (table 9-1). Some 10 to 15 percent are formally unemployed and another 15 percent may be grossly underemployed.[10] Employment in this sector is highly uncertain, wages are low, and the average level of education is low. It is difficult to move from the informal to the modern sector because entry is generally restricted along educational, racial, or more subtle social lines.

Ironically, the enormous growth of this informal sector has largely been caused by urban-rural migration in response to the large difference in wages between the modern sector and the countryside. A disproportionate number of these migrants are young people aged fifteen to twenty-four, and unemployment in this age group is about double the general rate in the urban areas of most LDCs.[11] Although members of the informal sector are knocking at the door of the modern sector, their economic interests truly lie with the suppressed rural population, since the capital-intensive strategy that denies resources to the countryside also denies productive employment to the informal sector.

Import substitution partially achieved some of its goals. Some imports have been replaced, urban industry has been expanded, and in some cases rapid economic growth has ensued for varying lengths of time. But I.S. has had several major negative effects.[12] In the first place, there has been a large increase in the need for imported intermediate and capital goods

Table 9-1. Structure of the urban work force in Ecuador around 1970

	Urban Labor Force (%)
A. *Modern sector*	
1. Property owners, managers, professional classes; high political, military, and religious officials	10
2. White-collar workers, skilled laborers, factory employees	30
Subtotal	40
B. *Informal sector*	
1. Small firms and repair shops, self-employed persons in petty services, craftsmen, casual laborers, servants, thieves, prostitutes, smugglers	50
2. Unemployed	10
Subtotal	60

Source: Keith Griffin, *Land Concentration and Rural Poverty* (New York: Holmes and Meier, 1976), p. 180.

and, sometimes, for the components that go into the finished article. I.S. has therefore generally worsened, rather than improved, the LDC balance of payments and debt situation. Because the major beneficiaries have been the foreign companies who established the new industrial plants, there has been a net flow of capital abroad in the form of purchases from the parent company, profits, royalties, and the like (see the section below on foreign investment). At the same time, emphasis on I.S. has been associated with neglect of agriculture, since industry has soaked up available investment and has required government subsidies in the form of incentives and protective tariffs on competing, and cheaper, foreign goods. Since the urban demand for food has been increasing rapidly, the consequent agricultural stagnation has caused widespread increases in food imports. Thus, I.S. has increased rather than reduced the dependency of LDCs on exports.

In the second place, I.S. has often been a costly way of obtaining the goods produced. It frequently requires protective tariffs against manufactured goods from abroad, which the domestic industry cannot compete with. The results are that consumers often pay more, sometimes for an inferior article, while resources have been attracted to inefficient industry by such subsidies. This has benefited the industrialists and workers directly involved but has taken scarce capital away from more appropriate investments.

Thirdly, I.S. has tended to run out of steam quite rapidly, leading to industrial and economic stagnation. This has been caused by the nature of the goods being sold, by the continued need for exports, and by the high costs of industry's products. The market for I.S. goods is the urban high-income group, and by its nature this minority is a very limited market in LDCs. It is also a market that grows slowly, partly because incomes have grown quite slowly, and partly because that growth has been accompanied by increasing inequality of income: since the majority of the population is excluded from the benefits of growth, mass markets do not develop. This is particularly the case when, even within the "modern" sector, the wages of the workers do not rise as rapidly as total income is rising. This is well illustrated by Brazil. Within the Brazilian manufacturing sector between 1955 and 1965, the income of wage earners increased by only 1.3 percent a year, while their productivity rose by 5.2 percent a year.[13] (More recently the ratio between the growth of incomes and of productivity was 1:2.) Thus the tremendous skew in incomes, both nationally and within the modern sector, and its consistent tendency to become worse, shuts down the very demand that is needed to maintain growth.

I.S. also constrains industrial growth by inhibiting the creation of forward "linkages" (see Chapter 7). By operating inefficiently behind protective barriers, the local industry produces high-priced goods. If these goods serve as inputs for other industry, that other industry is stifled. (Chapter 6 discussed as a prime example, albeit outside of industry, the way high fertilizer prices suppress agricultural growth.) Since many I.S. inputs are purchased from abroad, backward linkages are also suppressed.

Limits to growth also arise, paradoxically, from import substitution's appetite for more imports. The industrial plant needed to produce the substituted goods usually has to be imported. As I.S. works "backward" and begins to substitute for imported intermediate and capital goods, the capital intensity of industry increases, requiring yet more capital imports. In addition, such large-scale industry requires ever larger and well-organized domestic markets if it is to remain efficient, and these markets do not exist in most LDCs. (We discussed this problem in India in Chapter 7.) The very policies that stimulate I.S. have inhibited export production, making it more difficult for LDCs to pay for the imports needed for industrial expansion.[14]

The severe limits set to growth through import substitution have become apparent quite rapidly. They have been particularly evident in Latin America. Brazil's high growth rate for a decade provided the West with one of its favorite exemplars of capitalist-style development. Yet in spite of the influx of foreign investment, the creation of a capital goods industry, and the country's enormous natural wealth and entrepreneurial ability, the growth rate slowed down in the mid-1970s and is likely to remain low for some time. This situation can be maintained in the face of great rural poverty, high birth rates, and increasing unemployment only by strict authoritarianism. Similar limits are also quite evident in developing countries that have experienced much less growth than Brazil. The case of the Philippines is an example from Asia that is discussed by Ranis.[15]

Fourthly, and most seriously, import substitution has accentuated the internal structural distortions in the dual economy. Prices and tax and investment policies have favored urban industry and have suppressed agriculture in particular and the rural economy in general,[16] through the mechanisms discussed in Chapter 6 and 7. Lack of demand from the agricultural population has prevented development of rural industry and has deepened the chasm between the "modern" and "traditional" sectors and between town and countryside (figure 9-1). Indeed, under these policies the two sectors are in competition, for resources invested in agriculture or rural enterprises are resources taken way from urban industry.

Import substitution, especially through foreign companies, has increased the trend toward inappropriate capital-intensive development. In many instances government subsidies and incentives actively encourage capital-intensive technology. These incentives include subsidized credit, tax allowances for accelerated depreciation, tax "holidays," overvalued exchange rates, and other devices, all directed to large-scale modern industry. At the same time, traditional, small-scale, labor-intensive enterprises have virtually no access to institutional credit (in the same way that small farmers do not). The western-type consumer goods that are produced use largely imported, western, and therefore capital-intensive technology. As a result, I.S. has done very little to solve the growing problem of unemployment and has generated little in the way of additional linkages.[17]

Import substitution has also greatly increased income inequality.[18] It has done this both by yielding greater returns to the owners of capital than to workers, as we saw above for Brazil, and by increasing the inequality between those employed in the modern urban sector and those who are not. It has even been suggested that the poorest segment in the LDCs has generally suffered a decrease in *absolute* income, although this contention has been disputed. The figures are in any case stark. For example, during two decades of economic development in India, the proportion of Indians living below a fixed and very low poverty line did not decrease and may have increased: in the mid-1950s over half were impoverished; in the early 1960s about 40 percent were impoverished; in 1967/68 there was a peak of 57 percent below the poverty line, and the fraction thereafter declined somewhat. There has certainly been an increase in absolute poverty in some areas. The fraction of the rural population in poverty in Bangladesh increased in both the 1960s and 1970s, and the average real wage in agriculture fell by half in this period. Within India, in the State of Bihar, the real income of the rural population declined in the 1960s. Between 1961 and 1971 the proportion of the rural population below the poverty line increased from half (21 million) to 59 percent (30 million).[19]

The increase in inequality between town and countryside has been particularly serious in view of the need for a dynamic agriculture (Chapter 7). Lipton's analyses suggest that the real difference in income between urban and rural populations is larger than official data indicate. Urban incomes are likely to be about three times, perhaps even six times, higher than rural incomes, and there is clear evidence that the gap is increasing in a wide range of countries.[20] The increasing skew in income further distorts the pattern of demand for consumer and producer goods, making it more difficult yet to establish a balanced and integrated pattern of development.

It would be quite wrong, incidentally, to assume that such strong inequality, and increasing inequality, are inevitable features of early development. On the contrary, Lipton has shown that urban-rural inequality was much less in European countries at a comparable stage in development and that, after a brief temporary increase in poverty, the degree of inequality declined as development proceeded.[21]

Finally, import substitution has generally been associated with penetration of LDC manufacturing by foreign corporations. We will examine the consequences of this intrusion in some detail in the next section, but it should be noted here that it has tended to exacerbate the problems of I.S. It has stimulated the capital-intensive development, the use of inappropriate technology, the production of nonessential consumer goods, and dependence on the developed nations. It also has reinforced the outward orientation of the economy.[22]

It is worth looking at a couple of examples of how growth through urban industrialization has been growth without justice and with little real development. I have already described this for India in Chapter 7; the case of Pakistan is also illustrative.[23] Import substitution became official Pakistan development policy in 1948. Development was equated with economic growth and with industrialization, and the key was thought to be savings and physical investment. The government tried to ensure, through its economic policies, that a few large farmers, industrialists, and capitalists would save and invest. Even in the late 1950s and early 1960s, issues such as unemployment, absolute poverty, and income distribution were regarded as secondary to aggregate growth. In all of this, of course, Pakistan was quite typical.

The 1950s in Pakistan were not a success. GNP grew more slowly than population. But in the 1960s the strategy succeeded, by its own standards, when GNP increased by over 5 percent a year and exports grew at 8 percent a year. What was the result? Not development, certainly. Most of the increase in income accrued to a tiny fraction of the population. Furthermore, economic wealth and control over the economy had become even more dramatically concentrated. In 1968 Mahbub ul Haq, then Chief Economist of the National Planning Commission, pointed to "the growing concentration of industrial income and wealth in the hands of only 22 family groups...(who) controlled...about two-thirds of the industrial assets, 80% of banking, and 70% of insurance in Pakistan."[24] Economic growth had been accompanied by increasing unemployment, a worsening income distribution, increased absolute poverty, worsening social services, and a decline of about one-third in the real wages of even industrial workers, to say nothing of the drastic declines in the countryside. West Pakistan has always fared better than East Pakistan (now Bangladesh), but in the 1960s the disparity in per capita income between East and West Pakistan almost doubled.

These increasing distortions reached into every aspect of the economy. Between 1958 and 1968 Pakistan imported or assembled $300 million worth of private automobiles but only $20 million worth of public buses. In the same period 80 to 90 percent of private construction was, by LDC standards, luxury housing. Human resources were equally neglected. Education emphasized that hangover from colonialism, liberal education for a select few. In 1950, 18 percent of the population was literate; by 1970 the figure was 15 percent. While China was busily bringing about a revolution in health care by creating a vast network of paramedics, Pakistan *removed* intermediate levels of medical training and instead produced each year 800 highly trained doctors, 500 of whom looked for employment abroad and almost none of whom served the rural population.

Pakistan's experience has been repeated over the last two decades throughout Asia and Latin America, except that many nations never achieved Pakistan's aggregate growth rate. Some summary figures for Latin America give an idea of the tremendous inequalities that persist on the continent where economic growth has been greatest. In 1974 average per capita income on the continent was almost $900. Yet, of the roughly 300 million population, 100 million had a per capita income of about $70, and half of the population lived on $120 per year, or less. The new consumerism is restricted to a tiny fraction of the population: the top 10 percent eat 41 percent of the meat and get 44 percent of the clothes, 85 percent of the motor vehicles, 74 percent of the furniture, and half of the electrical appliances. The bottom half gets 12 percent of the meat, 13 percent of the clothes, 1 percent of the motor vehicles, 5 percent of the furniture, and 5 percent of the electrical appliances.[25]

Essentially, what the process of import substitution has achieved, apart from increasing the standard of living of an already privileged minority and slightly enlarging that minority, is the intensification and reinforcement of the structural distortions that already existed. The economy is still geared to the production of nonessential goods, which will not bring economic welfare to the mass of the population and will not allow them to participate in growth through productive employment. The pattern of urban industrialization has thus added to the forces of dualism that we saw operating in the agricultural setting in Chapters 6 and 7. Industrial development has tended to create "oases of growth in a desert of stagnation" because it does not stimulate growth in the rural sector or create increasing employment there:

> If the developing country believes that it is developing because of a geographical shift in the location of (industrial) plants to within its own boundaries, this merely shows that the planners and politicians, no less than the economists, have become the slaves of geography.... The industrial sector of the poor countries is really a periphery of the metropolitan industrial economies, critically dependent on them for the technology it uses.[26]

In summary, the fundamental problem with import substitution is that, in supplying the demand of a privileged minority, it transfers to the LDCs inappropriate products and means of production. It subverts real development because it neither provides the consumer goods that would satisfy the basic human needs of the mass of the population nor does it supply the tools, equipment, and infrastructure that would unleash their potential productivity.

RELATIONS WITH THE RICH NATIONS

So far we have concentrated on the internal distortions of the developing nations. But the plight of the LDCs and the immense difficulties they face cannot be understood without understanding also their place in the international economic system. That system not only holds the LDCs in a disadvantaged position, it also helps maintain the internal distortions we have been discussing.

International Inequality and Dependence

There are two crucial and interrelated features of the relationship between the rich and poor countries. First, the massive inequality between the two places the poor nations at a perennial disadvantage. Second, the poor countries are dependent upon the rich countries. The gross features of international inequality are portrayed in table 9-2. Notice that the per capita income of the rich nations is growing much faster than that of the poor, so that the differences are increasing. In 1960 the average per capita income in the rich nations was almost eleven times that in the LDCs and the absolute gap was over $1,200. By 1975 there was a twelvefold difference and the absolute gap was over $5,000. By then, the average income in the rich nations was forty times that of the 1.2 billion people in the poorest LDCs.

Table 9-2. International inequality in 1971

	Population (millions)	Population as percentage of world population	Per capita GNP ($)	Growth rate of per capita GNP (%)	Literacy (%)
Poorest 40 countries	1,005.9	26	96	1.3	20.5
Other LDCs	1,408.5	37	501	2.5	52.7
OPEC[a] countries	257.6	7	1,143	5.4	31.6
Developed countries	1,082.0	28	2,297	4.6	90.7

Source: Hans W. Singer and Javed A. Ansari, *Rich and Poor Countries* (London: Allen and Unwin, 1977), p. 16.

[a]Abu Dhabi, Algeria, Ecuador, Indonesia, Iran, Iraq, Kuwait, Libya, Nigeria, Qatar, Saudi Arabia, Venezuela. (Gabon is an associated member of OPEC.)

Even under optimistic projections of future growth, by 1990 that figure will be forty-six. By 1990, under this projection, the average annual per capita income in the rich nations will be almost thirteen times greater than that in the LDCs as a whole, and the absolute difference (in 1975 dollars) will be almost $10,000.[27]

The rapid growth of income in OPEC countries is pulling some of them out of the "poor" category. Whether this flood of capital will be used over the next twenty or thirty years to transform the economic structure of these countries, so that they can create sustained development for the benefit of their entire population, is another matter. What it is certainly doing is making development for the poorest nations more difficult. Non-OPEC developing countries will need to spend more than 20 percent of their export earnings to import oil over the next few years. On the other hand, about half of the extra earnings of the OPEC countries is being invested in the developed nations, thus effecting a transfer of capital from the capital-poor to the capital-rich nations.[28]

International inequality is so marked that it is generally not appreciated that its origin is quite recent. Before 1850 only Britain had shown much sign of economic growth and development. The world economy before then was essentially stationary, and before the nineteenth century the now-developed and the now-underdeveloped nations looked rather similar. They were largely agricultural, and "industry" consisted of handicrafts. By 1850 per capita income in the "rich" nations was only 70 percent higher than that of the poor; the difference was almost 1,000 percent by 1960. Thus the current economic differences between rich and poor countries have arisen mainly in the last century and a quarter.[29]

These differences are not merely of the gross quantitative type shown in table 9-2. The qualitative differences are equally important. Although agricultural output has risen by four- or fivefold in the rich nations since 1850, industrial output has increased fortyfold, and the output of capital goods (as distinct from consumer goods) has increased a hundredfold.[30]

Most important of all is the difference in levels of technology.* The development of highly sophisticated production technology and the ability to develop ever more sophisticated technology has occurred almost solely in the developed countries. Some 98 to 99 percent of world expenditure on research and development occurs within the rich nations. Thus the poor countries—if they wish to produce goods that require modern technical "know-how"—must import it, and they do not have the technical and educational sophistication to internalize that knowledge and create their

---

*Recall from Chapter 7 that technical innovation is the mainspring of economic growth because it leads to increases in productivity—that is, it lowers the cost of producing a given good.

own self-sustaining technology. The latter aspect is crucial, for while the poor nations are desperately scraping together the capital to import modern technology, the rich nations are busily rendering it obsolete and less efficient.

The result of this process is that the goods produced by the rich nations become cheaper than those produced by the LDCs. This further weakens the position of the LDCs in the international market, tends to drive up LDC imports from the rich nations, inhibits local industry, and creates the need to import more technology. The "technology gap" is thus self-regenerating, and there is little hope that the poor nations can produce soon an analogous technology-generating establishment to compete with that of the rich nations.

The developed nations thus have two commodities that the LDCs need: large amounts of capital to create industry, and advanced technology. It is these needs that create the dependence of the poor on the rich nations.

This dependence, however, is greater than it need be. It is *in large part the result of active choice by the poor nations.* Their ruling elites have chosen "modern" consumption goods and therefore have decided to import "modern" technology. It must be admitted, however, that this choice has not been entirely free. Many of these elites have owed, and still owe, their positions at least in part to western actions or western favor. Having become caught up in the international economic system, they require continued support from western nations and financial institutions. There has therefore been pressure on the elite to conform with western preferences.[31] Nevertheless, the elites could have chosen an inward-looking strategy emphasizing the interaction between agriculture and industry. Such a strategy creates its own capital and stimulates the development of technology that is suited to the resources of the poor countries and that at the same time leads to the internalization of the ability to innovate (Chapter 7). While this would not have removed the need to deal with the industrial world, it would have greatly reduced it.

The asymmetry between the rich and poor nations is greatly accentuated by the fact that *the poor countries need the rich ones more than the latter need the former,* so that the balance of bargaining power virtually always lies with the developed countries. This is amply illustrated by the pattern of world trade.

The LDCs, whether export enclave or semi-industrialized, are dependent on imports. As we shall see later, this dependence has also created a large foreign debt. The LDCs are therefore committed to exporting, and to exporting ever-increasing amounts, both to buy imports and to service their debts. By 1970 exports were, on average, 15 percent of the gross domestic product (GDP) of the non-Communist LDCs, and in some cases the proportion was 30 percent. (By contrast, the now-rich nations were never heavily dependent upon exports during their crucial early period of development, when exports probably represented 3 to 5 percent of the western nations' GDPs.)[32]

The poor nations are not only dependent upon exports, they depend upon exports to the western developed nations (table 9-3). By 1970, 71 percent of their exports went to the West and only 21 percent went to other LDCs. Since the economies of the developing nations in a region tend to be similar rather than complementary, there is little opportunity for trade even among poor nations in a given region. For example, inter-African trade accounts for less than 10 percent of all African trade.[33]

The dependence of individual LDCs upon the developed countries is even greater than these aggregate data suggest, since most of them rely on a very few products for most of their export earnings, many of them share this dependence, and they are therefore extremely vulnerable to falling or fluctuating prices. About half of the LDCs earn over half of their export earnings from a single primary commodity such as coffee, sugar, cocoa, or copper. About three-quarters of them earn 60 percent or more from three or fewer primary products. A few examples will suffice. Cuba and certain other Caribbean islands are almost totally dependent upon sugar exports.

Table 9-3. World trade: Origin and destination of exports

Exports from:		Exports to: Developed market[a] economies	Non-OPEC market[a] LDCs	OPEC nations	Communist nations
Developed market[a]	1960	69	25		4
economies	1970	77	16	3	4
	1978	71	15	9	5
Non-OPEC	1960	72[b]	22[b]		4[b]
market[a] LDCs	1970	71	19	2	8
	1978	68	19	7	6
OPEC nations	1960	—	—	—	—
	1970	80	17	1	2
	1978	76	21	1	2
Communist	1960	19	—	—	72
nations	1970	24	14	2	61
	1978	27	13	4	56

Sources: United Nations, *Monthly Bulletin of Statistics* 19, no. 3 (1965): special table E; 30, no. 8 (1976): special table C; 33, no. 6 (1979): special table C.

Note: Each number is the percentage of the exports from a given group of nations that goes to nations in the specified group.

[a]Market economies are non-Communist countries.

[b]Includes OPEC exports in 1960.

In Africa, copper supplies 90 percent of Zambia's foreign earnings and three-quarters of Zaire's. Ghana gets two-thirds of its foreign earnings from cocoa, Chad three-quarters from cotton, Uganda three-quarters from coffee and cotton, Malawi three-fifths from tobacco and tea, Kenya one-half from coffee and tea, Ivory Coast over one-half from cocoa and coffee. Five commodities (cocoa, coffee, oilseeds, cotton, and copper) make up half of the export earnings of Sub-Saharan Africa. In Asia, Sri Lanka gets over 60 percent of its foreign earnings from tea and natural rubber, and Burma earns over 70 percent from rice and wood.[34]

Whereas the poor need the markets in the rich countries, the LDCs are less important as markets for the rich nations (table 9-3). In fact, the rich trade mainly among themselves. In the 1970s between 70 and 77 percent of the exports of western nations went to other western nations and only 18 to 24 percent went to LDCs (including OPEC countries). Overall, the non-oil-exporting LDCs play a very small and decreasing role in world trade. In 1960 they contributed about 15 percent of the exports (by value) in world trade, compared with 67 percent by the West; by 1975 they contributed only 11 percent compared with 66 percent by the West.[35]

These figures do not mean that LDCs are absolutely unimportant to the West, or that the West can afford to lose markets there. For example, the United States sells a sizable fraction of its exports (27 percent in 1975) to non-OPEC LDCs.[36] This trade was crucial in helping to pay for America's huge oil import bill. Nevertheless, such exports are not as overwhelmingly important in the economy of the West as are exports to the developed countries in the economy of the LDCs.

These quantitative differences in trade are associated with important qualitative differences. The old "international division of labor" has been perpetuated: the LDCs export largely primary (raw) goods and import mainly manufactured goods (including equipment). In 1955, 87 percent of the LDC exports were primary goods, and this percentage was still about 80 percent in the 1970s. By contrast, in the 1970s almost 70 percent of their imports were manufactured goods.[37]

There is also a major qualitative difference between the manufactured goods imported and exported by the LDCs. Most of the manufactures they export are "basic manufactures"—generally yarn, cloth, woven goods, clothing, mats, rugs, and so on. Only a tiny fraction of their exports are "modern" goods—machinery, transport equipment, instruments, telecommunication equipment, chemical products, and the like—and these goods are exported by very few LDCs—mainly Brazil, Hong Kong, South Korea, Mexico, and Singapore. Even for these countries, modern goods form only 5 to 20 percent of exports. By contrast, such modern goods comprise the main bulk of the exports of developed nations, and they form the large majority of LDC imports. Transport equipment and machinery alone make up about half of the manufactured goods imported by the LDCs.

The significance of LDC dependence upon exports cannot be overemphasized. India has millions of people unemployed and underemployed. In the absence of an egalitarian, agriculture-based strategy of development, how is it to create employment? One way is to try to wrest from the rich nations more demand for Indian goods. For example, in September 1977, India's Minister of Industry visited London to try to convince the European Economic Community (EEC) countries to increase the quota for Indian textiles from the present 4 percent of their total annual imports.[38] He used the argument that this percentage was too small when one considers that India's population is enormous compared to Hong Kong's, which has a larger share of the textile market. The need for such cap-in-hand exercises clearly puts bargaining power on the side of the rich nations, which can extract favorable terms when they invest capital in India and elsewhere.

The dangers of tying economic growth in the LDCs, through exports, to continued expansion of the economies of the industrial West have been made depressingly clear in the 1970s. This strategy had already resulted in disastrous recession and stagnation in the LDCs when the West ran into economic difficulties in World War I and the Great Depression (Chapter 8). From 1950 until 1973 these dangers were pushed into the background as the industrial economies, and hence LDC exports, expanded rapidly. Since 1973, however, the economic growth rate of the industrial nations has slowed down by over 30 percent. This slowdown has persisted to the end of the decade and is not likely to be reversed soon because it results from structural changes in the economies of the developed countries. Reduced growth in the West has resulted in a great reduction in the growth rate of LDC exports. This rate has been cut almost in half in the period 1973–1979, compared with the preceding decade, and it has been combined with a general reduction in the price of LDC exports relative to their imports. The growth of exports has been cut both because of reduced growth in demand in the West and because increasing unemployment there has led to increasing protective barriers against LDC products. The reduced growth of LDC exports has in turn led to a drastic cut in the growth of their imports and in their overall economic growth rate.[39]

The response in the LDCs to the current stagnation in the West has been unusual. Growth of imports and overall economic growth in the second half of the 1970s have been greater than they would have been, because LDCs have borrowed heavily from international banks and institutions to make up, partially, for lagging exports. The result has been a rapid increase in debt. By 1977 external debt in the LDCs totaled over $250 billion and was growing about 20 percent a year. At the United Nations Conference on Trade and Development (UNCTAD) in Geneva in late 1979, it was estimated that the debt of the non-oil-exporting LDCs would reach $358 billion by the end of 1980. Such indebtedness itself reduces the rate of development because new earnings and loans must be spent on paying the debt instead of being invested.[40]

Having looked in general terms at inequality and dependence in the international economic system, let us now turn to the various pieces of machinery through which it acts: foreign trade, foreign investment, foreign borrowing, and foreign aid. In dealing with each of these mechanisms, I will emphasize how they create a net flow of resources from the poor to the rich nations, and how they tend to aggravate internal structural distortions.

Foreign Trade

A major issue here concerns the "terms of trade"—i.e., the amount of goods, say cotton, that a poor country must export to earn enough foreign exchange to buy, say, a tractor. Arguments rage over whether and when the terms of trade have deteriorated for the LDCs. But it must be stressed immediately that from the beginning, generally in colonial times, the poor nations were underpaid for their exports. Raw materials from mines and plantations cost very little in large part because extremely low wages were paid to the workers who produced them—wages a tenth or twentieth of what would have been paid to Europeans to do the same work. Table 9-4 shows the persistence of such wage differentials today. Since the terms of trade have not moved significantly in favor of the poor nations, there has in essence been an invisible transfer of resources from the poor to the rich nations, hidden in the low price of the goods exported by the LDCs. The same is now true of cheap manufactured goods imported from the LDCs; the high standard of living in the West is owing partly to the extraction of a surplus in the form of cheap labor in the LDCs.

There has no doubt been serious deterioration in the terms of trade for long periods for some countries. To choose a dramatic example, in 1968 the Senegalese peasant in West Africa got less than one-seventh of what he received in 1880 in terms of the value of the imported goods exchanged for each unit of groundnuts he produced. The French consumer therefore got ever cheaper groundnut oil by steadily further underpaying the Senegalese peasant. The overall picture is not as clear as this, and there have been some periods when the terms of trade improved. However, over the long haul it is likely that they have deteriorated: by 1973 the LDCs were exporting the equivalent of more than twice as much (in constant dollar value) to obtain the same amount (in constant dollar value) as they had obtained in

1913. The deterioration was strong in the 1950s and 1960s, and in recent years has been most marked for the poorest LDCs. The great exception is, of course, the OPEC countries for which the terms of trade improved with the large increase in the price of oil in 1974.[41]

Suppression of LDC export prices is often achieved by the fact that the buyers are only a handful of very large international firms with monopoly or oligopoly power over the market. This is spelled out in detail by Seidman for each major export from Sub-Saharan Africa.[42] She shows that a few firms buy virtually all of each of the major exported commodities. In addition, these firms are vertically integrated—i.e., they control the processing, manufacturing, and marketing of the goods, all of which take place in the developed countries. The producers of raw materials therefore have no choice but to sell to these few firms. To choose but one example, Seidman notes that in the 1960s the few major copper firms were "selling" (generally to other subsidiaries within the very same firms) Zambian crude

Table 9-4. Industrial wages in the United States and various poor countries in the 1960s

	Average hourly earnings abroad	Average hourly U.S. earnings	Ratio of U.S. earnings to earnings abroad
Consumer electronic products			
Hong Kong	$0.27	$3.12	11.6
Mexico	0.53	2.31	4.4
Taiwan	0.14	2.56	18.3
Office machine parts			
Hong Kong	0.30	2.92	9.7
Mexico	0.48	2.97	6.2
Korea	0.28	2.78	9.9
Singapore	0.29	3.36	11.6
Taiwan	0.38	3.67	9.7
Semi-conductors			
Hong Kong	0.28	2.84	10.1
Jamaica	0.30	2.23	7.4
Mexico	0.61	2.56	4.2
Netherlands Antilles	0.72	3.33	4.6
Korea	0.33	3.32	10.1
Singapore	0.29	3.36	11.6
Wearing apparel			
British Honduras	0.28	2.11	7.5
Costa Rica	0.34	2.28	6.7
Honduras	0.45	2.27	5.0
Mexico	0.53	2.29	4.3
Trinidad	0.40	2.49	6.2

Source: Gerald M. Meier, ed., Leading Issues in Economic Development, 3d ed. (New York: Oxford University Press, 1976) p. 677.

Note: Numbers reflect hourly earnings in U.S. dollars, of workers processing or assembling U.S. materials overseas and in the United States.

copper at almost exactly half of its selling price on the international market, thus greatly reducing Zambia's earnings while making additional profits by transferring copper within the company. (The next section expands on the question of oligopoly power.)

Trade with the rich nations, whether in raw materials or more sophisticated products, has accentuated inequalities within the poor countries. Income from trade accrues mainly to the owners of capital in the export enclave or to local industrialists who cooperate with the foreign manufacturing companies. Todaro reviews the consequences of international trade and concludes that:

> Third World countries have benefited disproportionately less from their economic dealings with developed nations and may have in fact even suffered absolutely from this association. . . . We can state almost without reservation that the principal benefits of world trade have accrued disproportionately to rich nations and within poor nations disproportionately to both foreign residents and wealthy nationals.[43]

Foreign Investment: The Transnational Corporations

The developing nations' need for investment capital and technology can be met in part through investment by foreign firms, which are attracted to the LDCs by high profit rates, new markets, cheap labor, tax benefits, and less stringent regulations. Indeed, the growing dominance by the transnational corporations (TNCs) has been the most dramatic change in the international economy in recent years.[44]* These firms now constitute the main machinery that makes this system operate, and they overwhelmingly dominate international investment. For example, 200 to 300 firms account for 75 percent of all U.S. foreign investment, 165 account for over 80 percent of U.K. foreign investment, and 82 account for over 75 percent of West German foreign investment. They also dominate international trade. For example in 1970, U.S. TNCs alone accounted for a quarter of all world exports, and this share has since increased:

> We are now heading towards a world of rapidly increasing international production, dominated by a few hundred private enterprises from the developed countries, with investment, trade and technology all coming under their aegis. "It is beyond dispute," in the view of the U.S. Tariff Commission, "that the spread of multinational business ranks with the development of the steam engine, electric

---

*It should be noted that the international corporations are *national* rather than *multinational* firms. They have a home country where the major stockholders and management live, to which profits return, and where the important decisions are made. These national firms operate across international boundaries and are thus properly called transnational corporations.

power, and the automobile as one of the major events of modern economic history."[45]

It is important to understand the nature of the TNCs. They are mainly in industries where research and development and marketing (e.g., advertising and "packaging") are important: petroleum, manufacturing, and mining. In LDC agriculture they are in export cash crops. As a consequence they are mainly in the more industrial LDCs, especially Latin America. (They are, however, relatively unimportant in India and Pakistan.) In the LDCs they operate through subsidiaries exporting, importing, or, frequently, manufacturing and selling goods within the country. Apart from their great size and global reach, three features are critical: their access to capital, to advanced technology, and to marketing techniques.

TNCs have privileged access to capital for investment abroad. They are closely associated with international banks (often sharing the same directors), which have twice as much money to lend as the total of all other international monetary institutions—for example, the World Bank and the International Monetary Fund. The TNC can therefore obtain capital for investing in an LDC more easily than the local government can. This does not mean that TNCs invest huge amounts of capital there. On the contrary, they prefer to invest a relatively small amount (12 percent of the initial capital has been average), to get the rest from local domestic savings, and thereafter to finance the LDC subsidiary with locally earned profits. Having established or taken over the subsidiary, the TNC usually does not relinquish control. For example, over 80 percent of the foreign subsidiaries of U.S. TNCs are either wholly owned or majority controlled by the TNC.

TNC control over research and development is perhaps the most powerful attribute. "TNCs produce, own and control the bulk of the most advanced technology in the world . . . and the LDCs as a whole are almost entirely dependent on them for access to such technology."[46] It should be noted, though, that much of this research is devoted to "product differentiation," i.e., to ringing changes on existing goods rather than creating truly innovative processes. The technology is protected by patent and can be sold to the LDC firm under license; however, whenever the market is stable the TNC will prefer to produce the product through a subsidiary, since this provides greater control over the "future stream of earnings."

Finally, the TNCs have great marketing expertise. They have the ability to carry out extensive market research, they can create and expand markets by advertising and promotion, they can develop additional products with ease, and they are adept at distributing the goods, all of which is greatly facilitated, particularly in Latin America, by the extent to which they have gained control over radio, T.V., and newspaper reporting.[47]

The great advantage that flows to the TNC from these features and from their organizational structure is *control,* an advantage that increases with size and success. Control over technology (which is often very specific to the product produced by the company) and over marketing gives the TNC monopolistic or oligopolistic power over markets. This allows it to ensure future earnings, to exclude smaller competitors, and to gain higher profits than under free competition.[48] Control also gives greater bargaining power against the local government.

Control and oligopolistic power over the market are increased by taking over smaller competitors in the LDC. For example, in the electrical industry in Brazil, foreign TNCs such as Westinghouse and Phillips took over forty-seven Brazilian firms between 1960 and 1974.[49] Of these, only one remained a Brazilian-controlled firm. The TNCs now have 77 percent of the industry, have increased the concentration of the market within a few firms, have prevented other firms from joining the industry, have reduced competition, and have held prices above what they would otherwise have been. This is *not* a reflection of greater efficiency on the part of the TNCs but of their economic power. The smaller firms were sophisticated; they were acquired because the advantages of the TNCs extend to the buying and selling of firms. Only where there is a very strong domestic industry can this power be withstood.[50]

As TNCs grow and their economic power increases, they become more and more hierarchical and the important decisions are taken in the central home country rather than in the local subsidiary. This means that the local people and government have less and less control over their own productive assets and over the economic decisions that have great import for their future welfare.[51]

The structure and power of the TNCs allow them to carry out various manipulations that are greatly to their own financial advantage and to the financial detriment of the LDC. First, oligopoly power produces high profits at the expense of the consumer. However, *declared* profits of the subsidiary in the LDC itself are often not remarkably high, because a second set of mechanisms enables the TNC to declare profits in countries other than where they were made. There are several reasons for doing this: the profits can be declared in a country (a tax haven) that has low taxes on profits; the TNC can reduce payments to the local LDC shareholders; local wages can be kept lower because declared profits are low.

The main mechanism for clandestine transfer of profits is "transfer pricing," which is made possible by the fact that transactions between countries take place between units of the same firm. The price that the LDC subsidiary pays for commodities, technology, and services can therefore be fixed artificially high. A reverse procedure can be used for goods or services bought in the LDC.

The most notorious example of transfer pricing is from a study by Vaitsos of the pharmaceutical industry in Colombia. In 1968 total profits were reported as only 6.7 percent of TNC investment. However, when overpricing of goods sold by TNCs to their own Colombian subsidiaries, plus royalties paid for the imported technology, were calculated, return on investment rose to 136 percent! Lall and Streeten confirm this situation. They found that on average the local subsidiaries paid (to other parts of the TNC) prices two and a half times too high. Actual profits were estimated to range from 21 to 272 percent, versus a declared range of a 7 percent loss to a 43 percent profit. The pharmaceutical industry in Colombia may be an atypical case, but transfer pricing undoubtedly occurs widely. It is not clear just how much additional profit is transferred in this way.[52]

Finally, since the TNC controls technology, much of which is specific to a particular make of product, the LDC frequently overpays for the technology, since there is no competitive market. Inflated "technical payments" by LDC firms to the TNCs are thus a way of extracting extra profits from the LDC; in fact, these are frequently more than half the size of declared dividends remitted to the home country.[53]

Having noted the various mechanisms by which TNCs remove profit from the LDCs, the question still remains: do the less developed countries nonetheless benefit financially from these activities? At the most obvious level they don't: the flow of resources out of the LDCs to the rich nations, via the transnationals, greatly exceeds the flow of capital into them. That, after all, is why TNCs invest there.[54] However, this misses the point that incomes and *some* profit remain, and we must ask, does the TNC generate more net national income by its activities than would have occurred in its absence? The notion here is that the TNC brings in more capital than would otherwise be obtained, perhaps freeing local capital for other uses, and that its technological and other expertise may create new opportunities for growth.

This question has been addressed by Lall and Streeten for over 150 firms in six developing countries. It is not at all obvious what measurements, calculations, and assumptions should be made, so the answer must be treated with caution. However, they concluded that for slightly more than half of the firms, there is a net financial gain to the LDC, and for less than half there is a net loss.[55]

Can we thus conclude that in spite of their financial manipulations, in at least half of the cases TNCs are "good for" the LDCs? That they are not, in fact, the main means by which underdevelopment is perpetuated by modern capitalism?[56] To resolve this question we need to examine the structural consequences of TNC investment, and these consequences cannot be converted to dollars and cents to be counted up. Unfortunately, standard economics is concerned mainly with what can be counted, but what is countable may not be everything that is crucial.

If one accepts the basic premise of this book, that structural aspects of LDC economies are overwhelmingly important, then there seems little doubt that the TNCs in general are an obstacle to real development. The basic problem is that the goals of the TNC do not conform to the requirements of real development, particularly the needs of the poor majority in the LDCs.

In essence, the problem is that the TNCs accentuate the distortions discussed throughout these last few chapters, and in doing so they deepen the dualism that prevents development.[57] First, because the TNC is interested in producing the same sorts of goods as it does in the West, using the same sorts of technology, it produces generally inessential and inappropriate goods in relation to LDC needs. It is the essence of TNC production and marketing techniques that these goods are oversophisticated, overelaborate, and highly packaged and promoted products. Rarely is the technology adapted to local needs and resources. The TNC employs capital-intensive technology that has a high requirement for imports, thereby generating relatively little local employment, creating few linkages, diverting local capital from investments that could respond to the needs of the poor, and increasing income inequality. While some of this technology is no doubt appropriate, it is clear that most of it is not.

Secondly, while the activities of TNCs increase the power of some small local groups, they inhibit local businesses and the development of domestic entrepreneurship. They do this through the mechanisms already discussed—soaking up local capital, dominating the technology, taking over local firms, and so on.[58]

Thirdly, TNC activities lead to a loss of national control over local productive assets and over important economic decisions, and there is evidence that this "denationalization" is increasing. "LDCs are more and more excluded from participation in the centralized use of power in the TNCs," according to one study.[59]

Fourthly, a major argument in support of TNC activities is that they bring modern technology to the LDCs. However, as we have seen, much of the technology is overpriced and inappropriate—it is capital- and import intensive. Furthermore, in recent years the TNCs have generally taken over, rather than set up, subsidiaries, and in many cases no technical changes are made in these firms.[60]

Finally, because they have economic power, TNCs are powerful social and political forces in many LDCs. At its most straightforward, this force is applied by making or withholding investments: as was noted earlier, investments have been withheld from leftist regimes and have expanded when rightist regimes took over. Political power accrues to the local groups that work closely with the TNCs, and at times this relationship has been bolstered by corporate bribery. In at least one case (ITT in Chile), there has been corporate collusion with the U.S. Central Intelligence

Agency (CIA) in overthrowing a socialist government. This is not to say that all TNCs interfere in the internal politics of LDCs. However, TNCs have had and will continue to have political influence in many LDCs. This political influence inevitably is used in support of regimes and groups that do not have the welfare of the poor as their prime concern and those with policies that deepen economic dualism.[61]

Foreign Loans and Foreign Debt

Capital for development can also come from loans, either from foreign commercial banks or from international institutions like the International Monetary Fund and the World Bank. International commercial banks charge higher interest and generally give loans for shorter periods, thus making the cost of debt service higher. About 60 percent of LDC debt is from such private sources; the main borrowers are Algeria, Brazil, Indonesia, Mexico, and Argentina, and the primary "low-income" borrower is Zaire. Generally, low-income borrowers tend to use the international institutions, India and Pakistan being the main debtors. Moreover, foreign debt is highly concentrated; only twenty LDCs account for 80 percent of the total LDC foreign debt.[62]

We need to distinguish two types of loans. Commercial loans are made at regular commercial interest rates by both commercial banks and international institutions. IMF loans and three-quarters of World Bank loans are of this sort. "Concessional" loans are made at lower than commercial interest rates, are usually long-term loans, and may have a grace period when no repayment is required. Most aid consists of concessional loans; one-quarter of the World Bank's lending is of this type. Such concessional loans, of course, still lead to debt that must be serviced by payments of interest and principal.

There is nothing wrong with LDCs being in debt; indeed, it can be an excellent way of getting capital for investment. Countries behind in development have always borrowed from more advanced nations, which have often had excess capital.[63] The dangers arise when debt is used for the wrong purposes, the debt is too great, or the creditor is able to impose unwise policies. Borrowed capital has indeed been misused, as we have seen, to import luxury consumer goods, to develop inappropriate industry, and to tie the country to future importation.

The debt of LDCs in the late 1970s may have become so large as to threaten their future economic growth. As noted earlier, stagnation in the developed countries and the ensuing limits on exports by the LDCs since 1973 have been major factors causing debt to increase rapidly. The total public debt of the non-oil-exporting LDCs in 1974 was $114 billion; by

1977 it exceeded $250 billion and by 1980 it will probably exceed $350 billion. In 1977 the cost of servicing this debt (paying the interest and repaying the principal) was equivalent to about 12 percent of the LDCs' export earnings in the same year. Of course, this average obscures the fact that there was a great deal of variation from country to country. Moreover, the cost of debt service is expected to rise to about 19 perent of export earnings in the 1980s. Still, there is disagreement about the significance of this debt. Some observers believe it will interfere strongly with economic growth because it will divert capital from investment. In fact, it has been claimed that this is already the case for Brazil. The World Bank, on the other hand, argues that most countries should be able to manage their debt and that those with particularly large debts should be able to expand their exports and continue to borrow. As we will see, however, there are serious structural problems that arise from indebtedness, even when repayment is not a problem.[64]

As in the case of investment by the TNCs, foreign lending and foreign debt have worsened the structural distortions in the LDCs. The commercial banks wield considerable power because they control much of the private savings and capital and the flow of foreign exchange, and through this power they can indirectly influence LDC economic policies. A striking example is provided by Chile. Before 1970, U.S. private suppliers and banks provided almost 80 percent of Chile's short-term credit. Five of the banks cut off all credit to Chile after Allende became president, and by 1972 loans from U.S. banks had been reduced by over 80 percent, greatly deepening Chile's financial crisis and thereby hastening the end of Allende's regime. However, the most direct interference in LDC economies is that of the International Monetary Fund (IMF). Private banks are more likely to lend to countries with policies approved by the IMF, so their influence tends to be indirect.[65]

The IMF works closely with the World Bank but plays the stronger role in shaping the economic policies of LDCs. The IMF began at the end of World War II as an institution to provide credit to countries with balance-of-payments problems but gradually has spread its activities to the general field of development. Although the technicalities of its money lending are different from those of the World Bank and of commercial banks, it basically gives loans. However, the Fund's importance is greater even than its considerable lending powers would suggest, because it acts essentially as a kind of super credit agency. In the field of multilateral aid, the Fund has been given the job of ensuring that the LDC economic policies are "appropriate" before aid is given, and in the area of commercial lending, loans from all sources follow more easily if the LDC has shaped its economic policies to meet the approval of the Fund's technical experts.[66]

The IMF is run by the developed nations and is dominated by the

United States. It is committed to encouraging international trade and to the removal of obstacles within countries that act as barriers to trade (including efforts by LDCs to slow down imports). It is also committed to free-market principles and to maintaining a good environment for foreign investment in the LDCs. Finally, "it is an explicit and basic aim of IMF programs to discourage local consumption in order to free resources for exports." In all of these respects IMF-approved policies accentuate the structural distortions in the LDCs, for reasons we have discussed at length, and they operate against social reform and a more egalitarian development strategy.[67]

Foreign Aid

It is important to place foreign aid in its proper historical perspective. I alluded earlier to the invisible transfer of capital from the poor to the rich nations that has taken place, over several centuries, in the form of cheap exports. Mahbub ul Haq has made the point forcefully in an ironical conversation with an imaginary Mr. Polanski. Mr. Polanski refuses to believe that there has ever been, or ever will be, any "meaningful partnership or aid relationship between the developed world and the developing countries." Mr. Haq notes, however, that there has indeed been extensive aid within the "partnership," leading to economic growth:

> I argued from the experience of India and Pakistan that, when we were associated with Britain in a partnership in the nineteenth century and the British had this slight problem about financing their industrial revolution and their structural transformation, we willingly brought out our gold and our diamonds and our agricultural produce for nominal prices and told them to go ahead and not lose the opportunity for a technological breakthrough. We cheerfully stayed on as an agrarian economy and applauded the industrial strides of our partner. In the modern terminology, such a thing will be called a transfer of resources, but the world was such a happy community at that time that we never even dreamed of such terms or asked for performance audits.
>
> Mr. Polanski, unreasonable as he is, wanted to know the magnitude of the transfer and I mentioned an off-the-cuff figure of $100 million—a modest estimate for which I may be disowned by my fellow economists in the subcontinent. I could not confirm to him whether this amount was 1 percent of our GNP at that time. Anyway, I argued that this amount could be treated as a voluntary loan, at 6 percent interest, which has been happily multiplying over the years so that it stands at $410 billion today. I also explained to him that, since the amount is doubling every twelve years, at this stage it is an advantage to leave it with Britain, as it will be $820 billion by 1982. We can always draw on this amount whenever we need to finance a bit of our delayed structural transformation. But Polanski, who does not understand the basic principles of sound inter-

national finance, kept on insisting that we must call up the loan immediately. I tried to reason that Britain is in no position to pay, and, being equal partners, we are in no position to collect. If we insist on quick repayment, the international community may have to do a bailing-out operation. I also told him that in matters like this we ought to be more generous and, at the very least, undertake the standard debt rescheduling exercise—for instance, we would forget the $10 billion and only ask for the remaining $400 billion.

But Polanski, I am afraid, remains unconvinced and I am at a loss how to explain to him the inherent logic and strength of our partnership in development.[68]

The developed countries have by now been lending aid to the LDCs for three decades. In 1975 such aid from the western nations reached $13.6 billion. This amounted to roughly one-third of 1 percent of the GNP of the developed nations. (The Communist developed countries contribute less than one-tenth of 1 percent of their GNP; the OPEC countries have given about 2.5 percent.) In the same year, world military expenditures reached $371 billion, or twenty-seven times the amount spent on aid. That $371 billion was roughly equivalent to the entire income of the poorest half of the world's population.[69]

Aid is not only a tiny fraction of the GNP in developed countries, it is a declining fraction: 0.52 percent in 1960 and only 0.31 percent in 1977. Much of this decline was attributable to the U.S. contribution, which has fallen from almost 0.5 percent of the U.S. GNP in 1965 to less than 0.25 percent in the late 1970s. America now contributes one of the smallest fractions of GNP among the developed nations. In real terms (i.e., constant dollars), net aid to LDCs from the developed world has actually declined—again particularly that of the United States, which fell by more than a third between 1965 and 1975.[70]

From the point of view of the (non-OPEC) LDCs, aid is a significant contribution but not a massive one. It has been equivalent to about 10 percent of total investment in the LDCs and to roughly a fifth of the foreign exchange earned by their exports.[71]

Aid is sometimes given for the highest moral reasons. Sweden's aid is over 0.8 percent of its GNP; it is given to countries most in need, generally with few strings attached. In general, however, the history of aid to the poor nations has not been a particularly creditable one for most developed nations. Most countries give aid only partly for humanitarian reasons. The other, perhaps main, aim is to gain political and economic advantage for themselves. Singer and Ansari conclude that "the overwhelmingly important determinants of aid allocation by the large donor countries are political considerations and colonial ties." U.S. bilateral economic aid (i.e., aid that does not go through international agencies) goes mainly to Latin America; to strategically important nations along the U.S.S.R. and Chinese borders (e.g., Turkey, Pakistan); to military dictatorships in Asia (e.g., South Korea, Indonesia, the Philippines); and to the Middle East (Israel, Egypt, Jordan). U.S. economic aid also goes mainly to countries that receive the most American military aid. Note that U.S. (and World Bank) aid was withheld from Brazil in the early 1960s but was renewed within days of the overthrow of the democratically elected government and the seizure of power by the army generals. Similarly, Indonesia received a flood of U.S. aid and a few weeks after Suharto took over from Sukarno and reversed Sukarno's nationalistic, anti-private enterprise and anti-foreign investment policies. Much of U.S. aid to India also reflects strategic considerations. By the same token, French aid goes mainly to the former French African colonies, which are closely tied to France through trade. Similarly, British aid goes mainly to Commonwealth countries. In each case a strong economic argument for such aid is that it is a way of developing a demand for the exports of the donor nations. This is clearly the case for aid that is tied (i.e., the money must be spent in the donor country), and most bilateral aid is tied.[72]

Regardless of these mixed motivations, foreign aid has undoubtedly contributed to economic growth in many developing countries. It has helped them build projects and import equipment and raw materials for industry. Technical assistance has helped them adopt new technologies. Aid has also fed, clothed, and sheltered starving and destitute people in times of emergency.

Unfortunately, aid has also had serious negative effects on the LDCs. For example, aid given as loans increases subsequent indebtedness and dependence. More serious and perhaps less obvious are the negative structural effects of such help upon LDCs. The existence of these ill effects had become quite widely recognized by the early 1970s both in and outside of aid agencies. As we will see, they have not proven easy to correct.[73]

To see how these effects arise, we need to look first at how aid is administered. Foreign aid can be extended directly from one country to another —this is bilateral aid. The U.S. Agency for International Development (AID) is an example of a bilateral aid agency. Because of the obvious opportunity in bilateral aid for the pursuit of the donor's self-interest, "multilateral" or international agencies have been created that pool aid from various countries and administer it. The largest and most important of these is the World Bank or, more precisely, the International Development Agency (IDA) of the Bank, the division that gives grants and low-interest loans. The Bank provides about a quarter of the net aid that goes from the West to the LDCs. However, its influence in the aid field is much greater than this figure suggests because the Bank has the largest body of expertise in development, it is the most important source of information on the economies of LDCs, and it has a large capacity for commercial lending in addition to aid. In addition, it operates together with its extremely powerful sister institution, the International Monetary Fund, in evaluating and giving a seal of approval to the economic policies of recipient LDCs.[74]

Official aid comes in various forms, food aid being about 15 percent of the total.[75] Some aid is in the form of technical assistance in which engineers, agronomists, and other experts are sent to the LDC at the expense of the donor government. Most aid, however, comes as grants or low-interest loans that are used to help finance development. This type of help takes two forms. The first is project aid, historically the most common kind of assistance. It is given for a specific purpose (e.g., building a dam, an electric power generating station, a highway). The World Bank has particularly favored project aid, but this has also been the most common form of bilateral assistance. In project aid the great majority of funds is given to buy goods (usually capital goods) from the developed nations—that is, the purpose of the aid is to help out the LDC with foreign exchange. This means, quite naturally, that these funds are spent in the developed countries. In bilateral relationships it has been the general rule for most aid to be tied; this does not occur in multilateral aid.[76]

The second major type is program aid, which has been less common. Here funds are given for the purpose of buying imports (again usually capital goods), but the spending is not tied to a particular project. Notice again that only a very small portion of funds can be spent buying goods produced in the recipient country. Project aid has been favored over program aid because it is easier to control and evaluate. However, program aid allows control on a broader scale because it involves approval at a high political level. Its acceptance generally requires that the LDC's economic policies conform to guidelines laid down by the international institutions involved, especially the IMF, as discussed above.

The negative structural effects of aid are by now well known. It has encouraged the growth of large-scale, capital-intensive, and import-intensive projects. This has occurred in a variety of ways. Such growth is an obvious consequence of project aid, has been reinforced by western technical advisers, and has been encouraged by the quite open use of aid as a stimulant to donor-country exports. The insistence that aid be mostly in the form of foreign exchange has reordered LDC priorities around large projects with a heavy import component. Even the organizational needs of aid agencies have encouraged this pattern: their aim is to transfer large amounts of aid with low administrative costs, and large-scale projects facilitate this. Since foreign aid comes to substitute for, rather than supplement, domestic savings, and since aid is easier to transfer in large bundles, "development assistance incentives make the extravagant project the most rational choice for an LDC country to make." Aid agencies themselves have gone into the business of *generating* projects, since it has turned out to be difficult to transfer resources to the LDCs quickly because of administrative and technical delays, and because of the difficulty LDCs experience in absorbing such transfers.[77]

Aid, while encouraging economic growth, has thus deepened the dualism in developing economies. It has helped commit LDCs to capital-intensive and import-intensive technologies, increasing the need for future requirements of imports for replacement parts and other associated western technology. It has deemphasized the creation of employment and has benefited mainly a small minority of industrialists, thereby increasing income inequality. It has led to greater dependence on the industrial world and has slowed the development of more suitable indigenous technology.[78]

It is clear that aid has played an important political as well as economic role in sustaining inequality and structural distortions in the LDCs.[79] This was noted above in discussing the major nations that receive bilateral aid. Military aid, of course, is the most direct form of such support, and military aid from the West (both overt and covert) helps support numerous reactionary governments that maintain the dual economy and suppress the living standards of the masses of their population (see Chapter 11).

In the 1970s there has been some attempt to overcome some of the worst aspects of nonmilitary economic aid programs. The World Bank was a leader in expressing a new sense of the importance of increased employment, and the need to redistribute income, to raise the living standards of the poorest segments of society, to introduce means of production more suited to the needs and resources of the LDCs, and to shift emphasis to rural development.[80] Unfortunately, it is easier to change the rhetoric and intentions than the results, and mere readjustments in aid policy, within the existing larger political and economic framework, are unlikely to make much difference.

The World Bank's experience in providing agricultural aid illustrates some of the difficulties.[81] Until recently agriculture received only a small proportion of total Bank lending; this fraction was less than 10 percent in the period 1948 to 1963 but rose to almost 40 percent in 1978. Unfortunately, from 1974 to 1978 the fraction of loaned funds that were actual aid (i.e., came from IDA) dropped from a half to a third, and in 1979 the fraction of Bank lending going to agriculture fell to 25 percent. Most of this lending in agriculture has been in support of large-scale production of livestock and export crops, rather than for food production. From 1964 to 1973, less than a quarter of lending in agriculture went to increase the production of domestic food crops.

The central aim of the new strategy, begun in the early and mid-1970s, is to increase the productivity of the millions of small farmers in the LDCs, especially their production of food. However, various difficulties have arisen. The first general problem is that as long as the new strategy injects aid into a system in which resources are already very unevenly distributed, it will likely cause an increase in inequality. The Bank is of course aware of this danger and has stated its support for land reform and other changes designed to help the poor. However, the Bank cannot force such reform but can only support it where it occurs.[82] Even then, as we saw in Chapter 6, land reform has almost always been only partial, and partial reform itself will usually lead to increased rural inequality.

The Bank has commented on the great practical difficulties it has experienced in getting help to the vast army of peasants and has acknowledged that, in spite of its intentions to help poor farmers, much of its effort will in fact continue to go to larger farmers. In the late 1970s almost half of its projects have still been in support of large farmers, and there is also a great "leakage" upward of benefits from projects designed to help the small farmer.

The Muda River Project in Malaysia provides a good example of how benefits move toward the better-off segments of society even when the aid is aimed at the poor.[83] This project was specifically focused on improving the standard of living of poor farmers. The project was begun in the late 1960s with a $45 million loan from the World Bank. It was designed to provide irrigation water for double cropping to 51,000 padi rice farm families living on 240,000 acres. In addition, rice-drying complexes were built and agricultural development centers established to provide extension and market services and better credit, and to supply physical inputs such as seeds and fertilizer. Double cropping has become standard and production has greatly increased.

The project has had two kinds of effects on the distribution of income and resources. First, farm incomes have increased, but unevenly. The richer farmers have benefited most, so that the distribution of income among farmers has worsened. Secondly, while the income of nonfarm rural workers has probably gone up, increased resources and welfare have flowed mainly to the towns and cities in the region, and primarily to the richest groups there. In particular, urban services (retail shops, transport) and financial institutions have benefited the most. Thus urban/rural inequality has increased.

An optimistic view of this and similar projects would stress that poor farmers did gain absolutely. Such a case has been made by the Bank's Director of Agriculture and Rural Development Programs.[84] But the price of these absolute gains is increasing inequality and a strengthening of dualism and its attendant obstacles to development. A more radical strategy, one that changed the basic distribution of productive resources, would provide much greater immediate and long-term benefits to the poor with a similar injection of resources. However, it is not within the political power of aid agencies to carry out such a radical strategy.

The second general problem with the strategy is that even in its conception, it does not go far enough in its attack on poverty. Even if the Bank and other aid agencies could achieve the goal of helping mainly the small farmer, serious negative as well as positive effects would probably follow. This strategy excludes the rural landless, who constitute 30 to 40 percent of the agricultural population in the LDCs and are generally the poorest group in the countryside. The landless can hope to benefit only indirectly, through increased employment. However, the small-farmer strategy is not likely to increase the agricultural employment of this group and it does nothing directly to create nonagricultural employment.[85] It therefore runs the risk of reinforcing the already marginal position of this class. The more general question is whether it is possible to help, selectively, people with no or few productive resources, *without first redistributing resources* (e.g., land, credit).

Thirdly, there remains the problem that western aid agencies, including the World Bank, still tend to view LDC problems with a bias toward "technocratic" and "free enterprise" solutions:

> Despite homages to labour-intensive and self-reliant development strategies in the new rhetoric, there have been few changes in the pattern of insisting on competitive international bidding on most contracts financed by Bank loans (rather than preferential inducements for local producers) and severe restrictions on local cost financing, thus encouraging capital-intensive imports.[86]

Of particular concern here is the expanding role of large agribusiness firms in penetrating LDC agriculture, especially in export production. The lending agencies of developed countries encourage this growth of agribusiness—for example, by lending funds for infrastructure in the development of export agriculture in Africa. The World Bank plays a critical role in this process.[87] The Food and Agriculture Organization of the United Nations (FAO) also has an Industry Cooperative Program or ICP, comprised of 100 international agribusiness firms; its purpose is to help LDC agricultural production. Among the agribusiness companies in ICP are those that have worsened the conditions of the rural population in various parts of the Third World (e.g., Gulf and Western, which dispossessed peasants in the Dominican Republic, and the three major banana TNCs of Latin America). Even if the company people concerned can set aside the direct interests of the corporation, they are not likely to recommend, and do not recommend, the sort of policies that will lead to a basic restructuring of agriculture in a more egalitarian mold. It is clear that in the majority of cases the activities of agribusiness firms in the LDCs do not increase the welfare of the rural poor. Put bluntly, in many cases there is good evidence that they reduce that welfare.[88]

In summary, the problem of poverty is an extremely difficult one for aid agencies to deal with. This in part is a result of aid policies themselves.

But even with the best of intentions and strong efforts to help the poor directly, aid programs wind up helping the better-off segments of society more than they help the poor. This is because giving occurs within strongly distorted economic systems, which aid agencies are largely powerless to change. There is thus a deep dilemma: the poor are in great need, but efforts to alleviate that need are likely to strengthen the very structure that maintains poverty.

Export Substitution: Limits to the Outward-oriented Strategy

I have already noted that the import substitution strategy is severely limited. It is limited internally because it responds to demand from only a very narrow segment of the population. It is limited also by its paradoxical dependence upon imported goods and technology and by the consequent need for expanding exports.

There are also very serious limits to exports of raw materials, with the exception of course of a few key commodities such as oil. In the developed countries the demand for many raw agricultural products is increasing only very slowly. Population is leveling off; new technology is continually using raw materials more efficiently so that manufacturing consistently grows faster than the extractive industries (see Chapter 10); new technology also is continually finding new substitutes, often synthetic, for existing raw materials.

By way of illustration, Seidman has developed the case for the five major exports of Sub-Saharan Africa, which together make up half of this area's exports.[89] The projected rates of growth of four of the commodities are about 3 percent or less; copper is only slightly higher. These rates will barely keep up with Africa's projected population growth and hardly provide hope for the accumulation of additional savings to fuel development.

In response to these difficulties and to problems of indebtedness, it has become common to suggest an elaboration of the strategy of export-based development. The modern strategy would extend exports to processed raw materials, where appropriate. Thus in addition to, or instead of, exporting raw materials, the developing country would carry out at least some of the processing and manufacturing, thereby developing linkages out into the economy from the export enclave and spreading employment and incomes. At the same time, the rich nations are to be exhorted to provide both stable prices for raw materials from the LDCs and expanded markets for their manufactured goods.

This strategy may work in some situations. Manufactured exports have been important in the economic booms of South Korea and Taiwan. They have also been important in Puerto Rico, although this has been a very special case.[90] It is not clear, however, that this could be a successful strategy for the LDCs in general: even though LDC-manufactured exports currently form only a small proportion of the total imports of the developed countries, and only a minuscule fraction of the total market for manufactured goods, the rich nations in the 1970s have already increased import barriers against these goods. Dependence upon trade with the rich nations means that economic growth in the poor nations will continue to rise and fall with events in the developed world, over which they have no control. In particular, the outlook for rapidly expanding exports in the near future looks bleak in view of the continuing slow growth of the developed nations.

This strategy also makes the poor nations dependent upon the good will of the rich nations, a commodity never strongly in evidence. The trade barriers of the rich nations are erected mainly against manufactured goods (to protect their own industry), and they discriminate particularly against the LDCs. In the industrial nations, tariff barriers (e.g., duty levied on imported goods, thereby making them less competitive with domestic goods) are higher on manufactured goods from the poor nations than from other rich countries. Equally important are nontariff barriers that include, for example, strict quotas on the amount of particular goods that can be imported, rules about procurement procedures, health and safety standards that may bear little relation to real needs, and other administrative and customs regulations.[91] The evidence from recent negotiations on international trade is quite unequivocal; it is clear that the rich nations do not intend to improve the situation to encourage the development of the LDCs.[92] The fifth UN Conference on Trade and Development ended in 1979 with no guarantee of improved access to developed markets.

Clearly, some trade with the developed countries is necessary and could be beneficial to the LDCs. It would be foolish to suggest that exports are never valuable for a developing country, or that a development strategy incorporating a substantial export sector is doomed to failure under all circumstances. It also makes sense to shift from the export of raw materials to the export of processed products whenever that can be done in a way that uses the abundant resources of the developing country and creates employment. The dangers are relying upon exports to provide the impetus for development; allowing the need for exports to dominate the internal structure; and substituting an export drive for the real basis of sustained development, which is the harnessing of the productive forces of the nation to create an internally integrated economy.

DEVELOPMENT AND SELF-RELIANCE

In the second part of this chapter I have tried to show how the relationship of LDCs with the developed countries fosters underdevelopment. There are two fundamental and essential causes of this process. First, the relationship between rich and poor countries is unequal. This creates dependence of the poor on the rich and hence a large amount of control for the rich over the poor. The direct control of colonial times has been replaced by a variety of less powerful but still substantial forms of indirect control. Second, the dependence of the LDCs on the rich nations is greatly increased by their own internal structure—the dual economy. By inhibiting the mobilization of internal resources, the elite of the LDCs place themselves in a position of supplication to the developed nations. The two sorts of distortions—internal and external—are therefore intimately and inextricably linked to each other. The problem of development cannot be solved unless both these issues are tackled.

The solution, however, cannot be simply for the LDCs to cut themselves off from the West and to rely on a strategy of pure self-reliance. No nation can be completely self-sufficient, and all LDCs need to import some things from the industrial world. It is also the case that the LDCs could benefit greatly from the right sort of contact with the West. In fact, the poor nations face a deep contradiction in their dealings with the rich nations. On the one hand, they can benefit by gaining access to the technological capacity of the rich nations. (Of course, this technology, and the ability to create new technology, must be used selectively and it must be adapted to LDC needs; nevertheless it could greatly accelerate development.) On the other hand, western capitalism, unbridled by a matching LDC strength, undermines independence and self-sufficiency and fosters underdevelopment by accentuating internal distortions.

LDC relationships with the industrial world are likely to improve, therefore, only when the LDCs can come to the interaction from a position of internal strength. That is, they need to develop their own productive capacities in order to reduce dependence upon the rich nations. This, in turn, requires the internal development of social and political forces that are strong enough to create the profound structural changes that will release these productive capacities. What is required of the rich nations, at the very least, is that they allow this process to happen.

The problem of underdevelopment is thus basically a political one. Economic processes are organized by those with economic and hence political power. Those who have power in the LDCs are precisely the people who want to maintain dualism and inequality. "Radical restructuring" thus implies no less than the transfer of this power so that the economy will be reordered to benefit those who are poor and presently lack access to productive resources. Alternatively, those who have power will need to be convinced to use it to their own financial detriment and for the benefit of those who lack power.

Chapter 11 pursues the question of how the dilemma of dependence and development can and should be resolved, and what political changes are required to allow a resolution to take place. Chapter 10 is a digression for those concerned with the environmental and resource aspects of development, population growth, and increasing food supplies. The reader wishing to follow the strict logic of the argument should go straight to the final chapter.

10

LIMITS TO GROWTH AND THE STRUCTURAL
CAUSES OF DETERIORATING ENVIRONMENTS

The claim that economic development is needed to solve the linked problems of population growth, inadequate food supply, and poverty raises two questions. Where will the material resources for development come from? And if they can be obtained, won't the associated environmental degradation act as a limiting factor? In particular, won't the pressure to produce more food now undermine agriculture's capacity to produce in the long term, so that in the end the effort will be self-defeating? We will take these two issues of resources and environment in order, in the first part of this chapter. The second part will examine the economic and political processes that lead to environmental degradation of marginal land.

LIMITING RESOURCES AND DEVELOPMENT

I dealt with resources for agriculture in the LDCs in Chapter 5 and deal here with overall resource and energy requirements. Will resource limits prevent development in the LDCs in the near future? This is the conclusion to be drawn from the early formulation of the limits-to-growth argument and from recent modifications made by those who consider the argument to be basically correct. The main conclusion is that global resource limitation is imminent, and the waiting time is only a few decades. The LDCs are not likely to escape these limits; indeed, since the rich nations have greater access to resources and (within the current international framework), economic growth of the LDCs depends on growth in the rich nations, the LDCs are bound to stagnate with the cessation of growth in the rich nations, if not before. Forrester even suggests that the current poverty of the LDCs is to their long-term advantage—since they may now be close to the ultimate low equilibrium standard of living, unlike the rich nations, they will not suffer major problems in readjusting to long-term scarcity.[1]

I believe not only that these conclusions about resources and development are incorrect but that the issue of physical limits to development is largely a red herring. It is worth looking first at the history of resource use, especially the experience of the rich nations.

Resources: Experience of the Rich Nations

The limits argument stresses the impossibility of continued exponential expansion of consumption in the face of fixed resources. It points also to the suddenness with which resource constraints become apparent in such a situation: if the number of lily pads in a pond grows exponentially and doubles each day, on the second-to-last day the pads cover only half of the pond, but on the next day they cover the entire pond. Thus the danger is that we will come to terms with resource limits in a very disorderly, indeed disastrous, way.[2] However, the history of changing technology, changing economics, and changing demand for resources as affluence increases shows that this is an oversimplification of the problem.

These changes affect, first of all, the amount of available resources. In spite of rapidly expanding use of materials, over the past century the amount of economically recoverable resources available at any given time has continually expanded. This has been caused by exploration, by economic growth, and by the creation of new technology, which makes it economically feasible, for example, to mine lower grades of ore. Cook has pointed out that forty years ago Americans were warned of the imminent depletion of major minerals yet, except for crude oil, the projected lifetimes of economically recoverable minerals are longer now than they were then. More striking is the fact that, in spite of the decreasing concentrations of the minerals being mined, the average real price of most minerals has declined or remained almost constant for eighty years, and the cost of actually mining them has declined. These costs are kept low through innovation.[3]*

This historical process of innovation and cutting of costs is likely to continue, with the important exception that energy may become more expensive. However, even the case of energy costs is not straightforward. The increase in the price of oil between 1973 and 1974, and the leveling off of per capita production, were caused not by an immediate absolute scarcity of oil, but by the cartel action of the Organization of Petroleum Exporting Countries (OPEC). The real price of oil hardly increased between 1974 and 1979. Furthermore, increases in energy prices would have little effect on the price of resources. Most energy used in the production of metal, for example, is used after the ore has been mined and "beneficated," so until the ore becomes extremely dilute, the amount of energy required to pro-

---

*It may be argued that the price of raw materials does not include the environmental costs of producing them. However, this was also true historically. While more earth now has to be moved to produce each ton of ore, reclamation techniques have improved. Furthermore, in the richer nations businesses *are* now forced to pay for some clean-up and reclamation, so some of the environmental cost is now figured into the price. This is not to say, of course, that such internalizing of environmental costs has gone far enough.

duce usable metal, such as steel, is not much affected by the grade of ore that is mined. Such extremely low grades are not likely to be exploited because other very abundant materials could be substituted for them.[4]

Changing technology and economics also strongly affect the demand for resources. The limits argument hinges on the projection into the future of current exponential growth rates in the demand for materials and energy. Such projection makes very little sense. This point is fundamental, for continued exponential growth in demand is the force that rams us so rapidly into the hypothetical brick wall of absolute resource limits. But continued unabated growth in the demand for physical resources is most unlikely, for several reasons.

First, as economies become technically more advanced, they use resources more efficiently. Two examples from the use of coal illustrate this. In the mid-twentieth century, it took less than one-sixth the amount of coal to produce a ton of cast iron as it did in the late eighteenth century; in the thirty years ending in 1970, the amount of coal needed to produce one kilowatt hour of electricity was cut almost by half. Recycling, miniaturization, and the substitution of lighter and stronger materials operate to reduce primary resource needs. As a result, the production of manufactured goods increases much faster than the need for physical resources. Between 1960 and 1978 the production of manufactured goods increased more than a third faster than the mining of raw materials. When oil and natural gas are removed from the mining figures, manufacturing grew more than twice as fast as mining.[5] These increases in efficiency have occurred in an era of cheap materials. For example, in the United States, nonfuel minerals account for less than half of 1 percent of the GNP; even energy costs are less than 1 percent. If and when the price of materials increases, the pressure to conserve them will also increase.

Secondly, it appears that the rate of increase in the per capita demand for material goods slows down as people become richer, and may now be close to leveling off in the richest nations. As people become more affluent, they spend a smaller fraction of their income on material goods. Furthermore, there simply appears to be a limit to the amount of goods one can use and enjoy, although the quality and sophistication of the goods may increase. According to Landsberg, the annual total amount of materials used per person in the United States, apart from energy, has not increased over the past two decades. Steel is the major industrial material, and annual U.S. per capita use has increased very little since 1950. Radcliffe suggests that as a general rule, per capita demand for many materials levels off (and even declines) around high-income levels such as those now reached in the West.[6]

The exceptional case of energy, noted by Landsberg, is important; yet it is precisely here that large-scale conservation is most obviously possible.

For example, a recent study examined the future requirements for energy in the United Kingdom under the assumption that more efficient technologies will gradually be introduced over the next few decades. The only technologies considered (e.g., better insulation, greater gas mileage in cars) were those that are available now or are expected by the manufacturers to be available in volume in the early 1980s, and those that are cost effective. The study shows that, even allowing for a greatly increased standard of living, mobility, personal comfort, and industrial production, the demand for energy can be much lower than the 1978 level and the use of primary fuel (oil, coal, etc.) could be cut to only half of the 1978 level. It should be recalled that per capita energy use in the United Kingdom is already less than half the level in the United States. Similarly, a study by the National Research Council concludes that U.S. energy consumption in 2010 could be 20 percent less than in 1975, even with a doubling of the standard of living. Japan has reduced its energy consumption since 1973 without reducing its economic growth rate.[7]

World Supply and Demand for Material Resources

A recent analysis by Ridker and Watson projects the future growth in world demand for resources. This projection uses 1973 UN population projections that are probably too high. It assumes that recycling of materials will not increase above the levels of 1973 to 1974. It makes very modest assumptions about conservation of energy and materials in the rich nations. It assumes that materials and energy use in the LDCs will follow the pattern in the industrial world (that is, there will be no special attempts to save either resource). Even then, the projections show that the world's rate of increase in materials use will decline significantly over the next four or five decades. The growth rate of energy demand, for example, is expected to be cut almost by half.[8] Serious efforts at conservation of energy and materials could certainly reduce these projections still further.

Even with the very modest efforts at conservation implied in Ridker and Watson's projections, the world should be able to meet its needs for fuel and nonfuel materials over the next fifty years. Indeed, sharp increases in real prices before 2025 are expected only for lead (around 2016), petroleum (around 2010), and natural gas (around 2024). (Of course, cartel action could push oil prices higher than demand and supply would warrant.) Ridker and Cecelski conclude that "depletion of minerals and fuels and rising world resource prices are not the central problems we face in the next century." The problems instead are transitional—adapting to higher oil prices and making substitutions occur smoothly. These conclusions are echoed in the other recent serious analyses of material resources.[9]

Over the long term there are no doubt limits to the amount of materials that can be used, and these limits certainly will occur well before the entire earth's crust has been transformed into human structures! But just where these eventual limits are is extremely difficult to determine. It is most likely that world population will stabilize (probably in the next century) well before physical limits are approached, and the evidence from the developed world suggests that demand will also level off before then. A more parsimonious use of resources, however, would ease transitions along the way. Perhaps the most likely limit to continued economic growth is not scarce resources, but a decision by the population that the environmental costs of obtaining and using more resources are unacceptable.[10]

Resources and Development

It can hardly be argued that LDC economic growth will place too great a strain on global resources. The LDCs, with over 70 percent of the world's population, produce about 20 percent of the world's goods and services. Even quite optimistic projections of LDC economic growth show this fraction rising to only 23 percent by the year 2000. The LDCs currently use about 16 percent of the world's commercial energy; this fraction is projected to rise to only 33 percent in 2000, and to less than half by 2025.[11] Clearly, if global physical resource limits were to prevent further development in the near future, this would be caused mainly by consumption in the rich nations.

In evaluating the physical potential for development in the LDCs, it is also useful to dispose of a common argument that goes roughly as follows. In the United States, per capita use of commercial energy and of selected minerals is twenty to thirty times that in the LDCs (see, for example, table 10-1).* To bring the world's present population up to current U.S. per capita levels of consumption would require an increase of about sevenfold in the total amount of energy and materials used in the world. Even more formidable, since future population growth in the LDCs is inevitable, bringing all of the world's population to current U.S. consumption levels fifty years from now would require more than a twelvefold increase in total production over fifty years. Were U.S. levels to continue increasing exponentially, bringing everyone up to American standards fifty years from now

*Table 10-1 shows for the LDCs both conventional (i.e., commercial) energy sources and nonconventional sources. The former include coal, oil, natural gas, nuclear and hydroelectric power. Nonconventional sources are mainly wood and dung collected in the countryside. Most calculations of LDC energy use, and most comparisons with the developed countries, ignore nonconventional sources.

would require about a hundredfold increase in annual production.* Again, to give everyone in the world in 1970 the use of the amount of steel available to the average person in the world's ten richest countries would require all the output from the world's iron ore mines over the next sixty years, and there would be none left over for losses or the continued demand of the rich nations.[12] It is then frequently inferred from such mind-boggling calculations that these consumption levels are impossible and therefore that the LDCs will *never* be developed.

This line of argument seems ill conceived for several reasons. First, there is no good reason for the LDCs to follow the rich nations' historical pattern of industrialization and urbanization, and many good reasons for them not to (Chapters 6 to 9). The pattern of development that is appropriate for the LDCs, which I outlined earlier, is energy and materials saving and would also greatly slow down the process of urbanization. No overall estimates are available for the energy and materials requirements of this type of development, but they are certainly low compared with the western pattern.

*The calculations are as follows. In 1970 total world consumption of commercial energy was equivalent to 6.8 billion tons of coal. U.S. per capita use was approximately 11 tons per year and LDC use was 0.3 tons per year. To bring the 1970 LDC population of 2.4 billion up to U.S. standards would have required 26.4 billion tons. For the rest of the world, including the United States, it would have required 13.2 billion tons, giving a total of almost 40 billion tons, or almost six times actual consumption. By 2020 the world population will likely be more than twice the 1970 population, giving a requirement over twelve times current consumption. Energy use in the United States in 1970 was growing at roughly 5 percent a year. In fifty years, this growth rate would give an annual consumption of about 134 tons per person. Even if world population were only twice the 1970 total by 2020, this would give a total use per year of 965 billion tons, which is well over 100 times greater than the 1970 annual consumption.

Table 10-1. Population and annual per capita consumption of energy and steel in 1970

	Population (billions)	Energy per capita[a]	Steel per capita (kg.)
United States	0.2	11.1	620
Other developed countries	0.8	4.5	516
"Intermediate" countries[b]	0.2	1.6	158
LDCs	2.4	{ 0.3 (conventional sources) 1.2 (all sources)[c]	21

Sources: H. Brown, "Human Materials Production as a Process in the Biosphere," *Scientific American* 223 (1970): 194–208; United Nations, *Statistical Yearbook* 1974.

[a]Energy is in metric tons of "coal equivalent."

[b]Intermediate countries had a per capita GNP between $600 and $1,200 in the early 1970s.

[c]Conventional sources are oil, nuclear energy, hydroelectric power, etc. Nonconventional sources are wood, dung, crop residues, etc.

Second, increased levels of material well-being in the LDCs are desirable even if they never reach the current U.S. level. For example, in the early 1970s, at average per capita income levels between $600 and $1,200, people in countries such as Yugoslavia, Spain, and Argentina were able to lead vastly more comfortable and healthy lives than do people in the LDCs. Furthermore, Chapters 2 and 3 have shown that at these intermediate income levels birth rates decline rapidly and continue to decline, provided income distribution is not too uneven. Thus, moving even partially along the development path can solve the population problem. Yet the per capita energy consumption needed to maintain these intermediate levels of income is only a seventh of that in the United States and is less than twice that in the LDCs. (See table 10-1. This calculation is based on the total energy available, including nonconventional energy.) To bring LDC per capita energy consumption up to such intermediate levels would require world energy production to increase by the equivalent of about 1 billion tons of coal, i.e., by less than 20 percent. Were the LDC population to increase threefold in fifty years (which was roughly the UN "medium" projection in 1973), world energy production would still need to increase only by half for the LDCs to reach and maintain the level of energy expenditure associated with this intermediate income level.

The per capita steel consumption of intermediate countries is likewise only a fourth that of the United States, though it is more than seven times greater than that of the LDCs (table 10-1). To raise LDC per capita steel consumption to the 1970 level of use in these intermediately rich countries would require the production of an extra 300 or so million tons, or roughly half of 1970 world production. In summary, even if development were to follow recent patterns of energy and materials use, decent standards of living for the poor could be reached with relatively modest increases in total world energy and materials production.

Finally, to the extent that resources limits do become a global problem, there is a clear case to be made for reduced consumption by the rich, rather than the poor nations. Indeed, if and when global resources come into short supply (as oil will do soon), their profligate use by the rich nations will drive up the price and hasten the day when conversion to more expensive alternatives is needed.

The analyses discussed in the previous section make it clear that a shortage of material resources should not interfere with development in the forseeable future, and it also seems likely that the cost of materials will not be a serious problem. The obvious exception to this latter statement is the price of oil, which increased in the early 1970s and has resulted in a large demand for foreign exchange in oil-importing LDCs. Since energy is also the key resource in assuring the supply of other materials and in sustaining development, it deserves special attention.[13]

Energy and Development

Numerous detailed studies of energy needs and resources have agreed in concluding that world energy resources are adequate to meet a long-term demand that is many times greater than current consumption, at prices not more than two or three times greater than those prevailing now.[14] (As with other materials, the likely problems will concern the transition from one form of energy to another.) Nevertheless, there is great opportunity in the LDCs for developing methods of energy production that are adapted to these nations' abundant labor and poor capital resources and would buffer them from transitional problems and from the uncertainties caused by the geographic concentration of oil and other fuels. This question was discussed to some extent in Chapter 5.

The first point to notice is that per capita energy consumption in the LDCs is much higher than most estimates, which count only conventional sources (table 10-1). On the basis of conventional accounting, energy use in the LDCs is about one-thirtieth of use in the United States and one-fourteenth of the use in other rich countries. But once we include the energy contained in the wood, crop residues, and dung that are used as fuel, the ratios become about one-tenth and one-fourth, respectively. Unfortunately the LDCs get very little useful energy (work) out of these unconventional sources because they are burned very inefficiently. The crucial point, however, is that these energy sources *can* be converted into useful work, and much of the technology for doing that is available.[15]

Secondly, the per capita energy expenditure actually needed to sustain the high income levels of the rich nations is certainly much lower than that shown in table 10-1. As noted earlier, the United Kingdom could continue to increase its level of material well-being on half the quantity of primary fuels it now uses, and the United States could double its standard of living and still cut its current energy use by 20 percent. Thus the energy available to the LDCs now is not very far from that needed for a decent standard of living.

Thirdly, many of the LDCs are in a position to tap unconventional sources of energy, such as solar energy, which do not even figure in table 10-1.

The following brief account presents just a few of the available technologies that can either produce energy efficiently from nonconventional sources or can carry out crucial activities at much lower energy costs than conventional technology. In each case these technologies also tend to be labor intensive, to rely largely on locally available resources, and to use scarce materials sparingly.

• Energy in the LDCs is used mainly for domestic purposes (cooking and heating), for agriculture (e.g., irrigation), and for industry. Most of the nonconventional use is for domestic purposes and rural manufacturing and represents about twice as much energy as is provided nationally by conventional fuels. Wood is the major nonconventional fuel, and there are two ways in which this energy source could be exploited more efficiently. First, wood production on village woodlots could produce the same amount of wood as is now used, but on only a fifth of the land. Secondary benefits would be a great reduction in the labor needed for wood gathering and an improved environment. Although the investment required is not large and would soon be repaid in firewood, the capital and local expertise are not generally available.[16]

The second way to increase efficiency would be to burn the wood in simple but better designed fires, furnaces, and cooking stoves. For example, cooking is a major use of fuelwood but typically in the LDCs it requires two to six times as much energy per person as does cooking with gas and electric stoves in the United States. A much-improved stove is being developed in India, and better cooking methods are being tested.[17]

• There is great opportunity for using the energy in biological materials other than wood. Through biogasification, weeds, straw, and the like, which are often simply burned off in the tropics, can be converted into fuel (methane gas), as discussed in Chapter 5. Biogas production in LDC agriculture could actually provide all of agriculture's energy requirements, plus an excess for use in industry.[18]

• Solar energy has also been adapted for LDC agriculture. For example, a technically sophisticated but robust solar pump (for raising water) that is long lasting, requires little maintenance, and fits well into a rural life style has been introduced into West Africa and Mexico.[19]

• In recent years a surprising range of successful energy-saving intermediate technology has been developed and introduced in the tropics. Small two-wheel tractors have been developed at the International Rice Research Institute in the Philippines and by industrial cooperatives in Sri Lanka; small-scale sugar factories are widespread in India. These and other examples are described in detail by Jéquier.[20]

• There is also enormous room for further innovation. For example, especially in the sunny drylands, small solar cookers present an obvious method of saving wood fuel and allowing dung, which is often burned as fuel, to be returned to the soil. However, people in the drylands prefer to cook when the sun has gone down, so a technique for storing the heat is required. Other potential uses of solar energy include its conversion to electricity for pumping irrigation water, heating domestic water using flat glass "collectors," solar dryers that heat air to dry grain, solar heating and cooling of buildings, solar evaporation for producing salt, making drinking water, and refrigerating food.[21]

We must stress again that without socio-economic change the introduction of such intermediate technology will probably fail. For example, the production of both fuelwood in village woodlots and of biogas for agricultural purposes requires a restructuring of rural society if the benefits are not to accrue to the rich, and these techniques will require social reorganization to ensure the participation of the poor. Similarly, while the production of biogas energy in excess of agriculture's needs can increase as food production does,* such increases require radical changes in the whole society (Chapters 6 and 9).

In summary, given an appropriate pattern of development and the imaginative use of nonconventional fuels, there is no reason why energy resources or costs should constrain overall development. Almost all of rural energy requirements, including expanded rural industry, could be met by unconventional sources, and the countryside can even supply energy to urban industry. Much of the energy use by urban industry is in any case for inappropriate purposes, and it occurs in an industrial system that is too large scale and energy intensive in relation to LDC resources. LDCs would gain by redirecting the current use of conventional fuels (Chapter 9).

ENVIRONMENTAL CONSIDERATIONS

Environmental problems abound in the rich and poor nations alike. Mining, processing, manufacture, transportation, and energy production all pollute air, water, and land and degrade the overall environment. New and poorly understood substances, some of them carcinogenic and mutagenic, are being released into air, soil, and water. Deforestation, soil erosion, eutrophication of lakes, and the spread of persistent pesticides accompany agriculture. The Aswan and other dams in the LDCs, while providing new farmland, irrigation, and power, disrupt ecosystems and help spread water-borne parasitic diseases. Parts of the most diverse ecological communities in the world are being destroyed as tropical rainforest falls before human expansion. On a global scale we are altering the climate, and risking self-annihilation through the spread of nuclear technology.

The purpose of this section is not to minimize the importance of these problems but to determine whether future development of the LDCs will be constrained by the extent to which it exacerbates present difficulties.†

*The excess available for other uses increases because plants capture solar energy more efficiently as yields increase (Makhijani, *Energy Policy*).

†Environmentalists and others may feel these problems *ought* to stop further economic growth in both rich and poor countries. Such views are sometimes based on the belief that nature is valuable in its own right or that humans have no "right" to demolish nature. This

Industrial Pollution

The two major sources of environmental degradation are industrial activity and agriculture. The effects of industrial growth in the LDCs are not likely to limit development. As with resources, industrial pollution is contributed mainly by the rich nations, and this will continue to be so for decades into the future. As with resource use, it makes no sense to assume that industrial pollution will expand exponentially into the future. In fact, in the rich nations there is clear evidence that some aspects of industrial pollution have declined with increasing affluence. In recent years there has been a reduction in the levels of pollutants such as carbon monoxide, particulates, hydrocarbons, sulfates, and suspended solids in water. The general level of air pollution in European cities such as London has greatly decreased over the past thirty years; even Los Angeles smog is less severe than in the 1950s; the Thames near London has been reinvaded by fish as water pollution has declined. The dangers of heavy metal pollution are now understood, following serious pollution episodes in the 1950s and 1960s, and improved effluent treatment and substitution should greatly reduce this problem. The health and safety of industrial workers are much greater than they were a century ago.[22]

Industrial pollution in the LDCs generally is less strictly controlled than in the developed countries, and we can expect pollution there to increase as economic growth continues. However, with affluence comes a desire to have a cleaner and healthier industrial environment, and we can expect pollution control technology to expand in the LDCs at markedly higher levels of industrial activity. Nor is the cost of pollution control very great. In the rich nations it now is on the order of 1 percent of GNP. Without such efforts, environmental damage would cost more than the controls, so it pays to control pollution.

Even the highest levels of various types of pollution that have occurred in the industrial nations have not been allowed to interfere with economic growth. While one may decry such an attitude, presumably a similar response would occur if the LDCs were to reach such levels.

The most intractable pollution problem is the climatic effects of burning fossil fuels. A major difficulty is that we are still uncertain as to just what the net climatic effects of further industrial growth will be. Here again, however, the main contributors are the developed nations and it can hardly be argued that the LDCs should forgo development to avoid global climatic effects.

---

position is defensible within a particular framework of values, but it is beside the issue I tackle here, which is whether the LDCs can sustain higher material standards of living over an indefinitely long period, in the face of the environmental damage created in attaining these standards.

Environmental degradation resulting from existing and expanding agricultural activities is more likely than industrial pollution to be a constraint on development for, as pointed out by Eckholm, the pursuit of ever more food production in some situations threatens actually to reduce, rather than increase, the land's future capacity to produce food.[23] We can distinguish two types of environmental degradation arising, respectively, from intensive and extensive farming.

Intensive Farming

Any agricultural activity can cause environmental degradation. But intensive agriculture, done properly, can and generally does improve the quality of agricultural land. Hundreds of generations of farmers in northwest Europe and throughout Asia have cultivated the land with ever-increasing intensity, and the land's ability to produce food has grown concomitantly. The Great Plains of the United States and Canada have been transformed into an enormous and intensive wheat-producing region by proper land use. In the American Midwest, the Morrow plots of the University of Illinois have been continuously cropped and fertilized at various levels for 100 years. During this period they have been closely monitored, and they show that fertilizer, properly used, does not harm the soil.[24]

Concentrating on high-yielding agriculture, where appropriate, can also help save natural environments by reducing the need to extend agriculture into new areas. As I have argued in Chapter 6 and elsewhere in this book the crux of a proper development strategy is to provide peasants with land and the financial resources that will enable them to invest in and improve that land.

The major environmental costs of intensive farming come from the production and use of chemical fertilizers and pesticides, especially insecticides, and from irrigation. Except for irrigation, these activities are on a much smaller scale in the LDCs than in the developed countries (Chapter 5), and the effects are correspondingly on a smaller scale.

In spite of the furor that has surrounded the use of fertilizers and pesticides, their projected rates of use in the LDCs are not likely to cause sufficient environmental disruption to affect seriously the continued growth of agriculture.[25] After all, Japan and some European nations use fertilizers and pesticides at much higher rates than the LDCs are likely to approach for many decades, yet the environmental consequences have not been great enough to restrain agriculture, and the agricultural productivity of the land is not only generally unimpaired but is ever increasing.

This certainly does not mean that these problems are unimportant or that they should be disregarded. In fact, they are frequently avoidable. Much insecticide pollution, in particular, results from overuse and misuse, and there is no doubt that it could be greatly reduced through increased application of integrated pest management techniques. In the LDCs these techniques, together with improved designs for cropping systems, could substitute labor-intensive and environmentally sound methods of pest control for insecticides that are expensive, require scarce foreign exchange, and are frequently either ineffective or even counterproductive. The FAO and the UN have begun several programs to develop integrated pest management in the tropics, but much more research is needed. Also, returning crop residues and dung to the soil (perhaps through biogasification) would save foreign exchange spent on chemical fertilizer, create employment, and improve the soil at the same time.[26]

Irrigation is the other activity of intensive farming that in some dry regions causes serious damage to agro-ecosystems. When an irrigation system is improperly maintained, waterlogging and/or soil salinization can easily occur, yields are reduced, and eventually farming may become impossible without expensive reclamation work. This problem has been most serious in Pakistan, where 20,000 to 45,000 hectares are seriously affected each year. Even in Pakistan, however, this is less than 0.3 percent of the country's total of 15 million irrigated hectares. The amount of irrigated land that is degraded each year in all the LDCs is probably about 100,000 hectares. This is a huge loss, but it is still only 0.05 percent of the total irrigated land (250 million hectares) and only about 1 percent of the amount added to irrigation systems each year, so that the area of land that is irrigated continues to grow rapidly (Chapter 5).[27]

Irrigation techniques, although sometimes quite complex, are well established, and while research can be expected to produce improvements, technology needed to maintain and repair irrigation systems is well understood. For example, 1 million acres of waterlogged irrigated land in Pakistan are now being reclaimed.[28] The problem is therefore one of applying these techniques.

Here we come to a crucial point: the collapse or decline of irrigation systems is frequently the result of economic factors. The peasant is too poor to construct drainage or to maintain the system; or the technology is available, but the farmers are illiterate and farm extension services are inadequate; or the distribution of land, land tenure arrangements, credit, or other "structural" features are such that there is either no means or no incentive for the peasant or landlord to maintain the system.[29] Thus environmental degradation caused by irrigation is generally attributable to economic or other structural conditions, a point discussed more fully later in this chapter.

Extensive Agriculture: Desertification

In the LDCs the major source of environmental degradation from agriculture is the use of two types of "marginal" land, namely drylands and steeply sloping land. Misuse of these lands causes soil erosion and desertification. The former is already a serious problem in some LDCs (e.g., Nepal, Bangladesh, Madagascar, El Salvador, Haiti). It is largely a consequence of poor soil management and of farming in unsuitable areas, and in general could be avoided. Desertification, which may be associated with erosion, is perhaps the most serious type of damage caused by extensive agriculture. It is often cited as a massive threat to human welfare, and we now pursue its causes in some detail.[30]

The world's drylands occur mainly in two broad belts that run between latitudes 15° and 30° north and south of the equator. In this band are found not only the major deserts of the world but also the notorious ruins of those civilizations—in North Africa, Iran, Pakistan—in the demise of which desertification, salinization, and clogged irrigation arteries seem to have played a major role. Excluding real deserts, potentially productive arid and semi-arid regions now cover 45 million km.[2], or almost a third of the world's land surface, in two-thirds of the world's nations.

Despite the skeletons of some past civilizations, populations pursuing traditional agriculture have lived for centuries in dryland areas, and between 600 and 700 million people now live there. The world's drylands produce huge amounts of cereals, fibers, meats, and hides. Some drylands can be highly productive, as is shown by large areas of intensive agriculture in the United States, Israel, and Australia. Thus, although dryland farming is not free of problems, desertification is certainly not the inevitable consequence of continuous farming of arid and semi-arid land.[31]

The general pattern of land use in drylands is as follows.[32] In the arid regions,* where there is a sparse natural vegetation of annual plants, perennial grasses, and long-lived, drought-resistant shrubs and trees, pastoral agriculture (the herding of grazing and browsing animals like cattle and goats) is dominant. The pastoralists tend to be nomadic. Moving away from the arid regions, the vegetation changes gradually to savanna. In these semi-arid regions the grazing is more reliable, and livestock is maintained by sedentary farmers who also grow crops that are planted in the wet season, often in a rotational system that requires long fallow times between cropping periods of a few years ("shifting" agriculture). The dryland farmers grow mainly cereals—wheat, sorghum, millet,

---

*Arid regions have an average rainfall of 200 to 300 mm. or less; semi-arid regions receive 200 to 600 mm.

etc. The area under rain-fed crops in the drylands is much less than that used by pastoralists, but the former supports much larger populations.

A third type of agriculture—large-scale, highly specialized, and mechanized commercial ranching and cash cropping—occurs generally on the better soils of semi-arid areas. Finally, both peasant and large-scale commercial farming occur in irrigated areas, as discussed earlier.

Desertification can result from any of these different agricultural systems, as well as from natural processes. For example, overgrazing, generally arising from a conjunction of drought and overstocking, reduces the vegetation cover. This in turn reduces the organic content of the soil, changing its structure. Rain followed by baking sun then tends to produce a thin surface crust of soil, which holds later rain on the surface. This water evaporates, which further reduces the soil moisture available to surviving plants and leads to further loss of vegetation. Then too, ground water levels may fall. Because of its poor structure, as the surface crust crumbles the soil is easily washed or blown away. The remaining soil is less fertile, has a poorer structure, and is less able to support plant life. This is desertification.

Cropping can also cause desertification, again often in combination with drought. Land that has little vegetation is especially vulnerable, and this condition occurs when dry weather continues after the land has been stripped of vegetation in preparation for planting, or when it is left fallow but has only sparse vegetation. When the rains fail to come such land is exposed to wind erosion, and when rain does come the poor soil structure (caused by a low organic content) may lead to crusting and further erosion by water.

Desertification can also arise as a gradual process resulting from too-intensive cultivation. Crops are grown year after year, without fertilizer or an intervening fallow period, and soil fertility gradually declines because nutrients are removed in the crops. Crops become thinner and thinner. Eventually the land must be abandoned, but by then it supports very little natural vegetation and is vulnerable to erosion. Cash cropping has often been a major culprit in this process, as in the Sahel. Cultivation is particularly a cause of desertification when, during wet years, it spreads onto land suited only for grazing.

Large-scale commercial agriculture has also caused desertification through ranching, excessive cash cropping, the use of too much heavy machinery, and, as discussed above, through badly managed irrigation.

Disaster in the Sahel

Perhaps the best way to get some feeling for the process and consequences of desertification is to look at the recent Sahelian drought by way of example. The famine in the Sahel, which was most acute in 1973, was triggered by drought in 1968, 1970, 1971, and 1972. Perhaps 100,000 people died of starvation and disease. The nomads suffered more than the farmers. There was a mass exodus of both nomads and farmers southward to towns and refugee camps. In the north of Niger more than 80 percent of the livestock died. In five of the Sahel countries (Mauritania, Upper Volta, Mali, Niger, and Chad), which were already extremely poor, the exodus represented a collapse of much of the subsistence agriculture. The damage in Senegal was severe but less disastrous. Two million nomads in the Sahel lost as much as half of their livestock; some lost over 90 percent. The harvests of 15 million farmers were cut by half during most of this period. Many of the surviving refugees will never return.[33] By 1973:

> Lake Chad had shrunk to one-third its normal size. . . . In the preceding winter, the Niger and Senegal rivers had failed to flood, leaving much of the best cropland in five countries (Niger, Mali, Upper Volta, Senegal and Mauritania) unwatered and barren. Failure of the rains meant the loss of valuable annual pastures in the northern Sahel, and as the drought continued and the water store became more depleted, there was widespread death of sustaining shrubs and trees. With the drying out of shallow and seasonal wells over much of the Sahel. . . famished and weakened livestock concentrated around larger watering points, where vegetation and soil were totally destroyed, or were driven southward in an often fruitless search for pasture. They left behind a stripped landscape, baking in the sun, where patches of newly-created desert seemed to grow and link up, producing an impression that the great Sahara desert was "marching southward." Further south. . . the traditional grazing of stubble was no longer available. Regional food stores were exhausted, with complete breakdown of the Sahelian livelihood systems.[34]

Although the drought played a major role, the Sahelian disaster was in large part man-made. Although the livestock density, at least in the nomadic zone of Niger, had been within the carrying capacity of the environment before the drought, it was clearly too high for the available grazing under the drought conditions. The modern deep wells, sunk with western planning and technology, provided a large supply of water at widely separated areas. However they did not provide a corresponding abundance of grazing, and so they attracted aggregations of cattle far in excess of the capacity of the local vegetation around the wells. There was overintensive cropping and overextension of cropping onto marginal land. Indeed, although the nomads suffered the most, desertification tended to occur away from the desert edge, at the margin of cultivated land, and it was probably the cattle and crops of the sedentary farmers that caused the most environmental damage. Within these activities, crop production probably caused more damage than grazing.[35]

Extent of Desertification

Drought and desertification, of course, are not problems confined to the Sahel. In Africa they occur also in the Sudan, Ethiopia, Somalia, Kenya, and southern Africa; they occur in South America and Asia, especially in the Rajasthan area in northwest India, and in some developed nations.[36]

Desertification is thus a widespread problem. However, the extent of the drylands and the large population they support should not lead us to overestimate its importance. Of the drylands population of 600 to 700 million, approximately 50 million people are under intermittent threat from desertification.[37] While this is a huge number of people, it is important to recall that it is only slightly more than 1 percent of the world's population, and only 5 percent of the 1 billion that are the world's poor. Similarly, although large tracts of land are involved, it is generally grazing land and marginal farming land, which contribute relatively little to overall world food production. In terms of feeding the world's population, or of setting a limit to development, the process of desertification is relatively unimportant.

None of the above, of course, provides any comfort to the 50 million people whose livelihood is directly threatened. However, there is no physical reason why this threat cannot be removed by appropriate investment in the agriculture of the nations in question; as we will see below, the essence of these problems is economic and political rather than physical.

Desertification: Some Clarifications

It is worthwhile to dispel some of the misconceptions that surround the problem of desertification, and I have collected here a miscellany of the more serious.

- The first, and rather startling, fact about desertification is that there are actually very few facts about its extent or seriousness. Indeed, while much is written about how desertification is a serious global problem, there is actually no strong *physical* evidence that this is the case. For example, although the farming population in the drylands area to the east of the Rajasthan desert in India is extremely dense by world dryland standards, and although the area is often regarded as a prime example of desertification, there are quite strong contrary opinions on whether or not the phenomenon is actually occurring there. Warren and Maizels are not even convinced that the Sahel shows desertification, when that process is defined as a *permanent* reduction in the area's ability to produce useful crops:

> The evidence for desertification is diffuse and almost impossible to quantify. There can be little reasonable doubt that many environments have suffered

serious damage, and this mostly by cultural practices, but the *persistence* of the effects is much more debatable. In particular, the losses that followed the recent droughts in the Sahel, and elsewhere, cannot be classed as desertification until clear evidence emerges that the yield of useful crops in the ensuing good years has been depressed beneath that of the preceding wet period, and that the losses are due to environmental causes.[38]

• There is a good deal of rubbish talked about the "carrying capacity" of drylands (and everywhere else) and the tendency for populations there to overshoot this carrying capacity. The capacity of the drylands to produce food, while often much lower than that of more humid areas, can be increased by proper management (and of course it can be vastly increased by irrigation). This can be seen from the fact that different areas with similar climates and environments support very different levels of population. Semi-arid areas of northern Nigeria support 180 persons per km.^{2} and drylands in India's Rajasthan area support 150 to 200 per km.^{2}, as a result of the farming systems that have evolved there. By contrast, the Sahelian-Sudanic zone and the Middle East support much lower population densities (around 10 to 20 per km.^{2}); yet there appears to be at least as much desertification in those areas.[39]

Kates and his co-authors point out that in many dryland areas there are problems of *under*-population. Many of the able-bodied men leave to work elsewhere and there is not enough labor to maintain and operate some of the labor-intensive aspects of cropping. Desertification has thus resulted from under-population when irrigation works or terracing have fallen into disrepair.[40]

• Desertification is not the result of the deserts "marching." Desertification usually occurs around centers of very intensive activity, such as over-cropped areas or around wells where livestock have cleared the vegetation. These areas sometimes coalesce with similar areas, giving an impression of "creeping" deserts. However, there is no particular tendency for desertification to occur at the edge of the real desert, and in fact it tends to occur mainly away from this edge at the margin of cultivated land.[41]

• Although nomads and their herds are often seen in popular myth as the culprits in desertification, farming is probably the major cause, and recent ecological analyses suggest that nomadic pastoralism is the optimal way to exploit the drylands beyond the areas suitable for cultivation. When they are not constrained, the grazing and management practices of the nomads *increase* the productivity of the pastures: moderate grazing increases the growth and vigor of the plants, and livestock speed up the nitrogen cycle. A study in the Amboseli area in Kenya has shown that the nomadic Masai are about twice as efficient at converting pasture to livestock as are nearby cattle ranches.[42]

• Finally, we are not helpless in the face of desertification, nor are we condemned simply to bear passively the vagaries of the dryland environment. Not only is desertification usually reversible, it will in general be economic to reverse it, since the benefits will exceed the costs.[43]

Desertification and Appropriate Technology

There is a great range of traditional and western technology (and a blend of the two) that has been applied successfully in the drylands and can be applied more widely. This technology need not be expensive. It can greatly increase the productivity of the drylands and reduce their vulnerability to degradation.[44] For example, terracing in Tunisia, a technology that is several thousand years old, is restoring the area's productivity to its ancient level. In crop farming, wind breaks, strip cropping (which prevents erosion), mulching with stubble (which improves soil structure), and planting legumes as fallow "crops" (which increases fertility) can all increase productivity and simultaneously prevent desertification. In grazing systems improved livestock strains, deferred grazing, rotational grazing, revegetation, and the provision of *well-distributed* watering places can all provide higher yields and protect the natural vegetation. Previously degraded irrigated land is being reclaimed in Iraq and Pakistan.

Environmental Degradation and the Food Supply

We can now bring together the conclusions about the effects of degradation of marginal land upon food production. Local production of food for some tens of millions of people living in marginal areas is threatened either continually or intermittently, mainly by desertification and/or erosion. As a consequence their livelihood is also threatened. Usually adequate food from elsewhere is available, but the marginal population is often too poor to buy it.

There is great scope for research on the management of marginal lands, but enough is already known to prevent most of the deterioration and to support current populations. However, there is simply not enough known to estimate how many more people marginal areas could support. Emigration from these areas is always occurring, sometimes dramatically in periods of severe disruption. As we will see below, some of the population on marginal lands has been pushed onto them, and it would probably be better both for the environment and for the people if some were able to move, or move back, to higher-quality land.

Thus, there are environmental problems in agriculture, especially in marginal areas. Although technical solutions exist, if the problems are ignored they will worsen and will cause increased suffering for the local populations in the affected areas. The question in these situations is whether LDC governments will make the economic and social changes that are prerequisite to solving the problems. In general, however, food production occurs overwhelmingly on land that is suitable for agriculture, is not deteriorating, and can become continually more productive under intensive use, if properly managed. It must be concluded, therefore, that environmental degradation should not pose a major threat to increasing the world's food supply or to increasing food production in the LDCs in particular.

Development and Natural Ecosystems

Development inevitably brings in its train the disruption and loss of natural ecosystems and of hundreds of thousands of species of plants and animals. To the ecologist, at least, these losses of insects, spiders, protozoa, mites, fungi, annelids, molluscs, crustacea, etc., no less than of the dodo or the condor, are tragedies. Each species is a unique product of nature and, once extinct, will never be seen again. The encroachment on tropical ecosystems is especially tragic, since they are so diverse.

For humanity in general there is also the problem that any species that is lost may contain genetic information that might be of use to us in the future. After all, the species that now provide our daily bread and rice would in other circumstances be considered weeds; wild strains of these or other similar species are still scattered around the world and may yet prove invaluable to plant breeding programs. The wild ungulate herds of the African plains may yet be the source of improved domesticated livestock. Some obscure plant in the Amazon rain forest may yet be a source of a crucial medicine; a leaf mold buried somewhere in Asia may yet provide a new antibiotic. Unfortunately, such genetic material, once lost, can never be reconstituted.

Yet we in the developed nations can hardly argue that the poor should forgo development for nature's sake, having destroyed most of our own natural heritage in the pursuit of wealth. Our own experience also tells us that quite depauperate natural communities (which can be found in England's countryside, for example) can be pleasant, interesting, and apparently able to provide such important "natural services"[45] as pollination of crops. Thus we have no grounds for arguing that some terrible catastrophe will befall the LDCs as they disrupt and remove large chunks of natural ecosystems.

Whether we are concerned with the loss of species or with some other environmental cost of development, the crucial question we must ask is: what are the different environmental consequences of different strategies for economic growth in the LDCs? Perhaps some people would prefer that the poor stay poor if that means protecting the natural environment. But preventing economic growth is not a real option, even if it were possible: indefinite increase in human population is the greatest ultimate threat to nature and, except for an omnipotent dictator or recurrent genocide, economic development is the only force that can stop this increase short of environmental disaster.

Without rural development, in particular, the poverty-stricken agrarian populations of the world will continue to expand onto and to destroy those wild ecosystems that still exist. By contrast, rural development, based largely on intensive farming, would restrict movement onto marginal land and would provide the agrarian population with the means to manage the land properly. It would thus help *save* natural environments. As a corollary, strategies of economic growth that continue to exploit the rural poor will exacerbate environmental problems. We examine several such examples in the next section.

ECONOMIC, POLITICAL, AND SOCIAL CAUSES OF ENVIRONMENTAL DEGRADATION OF MARGINAL LANDS

The first part of this chapter has examined the nature and immediate causes of ecological degradation in the LDCs and especially of marginal lands. We now examine the deeper causes of this environmental degradation. Does it arise simply from the pressures of a growing population upon a fragile environment, aided and abetted by unfavorable climate and inappropriate technology, or are there at work political and economic processes of the sort that we have already seen maintain population growth and constrain the food supply?

Hill-Farming in the Philippines

In the Philippines, some twenty or thirty miles from the famous International Rice Research Institute where "miracle" rice was developed, and at a similar distance from Manila, a cluster of hills overlooks a large lake called Laguna de Bay. These hills are farmed by formerly landless people who have moved into the area from the lowlands over the past forty years. These farmers plant crops on plots hacked out of the forest, on slopes with inclines of up to 80°. Banana trees dominate a rich mixture of crops that includes coffee, peppers, tubers of various sorts, tomatoes, and even rice, which is grown in the rainy season on small cleared areas. However, rice is obtained mainly by buying it from lowland farmers with money earned by selling bananas, peppers, and other produce.

Adjacent to the cropping areas are stands of rapidly growing trees.

These trees cover areas that were previously cropped but are now being left fallow. The trees are legumes that replenish the soil's fertility.* They are used for firewood and to some extent as fodder for livestock (mainly goats). Two families farm a small ravine that is being studied by the University of the Philippines, and when I visited the area one section of trees was being cut down to provide a new cropping area.

Although this is called shifting agriculture, the families remain in one area and rotate the land use within that area. Provided the fallow period is about twelve to fifteen years, the hills can probably sustain these families indefinitely under this traditional system of management. However, as more and more people need to wrest a livelihood from the area, pressure on the land is intensifying and the fallow period has now fallen to about seven or eight years. There is a danger that this period is too brief to replenish the soil nutrients and that future crop yields will decline. Even under the long fallow period the system is not self-sustaining; the people are extremely poor, large families are the rule, and there is a steady exodus from the hills into Manila, where unemployment is already high.

Here, it would seem, we have the epitome of the population/food/environment dilemma, exemplified the world over by shifting agriculture on hillsides.[46] Population growth pushes people on to marginal land; further growth, on both the hills and in the lowlands, pushes the hill population over the carrying capacity; the vulnerable environment deteriorates, bringing both a local decline in the capacity to sustain population and further pressure on already overburdened cities.

This dynamic process of "population pressure" on marginal areas, combined with mismanagement, is generally offered as the almost universal explanation of the widespread deterioration of marginal lands, whether they be hillsides or drylands:

> Whatever the root causes of suicidal land treatment and rapid population growth—and the causes of both are numerous and complex—in nearly every instance the rise in human numbers is the immediate catalyst of deteriorating food-production systems.[47]

Clearly, overintensive use is responsible in part for the deterioration of marginal systems, though often the land could sustain an even larger population if the farmers could afford appropriate technology, such as contouring land, adding fertilizers, and so on. There is also no doubt that in some circumstances rapid population growth, or high population density,

---

*Trees and other plants (e.g., clover and soybeans) that belong to the legume family have nodules on their roots. These contain bacteria that can incorporate nitrogen directly from the air. Thus when the roots are left behind and decay, nitrogen compounds are released into the soil and these can be taken up by crops planted in the soil. These plants thus act as natural nitrogen fertilizers.

or both, contribute strongly to the overintensive use of marginal land. But, as always, we need to view with skepticism the notion that such a simple and apparently obvious explanation is complete.

If the hill farmers above Laguna de Bay were to rest for a moment and gaze out towards the lake, they would see a vast gently undulating plain lying between the hills and the lake. The plain is covered with sugar cane. This enormous sugar cane plantation, with a factory at its center, is highly mechanized and run by minimal labor. It is owned by one man (a state of affairs that is officially illegal in the Philippines). The sugar cane is grown for export and the earnings provide virtually no benefits to the rural population (Chapter 6). Yet by growing mainly staple food crops on the plains, the local hill population could maintain and employ itself adequately on a small fraction of the estate.

This situation is starkly simple. In Latin America similar circumstances are probably more the rule than the exception.[48] Elsewhere, however, the socio-economic distortions that lead to excessive pressure on marginal land are less blatant. In the following account I have chosen to concentrate on the situation in semi-arid northern Africa as an example, because environmental degradation seems especially severe there and also because the generally available accounts of Africa's ecological problems suggest they arise from overuse (stemming from "population pressures"), a fragile environment, and a harsh climate.[49] We will begin with the Sahel and then will discuss eastern Kenya.

The Sahel

The literature on the Sahelian disaster is remarkable for the degree to which it concentrates on the immediate, and especially the physical, causes. The main points at issue tend to be whether the drought was natural or induced by man, whether it represents a long-term trend in the climate, the importance of misapplied technology, and so on. There is general agreement that western technology (medicine, veterinary medicine, deep wells) has encouraged uncontrolled growth of livestock and human populations, which is seen as the major cause. But apart from the political status of the nomads, especially their difficulties in getting food aid, little attention has been paid to the political, economic, social, and historical framework. These aspects are fundamental, for the ultimate cause of the Sahelian disaster was the destruction of a complex pattern of living arrangements that had previously allowed quite large numbers of people to live in a difficult environment.

I pointed out earlier in this chapter that, although attention has focused largely on the plight of the 2 million nomads and on overgrazing by their cattle, most of the environmental damage was caused by the farming and livestock of the 15 million sedentary peasants. Similarly, the underlying causes of desertification, including that caused by the nomads, are to be found in the history of both peasants and nomads—in the economic straits in which both groups find themselves, and in the disruption of the complex relationships that have existed for centuries between the two groups. Thus we can best lay bare the "structural" causes of the disaster by examining first the nomadic strategy for survival, second the history of the Sahelian peasant, and third the way in which the relationships between them have altered.

Nomadism and Environmental Uncertainty

The nomads have survived for centuries in the Sahel, where they have had to deal with resources that are very thinly and widely dispersed. Suitable vegetation occurs in patches, and in areas that are not entirely predictable. The amount of suitable vegetation also varies through time—from season to season and from year to year. In particular, runs of extremely bad drought years, inevitably years of local disaster, are known to be a recurrent and ineluctable part of life in the Sahel. They have been recorded in the folk history of the area for at least four centuries.[50]

Over this period the nomads developed a highly complex strategy to cope with their environment. Except in periods of disastrous and prolonged drought, the short-term local strategy has hinged on the livestock herds and has involved spreading risk and adapting to uncertainty.[51] First, the herds have been mixtures of different livestock species—camels, cattle, sheep, and goats—so that a wide spectrum of vegetation could be exploited. Staggered breeding patterns have provided milk throughout the year, and the goats have been an especially hardy reserve in poor years.

Secondly, movement has been a crucial part of the strategy. In the rainy season the herds have been moved from one communal pasture to another, depending upon where and when the rain has fallen. This strategy has also helped prevent overgrazing. These movements in the past were strictly controlled by the upper echelons of the nomadic hierarchy, so the strategy depended on internal social cohesion. In the dry season the herds have been concentrated in areas of permanent vegetation, for example at wells and wadis, and during this period there has been less movement. However, traditionally, part of the community has always undertaken much longer southward movements in the dry season, into the savanna area where the sedentary farmers live. Here the nomads have grazed their herds, often in the farmers' stubble in return for the livestock's manure, and have carried out extensive trading. This southward movement is the key to the long-term, large-scale strategy for coping with severe drought, but it has also been a regular ongoing part of the nomadic life.

Thirdly, the herds have served as food stores "on the hoof." The nomads have kept livestock in excess of current needs as a form of security (rather than merely for prestige, as is often thought). When drought has struck or food has become scarce, excess livestock have been slaughtered or traded for grain grown by sedentary farmers. The herds also have been used to build mutual reliance within nomadic society; there has been extensive loaning of animals to friends and relatives, a primitive insurance system for spreading risk.

Finally, when the herds became depleted in a series of bad years, the nomads have historically taken up gathering and hunting (mainly for gazelle), which they do with considerable skill and efficiency.

Existing alongside these more-or-less local and internal arrangements has been an equally important strategy based on a highly complex and geographically far-flung network of relationships with nonnomadic groups of people. These relationships have also provided the last resort in times of environmental disaster. Of particular importance have been relationships with the sedentary peasants to the south. Indeed, the nomads' desert edge and the peasants' savanna were until recently so closely integrated as to comprise a unified economic region, in which interaction was generally to the economic benefit of both groups.[52]

It is important to realize that trade with the savanna region to the south has been central to the nomadic economy; the nomads have been traders, not merely pastoralists, and they may even have been primarily traders. In part this was necessary because the savanna was the source of grain, and grain was and is an important part of the nomads' diet. But traditionally they also received most of their clothes, swords, and luxuries through trade. The "income" to buy these goods came from selling or trading livestock, and from extensive north-south trade. These trading earnings were made possible by the large differences in the price of various goods at the northern and southern ends of their trade routes. For example, they were able to buy salt and dates in the north (sometimes in exchange for grain bought in the south) and sell or trade them at higher prices in the south. They were thus part of the trans-Sahara commerce that linked the Mediterranean shores with Central Africa. This could be a very rewarding business: millet could be bought in the south, taken north, and traded for salt; when brought south, the salt would purchase eighty times as much millet as was bought initially.[53]

Nomadic penetration of the savanna, however, was much deeper than mere trade. The nomads dominated many savanna areas (often by force), controlled the grain farming, and obtained grain as taxes. Even more impressive, they invested in the savanna region profits made in the desert. They owned land and manufacturing businesses (i.e., handicrafts) there, and were deeply involved as brokers and merchants. Erstwhile nomads and their descendants were well represented in the savanna population.

This network of relationships was critical in the recurrent periods of environmental disaster. When prolonged severe droughts occurred, the capacity of the Sahel to support people—both nomads and farmers on the fringe—was greatly reduced. The economy was severely reduced and there was no recourse other than mass temporary exodus. During these periods the nomads retreated deep into the southern end of the trading area in the savanna, among the sedentary farmers.

As we will see below, the nomads' power, and hence their strategy, has been increasingly constrained in modern times. However, southward migration has remained critical and the economic and environmental good health of the peasants has thus been of crucial importance to the nomads as well as to the peasants themselves.

The Sahelian Peasant

The Sahel is not naturally highly productive, and is sensitive to overuse. Before colonial times, the peasants incorporated long fallow periods in each area between fairly brief periods of cultivation although, as noted above, the nomads' livestock did help to return nutrients to the soil when they grazed the stubble after harvest. In spite of the difficult environment, however, excess food production and the maintenance of large food reserves against drought years were standard practice.[54]

The French moved into the Sahel and the rest of West Africa during the early years of this century and had firm control of the southern farming region by 1914. Colonialism in West Africa was particularly harsh, especially during the period of military suppression in the first two decades of the century. This was probably worse to the south, in French Equatorial Africa, where military suppression and economic repression were so severe that most of the population was exterminated. The population of 15 million in 1900 was reduced, mainly through man-made famine, to just under 3 million in 1921.[55]

The sedentary farmers of the Sahelian area quickly came under French control. Revolts were suppressed and the resident military force had to be supported from the land. Taxes were imposed and increased continually (thus forcing the peasants into cash-crop production to pay the taxes). Subsistence agriculture and handicraft production were disrupted by the conscription of forced labor for road and rail building. These burdens were greatly increased during World War I, when compulsory quotas of food crops for shipment to France were extorted, special taxes were imposed, and more than 200,000 West Africans were marched off to fight in the trenches—all of this on top of a severe drought that began in 1912. Equally important was the rapid spread of cash crops, which the peasants were forced to grow for export to France. Senegal in particular was turned into a groundnut-producing estate, though this crop was also grown elsewhere in the Sahel.

Between the world wars, the French in Africa exploited their colonies without ever making substantial investment in them, and the poverty of the Sahel was deepened by this long period of exploitation and stagnation. The burdens of taxation, forced labor, and the production of cash crops sold at ridiculously low prices gradually worsened. In Senegal, for example, groundnut production became so extensive and food production so reduced that the peasants were forced to spend a third of their income on buying imported food. The area emerged from colonialism among the very poorest in the world; illiteracy was virtually universal and internal development nonexistent—even by the end of colonial rule there were almost no roads in the interior.

Conditions have remained relatively unchanged since independence, except that cash cropping has spread and has a firmer grip on the economies of the region, and the role of international agribusiness has expanded greatly. The main cash crops in the area are still groundnuts (Senegal, Mali, Upper Volta, and Niger) and cotton (Niger, Chad, Mali, and Upper Volta). Livestock is also exported. However, during the 1970s, international agribusiness firms have been planning and creating large-scale export enterprises in which modern labor-saving production is replacing or adding to peasant production and the range of exports is being extended. These enterprises include large ranching areas in Mauritania, Upper Volta, Mali, Niger, and Senegal, in addition to cotton and vegetables in Chad, Upper Volta, Senegal, and Niger. A major new project is to provide winter vegetables for the European market, much in the way agribusiness in Latin America does for the U.S. market.[56]

Bud Senegal, an affiliate of the U.S. agribusiness firm of Bud Antle, Inc., provides a good example of these operations. With the help of capital from the Senegalese government, the World Bank, and the German Development Bank, Bud Senegal has established huge irrigated "garden plantations" on land from which peasants have been moved. These plantations produce vegetables in the winter and feed for livestock (for export) in the summer. *None of this produce is eaten in Senegal.* The president of American Food Shares Company believes that "Africa is going to become the world's biggest producer of vegetables, not only to Europe but also to America." In this vision, however, Africa will not feed Africans, who cannot afford this produce.[57]

This process is occurring across all of North Africa. In Ethiopia, in an area where thousands of people were evicted to make way for agribusiness and then starved to death, international firms are producing alfalfa to feed livestock in Japan. The power of modern agribusiness is such that during the Sahelian famine the acreage planted to groundnuts in Senegal was increasing while that planted to sorghum and millet for local consumption was actually decreasing![58]

These changes wrought over the past seventy years have had profound direct and indirect consequences for the southern Sahelian environment.[59] From early colonial times, cash cropping has degraded the environment by its effects on soil fertility and soil erosion. The constraints of cash cropping have consistently forced the peasant to extend the cultivated period and reduce the fallow period. Furthermore, since organic material is continually removed in cash cropping and there is no stubble grazing, the fertility of the soil has declined and soil structure has deteriorated, a process that is hastened when commercial farming has introduced mechanization. This process becomes self-accelerating as the land is worked more intensively to make up for lost fertility, reducing fertility even further. Throughout the colonial period cash crops were mistakenly extended into unsuitable areas that were quickly degraded and abandoned. Cash cropping has thus been directly an agent of desertification.

The pressure to produce crops for cash and, more recently, the expansion of agribusiness, have forced peasants onto unsuitable marginal land for the production of both food and cash crops. This land is the most vulnerable to desertification and was most severely damaged in the recent disaster. In addition, peasant encroachment has reduced the grazing land available to nomads.

The pauperization of the Sahelian peasant has also led to environmental degradation indirectly. Since World War I, food production has been inadequate and malnutrition a constant fact of life. This has had two consequences. First, when drought has come and yields have fallen, the peasant has had no alternative but to exploit every available piece of land, no matter how badly it has deteriorated already, because there have been no food reserves. Second, poverty has prevented the peasant from investing in the land to increase its productivity and protect it from environmental degradation.

In a broader context, the poverty of the peasants has been a causal mechanism in the vicious circle of underdevelopment that has prevented the sustained growth of an integrated economy, which would in turn provide more income, greater employment, and more capital for investment (Chapters 7 and 9). Even the continued rapid growth of population, which undoubtedly exacerbates the environmental problems, has its origins in the structural poverty of the peasant. Thus environmental deterioration, like excessive birth rates and inadequate food production, arises in large part from this structural poverty.

The Collapse of the Nomadic Strategy

The French entry into the Sahel marked the beginning of a decline in the economic and political position of the nomads that has since proceeded relentlessly. Right from the earliest stages of the French occupation, the nomads had to bear an unusually heavy colonial load. A tax on livestock was added to the usual poll tax, and livestock were requisitioned to fill the needs of the French army. Particularly serious was the commandeering of camels by the French military, a practice that had a disastrous effect on trading and transport activities. Requisitioning was so increased during World War I that the nomads revolted and were suppressed with great ferocity.

The collapse of traditional nomadic trading was perhaps even more critical than direct taxation, requisitioning, and repression, for this destroyed the nomads' long-term strategy. By 1911 the trans-Sahara trade had already collapsed, and the salt and livestock trade was greatly disrupted by the loss of camels. The colonial administration also set up fixed trading points, run by three large international companies, and made it illegal to trade anywhere else, thus not only reducing nomadic trading but also arranging matters so that the companies could enforce their low monopoly buying prices. Finally, the French reoriented the peasants' trade toward the coast and the European market, thus breaking the traditional nomad/peasant trading link.[60]

The reduction of the nomads' political power and freedom of movement was equally serious. From the beginning of the colonial period the French imposed strict regulations on nomad movements. The nomads' military dominance over the sedentary farmer—and hence their ability to control land and grain production and to collect taxes—was destroyed. However, most of the interaction between nomad and farmer had been cooperative, and as the nomads' trading economy declined so too did their ability to invest in the farming area.

The nomads' freedom of movement has recently been further restricted by the arbitrary national boundaries drawn up at independence. The amount of available pasture has been reduced by the encroachment from the south of cash cropping and subsistence farming, and pasture has been destroyed by desertification when these activities have had to be abandoned. Dry-season grazing lands have been taken over for irrigated cash crops. The internal hierarchy of the nomads has been undermined through these various processes and by the efforts of the new governments to gain political control over them, so there is no longer adequate authority to enforce the traditional grazing patterns. The result is mismanagement of the restricted grazing that is now available. Game hunting by government officials, expatriates, and army personnel has so reduced game, especially gazelle, that the nomads can no longer depend on hunting in drought years.[61]

These changes in the economic status of the peasants and nomads, in the nomads' political status relative to that of the sedentary farmer, and in the agricultural practices of the peasants, have destroyed the ancient relationships that existed between nomad and peasant. In so doing, they have also destroyed the ultimate fallback in the nomads' strategy—the retreat far into the zone of sedentary farming where they could survive severe drought and where part of the herd could be maintained.

The exploration of these structural features and of the historical processes in the Sahel forces us to see the disaster in a different light from that cast by the usual simple explanations. Certainly the problem results from "pressure" on the land, from overuse and misuse of a difficult environment combined with a drastically varying climate. The problem surely would be less severe with a smaller and more slowly growing population. But similar environments elsewhere produce much more food and can maintain much higher populations. Agribusiness operations show that it is not land that is scarce, but the capital needed to make the land productive. The pressure and misuse have their origins in the poverty of the people, which in turn is a consequence of the political and economic framework in which they have been caught for eighty years.

Desertification and Famine in East Kenya

Famine and desertification in Africa are popularly associated with the Sahel. But there have also been recurrent disasters in East Africa, associated with a less spectacular but steady environmental deterioration. This has been studied in detail in eastern Kenya by Wisner, and by O'Keefe and Wisner.[62] Overgrazing and excessive cultivation have caused here the same sort of desertification as in the Sahel. Here I can present only the main processes in the history of the area, but Wisner's account is rich in detail.

The Current Plight of the Kamba

The major agricultural zones of Kenya are shown diagrammatically in figure 10-1. Kenya's southwest is an area of outstanding agricultural potential, among the best in Africa. The highlands (generally over 5,000 feet) have good soil and rainfall, a pleasant climate, and grow an enormous range of crops. This "core" agricultural area is surrounded by an arc of lower-lying land, generally between 1,000 and 5,000 feet, where rainfall is much sparser and very variable. In the absence of heavy invest-

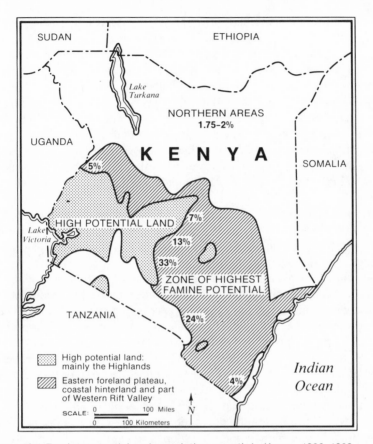

Figure 10-1 Famine potential and population growth in Kenya, 1962–1969

Source: Redrawn from Ben Wisner, "Man-Made Famine in Eastern Kenya: The Interrelationship of Environment and Development," *Institute of Development Studies Discussion Paper* no. 96, July 1976 (Brighton: University of Sussex).

Note: The percentages are rates of population increase in various areas.

ment—for example for irrigation—this area is best suited to extensive agriculture (grazing or shifting cultivation), except along river beds and other wet areas. The northern arid section of the arc is sparsely populated, but the area between the highlands and the coast, the Eastern Foreland Plateau, has a denser population and has recently been undergoing explosive population growth (figure 10-1). On the coast, the agricultural potential is again high and intensive cultivation possible. Thus, conditions for agriculture worsen as one moves away from the highlands or from the coast.

The Foreland Plateau is the area of Kenya most vulnerable to environmental deterioration and has the highest famine potential, in part because of its natural ecological situation but also because it is subjected to very intensive use. Wisner has described the Kamba as an example of how one tribe has fared in this vulnerable zone. They occupy the western side of the Plateau, where 90 percent of the land is less favorable semi-arid lowland and only 10 percent is more favorable hill zone.

The Kamba of the Foreland Plateau provide an example similar in many respects to the people of the Sahel. The majority of them are extremely poor and live in the lowlands, where their main security against drought and famine is provided by herds of livestock. This area is undergoing the typical ecological deterioration associated with severe overuse of marginal land by a rapidly growing population too poor to take corrective action.

Overstocking in the Kamba reserve was noted by the colonial Kenya Land Commission as early as 1934, and as population has increased the area has been caught in a classical vicious circle of overexploitation, degradation, production shortage, and related ills. The livestock, the main source of future security, destroy the vegetation, especially in drought years; the soil deteriorates, and hence the long-term vulnerability to drought, famine, and ecological disaster is increased. As a result, the Kamba are in a virtually perpetual state of near-famine, made especially severe in times of drought. For forty years the area has received a steady flow of what amounts to famine relief. From 1943 to 1963 there were seven years of serious famine; recently serious famines occurred in 1961 to 1962, 1965, and 1970 to 1974.

Yet there is no doubt that Kenya could easily produce more than enough food for its 12 million population, including the Kamba. Kenya is larger than France (population 52 million) and has large amounts of good farmland. Its population is less than Sri Lanka's, where the land area, one-ninth of Kenya's, is very mountainous but hunger is virtually unknown (Chapter 3). We must ask, therefore, why famine and desertification are so prevalent on the Foreland Plateau, why so many peasants are living on such a marginal area in the first place, and why the population there has been increasing at 20 to 30 percent a year when the national population growth rate is 3 percent.

The answer lies in the distorted economic structure and, particularly, in the process of "marginalization" of the Kenyan peasant. "Marginalized" peasants in this case are the landless classes that have been created and then pushed into the Kamba area from fertile highlands and from the better farming areas to the east.

Historical Origins

At the end of the nineteenth century, the Kamba lived at the edge of the highlands and the Plateau, mainly in those areas most suitable for agriculture—in the hills and beside rivers and other well-watered spots. Here their agriculture, including irrigation systems, was well developed; they raised a wide variety of crops and maintained large livestock herds. They also hunted and, most important, carried on very extensive trade with the Kikuyu in the highlands to the east, with other tribes to the west, and with the people of the coast. Drought years did occur, of course, and these were managed by the accumulation of large food stores in good years and by well-established and reliable trading with the Kikuyu, whose food production was much more assured. This state of affairs had persisted for at least 150 years.

The first major colonial impact on the Kamba occurred in the period 1908 to 1914, when large European ranches were established. These took over half of the Kamba's pasture land. In addition, at least 20 percent of their best farmland was taken over by settlers. Here, then, is the origin of overgrazing in the Kamba area. As elsewhere, the type of land ownership also changed, and within their colonial reserve the Kamba farmers were reduced to the status of tenants of the Crown. At the same time the colonists took over much of the Kamba's trade, particularly by means of the farmers' railway from Mombasa to Nairobi.[63] Finally, the poll tax was not only an extra financial burden but generally required that men go off and labor on settler estates at wages that declined throughout the 1930s, thus reducing the labor available at crucial times for maintaining subsistence farming.

Through the action of these various colonial policies, the Kamba economy showed the same signs of decline that typified East Africa:

> Down to 1912–13, African production had accounted for at least 70 per cent of exports. By 1928 it accounted for less than 20 per cent, and from 1925 absolute value of African export production declined as the reserves increasingly relapsed into subsistence farming to support their increasing populations.
>
> Under the conditions noted above—settler-imposed overstocking, lack of able-bodied men, heavy tax burdens—the pioneering Kamba in the lowlands found it hard-going. The famine of 1924–25 marked the emergence of marginality and famine vulnerability which has maintained its hold for 50 years.[64]

A particularly serious change brought about by colonialism was the disruption of trade with the Kikuyu. This exchange for food had been absolutely crucial in drought years, but it declined rapidly as the conditions in the highland Kikuyu reserve worsened throughout the 1930s under settler pressure (Chapter 8). The economic stresses of World War II, including the conscription of able-bodied men, exacerbated this situation, and the famine of 1943 to 1944 was devastating.

Since about 1950 the problems of the Kamba area have become more severe as a result of the rapid growth in population, *which has been caused largely by immigration into the area.* This immigration was brought about partly by colonial resettlement schemes, but mainly by the influx of marginalized landless peasants. This influx resulted from the overall agricultural policies of the colonial, and then of the independent, Kenya government; it began in the 1940s with the expulsion from the white-controlled highland farmlands of thousands of Kikuyu squatters.

Three policies in particular have led to marginalization: the introduction and spread of private land ownership, the concentration of investment and development around this new class of landowners, and the spread of cash crops for export. In the African reserves adjacent to the white settler areas, the colonial government set about establishing private ownership and registration of land by *Africans*. This created on the one hand a privileged group of African farmers, small holders, and ranchers who farmed high-potential land often with the aim of producing cash crops, and on the other hand large numbers of landless peasants who could no longer support themselves in the new economic framework. Thus, to the Kamba's own internal problem was added the immigration of landless Kikuyu, Luo, and other tribes.

From the mid-1950s the colonial government also pursued a policy of introducing cash crops to the best farming regions—first in the highlands but later in other upland areas, including the hilltops of the Kamba region. This accelerated the creation of deep class divisions among Africans, especially those between landowners and the landless. Some of the African profits from cash cropping were invested in large cattle herds in Kamba land. This created "cattle barons," deepened the schism between landowner and landless, and at the same time caused further overstocking. In the 1950s coffee profits were also invested in cotton production in the lowlands of the Kamba region. This scheme was eventually a failure, but not before it had degraded land previously used for food production. This and other commercial activities, including tourism, once more cut the grazing land available to lowland farmers, this time by one-third.

The independent Kenyan government since 1964 has simply extended these policies by "Africanizing" previously white areas without altering the basic policy of concentrating development on a restricted land-owning class in the areas with high potential farmland.[65] Thus a continuing stream of landless migrants has been forced to leave high-potential areas, which receive almost all the government investment in agriculture. These migrants exert ever-greater pressure on the marginal area of the Plateau, which has received virtually no investment to help deal with this influx. In the meantime, land farther east has been accumulated by large commercial enterprises involved in ranching, tourism, irrigated horticulture for export, and the stripping of scrubland to produce charcoal for export. The displaced dryland farmers are thus pushed westward toward ecologically vulnerable land that they must inevitably overexploit.

As Wisner notes, the result of these structural distortions in Kenya's rural economy has been the destruction of the peasant mode of existence. There has been increased economic welfare, choice, and security for the land-owning minority, reduced welfare and security for the mass of the peasants, and the steady erosion of marginal land in the process.

Causes of Environmental Degradation: Conclusions

There is obviously a strong temptation to assume that environmental degradation of marginal land through overuse and misuse is a result of "population pressure" caused by unchecked population growth. This temptation should be resisted. I do not claim that high population density is never a contributory factor in overuse; it sometimes is. But whenever one digs into the deeper causes of the degradation of marginal lands, the same forces that have been so important in maintaining high birth rates and constraining food production and economic development turn out to be dominant: the suppression of the welfare of the rural population, inequality within rural society, the impoverishment and marginalization of a large fraction of the peasants. Ecological deterioration in marginal food-producing areas in the LDCs is thus, in essence, a problem of poverty. Even if environmental degradation were the result "merely" of population pressure, it must be stressed that this, in turn, has its origins in the structural poverty of the rural population.

LIMITS TO GROWTH AND THE PATTERN OF ECONOMIC DEVELOPMENT

This chapter began with the question of whether or not the development of the LDCs is feasible in the face of finite resources and the inevitable environmental effects of economic growth. Its answer is that neither of these factors should prevent development for the foreseeable future. The extent and intensity of resource problems and of environmental degradation, however, depend on the *pattern* of development. Further economic growth rooted in rural inequality is likely to cause ever more severe deterioration of the environment; growth based on an egalitarian rural structure is likely to lead to an improved agricultural environment as peasants concentrate on the best land and invest in its care.

There are choices to be made among different strategies of development, both by the LDCs and by the various agencies of the rich nations that influence development. Different strategies will use different amounts and combinations of material resources and will have different effects on the environment. Most obviously, the classical strategy of the 1950s and 1960s, based on industrialization and maximum aggregate growth of GNP, would have consequences quite different from those of the agriculture-based egalitarian strategy recommended in this book.

The development strategy I have presented will reduce population growth rapidly by addressing first the economic welfare of the rural majority. Such a strategy, based on higher yields obtained through labor-intensive development, increased incomes, and evenly spread income, will provide economic opportunities and employment on the best land, will reduce the rate of movement onto marginal land, and will reduce the misuse of such land. An integrated, agricultural-based pattern of development will accelerate these processes by providing employment in labor-intensive rural industry. Such development will also reduce the flow of people to the cities.

A labor-intensive strategy in both agriculture and industry will reduce the energy requirements for development. Furthermore, such a strategy is more amenable to the use of intermediate technology, which would probably involve tapping abundant local materials and skills; it is also likely to be small scale, energy saving, and less environmentally disruptive. Thus the choice is *not* between development and the environment. Development, and development of the right sort, is needed to minimize future degradation of the environment.

A labor-intensive strategy, of course, does envisage the development of heavy industry, roads and railways, and sophisticated technology. I do not suggest that the perfect nation will consist entirely of idyllic villages, each grouped around its windmill and its solar power units. But I do suggest that moderate affluence can be reached by a path very different from the energy- and material-spending spree that has marked the development of Europe and the United States.

A consideration of resource limits and environmental effects thus leads to the same conclusions reached from an analysis of population growth, food supply, and poverty. The fundamental cause of these problems is the biases in the political, economic, and social structure of the LDCs, and in their relationships with the rich nations. Radical change in these structures is required to reduce environmental costs during development.

11

STANDING UP

> The Chinese people have stood up.
> *Mao Zedong*

Synthesis

I have sought to establish that rapid population growth and inadequate food supply are but the symptoms of poverty and that poverty itself is maintained by two basic and related causes. These are the internal political-economic structure of the LDCs and their strongly dependent and unequal relationship with the rich nations. I will first summarize the analysis that has led to these conclusions, then discuss what can be done to improve matters—in particular, what the rich nations ought to do.

Our point of departure was the massive increase in population in the LDCs, which is caused by persistent high birth rates in the face of greatly reduced death rates. The evidence is strong that these high birth rates result from poverty (Chapters 2 and 3). Large families make economic good sense for very poor people. This motivation for large families disappears as the family's level of economic welfare rises during development, and this is reflected in smaller families at higher levels of economic well-being. No single factor will explain all variation in family size, of course, and cultural features such as religion, the status of women, and family structure are likely to affect the timing of the demographic transition, i.e., the level of economic welfare at which average family size begins to decline. The rate of decline may also be increased by access to modern family planning techniques. However, the fundamental factors are economic.

Above the very lowest levels of national income, average family size falls sooner and faster when economic well-being is more evenly spread across the population (Chapter 3). Birth rates can be reduced, even at low income levels, if the nation or state uses its income to provide increased economic welfare and security to the entire population, as exemplified by China, Sri Lanka, and Kerala. Conversely, if the benefits of growth are very unevenly distributed, as in Mexico and Brazil, the national birth rate remains high even when national income is quite high and increasing rapidly. Thus, egalitarian patterns of development lead to more rapid population control. In particular, since the countryside is the great population dynamo, equality within rural society, and between rural and urban societies, is critical for reduced birth rates.

The maintenance of high birth rates, then, even in nations where *aggregate* income has increased at respectable rates, is caused by the persistent poverty of the majority, and particularly by rural poverty. I have called this *structural* poverty because it is the result of the economic, social, and political structure of society: the poor stay poor because they do not have access to productive resources.

A similar analysis applies to inadequate food supplies. The poor are malnourished either because they cannot afford to buy enough food or, where they are farmers, because they cannot afford the investment needed to grow more (Chapter 5). Since agricultural production is the major source of rural income, low agricultural productivity also causes rural poverty. The effects are widespread; low farm incomes mean low demand for nonfarm goods and therefore low employment for the off-farm rural population.

Two related sets of circumstances maintain the structural poverty of the rural population. Within rural society gross inequities exist in the distribution of land, water, credit, and technical innovations. The poor are thus prevented from making use of the available productive resources. In addition, the rural economy is suppressed because almost all LDCs have concentrated on developing urban industry at the expense of agriculture. A critical feature of this strategy has been the need for cheap labor, both in urban industry and in the production of exports that buy imported industrial goods. This cheap labor would be impossible without cheap food, but cheap food has required the suppression of agricultural incomes. Thus the rural population is exploited so that urban industry can be sustained (Chapter 6).

An important consequence of the suppression of agriculture is that this sector is then unable to contribute to overall economic development. Development requires a dynamic agriculture that can supply the needs of the nonfarm population and provide savings for investment. It also requires the integration of agriculture and *appropriate* industry through the meshing of supply and demand from both sectors. This integration is not possible within the distorted "dual economy" of the LDCs. The reason is that farm incomes are highly concentrated in a very small fraction of the farm population, and the demand generated by this group is for goods that are quite inappropriate to the needs and resources of the developing countries. As a result, there is no stimulus to small-scale industry that could provide goods to the farm population at large and could, in the process, make use of abundant local resources and employ many people (Chapter 7). This failure of agriculture is crucial: the LDCs cannot expect to develop without attacking the poverty of the rural majority, but the structural biases in most LDC economies maintain this poverty by distributing the costs of failure to the countryside and the benefits of progress to the cities. We thus have a "circular causal pathway" that is self-perpetuating and extremely difficult to break.

The fundamental cause of these problems is the unequal distribution of economic and political power in the LDCs. A small, mainly urban, elite controls the economy and ensures that it produces goods largely for a privileged minority. These goods are typically luxury items in the LDC context. They are inappropriate to LDC needs and are produced by large-scale, capital- and import-intensive industry that is generally inappropriate to LDC resources. This industrial strategy thus accentuates those biases within the LDCs that maintain poverty and underdevelopment. It squanders scarce capital, suppresses employment, increases income inequality, strengthens the position of the elite, and diverts resources from rural society and from the urban poor (Chapter 9).

Because development does not grow out of the internal dynamics of the dual economy, and because they have chosen the goal of creating "modern" industry quickly, the LDCs are dependent upon the industrialized nations for modern industrial goods and technology. These require foreign exchange, and so the LDCs depend upon the rich nations for markets for their exports, commercial loans, aid, and direct investment by foreign firms (Chapter 9). This pattern of dependence has its origins in colonial history and in the history of economic domination by the West (Chapter 8). It has been maintained in recent decades by the nature and aims of the LDCs' ruling elites, and by the unequal relationship between the rich and poor countries, particularly by the West's control over capital and modern technology.

Two important conclusions flow from these analyses. First, to reduce poverty and create sustained development, it is not enough to redistribute income and benefits. *Instead, there must be a redistribution of the productive resources (wealth) that produce income and benefits.* Second, basic changes within the LDCs require equally basic changes in their relationships with the rich nations. The exercise of economic and political power by the rich nations, which is made possible by the dependence of the LDCs, reinforces inequality *within* the poor nations and hence accentuates there the maldistribution of economic and political power—which in turn strengthens the dependent relationship. Thus the two sets of structural relationships—internal and external—must be seen as interlocked; *they have a joint historical origin and they are mutually reinforcing.*

Finally, the economic policies that interfere with real development in the LDCs are the natural result of the distribution of political power there. That political power in turn rests upon the uneven distribution of wealth. That is, the problems we have discussed have a political basis and require political solutions.

Pessimism is widespread over the prospects for controlling the population growth of the LDCs and for banishing hunger there. Such pessimism usually reflects a concern with the technical difficulties involved in controlling population, the technical difficulties in producing enough food, the physical inadequacy of tropical agriculture, the lack of physical resources, the likelihood of severe environmental disruption in ecosystems under pressure, and so on. Such pessimism is inappropriate. There is every reason to be optimistic about the physical and technical aspects of the problem, and if these were truly the heart of the matter there would be ample basis for optimism about population growth, food supply, and poverty in general. The snag is that these technical issues are not the heart of the matter. The original pessimism is misplaced, but there seems to be little reason for optimism when we confront the true nature of the problem.

The real issue underlying the population and food problem is how the LDCs can be transformed into integrated, self-sustaining, and more egalitarian economies that will continue to create real economic development which greatly improves the welfare of their poorest people. If this does not occur, birth rates will decline very spottily and slowly, food production will continue to lag, and agriculture's task will become ever harder. But this transformation requires a drastic restructuring of the internal economic framework of the LDCs, and this in turn requires a major redistribution of political power. Unfortunately, the prospects for such change within LDCs, and for appropriate changes in international relationships which would allow it to occur, seem poor. Here is the true basis for pessimism about the problems of population, food supply, and poverty.

The Relevance of Ecology

There are explanations of the population-and-food problem that largely eschew questions of economics and politics and focus instead upon what one might call "ecological" explanations. Indeed, ecological or environmental ideas sustain some of the most influential writing about food and population. It has even been suggested that ecological principles can provide a conceptual framework for analyzing the social and ethical aspects of food and population problems, and for deciding upon optimal arrangements for a sustainable human society.

The scientific discipline of ecology *does* have useful things to say about various technical aspects of the food and population problem and about the environmental consequences of economic growth. But it is not an appropriate discipline for analyzing the social, economic, and political aspects of these issues. Furthermore, the particular "ecological principles" usually called upon have very little relevance (even to technical issues), some are vacuous, and others are incorrect, or at least controversial among professional ecologists. (In this last regard, ecology has developed rapidly over the past twenty years, and its popularizers appear not to have caught up with the changes.)

I have found five major "ecological principles" commonly referred to for guidance in dealing with human problems and environmental questions.[1] The two principles most empty of useful content are: (1) "everything is connected to everything else," or "we can never do merely one thing," and (2) indefinite exponential growth is impossible in a limited environment.

Both "principles" are obvious without the benefit of ecology. The first is irrelevant except as an admonition to look beyond the immediate effects of one's actions; it is false if taken to mean that all connections are significant or that every action is so fraught with hidden dangers that it is best to do nothing (even if it were possible to do nothing). Building the Aswan dam greatly reduced the flow of silt to the delta (this was acknowledged before it was built), but it did not significantly affect, say, the diversity of rainforest trees in northern Queensland. The whole point of sound environmental management is to recognize probable *significant* effects—to find the sense between the nonsense that nothing is connected to anything else and the nonsense that everything is connected to everything else.

The second principle is irrelevant unless we are close to the limits of the environment's capacity to support us. I have tried to show that we are far short of these limits (Chapters 5 and 10). This principle is often stated in terms of the environment's "carrying capacity" and the likelihood that we will exceed it and suffer catastrophe. Such usage often suggests that the carrying capacity is a fixed property of the environment. While this is true for most nonhuman populations, the success of the human race is owing precisely to its ability to increase this capacity.

The three other principles are:

3. Diversity begets stability (often used as an analogy for human societies and as an argument against some types of agriculture).
4. Natural systems develop, through ecological succession, to climax ecosystems that are the most diverse and are "protective" of the physical environment. Forests are often given as an example. (This principle is generally used in arguments about the destruction of "life support systems" and particularly against the expansion of agriculture.)
5. "Homeostasis" or "balance" characterizes natural systems. This principle is used in the same way as principle 4.

The only "evidence" for principle 3 is that artificial ecosystems (e.g., cornfields) are simpler and less stable than natural ones. However, this says merely that ecosystems that already exist are more stable than those we must put together, which is hardly surprising. There is no evidence that simple artificial systems are less stable than diverse artificial systems, *or that simple natural systems are less stable than diverse natural systems.* [2]

Principle 4 appears to be false: climax systems (if they exist) tend to be *less* diverse than the intermediate steps preceding them.[3] (Nor is there any evidence that evolution "favors" diverse over simple ecosystems.) Principle 5 is certainly false as a general statement: drastic disturbance is a recurrent feature of many, perhaps most, natural ecosystems, and these disturbances are actually essential to prevent the extinction of some species by superior competitors. In fact, the *local* extinction of superior competitor species is often needed to allow the persistence of poorer competitors, which survive by filling, temporarily, the spaces left by recurrent ecological devastation.[4]

In summary, an ecological approach to particular problems, such as pollution and pest control, is essential. But ecology is a poor discipline for providing the framework for socio-economic decision making. The danger in using such a framework is that, like the "invisible hand" of the early economists, it is politically defeatist and escapist. Hunger, population, and poverty are human problems requiring the application of human values, human judgment, and human reason.

The neo-Malthusian explanation of food and population is a particularly simple-minded one that leans heavily on some ecological principles, such as the impossiblity of indefinite growth in a limited environment. It requires comment because its provision of facile answers to difficult questions has sidetracked the public debate and won acceptance for a barbarous view of population and food supply. In this view, population keeps getting ahead of food supply in the LDCs. Its proponents regard both poor agriculture and the innate capacity of humanity to increase as explanations rather than as symptoms, and they do not seek underlying mechanisms. As one observer says: "It is neither capitalism, as Marx believed, nor communism, as many Westerners maintain, that fosters poverty and misery. It is the tragic imbalance between population and resources."[5]

The major policy recommendations of the neo-Malthusian school tend to center on the need for population control, particularly through the spread of family planning techniques, but also by implementing population control programs in which coercion may feature strongly, and by allowing death rates due to food shortage to rise. The neo-Malthusians scorn "guilt-ridden" and "bleeding heart" approaches to the poor, confusing the callousness of their own views with objectivity and hard-headedness. It should be obvious to anyone who has read the preceding chapters that the neo-Malthusian view is hopelessly superficial and can hardly be maintained when we analyze the interacting nature of the problems of population, food supply, and poverty. To quote Talleyrand, "these policies are worse than criminal: they are mistaken."[6]

As an interesting sidelight, popularizers of this view have tended to substitute analogies and metaphors for analysis. In addition to the race metaphor discussed in Chapter 1, we have "triage" on the battlefield, the food/population "escalator," lifeboats, and the human population as a cancer. Harking back again to ecological analogies, the human population is compared, for example, to an island deer population that, lacking predators, exhausts its food supply and suffers catastrophic decline. But human societies are not cancers or deer populations, we do not live in lifeboats, and food production is not trench warfare. These analogies, in fact, obscure more than they clarify the issues. The fallacies and dangers inherent in such argument by metaphor have been discussed in detail by Murdoch and Oaten.[7]

We now turn to the final issue: what can or should be done to solve the joint problems of population, food supply, and poverty?

Internal Solutions: Reformism or Revolution?

I have argued that solving these problems requires drastic restructuring of the LDC economy along much more egalitarian lines, including a fundamental shift in the distribution of wealth and power.* Barring benevolent dictatorship, there are basically two ways in which such changes might be achieved—either gradually, through "creeping reformism," or suddenly, through the accession to power of a radically socialist government. The latter could occur through either democratic election or revolution. Let us turn first to the possibilities of reformism.

Liberal development economists have proposed that the needed changes can be brought about gradually by "reformist coalitions" that would be able "to trade on the fears and realizations of the privileged that they must give something away in the short run in order to survive in the future." The coalition, once in power, would implement reformist (redistributive) policies, even though some members of the coalition would stand to lose, because in doing so the coalition would remain in control of the economy over the long run. The strategy is delicate and fragile and is likely to pro-

---

*There may well be some LDCs that can sustain economic growth and also reduce the fraction of their population in poverty without radical restructuring, through the sheer increase in national income that would be derived from their enormous natural wealth, coupled with mild reformism. The richer oil-exporting nations and Brazil, Mexico, and Malaysia are possible examples.

ceed by nibbling away at the problems, with the coalition "maneuvering all the while to stay in power."[8]

It is not altogether clear who might make up such coalitions. One possibility is those administrators, planners, and business people who see the need for a more dynamic agriculture as a complement to industry, and who might therefore join with moderate rural groups, such as small-farmer cooperatives. Such a coalition might attempt, for example, to force reform upon rural landlords.

Unfortunately, as we have seen in preceding chapters, and as Fagen points out, the pattern of development over the past few decades has made the success of such a strategy very unlikely.[9] As LDCs have developed "modern" sectors, power has shifted somewhat from the land owners to the new class that dominates financing, production, and distribution in the modern sector. This sector is driven by private capital, committed to growth, and highly "internationalized"—that is, dependent on foreign capital and technology and often deeply penetrated by the transnationals. None of these characteristics makes this sector, or the privileged class controlling it, a likely force for equality, and the recent history of increasing inequality in the LDCs has substantiated this expectation. Fagen notes that Mexico provides a prime example of a nation in which government has long advocated increasing egalitarianism yet has signally failed to achieve it.

Reformist changes within bimodal agricultural systems are even likely to deepen rural problems, as discussed in Chapters 6 and 9. For example, the new reformist rural development strategies, with their emphasis on the small farmer, are quite capable of increasing inequality and worsening the situation of the poorest groups. On the one hand, they can create a relatively small privileged class of richer land-owning peasants who add strength to the forces that deny the remaining rural population access to productive resources; on the other hand, by the maintenance and expansion of a system with many farms that have too little land or too few resources, these strategies can lead to an increase in the exploited class of small farmers.

The prognosis for a reformist solution is thus poor. "Although some among [the LDC elites] may genuinely wish to assault class privilege and maldistribution, they are relentlessly pulled back toward policies that favor the few rather than the many...sustained progress [toward equitable distribution] is structurally out of the question. Only profound changes in the developmental strategies currently in use (and most probably in the elites currently in power) will significantly alter this situation."[10]

But is the prognosis any more positive for drastic restructuring through sudden socialism? Probably not. Radical change in the LDCs brought about through democratic processes appears to be highly unlikely. Democracy is a rare phenomenon in the LDCs, and there is no evidence that it is spreading. Even within democratic systems there is little evidence of actual erosion of the power of the elite. Here and there, however, there are some small glimmerings of hope. For example, there is evidence that the Indian peasants are organizing in some states to gain political power through cooperatives and the ballot.[11] Whether such organizations can achieve anything remains to be seen.

There is also little reason to expect widespread successful revolutions by the peasants and the urban poor of the LDCs. The elite groups have had several decades of power in which to consolidate their economic and political position. Gerard Chaliand, a participant-observer in several recent revolutions, notes that "for all the prevailing poverty, the situation is not explosive in most Asian, African and Latin American countries." Nor can the successful Chinese or Vietnamese peasant revolutions be taken as a paradigm, for they arose out of the turmoil and disarray of international war and the struggle for national independence. Such a background of turmoil appears to be essential for successful revolution:

> Contemporary history provides virtually no instance of a class struggle in a backward country managing, by itself, without recourse to nationalism, to mobilize the population to achieve the proclaimed goals of socialism. On the contrary, patriotic exaltation in circumstances of foreign aggression, occupation, of general domination, proved to be decisive.[12]

In most areas, however, the wars of national liberation are over.

The Nicaraguan revolution of 1979 provides a partial counterexample to this view. The revolutionary forces were mainly a combination of the urban poor and the disaffected urban industrial workers, together with elements of the middle class. However, the new government is made up largely of representatives from business and the professions and has chosen economic policies that are likely to lead to the continuing dominance of private business and foreign interests.[13]

As Chaliand further observes, very few of the revolutions that have occurred have resulted in radical restructuring of the economy. The revolutions of the past thirty years have been undertaken mainly by the small middle class (often led by the intellectuals) when that class has been prevented from promoting and benefiting from economic growth. As a consequence, most revolutions have occurred only at the top of society and have not resulted in thoroughgoing social change. There is also the question of whether the rich nations, singly or jointly, would allow revolutionary socialist governments to persist, an issue discussed below.

External Relations: Cooperation or Self-Reliance?

The internal distortions in the LDCs are the greatest impediment to development and the removal of poverty. Most analysts, whether reformist or radical, agree that internal change is the key; without it, reform of the international system will have little effect on the poor. However, the international economic system does have powerful effects on the LDCs, particularly on their dual structure, and it also makes radical internal changes more difficult. We must therefore examine the possibilities for change in the relationships between the poor and rich nations.

Revolutionary or other change to a noncapitalist economy in the industrialized West hardly seems imminent. The reformer, radical or otherwise, here or in the LDCs, would surely be unwise to pin any hopes on such an event. The LDCs will most likely continue to be constrained within the framework of a world dominated by capitalist or "mixed" economies. So the question is, what should be the international strategy of the LDCs in these conditions, given that their goal ought to be economic development based on broad egalitarian participation? To answer that question we first need to resolve a basic issue: are the interests of the LDCs and the rich nations irreconcilably in conflict, or can they be made congruent? And immediately one must add: *whose* interests within the LDCs will be served by cooperation?

There are, again, two major viewpoints among those who see the need for change in the international economy. The reformist view is basically that the long-run interests of the two groups of nations are compatible within the broad structural relationships that exist. This view holds that changes can (and must) be made within the existing structures so that rapid economic growth is not only possible for both rich and poor countries but the growth of each can reinforce the economy of the other. It holds that this joint growth is central to the removal of poverty in the LDCs.

A critical condition for this mutual enhancement is more "liberal" international trade. The LDCs need to concentrate more on producing manufactured goods for exports (rather than on more import substitution for domestic consumption), and they need to reduce barriers to industrial imports. That is, they need to become more outward looking. The rich nations, for their part, need to reverse the recent trend toward raising barriers against imports of LDC-manufactured goods, and they need to achieve high economic growth rates again (to provide a growing market for LDC exports). The LDCs stand to gain greater economic growth through expanding exports. They also stand to gain greater employment, since producing manufactured exports tends to be more labor intensive than import substitution. The rich nations stand to gain both an increase in cheap imports and larger markets for their own exports as a result of freer trade and increasing LDC incomes. Increasing incomes in the West should also reverse the trend towards shrinking aid to the LDCs. Provided these policies are successful, that some changes are made in the system of giving official loans, that private loans and investment continue to grow, and that aid is increased, most LDCs should be able to avoid serious debt problems while expanding their economies.[14]

This view recognizes that changes are needed in international economic relationships. But it holds that with negotiation, accommodation, and some reforms, the areas of global common interest between the rich and poor nations can serve as a basis for cooperation. It is expected that these mutual benefits can be gained, and the needs of LDCs met, "in ways that disturb as little as possible the existing market forces that (purportedly) are conducive to the most efficient allocation of global resources," and that "a way can be found to give fairer shares to the [LDCs] without upsetting the international applecart as currently constructed."[15]

The focus of recent discussions on international reform is the resolution passed by the United Nations in 1974, expressing the determination of the member states, including the rich nations, to establish a more equitable New International Economic Order. This resolution was passed in response to the clear evidence that the rich nations up until then had made no serious attempt to implement previously adopted UN development strategies.[16] Under the proposed New Order, higher and steadier prices for raw materials and broader markets for LDC-manufactured exports would be achieved through trade negotiations; the LDC debt burden would be eased; aid and investment would be increased; and a number of less well-defined improvements made. Most attention has been directed, by LDCs and developed nations alike, to the questions of aid and investment.

The various particular reforms suggested since 1974 have differed in detail, but there is substantial agreement among liberal economists as to their general form.[17] First, the exports of the LDCs need to be expanded, in part by removing the rich countries' barriers to developing countries' exports. This expansion of manufactured exports is fundamental to the entire reform strategy. Without it, the other problems of development—debt repayment, industrialization, etc.—cannot be solved. Second, the supply of credit to LDCs needs to be assured by various improvements in the international lending institutions. Notice that the provision of credit does not remove the need to expand exports; in fact, it increases it because future exports must grow more rapidly than imports to repay the growing debt. If, instead, export growth is restricted, the response in the LDCs will be to reduce industrial imports and the growth they create, which will lead to increased unemployment and lower real wages. In other words, it is the poor who will suffer most, given the present structure of the LDCs.[18]

Third, a scheme such as an international tax on exploitation of common ocean resources is needed to provide capital to the poorest countries, who are poor debt risks. Fourth, some form of international regulation of TNC activities is needed, perhaps by having an international center in which TNCs would deposit information about their activities, including pricing, so that LDC governments could get this information.

Thus the reformist view recognizes that historically there has been international inequality, but it rejects the radical and especially the Marxist view that exploitation of the poor nations by the rich nations is inevitable. It sets for itself "the task of defining new rules [which] must incorporate seriously for the first time the claims of the developing world."[19] This view does not claim that such reforms will solve all problems; on the contrary, it stresses that redistributive policies *within* the LDCs are of paramount importance. However, it does claim that participation in trade can have an internal equalizing effect if exports are labor intensive and if the earnings are distributed equally.

There is no suggestion that this task will be easy. It requires "bold policy reforms" on the international scene, a quick recovery to rapid economic growth in the industrialized nations, and internal reform and sustained effort in the developing countries. Indeed, while championing the export-driven strategy for LDC development in its 1979 *World Development Report*, the World Bank, in its 1979 *Annual Report*, cautions that:

> the economic difficulties of the industrialized countries, the instability of exchange rates, and the prevailing atmosphere of uncertainty about the growth of international trade and the future movements of capital suggest that it will be more difficult for the developing countries to expand their economies in the coming decade than it has been in the past 25 years; and that even to maintain their present rate of progress, developing countries will need larger inflows of foreign capital, while undertaking vigorous efforts to withstand protectionist pressures and to stimulate the productivity of their agriculture sector.[20]

Nor should the potential benefits of this strategy be overestimated. The World Bank has made several alternative projections of the future. The most optimistic assumes that the changes discussed above will occur quickly. In 1990, under this high economic growth projection, the average annual income of over 1 billion people in the poorest LDCs will be $232, compared with $157 in 1976. In the LDCs as a whole, by the year 2000 almost half a billion people will still be in absolute poverty. In the pessimistic projection, which is largely a continuation of the conditions of the late 1970s, the average income in the poorest LDCs in 1990 will be $200, and in 2000 A.D. over 700 million people will be in absolute poverty.

We are now in a position to step back and evaluate the reform strategy. Its elements have been clearly laid out for at least a decade, and there has been ample time for the various parties to respond.

First, as discussed at length in Chapters 7 and 9, the LDCs have not been making great strides in internal reform. On the contrary, dualism has been deepening. Secondly, there has been no noticeable improvement, from the LDCs' point of view, in the international economic order. Following the 1974 UN resolution, the West certainly leapt into the discussion of the New International Economic Order with great gusto. The LDCs themselves, the OPEC nations excepted, also responded with reasonableness. Since then, however, there has been a downhill course. By the end of 1979, even talk on the New Order had run out of steam.[21]

During the latter half of the 1970s, the terms of trade went against the LDCs. As LDC-manufactured goods and steel invaded western markets, the rich nations responded by raising their trade barriers. (At the same time, the more advanced LDCs that produce these goods cannot find other markets. Because incomes in these semi-industrialized nations are highly concentrated and their own domestic demand is limited, and because the other LDCs remain undeveloped, they also cannot provide markets.) Aid in real terms has declined throughout most of this period.[22]

In late 1979, Mahmoud Mesteri, a UN spokesman on economic issues for the LDCs, concluded that "the basic problem is the refusal of most of the developed countries, and particularly the principal industrialized countries, to commit themselves seriously to economic reform." Albert Fishlow, who earlier clearly articulated the reform strategy, has since noted sadly that its prime requirement is lacking: "a liberal trade regime capable of absorbing the increasingly competitive exports of manufactures from the developing countries now seems more remote than ever." Clearly, "the rich countries have no intention of tackling the question of world poverty on a systematic and concerted basis."[23]

Even if the LDCs were to "win" at the international bargaining table, it is not at all clear that the poor in the LDCs would thereby gain. In the first place, it is the richer countries among the LDCs who stand to gain by far the greatest share of any improvements in trade and international credit; the poorer LDCs stand to gain hardly at all.[24] More importantly, it is also unlikely that the majority of people in any given LDC would gain significantly "if fairer shares of global product and opportunities [were to be] won by the elites ostensibly speaking in their name."[25] These elites, after all, represent interests, both at home and abroad, that are basically satisfied with the economic structure as it is, even though they may want a larger share of the product. Consequently, growth that is tied to the international economic system is likely to lead mainly to a small expansion of the elite in the LDCs, not to a broad upgrading of the poor majority. And intensified interaction with the rich nations is likely to reinforce these elites and thus accentuate the internal dualism that is at the root of the problems of population, food supply, and poverty.

The alternative and radical view of international relationships holds that, in the present circumstances, the interests of the poor in the LDCs are in conflict with the interests of the major economic forces in the developed world. (It recognizes that, over the long term, real development can be beneficial to both rich and poor countries.) This view does not deny that some individuals or groups, such as technical experts or aid-giving agencies, have the best interests of the LDCs at heart. It does assert that on balance interaction with the rich nations will be unfavorable to the LDCs— that is, it will be unfavorable to the economic welfare of the masses of the poor when compared with a strategy that emphasizes internal integration and therefore a maximum of self-reliance (Chapter 7).

No simple set of tactics flows from such a strategy. Complete isolation from the rich nations is not feasible. China, for example, while it turned inward and emphasized self-reliance, has always continued to trade on a small scale with the West—but always with independence and internal strength as prime objectives.

The essence of a self-reliant strategy is the mobilization of internal resources in the service of development, aimed first at raising the welfare of the majority—that is, it would greatly change what is produced and how it is distributed. Such a reorganization might mean a period of nearly total isolation from the developed nations, but it would soon require a return to trade for essential materials or goods that could not be produced efficiently at home. The demand, however, would then be for appropriate goods.

This is hardly the place to attempt to lay out development plans for an enormous array of LDCs; however, some features are probably generally applicable. The preferred strategy would seek to minimize dependence on foreign capital, at least during the early stages of development; where possible, it would use locally abundant resources rather than imports; it would greatly reduce foreign investment, especially by transnational corporations; it would minimize foreign loans that required western-oriented economic policies, foreign aid that the LDCs could not control, or foreign aid that accentuated internal biases or external dependence. Trade with other LDCs, especially regional trade, would be emphasized, where appropriate, since this would help to avoid dominance by foreign capital-rich nations. Where western technology had to be imported it would be analyzed, modified, and adapted (as the Japanese did so brilliantly) so that local technical skills would be developed, paving the way for the creation of indigenous technology in the future.

All of this would depend for its success, of course, on a radical redistribution of internal political power. However, once such a transformation were achieved, dependence would be reduced and the LDCs would come to the international bargaining table in a much stronger position.[26]

Overview of Reformist versus Radical Strategies

In the two previous sections, dealing respectively with internal and external changes, I have presented a reformist and a radical set of solutions to the problems facing the LDCs. In both cases, the issues and evidence are complex, and predictions about the future are surrounded by uncertainty. Nevertheless, I believe that the evidence points clearly to the need for the radical approach. With regard to the need for basic redistribution within the LDCs, governments able to bring about the profound internal structural changes that are required will need, at the least, to have a strong socialist bent. With regard to relations with the developed world, it seems clear that the effort to get a new international order by negotiation is largely failing and, further, that the general strategy of hitching the LDC wagon to the rich nations' star is in any case a poor one.

Having said this, it must quickly be added that the likelihood of radical solutions appears small. Sudden socialism in most LDCs is not looming on the horizon. Thus, while reformist change is somewhat more likely to occur, it is not likely to be successful; while radical change would more likely be successful, it has little chance of occurring.

Much of the gloom over the chances for radical change is cast by the rich nations and we turn, finally, to look at their possible role in the solution of the problem of poverty.

What Can the Rich Nations Do?

The rich nations will probably continue to be predominantly capitalist for the foreseeable future. Within this constraint, what might they do, and what is it reasonable to expect them to do, to help solve the problems of the poor in the LDCs?

Those people in the rich nations who wish to help the poor in the LDCs face a truly perplexing dilemma. Because our activities occur within highly interconnected and strongly biased international and internal economic structures, it is hard to set out simple changes that will improve matters. As we have seen, the typical LDC with which we interact has a politically repressive, authoritarian, and highly nonegalitarian government that uses its internal and foreign policies to remain in power and to improve the conditions of the privileged minority it represents. The obvious well-intentioned efforts we might make within this framework are likely to worsen this structural problem. "Fair shares" (e.g., through trade) for the LDCs, while providing some additional aggregate income, will benefit mainly the richer LDCs and the entrenched elites. Similarly, foreign aid almost inevitably benefits the richer segments of society (Chapter 9). It is extremely difficult to ensure that benefits intended for the poor do not flow to the rich.

Because it is difficult, perhaps impossible, to make sure that well-intentioned acts and projects have beneficial consequences when they take place within a larger economic framework that is highly distorted, one sensible piece of advice to rich nations is that they do "little or nothing; just try to avoid creating damage."[27] The difficulty here is that international ties are strong and pervasive and any probable policy of disengagement would still leave much interaction for the foreseeable future. Our actions will inevitably affect the future of the LDCs and our problem is therefore to try to make those actions more beneficial, or at least less harmful.

To achieve this aim, we need to be guided by a clear idea of what we believe to be in the best interests of the poor in the LDCs. I have argued that this should be a radical restructuring of the dual economy. If this is correct, the West must face squarely a truth it has long avoided: the radical, socialist, Communist, or "leftist" forces within developing countries represent the best hope for restructuring dual economies along egalitarian lines. The evidence is now in—for example from Cuba, Chile, China, and Tanzania—that radical socialist governments do assault the structural basis of poverty.[28]

Among the LDCs, Taiwan and South Korea are apparent exceptions to this claim. There, nonsocialist governments have overseen rapid economic growth combined with a large degree of economic egalitarianism and a general avoidance of the distortions of dualism (Chapters 6 and 7). However, because of the highly unusual nature of Japanese colonialism, and the immediate post-war reforms, these two nations gained independence with a relatively egalitarian structure and a highly developed agriculture (Chapters 7 and 8); they have not needed to overcome the deep-seated dualism which, I have argued, requires radical attack.

Like the aspiring physician, our first aim, above all, should be to do no harm. This requires that, at the least, the West needs to take a nonhostile and neutral attitude toward radical socialist movements in the LDCs. In turn, this would require a major reversal of foreign policy, especially in the United States. It implies a "major movement towards the demilitarization of foreign policy, close public control over intelligence operations, substantial decoupling of business and corporate interests from the conduct of foreign policy, and undoubtedly much more."[29] It requires recognizing that stability in the LDCs is not necessarily good and temporary turmoil not necessarily bad, that the interests of the majority in an LDC may be contrary to and more important than a "favorable climate for investment."

We need to recognize just how deep a change in policy is involved. The present policies of the West help maintain governments around the world that represent only a small minority of their population. Our current policies, of course, are rarely stated in such terms. Usually they are couched in terms of support for allies, the maintenance of "stability," and so on. But whether it is overt and covert military intervention, providing secret-police training, or giving military or economic aid, the general result is the support of regimes that pursue inequitable policies.

The United States is not unique in having these policies, but it has certainly been the major force against the accession of egalitarian governments, mainly in the name of anti-Communism: "American intervention in the name of anti-communism has been the most persistent phenomenon of U.S. foreign policy since the end of World War II."[30]

There are many instruments for carrying out these policies, but their pervasiveness can be seen by looking at only one, namely the *known* CIA covert activities in LDCs over the past three decades. The CIA has sponsored coups d'etat, some of them successful, in Iran, Guatemala, Indonesia, Cuba, Vietnam, Chile, and probably Greece. It has covertly helped to suppress revolutionary movements in the Philippines, prerevolutionary Cuba, Vietnam, the Congo (now Zaire), Bolivia, Peru, and Laos. (In Laos the CIA maintained, at least until the early 1970s, an army of about 50,000 men, which also operated in Burma, Cambodia, and Thailand.) Between 1949 and the late 1960s, the CIA sponsored guerrilla raids into China, supported a Nationalist Chinese army in Burma, and trained Tibetan guerrillas. In 1958, 1964, and 1970 (together with ITT), it interfered secretly to prevent Salvador Allende from winning elections in Chile, and it spent millions of dollars in Brazil in the 1960s to prevent leftist control of the Brazilian Congress. In addition, the CIA has indirectly aided coups and altered government policy in probably a score of nations through covert financing and penetration of political parties, the media, the military and organized labor.[31] This account includes only those covert activities that have come to light; presumably there are others that still remain secret.

Such activity is supposedly becoming less common, and this is likely to be true for the larger scale paramilitary operations that are difficult to keep secret. In 1974 the Hughes-Ryan Amendment required that various congressional committees were to be apprised of some covert activities. However, even in 1975, after passage of this law, the CIA ran a large-scale secret military operation in Angola against the Communist forces: it supplied arms, supported mercenaries, and flew them into Angola in CIA planes. (This activity was later denied by both Henry Kissinger and William Colby [then head of the CIA] before congressional committees.)[32]*

*As this book goes to press in early 1980, great pressure is building to relax the constraints on the CIA.

The CIA, of course, is not the only agent of western (or U.S.) military interference. U.S. troops were sent to Lebanon and the Dominican Republic. As recently as 1978, French and Belgian paratroopers (the latter carried in U.S. aircraft from British bases) were in Zaire helping to maintain the viciously repressive dictatorship of Mobutu. (In this case the reason for interference is particularly clear: access to copper, cobalt, industrial diamonds, and, more importantly, uranium.)[33]

I have already noted how other policies of the West operate against egalitarian forces in the LDCs (Chapter 9). Military aid goes generally to rightist regimes, and economic aid tends to follow a similar pattern. (Sweden is unusual in this regard and has in the past given all of its Latin American aid to Cuba and Allende's Chile.)[34]

A special problem is posed by the transnational corporations. While these have certainly on occasion been involved in covert political activities (as in Chile), their political influence in general is more subtle, operating primarily through their influence over the distribution of economic power and also through bribery.[35] In many cases only the governments of the developed nations are powerful enough to control these international giants, and it seems unlikely that they can do so without greatly cutting down their size.

To bring about a radical realignment of these policies would require a profound change in the world view of most people in the West. The United States in particular needs to reeducate itself out of the state of virtual paranoia over Communism that has seized it since the late 1940s, and it needs to learn to keep clear the distinction between the legitimate aspirations of the masses in some developing country, manifested in a revolutionary movement, and Russian nationalism and great-power competition in the guise of Communism. There is almost no public discussion in the United States of socialist alternatives for the LDCs (or for America itself), and the discussion we do hear often is hardly rational.*

In addition to an about-face in foreign policy, there are positive things that the West can do to help create real development in the LDCs. Unfortunately, most of these actions are likely to have only limited success, and always they carry with them the danger of structural harm as long as internal dualism remains in LDCs.

One improvement that is certainly in the power of the rich nations is to reduce greatly the sale of arms (and the giving of arms, which stimulates more sales) to the LDCs. Since the rich nations have a virtual monopoly of production and since their policies and salesmen create much of the de-

---

*For example, the July 2, 1979, issue of *Time* magazine sees the reduction of the free rice ration and the dismantling of the welfare state in Sri Lanka solely in terms of yet another victory in capitalism's world-wide war against socialism.

mand, they are in a position to reduce this disastrous squandering of scarce resources.

Our standard of living in the West depends in part on our exploitation of cheap labor and resources in the LDCs, and there is a clear need for fairer international trade. Although improvements in trade may further entrench the elites in the LDCs, one can hardly maintain that it is good for the LDCs for us to continue to shortchange them for their labor and resources.

The purpose of foreign commercial loans and investment is to gain financial return, so there is little chance that these will go specifically to benefit the poor. There are some steps the rich nations could take, however, to ameliorate the negative effects of their activities. The two main official international lending agencies—the World Bank and the International Monetary Fund (IMF)—are essentially run by the West. The IMF in particular has often required the LDCs to pursue inequitable internal policies, and policies that help foreign business, before making loans. The best that could realistically be hoped for here is that in their lending policies the two institutions will be neutral towards an LDC government's egalitarian measures. Ameliorating the effects of the transnational corporations and the international commercial banks is a much more difficult problem. As long as the West is committed to corporate capitalism, these institutions are not likely to be nationalized, or to be greatly reduced in size. Hence attempts to regulate them are likely to be ineffectual.

Foreign aid for development poses probably the most difficult problem of all. A strategy consistent with the aims outlined above would give aid only to those governments with a clear goal of improving the economic welfare of their people. Such aid should be given largely without strings, on the grounds that these governments probably know better than we do how to use it. The aid should be given as grants rather than as loans since this avoids future indebtedness. On the other hand, aid (other than emergency aid) would be withheld from governments pursuing nonegalitarian policies, on the grounds that such aid simply strengthens the position of the elites. The hope would be that, helped by other changes in foreign policy, the number of countries qualifying for aid would rapidly increase.

It must be admitted that this aid strategy is not likely to be followed, if for no other reason than the fact that there are many people in the West who genuinely care about the poor in the typical LDCs and want to do something positive for them. Aid programs to nonegalitarian LDCs will no doubt therefore continue, but within this framework several ameliorative steps might be taken. Nongovernmental aid agencies (such as Oxfam) appear to be quite successful at reaching the poor without exacerbating local structural distortions, and they could use more support. Official aid agencies probably would do better to give up the goal of optimal efficiency in transferring large amounts of aid and concentrate instead on efforts that are less easily distorted in the recipient nation. Such efforts are likely to be small scale and they need to be aimed directly at the poor, particularly the rural poor. Then too, it does seem that the rich nations could play a particularly useful role in the development of appropriate technology. Here, though, care needs to be taken to do the work in conjunction with people from the LDCs, and probably in the LDCs, so that the technology is truly appropriate and the technological skills involved become internalized.

It must be stressed again that these reforms in lending, investment, and aid would hardly have a major impact in the absence of the overarching changes needed in the West's foreign policy and in its tolerance of socialist movements and regimes.

The most important action that those of us in the rich nations can take to help the poor in the developing world is to bring about basic change in the policies of our own governments. Although the future of the poor is not solely, perhaps not even largely, in the hands of the developed nations, we nevertheless have a powerful effect on events in the LDCs, and we have the capacity to make it easier for the poor to help themselves. Our policies must become, at the very least, neutral with respect to movements in the poor countries that aim at a more egalitarian society through radical re-structuring of the economy. Furthermore, real development for the poor is not only a moral imperative, it is in our own long-term interest. Since most of the rich nations are democracies, the potential exists for changing our governments' aims to coincide with those of the world's poverty-ridden majority.

As a first step in bringing about such change, we need to understand the connections between rapid population growth, inadequate food sup-ply, and poverty in the LDCs; we also need to understand the connection between our nations' actions and the persistence of poverty in the develop-ing world. It has been the aim of this book to expose these connections.

APPENDIX A: A NOTE ON DEMOGRAPHY

The most readily available measure of a nation's fertility in a given year is its *crude birth rate* (CBR). This is simply the total number of babies born per year divided by the total population, multiplied by 1,000. So it is the number of births per thousand people per year. When we also know the *crude death rate* (CDR), then we know the growth rate of the population that year (growth rate per 1,000 = CBR–CDR).

The CBR is determined mainly by two factors: the number of babies born to the average reproductive-aged woman and the fraction of the female population that is of reproductive age (the sex ratio has a small effect). Thus, the population's age distribution affects its birth rate. Women's reproductive age ranges roughly from fifteen to forty-five, and most reproduction is done by women aged fifteen to twenty-nine. Therefore, a population that has increased rapidly for thirty years will likely have a larger fraction of reproductive-aged women than a population that has been constant for thirty years.

When we want to know how fast the population is growing, we need to know the CBR. However, if we want to know about the fertility behavior of the women in the population, the CBR may mislead us because it is influenced by the age distribution. It will also mislead us if we want to know how fast the population will grow over the next few decades as the age distribution changes.

There are several methods of measuring women's fertility that are not affected by age distribution. The most readily understandable is the *average completed family size*. This is determined by sampling or censusing those women in the population who have lived beyond the reproductive years and are still alive; it is the average number of children ever born to such women. This, however, tells us about *past* fertility behavior; if the conditions affecting fertility have been changing, this will not be a reliable guide to the average completed family size that the currently reproductive women will have. In developing countries we would in general expect this figure to overestimate future completed family size.

A measure of *current* fertility behavior that is somewhat analogous to completed family size is the *total fertility rate* (TFR). The TFR measures, in a given year, the fertility of women of all reproductive ages. Thus, to measure the TFR in the United States in, say, 1980, we begin by determining how many children were born to women aged fourteen to fifteen.

We then divide this by the number of women aged fourteen to fifteen to get the number of children born per woman in this age bracket. This rate might be about .001 (i.e., 1 child per 1,000 women). We do this for each year class. For example, women aged twenty to twenty-one might have .12 children on average (120 children for every 1,000 women). The TFR for 1980 is then the number of children a woman would have if she were to go through her entire reproductive life span having children according to the pattern set by 1980 women. Thus, we would imagine her having .001 of a child in her fifteenth year, gradually increasing to .12 of a child in her twenty-first year, and so on. Adding up these "parts" of children would in the end produce, over her lifespan, probably about 1.8 children. In the United States in 1976 the TFR was 1.8; it was 3.4 in Sri Lanka in 1974 and 6.3 in Pakistan in 1975.

Notice that the TFR measures the fertility of all women in the reproductive ages, whether they are married or not and whether they are sterile or fecund. These features are all averaged out.

In a population that has been a constant size for a long time, a TFR of just over 2 is needed to keep the numbers constant (this is "replacement" TFR). The TFR must be just over 2, rather than precisely 2, because some women die before getting to the end of their reproductive years. *Actual completed family size of women who marry* needs to be slightly greater again (about 2.1 in the West) because some women do not marry and do not have children.

Although the TFR in the United States has been below 2 in recent years, the population has continued to grow because there has been a large proportion of reproductive-aged women (and because of immigration). The youthfulness of the population, in turn, is a result of previous high fertility. For example, in 1955 the U.S. TFR was 3.6, slightly higher than Sri Lanka's rate in 1974.

The TFR is a better index of fertility behavior than the CBR because the former is not affected by age distribution. However, the CBR is generally easier to determine. Fortunately, in recent decades the two measures have been highly correlated—that is, most of the observed changes in the CBR in the less developed countries have been caused by changes in fertility behavior; changes in the age distributions have not been great enough to have large effects on changes in the birth rate. Those changes that have occurred in the age distribution have tended to *increase* the CBR.

The CDR is analogous to the CBR. It is the number of people dying in a given year divided by the number in the population, multiplied by 1,000. The death rate is of course strongly affected by the age distribution. In rapidly growing populations young people preponderate, and even in the LDCs young people are less likely to die than are old people. Thus the CDRs of LDCs are lower than one would expect. For example, in Austria in 1977 the CDR was 13 per 1,000. Life expectancy at birth was seventy-one years. The CDR in India in 1977 was also 13 per 1,000, but life expectancy at birth was only fifty years. In Austria only 24 percent of the population was younger than fifteen years, while in India 40 percent was less than fifteen years old.

Several countries now have TFRs very close to the replacement level. If these were exactly replacement TFRs, and if death rates were to stay as they are now, the population would gradually settle down into a *stable age distribution* (actually a special stable age distribution that occurs in stationary populations, namely a *stationary age distribution*). Quite soon the population would exactly replace itself in each generation, population size would not change, and the fraction of the population in any given age group would stay constant with time.

For example, suppose life expectancy at birth were to remain at its present value of seventy-one years. Then, each year, 1/71 of the population would die. This would give a crude death rate of $1/71 = 14/1,000$/year. Since the population exactly replaces itself, the crude birth rate would be 14/1,000 also. Thus if the rich nations soon achieve and maintain replacement fertility, their crude death rates will rise (they are now about 9/1,000 or less) and their crude birth rates (16/1,000 in 1979) will decline slightly, both changes resulting from the settling down of the age distribution and, in particular, from an increase in the fraction of older people in the population.

APPENDIX B: A NOTE ON "EXPLAINING VARIABILITY"

Chapters 2 and 3 discuss how per capita income and other variables "explain" a given percentage of the variation in birth rates among a number of different countries. Readers who are unfamiliar with statistics are due some explanation of this idea.

Table B-1 gives the information on forty-six developing countries that was presented and analyzed in figures 2-5, 3-1, 3-2, and 3-3. The average birth rate in these countries is 39.1 births per 1,000 population per year. Notice that not one of the forty-six countries has precisely this average birth rate; each country's birth rate differs, or deviates, from the average. For example, for Tanzania the deviation from average is + 11.0, for Taiwan it is − 14.8. If all countries had the same birth rate, obviously there would be no variation to explain. Our problem is to explain why there is variation about the average.

We could measure the total amount of variation by adding up all of the individual deviations, ignoring negative signs, to get the total deviation. However, for statistical reasons we actually first square each deviation and then add them up. Thus the squared deviation for Tanzania is 121 and the squared deviation for Taiwan is 219.04. Notice now that all the numbers are conveniently positive. When we do this for the countries in table B-1, we find that the total of the squared deviations is 4847.2. This total, then, is the amount of variation we must try to explain.

The first idea examined in Chapter 2 was that countries with higher per capita incomes would have lower birth rates and those with lower incomes would have higher birth rates. This relationship is shown in figure 2-5, which indicates that indeed there is some tendency for it to occur. Our next question is, how strong is this tendency? It is clearly not perfect, for some countries with low incomes have low birth rates and some with high incomes have high birth rates. We can measure the strength of the tendency by asking: how much of the variation in birth rates among countries is explained by differences in income?

The amount of variability explained is calculated as follows. First, we state precisely what we think the relationship is between birth rate and income. The simplest guess would be that the birth rate falls a given amount for each $100 increase in per capita income. (This assumes a straight line relationship between birth rate and income.) We then calculate and draw

Table B-1. Income and fertility in selected LDCs

Country	Per capita income in 1965 (U.S. $)	Degree of inequality (Gini)	Income per head of poorest 40% (U.S. $)	Birth rate
Puerto Rico	936	0.44	320.58	25.6
Venezuela	830	0.52	201.28	36.8
Argentina	787	0.42	340.38	21.8
Trinidad and Tobago	704	0.44		23.9
Greece	585	0.37	307.13	14.0
Spain	572	0.38	243.10	19.5
South Africa	552	0.56	85.56	43.1
Uruguay	497	0.42	177.68	20.4
Panama	490	0.48		37.1
Lebanon	446	0.52	144.95	39.8
Mexico	434	0.58	110.67	43.4
Jamaica	420	0.56	86.10	34.8
Chile	419	0.49	136.18	25.0
Yugoslavia	415	0.33	191.94	18.2
Costa Rica	360	0.43	132.30	33.8
Ivory Coast	179	0.43	78.31	45.6
Sri Lanka	142	0.37	60.35	28.6
Peru	289	0.57	46.96	41.8
Iraq	249	0.61	42.33	49.2
El Salvador	240	0.45	76.20	42.1
Colombia	228	0.54	53.58	44.6
Iran	218	0.47		45.3
Brazil	216	0.61	35.10	37.8
Taiwan	201	0.32	102.51	24.3
Tunisia	198	0.50	51.98	41.0
Ecuador	195	0.66	31.20	44.9
Senegal	192	0.56		48.0
Zambia	179	0.49		51.5
Morocco	179	0.50		49.1
Philippines	149	0.50	43.21	43.6
Ghana	155	0.62		48.8
Sierra Leone	135	0.56	78.31	44.7
Bolivia	124	0.53		44.0
South Korea	123	0.36	55.35	28.7
Thailand	110	0.50	35.48	43.7
Kenya	95	0.50		47.3
Sudan	88	0.43	31.24	47.8
Pakistan	84	0.37	36.75	47.6
India	84	0.46	29.40	41.2
Uganda	83	0.38	35.48	46.9
Niger	81	0.34		52.0
Nigeria	74	0.51		49.3
Dahomey	73	0.42		50.0
Chad	68	0.35		44.0
Burma	64	0.35		39.5
Tanzania	67	0.48	23.45	50.1

Sources: Income statistics are from Hollis Chenery and Moises Syrquin, *Patterns of Development, 1950–1970* (London: Oxford University Press, 1975), p. 103. Birth rates are from the text.

Note: These are the countries for which sufficient data were available in 1965 and 1970.

the straight line that passes through the points in figure 2-5, with the constraint that the line should pass "as close as possible to all the points." This procedure was done with the data in figure 2-5, but I have not drawn in the line. It also seems reasonable to assume, however, that as income becomes high the reduction in the birth rate may become small—after all, the birth rate is not going to go much lower than about 10 per 1,000, no matter how high the income. So, it seems reasonable to use a simple curve that tends to "bottom out," rather than a straight line. The rule here, roughly, is to use as simple a curve as possible. The one in figure 2-5, for example, is a parabola.

As with the straight line, we calculate and draw the curve such that it passes as close as possible to the points. This is shown in figure 3-1. This figure also shows, as dashed vertical lines, the deviation of each country from the curve. The curve that is "as close as possible" to the data is the one that produces the smallest total when we first square and then add up these deviations.

The curve in figure 3-1 represents our idea of how births and income are related. It says, for example, that we expect (on the basis of this idea) that Tanzania's birth rate should be 47.4. Tanzania's birth rate is actually 50.1, so the deviation from what is expected is 2.7 births. Tanzania's deviation from the *average* birth rate was 11, so in this case it is clear that low income (or something associated with it) has explained most of the difference (11 − 2.7 = 8.3) between Tanzania's birth rate and the average birth rate. Taiwan's birth rate, on the basis of income, is expected to be 41.5. Its actual birth rate is 24.3, so the deviation from the expected is − 17.2, which is even greater than its deviation (− 14.8) from the average birth rate. Clearly, Taiwan is one of the countries that weakens the relationship between birth rate and income.

We can now get, finally, a measure of the amount of variation in births that is explained by differences in income. Each deviation from the curve in figure 3-1 is squared and then all the squared deviations are summed. We find now that the total of the new squared deviations is 2606.6. The relationship between births and income thus explains 4847.2 − 2606.6 = 2240.6 of the variation. As a percentage this is 46 percent (2240.6 / 4847.2 × 100).

If all the points in figure 3-1 had fallen precisely on the curve, we would have had a complete explanation, with zero unexplained variation left. However, we still have 54 percent of the original variation remaining. By a precisely analogous procedure to that used above, we now therefore proceed to examine the second idea, which is that the deviations in birth rates *from those expected on the basis of average income* arise beçause some countries have an even distribution of income while others have an uneven distribution of income. This gives us figure 3-2. In this case, for Taiwan, the difference between the actual birth rate (24.3) and the expected birth rate based on the Gini coefficient (32.3) is reduced to 8.0, showing that the distribution of income contributes to the explanation of Taiwan's low birth rate, but does not completely account for it. Overall, income and Gini together reduce the unexplained total squared deviations to 1295.2, so that the amount of variability explained is 73 percent (3552.0/4847.2 × 100).

APPENDIX C: CLASSIFICATION OF THE WORLD'S NATIONS

The following classification is used by the United Nations:

(i) Economic Classes and Regions

Developed Countries

Developed Market Economies

North America: Canada, United States.

Western Europe: Andorra, Austria, Belgium-Luxembourg, Denmark, Faeroe Islands, Finland, France, Federal Republic of Germany (incl. West Berlin), Gibraltar, Greece, Holy See, Iceland, Ireland, Italy, Liechtenstein, Malta, Monaco, Netherlands, Norway, Portugal (incl. Azores and Madeira), San Marino, Spain, Sweden, Switzerland, United Kingdom (incl. Channel Islands and Isle of Man), Yugoslavia.

Oceania: Australia, New Zealand.

Other developed Market Economies: Israel, Japan, South Africa.

Eastern Europe and USSR: Albania, Bulgaria, Czechoslovakia, German Democratic Republic (incl. East Berlin), Hungary, Poland, Romania, USSR.

Developing Countries

Developing Market Economies

Africa: Algeria, Angola, Benin, Botswana, British Indian Ocean Territory, Burundi, Cameroon, Cape Verde, Central African Empire, Chad, Comoros, Congo, Djibouti, Equatorial Guinea, Ethiopia, Gabon, Gambia, Ghana, Guinea, Guinea-Bissau, Ivory Coast, Kenya, Lesotho, Liberia, Madagascar, Malawi, Mali, Mauritania, Mauritius, Morocco, Mozambique, Namibia, Niger, Nigeria, Reunion, Rhodesia, Rwanda, St. Helena, São Tomé and Principe, Senegal, Seychelles, Sierra Leone, Somalia, Spanish North Africa, Swaziland, Tanzania, Togo, Tunisia, Uganda, Upper Volta, Western Sahara, Zaire, Zambia.

Latin America: Antigua, Argentina, Bahamas, Barbados, Belize, Bolivia, Brazil, Cayman Islands, Chile, Colombia, Costa Rica, Cuba, Dominica, Dominican Republic, Ecuador (incl. Galapagos Islands), El Salvador, Falkland Islands (Malvinas), French Guinea, Grenada, Guadeloupe, Guatemala, Guyana, Haiti, Honduras, Jamaica, Martinique, Mexico, Montserrat, Netherlands Antilles, Nicaragua, Panama, Panama Canal Zone, Paraguay, Peru, Puerto Rico, St. Kits-Nevis-Anguilla, St. Lucia, St. Vincent, Surinam, Trinidad and Tobago, Turks and Caicos Islands, Uruguay, Venezuela, Virgin Islands (U.K.), Virgin Islands (U.S.).

Near East: Africa: Egypt, Libya, Sudan. Asia: Afghanistan, Bahrain, Cyprus, Gaza Strip (Palestine), Iran, Iraq, Jordan, Kuwait, Lebanon, Oman, Qatar, Saudi Arabia, Syria, Turkey, United Arab Emirates, Yemen Arab Republic, Democratic Yemen.

Far East: Bangladesh, Bhutan, Brunei, Burma, East Timor, Hong Kong, India, Indonesia, Republic of Korea, Lao, Macau, Malaysia (Peninsular Malaysia, Sabah, Sarawak), Maldives, Nepal, Pakistan, Philippines, Sikkim, Singapore, Sri Lanka, Thailand.

Other developing Market Economies: America: Bermuda, Greenland, St. Pierre and Miquelon. Oceania: American Samoa, Canton and Enderbury Islands, Christmas Island (Aust.), Cocos (Keeling) Islands, Cook Islands, Fiji, French Polynesia, Gilbert Islands, Guam, Johnston Island, Midway Islands, Nauru, New Caledonia, New Hebrides, Niue Island, Norfolk Island, Pacific Islands (Trust Territ.), Papua New Guinea, Pitcairn Island, Samoa, Solomon Islands, Tokelau, Tonga, Tuvalu, Wake Island, Wallis and Futuna Islands.

Asian Centrally Planned Economies: China, Democratic Kampuchea, Democratic People's Republic of Korea, Mongolia, Viet Nam.

(ii) Developing Market Economies Classified as MSA (Most Seriously Affected).

MSA Countries: Afghanistan, Bangladesh, Benin, Burma, Burundi, Cameroon, Cape Verde, Central African Empire, Chad, Egypt, El Salvador, Ethiopia, Gambia, Ghana, Guatemala, Guinea, Guinea-Bissau, Guyana, Haiti, Honduras, India, Ivory Coast, Kenya, Lao, Lesotho, Madagascar, Mali, Mauritania, Mozambique, Nepal, Niger, Pakistan, Rwanda, Senegal, Sierra Leone, Somalia, Sudan, Sri Lanka, Tanzania, Uganda, Upper Volta, Samoa, Yemen Arab Republic, Democratic Yemen.

In addition to the MSAs, countries that may be called "Fourth World" include Bhutan, Botswana, Cambodia (Khmer Republic), Malawi, and Maldives (James W. Howe, *The U.S. and World Development: Agenda for Action 1975* [New York: Praeger, 1975]). Fourth World nations are those recognized by the UN as the least developed in terms of per capita income, level of manufacturing, and literacy, plus a number of countries, such as India, that have been most seriously affected by recent world recession and inflation.

Source: Food and Agriculture Organization, *The Fourth World Food Survey,* Statistics Series no. 11 (Rome, FAO, 1977), pp. 67, 68.

NOTES

CHAPTER 1

1. Paul Bairoch, *The Economic Development of the Third World since 1900* (Berkeley and Los Angeles: University of California Press, 1975); John W. Mellor, *The New Economics of Growth: A Strategy for India and the Developing World* (Ithaca, N.Y.: Cornell University Press, 1976), p. 6.

2. J. de Hoogh et al., "Food for a Growing World Population," *European Review of Agricultural Economics* 3 (1977): 459-99.

3. National Research Council, *World Food and Nutrition Study: Interim Report* (Washington, D.C.: National Academy of Sciences, 1975).

4. International Food Policy Research Institute, *Food Needs of Developing Countries: Projections of Production and Consumption to 1990* (Washington, D.C.: International Food Policy Research Institute, 1977), Research Report no. 3.

5. Selwyn Enzer, Richard Drobnick, and Steven Alter, "Neither Feast nor Famine," *Food Policy* 3 (1978): 3-17.

6. The first quote is from Paul R. Ehrlich, "Human Population and Environmental Problems," *Environmental Conservation* 1 (1974): 15. For a more recent and detailed presentation of Ehrlich's views see Paul R. Ehrlich, Anne H. Ehrlich, and John P. Holdren, *Ecoscience: Population, Resources, Environment* (San Francisco: W. H. Freeman and Co., 1977). The second quote is from the Environmental Fund, in the *Wall Street Journal* of October 30, 1975.

7. The first quote is from the Environmental Fund, ibid., the second from the National Academy of Sciences, *Population and Food: Crucial Issues* (Washington, D.C.: National Academy of Sciences, 1975), p. v.

8. James R. Echols, "Population vs. the Environment: A Crisis of Too Many People," *American Scientist* 64 (1976): 165.

9. Lester R. Brown, *In the Human Interest: A Strategy to Stabilize World Population* (New York: W. W. Norton and Co., 1974), p. 53. A similar analysis is presented in Sterling Wortman and Ralph W. Cummings, Jr., *To Feed This World: The Challenge and the Strategy* (Baltimore: Johns Hopkins University Press, 1978), pp. 4, 203.

10. Environmental Fund (see note 6).

11. Garrett Hardin, "Living on a Lifeboat," *Bioscience* 24 (1974): 561-68; William C. Paddock and Paul Paddock, *Famine '75* (Boston: Little, Brown and Co., 1967).

12. Garrett Hardin, "Not Peace, but Ecology," in *Diversity and Stability in Ecological Systems, Brookhaven Symposium in Biology,* no. 22 (1969), pp. 151-61.

13. Mahmood Mamdani, *The Myth of Population Control* (New York: Monthly Review Press, 1972).

14. Nancy Birdsall, "Analytical Approaches to the Relationship of Population Growth and Development," *Population and Development Review* 3 (1977): 63-102.

15. Pan A. Yotopoulos, "Population and Agricultural Development: Selected Relationships and Possible Planning Uses," no. 2, "The Population Problem and the Development Solution" (Rome: Food and Agriculture Organization, 1978), ES:DP/INT/73/PO2, Technical Paper no. 2; Julian L. Simon, *The Economics of Population Growth* (Princeton, N.J.: Princeton University Press, 1977).

16. Simon, *Economics of Population Growth,* p. 107.

17. Hollis Chenery et al., *Redistribution with Growth* (London: Oxford University Press, 1974), p. 7.

18. Rakesh Mohan, "Urban Land Policy, Income Distribution, and the Urban Poor," in Charles R. Frank and Richard C. Webb, eds., *Income Distribution and Growth in the Less-Developed Countries* (Washington, D.C.: The Brookings Institution, 1977); A.L.O. de Almeida, "Share Tenancy and Family Size in the Brazilian Northeast," unpublished ms., Stanford University, 1977.

CHAPTER 2

1. U.S. Bureau of the Census, *Illustrative Projections of World Populations to the 21st Century,* Special Studies Series P-23, no. 79 (Washington, D.C.: U.S. Bureau of the Census, 1979), p. 81.

2. B. D. Misra et al., "The Dilemma of Family Planning in a North Indian State," *Studies in Family Planning* 7 (1976): 66–74.

3. Frank W. Notestein, "Population: The Long View," in Theodore W. Schultz, ed., *Food for the World* (Chicago: University of Chicago Press, 1945).

4. Ansley J. Coale, ed., *Economic Factors in Population Growth: Proceedings of a Conference* (New York: John Wiley and Sons, 1976).

5. Michael S. Teitlebaum, "Relevance of Demographic Transition Theory for Developing Countries," *Science* 188 (1975): 420–25; Richard A. Easterlin, "An Economic Framework for Fertility Analysis," *Studies in Family Planning* 6 (1975): 54–63.

6. Gary S. Becker and Nigel Tomes, "Child Endowments and the Quantity and Quality of Children," *Journal of Political Economy* 84, no. 4, Part 2 (1976): S143–S162; Richard A. Easterlin, "An Economic Framework for Fertility Analysis," *Studies in Family Planning* 6 (1975): 54–63; Richard A. Easterlin, "Population Change and Farm Settlement in the Northern United States," *Journal of Economic History* 36 (1976): 45–75; Harvey Leibenstein, *Economic Backwardness and Economic Growth* (New York: John Wiley and Sons, 1957); Harvey Leibenstein, "Socio-economic Fertility Theories and Their Relevance to Population Policy," *International Labour Review* 109 (1974): 443–57; Harvey Leibenstein, "An Interpretation of the Economic Theory of Fertility: Promising Path or Blind Alley?" *Journal of Economic Literature* (1974): 457–79; Theodore W. Schultz, *Economics of the Family: Marriage, Children, and Human Capital* (Chicago: University of Chicago Press, 1975). On the general agreement among these theories, see Warren C. Sanderson, "On Two Schools of the Economics of Fertility," *Population and Development Review* 2 (1976): 469–77.

7. John C. Caldwell, "Toward a Restatement of Demographic Transition Theory," *Population and Development Review* 2 (1976): 340; John C. Caldwell, "The Economic Rationality of High Fertility: An Investigation Illustrated with Nigerian Survey Data," *Population Studies* 31 (1977): 9.

8. Pan A. Yotopoulos, "Population and Agricultural Development: Selected Relationships and Possible Planning Uses," no. 2, "The Population Problem and the Development Solution" (Rome: Food and Agriculture Organization, 1978), ES:DP/INT/73/P02, Technical Paper no. 2.

9. Judith Bannister, "Implementing Fertility and Mortality Decline in the People's Republic of China: Recent Official Data," from *The Current Vital Rates and Population Size of the People's Republic of China and Its Provinces,* Ph.D. dissertation, Stanford University, 1977. Paper presented at the annual meeting of the Population Association of America, St. Louis, April 1977; Lee-Jay Cho and R. D. Retherford, "Comparative Analysis of Recent Fertility Trends in East Asia," International Population Conference, Liege (1973), vol. 2, pp. 163–81; Yotopoulos, "Population and Agricultural Development"; W. Parker Mauldin and Bernard Berelson, "Conditions of Fertility Decline in Developing Countries, 1965–75," *Studies in Family Planning* 9 (1978): 89–147.

10. C. Stephen Baldwin, "Policies and Realities of Delayed Marriage: The Cases of Tunisia, Sri Lanka, Malaysia, and Bangladesh," *PRB Report* 4 (1977): 1–11; World Fertility Survey, "The Nepal Fertility Survey, 1976: A Summary of Findings" (The Hague: Interna-

tional Statistical Institute, 1978); World Fertility Survey, "The Pakistan Fertility Survey, 1975: A Summary of Findings" (1977); World Fertility Survey, "The Sri Lanka Fertility Survey, 1976: A Summary of Findings" (1978).

11. Julian L. Simon, *The Economics of Population Growth* (Princeton, N.J.: Princeton University Press, 1977).

12. Some examples, in addition to references given earlier, include Alain de Janvry and Carlos Garramón, "The Dynamics of Rural Poverty in Latin America," *Journal of Peasant Studies* 4 (1977): 206-16; Mahmood Mamdani, *The Myth of Population Control* (New York: Monthly Review Press, 1972); John W. Mellor, *The New Economics of Growth: A Strategy for India and the Developing World* (Ithaca, N.Y.: Cornell University Press, 1976); Moni Nag et al., "Economic Value of Children in Two Peasant Societies" (Mexico City: Paper Prepared for General Conference of the International Union for the Scientific Study of Population, August 8-13, 1977), data presented in Thomas J. Espenshade, "The Value and Cost of Children," *Population Bulletin*, vol. 32 (Washington, D.C.: Population Reference Bureau, 1977). On Bangladesh specifically, see M. T. Cain, "The Economic Activities of Children in a Village in Bangladesh," *Population and Development Review* 3 (1977): 201-28.

13. Epsenshade, "The Value and Cost of Children."

14. Mellor, *New Economics*, p. 258.

15. Robert W. Morgan and P. O. Odhadike, "Fertility Levels and Fertility Change," in J. C. Caldwell, ed., *Population, Growth, and Socioeconomic Change in West Africa* (New York: Columbia University Press, 1975); John C. Caldwell and Pat Caldwell, "The Role of Marital Sexual Abstinence in Determining Fertility," *Population Studies* 31 (1977): 193-213.

16. Morgan and Odhadike, "Fertility Levels and Fertility Change"; Simon, *Economics of Population Growth;* Espenshade, "The Value and Cost of Children."

17. John C. Caldwell, "Towards a Restatement of Demographic Transition Theory," in John C. Caldwell, ed., *The Persistence of High Fertility: Population Prospects in the Third World,* Changing African Family Project, Family and Fertility Change Monograph Series no. 1, Department of Demography, the Australian National University, Canberra, 1977, pp. 26-27.

18. See, for example, Mamdani, *The Myth of Population Control.,*

19. Ronald Freedman, "Norms for Family Size in Underdeveloped Areas," in B. Nam, ed., *Population and Society* (Boston: Houghton Mifflin Co., 1968).

20. Eva Mueller, "The Economic Value of Children in Peasant Agriculture," in Ronald G. Ridker, ed., *Population and Development: The Search for Selective Interventions* (Baltimore: Johns Hopkins University Press, 1976); Albert I. Hermalin, "Empirical Research in Taiwan on Factors Underlying Differences in Fertility," *Studies in Family Planning* 5 (1974): 314-24.

21. John C. Caldwell and Pat Caldwell, "The Achieved Small Family: Early Fertility Transition in an African City," *Studies in Family Planning* 9 (1978): 1-18.

22. Yotopoulos, "Population and Agricultural Development."

23. See also William Rich, *Smaller Families Through Social and Economic Progress* (Washington, D.C.: Overseas Development Council, 1973), monograph no. 7.

24. Yotopoulos, "Population and Agricultural Development."

25. Frank W. Oechsli and Dudley Kirk, "Modernization and the Demographic Transition in Latin America and the Caribbean," *Economic Development and Cultural Change* 23 (1975): 391-419.

26. Dudley Kirk, "A New Demographic Transition?" in National Academy of Sciences, *Rapid Population Growth: Consequences and Policy Implications* (Baltimore: Johns Hopkins University Press, 1971).

27. Oechsli and Kirk, "Modernization and the Demographic Transition."

28. Barry Edmonston and Frank W. Oechsli, "Fertility Decline and Socio-economic Change in Venezuela," *Journal of Interamerican Studies and World Affairs* 19 (1977): 369-92. Some analyses show a slight turn up in fertility at the highest levels of per capita income—e.g., Julian L. Simon, *The Effects of Income on Fertility* (Chapel Hill, N.C.: Carolina Population Center, 1974).

29. United Nations, Department of Economic and Social Affairs, *World Population Trends and Policies: 1977 Monitoring Report*, vol. 1 (ST/ESA/SER.A/62), 1979.

30. See also Steven E. Beaver, *Demographic Transition Theory Reinterpreted: An Application to Recent Natality Trends in Latin America* (Lexington, Mass.: Lexington Books, 1975).

31. Oechsli and Kirk, "Modernization and the Demographic Transition"; T. Paul Schultz, *Fertility Determinants: A Theory, Evidence, and an Application to Policy Evaluation* (Santa Monica, Calif.: The Rand Corporation, 1974), R1016–RF/AID; K. S. Srikantan, *The Family Planning Program in the Socioeconomic Context* (New York: The Population Council, 1977); Beaver, *Demographic Transition;* Anne D. Williams, *Effects of Economic Development on Fertility: Review and Evaluation of the Literature* (Washington, D.C. and Santa Barbara, Calif.: General Electric Co.-Tempo, 1974), GE74TMP-32.

32. Caldwell and Caldwell, "The Achieved Small Family."

33. Yotopoulos, "Population and Agricultural Development."

34. Nancy Birdsall, "Analytical Approaches to the Relationship of Population Growth and Development," *Population and Development Review* 3 (1977): 63–102; Schultz, *Economics of the Family;* Srikantan, *The Family Planning Program.* See also the various country-by-country World Fertility Surveys.

35. Population Reference Bureau, "Literacy and World Population," *Population Bulletin*, vol. 30 (Washington, D.C.: Population Reference Bureau, 1975).

36. Barry Edmonston and Susan K. McGinnis, "Migrant-nonmigrant Fertility Differentials in Metropolitan Areas of Latin America," in Interdisciplinary Communications Program, Smithsonian Institution, Occasional Monograph Series no. 5, vol. 1: 277–85; Edmonston and Oechsli, "Fertility Decline"; Beaver, *Demographic Transition;* Oechsli and Kirk, "Modernization and the Demographic Transition"; Williams, *Effects of Economic Development;* Simon, *The Effects of Income,* p. 116.

37. Edmonston and McGinnis, "Migrant-nonmigrant Fertility"; Williams, *Effects of Economic Development.*

38. Schultz, *Fertility Determinants,* pp. 40, 41.

39. Birdsall, "Analytical Approaches"; Schultz, *Fertility Determinants,* pp. 32–46; Williams, *Effects of Economic Development.*

40. Bannister, "Implementing Fertility"; United Nations, Department of Economic and Social Affairs, *Poverty, Unemployment, and Development Policy: A Case Study of Selected Issues with Reference to Kerala* (ST/ESA/29), 1975.

41. Birdsall, "Analytical Approaches"; Simon, *The Effects of Income;* Baldwin, "Policies and Realities"; Bannister, "Implementing Fertility."

42. John D. Kasarda, "Economic Structure and Fertility: A Comparative Analysis," *Demography* 8 (1971): 307–18; Williams, *Effects of Economic Development;* World Fertility Survey, "The Thailand Fertility Survey, 1975: A Summary of Findings" (1978).

43. Oechsli and Kirk, "Modernization and the Demographic Transition"; Simon, *The Effects of Income;* Williams, *Effects of Economic Development;* World Health Organization, "Health Trends and Prospects in Relation to Population and Development," in United Nations, Department of Economic and Social Affairs, *The Population Debate: Discussions and Perspectives,* vol. 1 (ST/ESA/SER.A/57) Beaver, *Demographic Transition;* Birdsall, "Analytic Approaches"; Srikantan, *The Family Planning Program.*

44. Caldwell, "Towards a Restatement"; Jean Trevor, "Family Change in Sokoto: A Traditional Moslem Fulani/Hausa City," in John C. Caldwell et al., eds., *Population Growth and Socioeconomic Change in West Africa* (New York: Columbia University Press, 1975), p. 253.

45. Hollis Chenery and Moises Syrquin, *Patterns of Development, 1950–1970* (London: Oxford University Press, 1975), pp. 56–59; Robert Repetto, "The Interaction of Fertility and the Size Distribution of Income" (Cambridge, Mass.: Harvard University Center for Population Studies, 1974), Research Paper no. 8; Birdsall, "Analytical Approaches."

46. Beaver, *Demographic Transition.*

47. World Health Organization, "Health Trends."

48. Caldwell and Caldwell, "The Role of Marital Sexual Abstinence."

49. Carl E. Taylor, "Nutrition and Population in Health Sector Planning," *Stanford Food Research Institute Studies* 16 (1977): 77–90; Caldwell et al., eds., *Population Growth in West Africa;* Srikantan, *The Family Planning Program;* Carl E. Taylor, J. S. Newman, and N. V. Kelly, "Interactions between Health and Population," *Studies in Family Planning* 7 (1976): 94–100.

50. T. Paul Schultz, "Explanation of Birth Rate Changes Over Space and Time: A Study of Taiwan," *Journal of Political Economy,* 81, no. 2, part 2 (1973): S238–S274.

51. Chenery and Syrquin, *Patterns of Development,* p. 56.

52. Marc B. Glassman and John A. Ross, "Two Determinants of Fertility Decline: A Test of Competing Models," *Studies in Family Planning* 9 (1978): 193–97.

53. Garrett Hardin, "Not Peace, But Ecology," in *Diversity and Stability in Ecological Systems, Brookhaven Symposium in Biology,* no. 22 (1969), pp. 151–61.

54. Alan Berg, *The Nutrition Factor* (Washington, D.C.: The Brookings Institution, 1972); United Nations, *World Population Trends,* pp. 53, 206.

55. United Nations, *World Population Trends,* pp. 65–72.

56. Yotopoulos, "Population and Agricultural Development."

57. Chenery and Syrquin, *Patterns of Development,* p. 58; Beaver, *Demographic Transition.*

58. Simon, *The Effects of Income,* p. 106.

59. Beaver, *Demographic Transition.*

60. J. Chamie, "Religious Differentials in Fertility: Lebanon 1971," *Population Studies* 31 (1977):365.

61. Dudley L. Poston and Joachim Singelmann, "Socioeconomic Status, Value Orientations, and Fertility in India," *Demography* 12 (1975): 417–30.

62. Beaver, *Demographic Transition,* pp. 57, 58; Caldwell, "Towards a Restatement."

63. Beaver, *Demographic Transition,* p. 121.

64. Caldwell, "Towards a Restatement."

65. Althea Hill, "The Fertility of the Asian Community of East Africa," *Population Studies* 29 (1975): 355–72; Cho and Retherford, "Comparative Analysis."

66. T. Scarlett Epstein and Darrell Jackson, eds., *The Feasibility of Fertility Planning* (New York: Pergamon Press, 1977), p. 3.

67. A. Mitra, "National Population Policy in Relation to National Planning in India," *Population and Development Review* 3 (1977): 297–306.

68. Epstein and Jackson, *Feasibility of Family Planning.*

69. J. Wyon and J. Gordon, *The Khanna Study* (Cambridge, Mass.: Harvard University Press, 1971); Mamdani, *The Myth of Population Control.*

70. John C. Caldwell and H. Ware, "The Evolution of Family Planning in an African City: Ibadan, Nigeria," *Population Studies* 31 (1977): 487–508.

71. Ronald Freedman and Bernard Berelson, "The Record of Family Planning Programs," *Studies in Family Planning* 7 (1976): 1–40; Srikantan, *The Family Planning Program.*

72. Ronald Freedman and John Y. Takeshita, *Family Planning in Taiwan* (Princeton, N.J.: Princeton University Press, 1969).

73. Wen L. Li, "Temporal and Spatial Analysis of Fertility Decline in Taiwan," *Population Studies* 27 (1973): 97–104; Schultz, "Explanation of Birth Rate Changes", p. 254; Srikantan, *The Family Planning Program;* Albert I. Hermalin, "Spatial Analysis of Family Planning Program Effects in Taiwan" (paper presented at Population Seminar, East-West Population Institute, Honolulu, June 1976).

74. Arthur M. Conning, "Latin American Fertility Trends and Influencing Factors" (Leige: International Population Conference, 1973), vol. 2, pp. 125–47; see also Williams, *Effects of Economic Development;* Freedman and Berelson, "The Record of Family Planning Programs," p. 19. Freedman and Berelson's conclusion is supported by Mauldin and Berelson, who reach a similar if somewhat stronger position in support of the efficacy of family planning programs. See Mauldin and Berelson, "Conditions of Fertility Decline."

75. Freedman and Berelson, "The Record of Family Planning Programs"; Srikantan, *The Family Planning Program.*

76. Amy Ong Tsui and Donald J. Bogue, "Declining World Fertility: Trends, Causes, and Implications," *Population Bulletin,* vol. 33 (Washington, D.C.: Population Reference Bureau, 1978).
77. Ibid.
78. Ibid., p. 5.

CHAPTER 3

1. See also William Rich, *Smaller Families through Social and Economic Progress* (Washington, D.C.: Overseas Development Council, 1973), monograph no. 7; Pan A. Yoto-poulos, "Population and Agricultural Development: Selected Relationships and Possible Planning Uses," no. 2, "The Population Problem and the Development Solution" (Rome: Food and Agriculture Organization, 1978), ES:DP/INT/73/PO2, Technical Paper no. 2.
2. W. Hicks, "Comments on Daniel A. Seiver's 'Recent Fertility in Mexico: Measurement and Interpretation,' " *Population Studies* 31 (1977): 175-76; D. A. Seiver, "Recent Fertility in Mexico: Measurement and Interpretation," *Population Studies* 29 (1975): 341-54; D. A. Seiver, "A Reply to W. Hicks's Comments," *Population Studies* 31 (1977): 176-77.
3. Seiver, "Recent Fertility in Mexico"; Ansley J. Coale, ed., *Economic Factors in Population Growth: Proceedings of a Conference* (New York: John Wiley and Sons, 1976).
4. Seiver, "Recent Fertility in Mexico."
5. Richard Weisskoff, "Income Distribution and Economic Growth in Puerto Rico, Argentina, and Mexico," *Review of Income and Wealth* 17 (1970): 303-32; Barbara H. Tuckman, "The Green Revolution and the Distribution of Agricultural Income in Mexico," *World Development* 4 (1976): 17-24.
6. Seiver, "Recent Fertility in Mexico"; Barry Edmonston and Susan K. Mc Ginnis, "Migrant-nonmigrant Fertility Differentials in Metropolitan Areas of Latin America," in Interdisciplinary Communications Program, Smithsonian Institution, Occasional Monograph Series no. 5, vol. 1: 277-85.
7. Kirk's threshold levels are described in Dudley Kirk, "A New Demographic Transition?" in National Academy of Sciences, *Rapid Population Growth: Consequences and Policy Implications* (Baltimore: Johns Hopkins University Press, 1971). Estimates of Mexico's recent birth rates come from W. Parker Mauldin, "Patterns of Fertility Decline in Developing Countries 1950-1975," *Studies in Family Planning* 9 (1978): 75-84, and from United Nations, Department of Economic and Social Affairs, *World Population Trends and Policies: 1977 Monitoring Report,* vol. 1 (ST/ESA/SER.A/62), 1979.
8. Rakesh Mohan, "Urban Land Policy, Income Distribution, and the Urban Poor," in Charles R. Frank and Richard C. Webb, eds., *Income Distribution and Growth in the Less-Developed Countries* (Washington, D.C.: The Brookings Institution, 1977).
9. Information on income inequality and changes in inequality come from M. S. Ahluwalia, "Inequality, Poverty, and Development," *Journal of Development Economics* 13 (1976): 3-37; M. S. Ahluwalia, "Rural Poverty and Agricultural Performance in India," *Journal of Development Studies* 14 (1978): 298-323; Edmar L. Bacha and Lance Taylor, "Brazilian Income Distribution in the 1960s: 'Facts,' Model Results and Controversy," *Journal of Development Studies* 14 (1978): 271-97; Amit Kumar Bhattacharyya, "Income Inequality and Fertility: A Comparative View," *Population Studies* 29 (1975): 5-19; G. S. Fields, "Who Benefits from Economic Development? A Reexamination of Brazilian Growth in the 1960s," *American Economic Review* 64 (1977): 570-82; Albert Fishlow, "Brazilian Size Distribution of Income," *American Economic Review* 62 (1972): 391-401; John W. Mellor, *The New Economics of Growth: A Strategy for India and the Developing World* (Ithaca, N.Y.: Cornell University Press, 1976); Felix Paukert, "Income Distribution at Different Levels of Development: A Survey of Evidence," *International Labour Review* 108, nos. 2 and 3 (1973): 97-125; Robert Repetto, "The Interaction of Fertility and the Size Distribution of Income" (Cambridge, Mass.: Harvard University Center for Population Studies, 1974), research paper no. 8; Frederick C. Roche, "The Demographic Transition in Sri Lanka: Is Development Really a Prerequisite?" *Cornell Agricultural Economics Staff Paper*

no. 76-5, January 1976; T. N. Srinivasan, "Development, Poverty, and Basic Human Needs: Some Issues," *Stanford Food Research Institute Studies* 16, no. 2 (1977): 11-28; Tuckman, "The Green Revolution"; D. J. Turnham, "Income Distribution: Measurement and Problems," in *International Development 1971* (New York: Oceana Publications, 1972); R. Weisskoff, "Income Distribution."

10. Ibid.

11. Mauldin, "Patterns of Fertility Decline." Indian government statistics put India's 1975 birth rate at 36. However, the government estimates are consistently low (Arjun Adlakha and Dudley Kirk, "Vital Rates in India 1961-71 Estimated from 1971 Census Data," *Population Studies* 28 [1974]: 381-400), and the true birth rate is probably higher, at least 38 (United Nations, Department of Economic and Social Affairs, *Levels and Trends of Fertility Throughout the World, 1950-1970* [ST/ESA/SER.A/59], 1977).

12. International Bank for Reconstruction and Development, *World Bank Atlas* (Washington, D.C.: World Bank, 1972). The World Bank estimate of Sri Lanka's income is lower than that made by the United Nations (about $140). World Bank data files put Sri Lanka's 1970 income at about $130.

13. Information on the spread of benefits in Sri Lanka comes from Roche, "The Demographic Transition in Sri Lanka."

14. C. Stephen Baldwin, "Policies and Realities of Delayed Marriage: The Cases of Tunisia, Sri Lanka, Malaysia, and Bangladesh," *PRB Report* 4 (1977): 1-11; N. Gunasinghe, "Underdevelopment and Declining Fertility in a Kandyan Village," in T. Scarlett Epstein and Darrell Jackson, eds., *The Feasibility of Fertility Planning* (New York: Pergamon Press, 1977).

15. World Fertility Survey, "The Sri Lanka Fertility Survey, 1976. A Summary of Findings" (The Hague: International Statistical Institute, 1978).

16. W. M. Tilakaratne, "A Sri Lankan Village on the Verge of a Demographic Transition," in Epstein and Jackson, eds., *Feasibility of Fertility Planning*; Gunasinghe, "Underdevelopment and Declining Fertility"; World Fertility Survey, "Sri Lanka."

17. Dallas F. S. Fernando, "A Note on Differential Fertility in Sri Lanka," *Demography* 11 (1974): 441-56.

18. Martin Walker, "Sri Lanka Goes for Growth," *The Guardian* (London), August 1, 1978.

19. Information on Kerala comes from United Nations, Department of Economic and Social Affairs, *Poverty, Unemployment, and Development Policy: A Case Study of Selected Issues with Reference to Kerala* (ST/ESA/29), 1975; Government of Kerala, Bureau of Economics and Statistics, "Demographic Report of Kerala 1901-61, with an Addendum for 1971," Demographic Research Center, Trivandrum, 1976. The equalizing effects of food rationing are discussed by P. S. George, "Public Distribution of Foodgrains in Kerala—Income Distribution Implications and Effectiveness," *International Food Policy Research Institute* (Washington, D.C., 1979), Research Report no. 7.

20. Alexander Eckstein, *China's Economic Revolution* (Cambridge: At the University Press, 1977).

21. Thomas E. Weisskopf, "China and India: A Comparative Survey of Performance in Economic Development," *Economic and Political Weekly,* Annual Number (1975): 177.

22. For data on China, see Nicholas R. Lardy, "Economic Planning in the People's Republic of China: Central-Provisional Fiscal Relations," in U.S. Congress, Joint Economic Committee, *China: A Reassessment of the Economy,* 94th Congress, 1st session, 1975. For India, see John W. Mellor, *New Economics*; J. S. Sarma, "India—A Drive Towards Self-Sufficiency in Food Grains," *American Journal of Agricultural Economics* 60 (1978): 859-64. See also Chapter 7.

23. Henry J. Groen and James A. Kilpatrick, "Chinese Agricultural Production," in U.S. Congress, Joint Economic Committee, *Chinese Economy Post-Mao,* vol. 1, *Policy and Performance,* 95th Congress, 2d session, 1978, p. 649; Sarma, "India—A Drive Toward Self-Sufficiency"; Food and Agriculture Organization, *The Fourth World Food Survey,* Statistics Series no. 11 (Rome, FAO, 1977), p. 78; 1978 data from U.S. Department of Agriculture.

24. Leo A. Orleans, "China's Environomics: Backing into Ecological Leadership," in

U.S. Congress, *China: A Reassessment*; Eckstein, *China's Economic Revolution*; Nicholas R. Lardy, "Economic Planning in the Peoples Republic of China"; T. Weisskopf, "China and India."

25. Lardy, "Economic Planning in the People's Republic of China"; Carl Riskin, "Workers Incentives in Chinese Industry," in U.S. Congress, *China: A Reassessment*.

26. Penny Kane, "Population Planning in China: The Individual and the State," in Epstein and Jackson, eds., *Feasibility of Fertility Planning*; Judith Bannister, "Kiangsu and the East China Provinces," from *The Current Vital Rates and Population Size of the People's Republic of China and Its Provinces*, Ph.D. dissertation, Stanford University, 1977; Victor W. Sidel and Ruth Sidel, "The Delivery of Medical Care in China," *Scientific American* 230 (1974): 19–27; see Barry M. Richman, *Industrial Society in Communist China* (New York: Random House, 1969), pp. 551–54.

27. Kane, "Population Planning in China."

28. Keith Griffin, *The Political Economy of Agrarian Change* (Cambridge, Mass.: Harvard University Press, 1974); R. Albert Berry and William R. Cline, *Agrarian Structure and Productivity in Developing Countries* (Baltimore: Johns Hopkins University Press, 1979), pp. 38–39; Mahmood Mamdani, *The Myth of Population Control* (New York: Monthly Review Press, 1972).

29. R. H. Tawney, *Land and Labor in China* (Boston: Beacon Press, 1966, originally published 1932), pp. 72–73, 76–77.

30. Kane, "Population Planning in China," p. 213; Riskin, "Workers Incentives"; Notes and Comments, "Fertility Control and Public Health in Rural China: Unpublicized Problems," *Population and Development Review* 3 (1977): 482–85; Judith Bannister, "Implementing Fertility and Mortality Decline in the People's Republic of China: Recent Official Data," from *The Current Vital Rates and Population Size of the People's Republic of China and Its Provinces*, Ph.D. dissertation, Stanford University, 1977. Paper presented at the annual meeting of the Population Association of America, St. Louis, April 1977.

31. Eckstein, *China's Economic Revolution*, pp. 149–51; Dennis L. Chinn, "Income Distribution in a Chinese Commune," *Journal of Comparative Economics* 2 (1978): 246–65.

32. Lardy, "Economic Planning in the People's Republic of China"; Charles R. Roll, Jr., and Kung-Chia Yeh, "Balance in Coastal and Inland Industrial Development," in U.S. Congress, *China: A Reassessment*, p. 93; Eckstein, *China's Economic Revolution*, p. 123.

33. Tawney, *Land and Labor*.

34. T. Weisskopf, "China and India", p. 181.

35. G. W. Barclay, et al., "A Reassessment of the Demography of Traditional Rural China," *Population Index* 42 (1976): 606–35; John S. Aird, "Recent Provincial Population Figures," *The China Quarterly* 73 (March 1978): 1–44; Bannister, "Implementing Fertility."

36. Leo A. Orleans, *Every Fifth Child: The Population of China* (Stanford, Calif.: Stanford University Press, 1972); Judith Bannister, "Mortality, Fertility, and Contraceptive Use in Shanghai," *The China Quarterly* 70 (1977): 255–95.

37. The 1953 data are from Orleans, *Every Fifth Child*. Other data are from Bannister, "Kiangsu and the East China Provinces" and "Mortality, Fertility, and Contraceptive Use in Shanghai."

38. Bannister, "Implementing Fertility"; John S. Aird, Letter to *People* 4 (1977), no. 2, pp. 49–51.

39. Adlakha and Kirk, "Vital Rates in India."

40. Bannister, "Kiangsu and the East China Provinces."

41. Bannister, "Implementing Fertility"; Kane, "Population Planning in China."

42. Carl Djerassi, "Some Observations on Current Fertility Control in China," *The China Quarterly* 57 (1974): 40–59; Pi-chao Chen and Ann E. Miller, "Lessons From the Chinese Experience: China's Planned Birth Program and Its Transferability," *Studies in Family Planning* 6 (1975): 354–66.

43. Chen and Miller, "Lessons From the Chinese Experience"; Bannister, "Implementing Fertility."

44. Chen and Miller, "Lessons from the Chinese Experience"; Kane, "Population Planning in China," p. 217.

45. Michael P. Todaro, *Internal Migration in Developing Countries: A Review of Theory, Evidence, Methodology, and Research Priorities* (Geneva: International Labour Office, 1976), p. 368.

CHAPTER 4

1. United Nations, Department of Economic and Social Affairs, *World Population Prospects as Assessed in 1973* (ST/ESA/SER.A/60), 1977.
2. Thomas Frejka, *The Future of Population Growth: Alternative Paths to Equilibrium* (New York: John Wiley and Sons, 1973). Recall that population keeps growing after replacement family size occurs because for a while the age distribution remains young and there is a high fraction of people who are having children (appendix A).
3. U.S. Bureau of the Census, *Illustrative Projections of World Populations to the 21st Century,* Special Studies Series P-23, no. 79 (Washington, D.C.: U.S. Bureau of the Census, 1979), pp. 81, 92.
4. United Nations, Department of Economic and Social Affairs, *World Population Prospects as Assessed in 1968* (ST/SOA/SER.A/53), 1973; United Nations, *World Population Prospects as Assessed in 1973.*
5. Amy Ong Tsui and Donald J. Bogue, "Declining World Fertility: Trends, Causes, and Implications," *Population Bulletin,* vol. 33 (Washington, D.C.: Population Reference Bureau, 1978), pp. 1-56.
6. United Nations, Department of Economic and Social Affairs, *Levels and Trends of Fertility Throughout the World, 1950-1970* (ST/ESA/SER.A/59), 1977; W. Parker Mauldin, "Patterns of Fertility Decline in Developing Countries 1950-1975," *Studies in Family Planning* 9 (1978): 75-84; Tsui and Bogue, "Declining World Fertility."
7. Dudley Kirk, "A New Demographic Transition?" in National Academy of Sciences, *Rapid Population Growth: Consequences and Policy Implications* (Baltimore: Johns Hopkins University Press, 1971).
8. Tsui and Bogue, "Declining World Fertility"; Felix Paukert, "Income Distribution at Different Levels of Development: A Survey of Evidence," *International Labour Review* 108, nos. 2 and 3 (1973): 97-125.

CHAPTER 5

1. Food and Agriculture Organization/World Health Organization, Report of a Joint ad hoc Expert Committee, *Energy and Protein Requirements,* WHO Technical Report Series no. 522 (Rome: FAO/WHO, 1973); National Research Council, *Recommended Dietary Allowances,* 8th ed. (Washington, D.C.: National Academy of Sciences, 1974).
2. Nevin S. Scrimshaw and Vernon R. Young, "The Requirements of Human Nutrition," *Scientific American* 235 (1976): 50-73; Shlomo Reutlinger and M. Selowsky, "Malnutrition and Poverty: Magnitude and Policy Options," *World Bank Staff Occasional Paper* 23 (Baltimore: Johns Hopkins University Press, 1976).
3. Thomas T. Poleman, "World Food: A Perspective," *Science* 188 (1975): 510-18; National Research Council, *Supporting Papers: World Food and Nutrition Study,* vol. 4, Study Team 9, *Nutrition* (Washington, D.C.: National Academy of Sciences, 1977), p. 81.
4. National Research Council, *Nutrition,* p. 78; E. M. de Maeyer, "Protein-Energy Malnutrition," in G. H. Beaton and J. M. Bengoa, eds., *Nutrition in Preventive Medicine,* World Health Organization Monograph Series no. 62, 1976.
5. Nick Eberstadt, "Myths of the Food Crisis," *New York Review of Books* 23 (1976): 32-37; United Nations, World Food Conference, *Assessment of the World Food Situation: Present and Future* (E/Conf. 65/3), Rome, 5-16 November 1974.

6. Food and Agriculture Organization, *The Fourth World Food Survey,* Statistics Series no. 11 (Rome: FAO, 1977), pp. 15-28.

7. Eberstadt, "Myths of the Food Crisis"; J. de Hoogh et al., "Food for a Growing World Population," *European Review of Agricultural Economics* 3 (1977): 459-99.

8. FAO, *Fourth World Food Survey;* James D. Gavan and John A. Dixon, "India: A Perspective on the Food Situation," *Science* 188 (1975): 541-49.

9. FAO, *Fourth World Food Survey.*

10. FAO, *Fourth World Food Survey;* Alan Berg, *The Nutrition Factor* (Washington, D.C.: The Brookings Institution, 1972); Michael C. Latham, "Nutrition and Infection in National Development," *Science* 188 (1975): 561-65.

11. National Research Council, *Nutrition,* p. 63.

12. FAO, *Fourth World Food Survey,* and compare tables 5-5 and 5-6.

13. John W. Mellor, "The Agriculture of India," *Scientific American* 235 (1976): p. 46.

14. R. T. Maddock, "The Economic and Political Characteristics of Food as a Diplomatic Weapon," *American Journal of Agricultural Economics* 24 (1978): 31-41; T. Schell, "The Time of Illusion," *The New Yorker,* June 23, 1975, pp. 60-91.

15. S. J. Maxwell and H. W. Singer, "Food Aid to Developing Countries: A Survey," *World Development* 7 (1979): 225-47.

16. Maxwell and Singer, "Food Aid to Developing Countries."

17. P. H. Trezise, *Rebuilding Grain Reserves* (Washington, D.C.: The Brookings Institution, 1976). Other ideas for increasing food security in the LDCs include insurance schemes, with or without modest grain reserves. See, for example, Panos Konandreas, Barbara Huddleston, and Virabongsa Ramangkura, *Food Security: An Insurance Approach* (Washington, D.C.: International Food Policy Research Institute, 1978), Research Report no. 4.

18. Trezise, *Rebuilding Grain Reserves.*

19. de Hoogh et al., "Food for a Growing World Population."

20. de Hoogh et al., "Food for a Growing World Population," p. 488; FAO, *Fourth World Food Survey.*

21. FAO, *Fourth World Food Survey,* pp. 93-108.

22. Ibid., p. 6.

23. United Nations, *Assessment of the World Food Situation;* U.S. Department of Agriculture, *The World Food Situation and Prospects to 1985,* Foreign Agricultural Economic Report no. 98 (Washington, D.C.: U.S. Department of Agriculture, 1974); University of California Food Task Force, *A Hungry World: The Challenge to Agriculture* (Berkeley and Los Angeles: University of California Press, 1974); de Hoogh et al., "Food for a Growing Population"; International Food Policy Research Institute, *Food Needs of Developing Countries: Projections of Production and Consumption to 1990* (Washington, D.C.: International Food Policy Research Institute, 1977), Research Report no. 3.

24. See also U.S. Department of Agriculture, "Agricultural Situation: People's Republic of China, Review of 1978 and Outlook for 1979," supplement 6 to WAS-18 (Washington, D.C.: U.S. Department of Agriculture, 1979); Reutlinger and Selowsky, "Malnutrition and Poverty"; de Hoogh et al., "Food for a Growing Population."

25. International Food Policy Research Institute, *Food Needs of Developing Countries.*

26. Roger Revelle, "The Resources Available for Agriculture," *Scientific American* 235 (1976): 177.

27. . Buringh, H.D.J. van Heemst, and G. J. Staring, *Computation of the Absolute Maximum Food Production of the World* (Wageningen: Agricultural University, 1975); David Norse, "Development Strategies and the World Food Problem," *Journal of Agricultural Economics* 27 (1976): 137-58; M. Mesarovic and E. Pestel, *Mankind at the Turning Point: The Second Report to the Club of Rome* (New York: E. P. Dutton, 1974); National Research Council, *Supporting Papers: World Food and Nutrition Study,* vol. 2, Study Team 4, *Resources for Agriculture* (Washington, D.C.: National Academy of Sciences, 1977); Revelle, "The Resources Available for Agriculture."

28. President's Science Advisory Committee, *The World Food Problem,* vol. 2, *Report of the Panel on the World Food Supply* (Washington, D.C.: U.S. Government Printing Office, 1967).

29. P. A. Sanchez and S. W. Buol, "Soils of the Tropics and the World Food Crisis," *Science* 188 (1975): 598-603.

30. W. David Hopper, "The Development of Agriculture in Developing Countries," *Scientific American* 235 (1976): 196–204.

31. P. Buringh, "Food Production Potential of the World," *World Development* 5 (1977): 477–85.

32. National Research Council, *Resources for Agriculture*.

33. Ibid., p. 81.

34. Quoted in D. Gale Johnson, *World Food Problems and Prospects* (Washington, D.C.: American Enterprise Institute for Public Policy Research, 1975).

35. National Research Council, *Resources for Agriculture*.

36. Ibid.; Sterling Wortman and Ralph W. Cummings, Jr., *To Feed This World: The Challenge and the Strategy* (Baltimore: Johns Hopkins University Press, 1978).

37. D. Gale Johnson, "Food for the Future: A Perspective," *Population and Development Review* 2 (1976): 1–19; Wortman and Cummings, *To Feed This World*, pp. 50, 67; United Nations, *Assessment of the World Food Situation*.

38. Johnson, "Food for the Future."

39. Wortman and Cummings, *To Feed This World*, p. 147.

40. Hopper, "The Development of Agriculture"; Food and Agriculture Organization, *Monthly Bulletin of Statistics* 1, no. 11 (1978): 31.

41. Mellor, "The Agriculture of India," p. 155.

42. Gavan and Dixon, "India: A Perspective on the Food Situation"; National Research Council, *Resources for Agriculture*.

43. David Norse, "Natural Resources, Development Strategies, and the World Food Problem," in Margaret R. Biswas and Asit K. Biswas, eds., *Food, Climate, and Man* (New York: John Wiley and Sons, 1979).

44. Hopper, "The Development of Agriculture"; Keith Griffin, *The Political Economy of Agrarian Change* (Cambridge, Mass.: Harvard University Press, 1974); Wortman and Cummings, *To Feed This World*.

45. National Research Council, *World Food and Nutrition Study: The Potential Contributions of Research*, final report (Washington, D.C.: National Academy of Sciences, 1977).

46. Ibid.; Wortman and Cummings, *To Feed This World*, pp. 59–61; Norse, "Natural Resources."

47. United Nations, World Food Conference, *Assessment of the World Food Situation;* Asian Development Bank, *Asian Agricultural Survey* (Seattle: University of Washington Press, 1969); National Research Council, *Resources for Agriculture;* Norse, "Development Strategies."

48. National Research Council, *Resources for Agriculture*, p. 131.

49. National Research Council, *World Food and Nutrition Study*, final report, p. 132; Norse, "Natural Resources."

50. Revelle, "The Resources Available for Agriculture."

51. Food and Agriculture Organization, *Annual Fertilizer Review* (Rome: FAO, 1975); Wortman and Cummings, *To Feed This World*, pp. 67, 68; Norse, "Natural Resources."

52. H. R. von Uexküll, "Recent Fertilizer Problems in Asia," *Extension Bulletin* 59 (Taipei, Taiwan: Food and Fertilizer Technology Center, 1975).

53. R. B. Reidinger, "World Fertilizer Review and Prospects to 1980/81," *Foreign Agricultural Economic Report*, no. 115 (Washington, D.C.: U.S. Department of Agriculture, Economic Research Service, 1976); National Research Council, *World Food and Nutrition Study*, final report; United Nations, Industrial Development Organization, *World-Wide Study of the Fertilizer Industry 1975–2000* (Vienna: U.N. Industrial Development Organization, 1977); A.J.G. Northolt, "Phosphate Rock: World Production, Trade, and Resources," *Proceedings of the 1st Industrial Minerals International Congress, Metal Bulletin* (London, 1975); G. D. Emigh, *Phosphate Rock Industrial Minerals and Rocks* (New York: American Institute of Mining and Petroleum Engineers, 1975); National Research Council, *Resources for Agriculture*.

54. Reidinger, "World Fertilizer Review"; see also recent issues of U.S. Department of Agriculture, *World Agricultural Situation* (Washington, D.C.: U.S. Department of Agriculture); National Research Council, *World Food and Nutrition Study*, final report.

55. Johnson, "Food for the Future."

56. Ibid.

57. See various issues of U.S. Department of Agriculture, *World Agricultural Situation.*

58. National Research Council, *World Food and Nutrition Study,* final report.

59. International Bank for Reconstruction and Development, *Organic Fertilizers: Problems and Potential for Developing Countries. Background Paper* no. 4 (Washington, D.C.: World Bank, 1974).

60. Gerald Leach, *Energy and Food Production* (Guildford, U.K.: IPC Science and Technology Press, 1975); Food and Agriculture Organization, "Energy for Agriculture in Developing Countries," *Monthly Bulletin of Agricultural Economics and Statistics* 25, no. 2 (1976). These estimates of energy use in LDC crop production probably underestimate the use of nonconventional energy; see Chapter 10.

61. Food and Agriculture Organization, "Energy for Agriculture"; Organization for Economic Cooperation and Development, *World Energy Outlook* (Paris: OECD, 1977); National Research Council, *World Food and Nutrition Study,* final report.

62. Organization for Economic Cooperation and Development, *World Energy Outlook;* Revelle, "The Resources Available for Agriculture."

63. A. Makhijani, *Energy Policy for the Rural Third World* (London: International Institute for Environment and Development, 1976); Revelle, "The Resources Available for Agriculture"; National Research Council, *U.S. Science and Technology Development: A Contribution to the 1979 U.N. Conference* (Washington, D.C.: U.S. Department of State, 1978); Brace Research Institute, *A Handbook on Appropriate Technology* (Ottawa: Brace Research Institute, 1976).

64. C. D. Finney and R. S. Evans, "Anaerobic Digestion: The Rate Limiting Process and the Nature of Inhibition," *Science* 190 (1975): 1088-89; Jyoti K. Parikh and S. Kirit, "Mobilization and Impacts of Biogas Technologies," *Energy* 2 (1977): 441-56; A. Williams, "Methane Digesters in Remote Rural Areas," in T. Nejat Veziroglu, ed., *Alternative Energy Sources: An International Compendium,* vol. 3, *Solar Energy* (New York: Hemisphere Publishing Co., 1978), pp. 1273-84; National Research Council, *Resources for Agriculture.*

65. Elizabeth Cecelski, Joy Dunkerley, and William Ramsey, *Household Energy and the Poor in the Third World* (Washington, D.C.: Resources for the Future, 1979); Roy Meader, *Future Energy Alternatives* (Ann Arbor, Mich.: Ann Arbor Publishers, 1978); Vaclav Smil, *China's Energy* (New York: Praeger, 1976).

66. Cecelski et al., *Household Energy;* Makhijani, *Energy Policy:* Parikh and Kirit, "Mobilization of Biogas."

67. Cecelski et al., *Household Energy;* Smil, *China's Energy.*

68. National Research Council, *Supporting Papers: World Food and Nutrition Study,* vol. 4, Study Team 12, *New Approaches to the Alleviation of Hunger* (Washington, D.C.: National Academy of Sciences, 1977); National Research Council, *Resources for Agriculture;* Makhijani, *Energy Policy;* A. Eggers-Lura, *Solar Energy in Developing Countries* (New York: Pergamon Press, 1979); Meader, *Future Energy Alternatives.*

69. Brace Research Institute, *Handbook on Appropriate Technology;* P. Warpeha, "Methane Generator in Ecuador: Appropriate Success," *Alternative Sources of Energy* 24 (1977): 30-33; Williams, "Methane Digesters in Remote Rural Areas."

70. Wortman and Cummings, in *To Feed This World,* provide a detailed discussion of the research on high-yielding varieties. See also Norse, "Natural Resources."

71. National Research Council, *Supporting Papers: World Food and Nutrition Study,* vol. 5, Study Team 14, *Agricultural Research Organization* (Washington, D.C.: National Academy of Sciences, 1977).

72. National Research Council, *Supporting Papers: World Food and Nutrition Study,* vols. 1-5 (Washington, D.C.: National Academy of Sciences, 1977).

73. United Nations, World Food Conference, *Proposals for National and International Action* (E/Conf. 65/3), Rome, 5-16 November 1974; Hopper, "The Development of Agriculture"; National Research Council, *World Food and Nutrition Study,* final report.

74. Revelle, "The Resources Available for Agriculture"; Buringh, van Heemst, and Staring, *Computation of the Absolute Maximum Food Production.*

75. See Chapter 4, and especially Thomas Frejka, *The Future of Population Growth: Alternative Paths to Equilibrium* (New York: John Wiley and Sons, 1973); U.S. Bureau of

the Census, *Illustrative Projections of World Populations to the 21st Century,* Special Studies Series P-23, no. 79 (Washinigton, D.C.: U.S. Bureau of the Census, 1979); United Nations, Department of Economic and Social Affairs, *World Population Trends and Policies: 1977 Monitoring Report,* vol. 1 (ST/ESA/SER.A/62), 1979.

76. Eberstadt, "Myths of the Food Crisis."

77. Lawrence Hewes, *Rural Development: World Frontiers* (Ames, Ia.: Iowa State University Press, 1974); Food and Agriculture Organization, *Monthly Bulletin of Agricultural Economics and Statistics* 26, no. 7–8 (1977): 22, 23.

CHAPTER 6

1. Willard W. Cochrane, *The City Man's Guide to the Farm Problem* (Minneapolis: University of Minnesota Press, 1965); Willard W. Cochrane and Mary E. Ryan, *American Farm Policy 1948–1973* (Minneapolis: University of Minnesota Press, 1976).

2. Ibid.

3. P. J. Isenman and H. W. Singer, "Food Aid: Disincentive Effects and the Policy Implications," *Economic Development and Cultural Change* 25 (1977).

4. A broad range of Asian countries is analyzed by Keith Griffin, *The Political Economy of Agrarian Change* (Cambridge, Mass.: Harvard University Press, 1974). India is discussed in detail by John W. Mellor, *The New Economics of Growth: A Strategy for India and the Developing World* (Ithaca, N.Y.: Cornell University Press, 1976). Latin America countries are discussed by Solon Barraclough and Juan Collarte, *Agrarian Structure in Latin America* (Lexington, Mass.: Lexington Books, 1973); Celso Furtado, *Economic Development of Latin America,* 2d ed., *Cambridge Latin American Studies* 8 (Cambridge: At the University Press, 1976); Alain de Janvry and Lynn Ground, "Types and Consequences of Land Reform in Latin America," *Latin American Perspectives* 19 (1978): 90–112. African countries are discussed in E. A. Brett, *Colonialism and Underdevelopment in East Africa* (New York: NOK Publishers, 1973); Ann Seidman, *Comparative Development Strategies in East Africa* (Nairobi: East African Publishing House, 1972); Ann Seidman, *Planning for Development in Sub-Saharan Africa* (New York: Praeger, 1974); and R.M.A. van Zwanenberg and A. King, *An Economic History of Kenya and Uganda, 1800–1970* (London: Macmillan, 1975). Keith Griffin, *Land Concentration and Rural Poverty* (New York: Holmes and Meier, 1976) discusses several African, Latin American, and Asian countries. R. Albert Berry and William R. Cline, *Agrarian Structure and Productivity in Developing Countries* (Baltimore: Johns Hopkins University Press, 1979), presents detailed results for over twenty countries on all three continents.

5. United Nations, Department of Economic and Social Affairs, *Progress in Land Reform,* 6th Report (ST/ESA/32), 1976, p. 83.

6. Griffin, *Political Economy;* Berry and Cline, *Agrarian Structure;* van Zwanenberg and King, *Economic History of Kenya and Uganda;* United Nations, *Progress in Land Reform.*

7. Berry and Cline, *Agrarian Structure;* Barraclough and Collarte, *Agrarian Structure in Latin America.*

8. Bruce F. Johnston and Peter Kilby, *Agricultural and Structural Transformation: Economic Strategies in Late-Developing Countries* (London: Oxford University Press, 1975).

9. Berry and Cline, *Agrarian Structure*; Griffin, *Land Concentration.*

10. International Bank for Reconstruction and Development, *Land Reform,* World Bank Paper-Rural Development Series (Washington, D.C.: World Bank, 1974), p. 60; Raisuddin Ahmed, "Agriculture in Integrated Rural Development: A Critique," *Food Policy* 2 (1977): 140–47; Richard Norton-Taylor, *The Guardian* (London) June 4, 1979, p. 12.

11. Griffin, *Political Economy,* p. 13.

12. A. Rudra, "Organization of Agriculture for Rural Development: The Indian Case," *Cambridge Journal of Economics* 2 (1978): 381–406; *London Observer,* 6 November 1977.

13. Barraclough and Collarte, *Agrarian Structure in Latin America.* One change that has

been occurring in this system is that cash is replacing labor as the payment for rent (de Janvry and Ground, "Types and Consequences of Land Reform").

14. Alain de Janvry, "Material Determinants of the World Food Crisis," *Berkeley Journal of Sociology* 21 (1976): 3-26; Furtado, *Economic Development of Latin America*; James E. Kocher, *Rural Development, Income Distribution, and Fertility Decline* (New York: The Population Council, 1973), p. 47; Berry and Cline, *Agrarian Structure*, pp. 25-27.

15. Carl H. Gotsch, "Technical Change and the Distribution of Income in Rural Areas," *American Journal of Agricultural Economics* 52 (1972): 326-41; United Nations, *Progress in Land Reform*; G. Rosen, *Peasant Society in a Changing Economy: Comparative Development in Southeast Asia and India* (Chicago: University of Illinois Press, 1975); P. R. Shaw, *Land Tenure and the Rural Exodus in Chile, Colombia, Costa Rica, and Peru* (Gainesville: University of Florida Press, 1976); de Janvry and Ground, "Types and Consequences of Land Reform."

16. Griffin, *Political Economy*; Michael Lipton, "Agricultural Finance and Rural Credit in Poor Countries," *World Development* 4 (1976): 543-53; Mellor, *New Economics*; Johnston and Kilby, *Agricultural Transformation*; Seidman, *Comparative Development Strategies*; Berry and Cline, *Agrarian Structure*, chapter 4.

17. Griffin, *Political Economy*, pp. 17-27; Mellor, *New Economics*, pp. 36, 84-85.

18. Griffin, *Political Economy*; Lipton, "Agricultural Finance"; A. Bhaduri, "A Study in Agricultural Backwardness Under Semi-Feudalism," *The Economic Journal* 83 (1973): 120-37; Mellor, *New Economics*.

19. Mellor, *New Economics*, p. 36.

20. W. P. Falcon, "The Green Revolution: Generations of Problems," *American Journal of Agricultural Economics* (1970); Berry and Cline, *Agrarian Structure*, chapter 4; Uma J. Lele, "The Roles of Credit and Marketing in Agricultural Development," in Nurul Islam, ed., *Agricultural Policy in Developing Countries* (London: Macmillan, 1974); Griffin, *Political Economy*.

21. Mahabub Hossain, "Farm Size, Tenancy, and Land Productivity," *Bangladesh Development Studies* (1977): 300-33.

22. Griffin, *Political Economy*, p. 17; Gotsch, "Technical Change."

23. United Nations, *Progress in Land Reform*, p. 6.

24. Ibid., p. 83.

25. Solon Barraclough, "Comment," *World Development* 4 (1976): 557-59; Bhaduri, "A Study in Agricultural Backwardness"; Rudra, "Organization of Agriculture."

26. Robert Eric Frykenberg, ed., *Land Control and Social Structure in Indian History* (Madison: University of Wisconsin Press, 1969); Mahmood Mamdani, *The Myth of Population Control* (New York: Monthly Review Press, 1972); Seidman, *Planning for Development*; United Nations, *Progress in Land Reform*, p. 12; Rudra, "Organization of Agriculture," p. 12.

27. Griffin, *Political Economy*, p. 51.

28. D. J. Greenland, "Bringing the Green Revolution to the Shifting Cultivator," *Science* 190 (1975): 841-44.

29. Lipton, "Agricultural Finance."

30. Berry and Cline, *Agrarian Structure*.

31. Griffin, *Political Economy*, p. 32 n.

32. Lipton, "Agricultural Finance."

33. Griffin, *Political Economy*, p. 32 n.

34. Berry and Cline, *Agrarian Structure*, chapters 3 and 4 and appendix A; Griffin, *Political Economy*, p. 39.

35. Michael Lipton, "Rural Poverty and Agribusiness," Discussion Paper no. 104, (Brighton: Institute of Development Studies, 1977); Barraclough and Collarte, *Agrarian Structure in Latin America*, p. 28.

36. The example of Brazil is discussed in detail by John H. Sanders and Vernon W. Ruttan, "Biased Choice of Technology in Brazilian Agriculture," in Hans P. Binswanger and Vernon W. Ruttan, *Induced Innovation: Technology, Institutions, and Development* (Baltimore: Johns Hopkins University Press, 1978).

37. Kocher, *Rural Development*, p. 28.

38. For Thailand and Indonesia see Griffin, *Political Economy,* p. 37 n; for Taiwan and Indonesia see Edgar Owens and Robert Shaw, *Development Reconsidered* (Lexington, Mass.: Lexington Books, 1972); for Bangladesh see Mahabub Hossain, "Farm Size and Productivity in Bangladesh Agriculture: A Case Study of Phulphur Farms," *The Bangladesh Economic Review* 2 (1974): 469-500, and Hossain, "Farm Size, Tenancy, and Land Productivity"; for India see Mellor, *New Economics,* p. 82; for Latin America see Barraclough and Collarte, *Agrarian Structure in Latin America,* and Berry and Cline, *Agrarian Structure.*

39. Barraclough and Collarte, *Agrarian Structure in Latin America*, p. 25; Berry and Cline, *Agrarian Structure.*

40. Berry and Cline, *Agrarian Structure*; Griffin, *Political Economy.*

41. Berry and Cline, *Agrarian Structure.*

42. Griffin, *Political Economy*, p. 73 n; Michael Lipton, "Urban Bias and Food Policy in Poor Countries," *Food Policy* 1 (1975): 41-52; United Nations, *Progress in Land Reform*; Barbara Tuckman, "The Green Revolution and the Distribution of Agricultural Income in Mexico," *World Development* 4 (1976): 17-24; Rudra, "Organization of Agriculture"; T. N. Srinivasan, "Development, Poverty, and Basic Human Needs: Some Issues," *Stanford Food Research Institute Studies* 16, no. 2 (1977): 11-28; Mellor, *New Economics,* p. 82.

43. Rudra, "Organization of Agriculture," p. 336.

44. D. W. Adams, "The Economics of Land Reform," *Stanford Food Research Institute Studies* 12 (1973): 133-38; Berry and Cline, *Agrarian Structure*, pp. 135-37; de Janvry and Ground, "Types and Consequences of Land Reform"; F. Dovring, "Land Reform: A Key to Change in Agriculture," in Nurul Islam, ed., *Agricultural Policy in Developing Countries* (London: Macmillan, 1974); Johnston and Kilby, *Agricultural Transformation,* pp. 165, 218, 248 n; Shlomo Eckstein et al., "Land Reform in Latin America: Bolivia, Chile, Mexico, Peru, and Venezuela," World Bank Staff Working Paper No. 275 (Washington, D.C.: World Bank, 1978); D. Warriner, "Results of Land Reform in Asian and Latin American Countries," *Stanford Food Research Institute Studies* 12 (1973): 115-31.

45. Berry and Cline, *Agrarian Structure;* United Nations, *Progress in Land Reform*; de Janvry and Ground, "Types and Consequences of Land Reform."

46. de Janvry and Ground, "Types and Consequences of Land Reform"; see also Eckstein et al., "Land Reform in Latin America."

47. Ibid. See especially pp. 92 and 93 in Eckstein et al.

48. de Janvry and Ground, "Types and Consequences of Land Reform"; J. Kirby, "Venezuela's Land Reform, Progress and Change," *Journal of Interamerican Studies and World Affairs* 15 (1973): 205-20; Solon Barraclough, *The Guardian* (London), August 13, 1979, p. 8.

49. de Janvry and Ground, "Types and Consequences of Land Reform"; P. Chopra, *The Guardian* (London), July 10, 1979, p. 15.

50. A. A. Saleh, "Disincentives to Agricultural Production in Developing Countries: A Policy Survey," U.S. Department of Agriculture, *Foreign Agriculture* (March 1975).

51. Nick Eberstadt, "Myths of the Food Crisis," *New York Review of Books* 23 (1976): 32-37.

52. Michael Lipton, *Why Poor People Stay Poor: Urban Bias and World Development* (Cambridge, Mass.: Harvard University Press, 1977).

53. W. L. Peterson, "International Farm Prices and the Social Cost of Cheap Food Policies," *American Journal of Agricultural Economics* 61 (1979): 18-19.

54. U.S. Department of Agriculture, "Agricultural Situation: Asia, Review of 1978 and Outlook for 1979," supplement 2 to WAS-18 (Washington, D.C.: U.S. Department of Agriculture, 1979); U.S. Department of Agriculture, "Indices of Agricultural Production for Asia and Oceania, Average 1961-65 and Annual 1969-78," (Washington, D.C.: U.S. Department of Agriculture, 1979); Food and Agriculture Organization, Statistical Bulletin 619 *Monthly Bulletin of Statistics* 1, no. 11 (1978); Mellor, *New Economics,* appendix 4; John B. Parker, "Changes in India's Agricultural Policy Have Spurred Productivity," *Highlight,* September 14, 1979; Sterling Wortman and Ralph W. Cummings, Jr., *To Feed This World: The Challenge and the Strategy* (Baltimore: Johns Hopkins University Press, 1978), p. 65.

55. Griffin, *Political Economy,* p. 103 n. Government food distribution often rubs salt in the wound of urban bias. In Bangladesh not only is the farmer squeezed through low prices,

but the rural population fares badly in the distribution of government food rations. Two-thirds of all public foodgrains go to the 9 percent of the population that is urban, even though there are about two and a half times as many "extremely poor" rural as extremely poor urban residents. See Raisuddin Ahmed, *Foodgrain Supply, Distribution, and Consumption Policies within a Dual Pricing Mechanism: A Case Study of Bangladesh* (Washington, D.C., International Food Policy Research Institute, 1979), Research Report no. 8.

56. Griffin, *Political Economy*.

57. Griffin, *Political Economy*, pp. 105-20; United Nations, *Progress in Land Reform*, p. 8; Barraclough and Collarte, *Agrarian Structure in Latin America*, p. 30.

58. Griffin, *Political Economy*, pp. 119-22; United Nations, *Progress in Land Reform*.

59. E. F. Szczepanik, "The Size and Efficiency of Agricultural Investment in Selected Developing Countries," Food and Agriculture Organization, *Monthly Bulletin of Agricultural Economics and Statistics* 18, no. 12 (1969): 1-13; Lipton, "Agricultural Finance."

60. W. David Hopper, "The Development of Agriculture in Developing Countries," *Scientific American* 235 (1976): 196-204; Mellor, *New Economics*.

61. Lipton, *Why Poor People Stay Poor;* Institute of Development Studies, *Ten-Year Review and Annual Report 1976* (Brighton: Institute of Development Studies, 1976).

62. M. Osterrieth and J. Waelbroeck, "Agricultural Prospects of Developing Countries," presented at 4th IIASA Global Modelling Symposium (Laxenburg, Austria, September 1976).

63. Paul Bairoch, *The Economic Development of the Third World since 1900* (Berkeley and Los Angeles: University of California Press, 1975); United Nations, *Progress in Land Reform*; M. F. Lofchie, "Political and Economic Origins of African Hunger," *Journal of Modern African Studies* 13 (1975): 551-67.

64. Wortman and Cummings, *To Feed This World*, pp. 144-50; Mellor, *New Economics*, p. 58; Food and Agriculture Organization, *Indicative World Plan for Agricultural Development* (Rome: FAO, 1969); David Norse, "Natural Resources, Development Strategies, and the World Food Problem," in Margaret R. Biswas and Asit K. Biswas, eds., *Food, Climate, and Man* (New York: John Wiley and Sons, 1979); Bairoch, *Economic Development;* United Nations, *Progress in Land Reform*.

65. J. Pastore, "Brazilian Agricultural Research," *Food Policy* 2 (1977): 217-27.

66. E. Feder, *Strawberry Imperialism: An Enquiry into the Mechanisms of Dependency in Mexican Agriculture* (The Hague: Institute of Social Studies, 1977); Frances Moore Lappé and Joseph Collins, *Food First: Beyond the Myth of Scarcity* (Boston: Houghton Mifflin Co., 1977); R. E. Stryker, "The World Bank and Agricultural Development: Food Production and Rural Poverty," *World Development* 7 (1977): 325-36.

67. Seidman, *Comparative Development Strategies;* Lofchie, "Political and Economic Origins of African Hunger"; C. Eicher et al., "Employment Generation in African Agriculture," in Gerald M. Meier, ed., *Leading Issues in Economic Development*, 3d ed. (New York: Oxford University Press, 1976).

68. Lofchie, "Political and Economic Origins of African Hunger," p. 553 (italics added).

69. Ibid., p. 554 (italics added).

70. Lofchie, "Political and Economic Origins of African Hunger"; Seidman, *Comparative Development Strategies;* Seidman, *Planning for Development*, and see Chapter 10.

71. Lofchie, "Political and Economic Origins of African Hunger," p. 560.

CHAPTER 7

1. Simon Kuznets, *Modern Economic Growth*, (New Haven, Conn.: Yale University Press, 1966), pp. 80, 81.

2. Ibid., pp. 81, 82.

3. Ibid., pp. 82, 83.

4. Paul Bairoch, *The Economic Development of the Third World since 1900* (Berkeley and Los Angeles: University of California Press, 1975), p. 49; V. D. Lippit, "Economic De-

velopment in Meiji Japan and Contemporary China: A Comparative Study," *Cambridge Journal of Economics* 2 (1978): 55-81; J. E. Nickum, "Labour Accumulation in Rural China and Its Role Since the Cultural Revolution," *Cambridge Journal of Economics* 2 (1978): 273-86.

   5. John W. Mellor, *The New Economics of Growth: A Strategy for India and the Developing World* (Ithaca, N.Y.: Cornell University Press, 1976), p. 17.

   6. Ibid., pp. 2-6.

   7. Ibid., p. 107 n.

   8. Ibid., pp. 120-22.

   9. Ibid., p. 116.

   10. A. Rudra, "Organization of Agriculture for Rural Development: The Indian Case," *Cambridge Journal of Economics* 2 (1978): 381-406; Mellor, *New Economics,* p. 42.

   11. John W. Mellor, "The Agriculture of India," *Scientific American* 235 (1976): 154-63; W. David Hopper, "The Development of Agriculture in Developing Countries," *Scientific American* 235 (1976): 196-204; J. S. Sarma, "India: A Drive towards Self-Sufficiency in Food Grains," *American Journal of Agricultural Economics* 60 (1978): 859-64; Rudra, "Organization of Agriculture."

   12. Mellor, *New Economics,* pp. 137-41.

   13. Alexander Eckstein, *China's Economic Revolution* (Cambridge: At the University Press, 1977), pp. 125, 202; Bairoch, *Economic Development,* p. 91.

   14. David Selbourne, *An Eye to India* (Harmondsworth: Pelican Books, 1977), p. 6.

   15. Mellor, *New Economics,* pp. 122, 123.

   16. Ibid.

   17. Keith Griffin, *The Political Economy of Agrarian Change* (Cambridge, Mass.: Harvard University Press, 1974); Mellor, *New Economics,* pp. 76-106; Barbara H. Tuckman, "The Green Revolution and the Distribution of Agricultural Income in Mexico," *World Development* 4 (1976): 17-24; R. Albert Berry and William R. Cline, *Agrarian Structure and Productivity in Developing Countries* (Baltimore: Johns Hopkins University Press, 1979); Rudra, "Organization of Agriculture."

   18. Bruce F. Johnston and Peter Kilby, *Agricultural and Structural Transformation: Economic Strategies in Late-Developing Countries* (London: Oxford University Press, 1975).

   19. Michael Lipton, *Why Poor People Stay Poor: Urban Bias and World Development* (Cambridge, Mass.: Harvard University Press, 1977).

   20. Johnston and Kilby, *Agricultural Transformation,* pp. 358 n.

   21. Ibid.

   22. Johnston and Kilby, *Agricultural Transformation;* Tuckman, "The Green Revolution."

   23. B. F. Johnston and J. W. Mellor, "The Role of Agriculture in Economic Development," *American Economic Review* 51 (1961): 566-93; B. F. Johnston, "Agriculture and Structural Transformation in Developing Countries: A Survey of Research," *Journal of Economic Literature* 8 (1970): 369-404; Johnston and Kilby, *Agricultural Transformation;* Paul Bairoch, "Agriculture and the Industrial Revolution 1700-1914," in C. M. Cipolla, ed., *The Fontana Economic History of Europe: The Industrial Revolution* (London: Collins, Fontana, 1973); Mellor, *New Economics;* Kuznets, *Modern Economic Growth;* W. H. Nicholls, "The Place of Agriculture in Economic Development," in C. Eicher and L. Witt, eds., *Agriculture and Economic Development* (New York: McGraw Hill, 1964); K. Ohkawa and H. Rosovsky, "The Role of Agriculture in Modern Japanese Economic Development," in Eicher and Witt, eds., *Agriculture and Economic Development.*

   24. Bairoch, "Agriculture and the Industrial Revolution"; Robert Brenner ("The Origins of Capitalist Development: A Critique of Neo-Smithian Marxism," *New Left Review* 104 [1977]: 75-78) argues convincingly that the necessary prerequisite to the increasing productivity of the agricultural revolution in technology was the preceding social revolution in English agriculture. Through this revolution serfdom had been destroyed by the end of the fifteenth century, and a capitalist class structure had arisen, consisting of landlords, capitalist (rent-paying, profit-making) tenants, and free wage laborers.

   25. Maurice Dobb, *Studies in the Development of Capitalism* (New York: International Publishers, 1963).

26. Michael P. Todaro, *Economic Development in the Third World: An Introduction to Problems and Policies in a Global Perspective* (New York: Longman, 1977), p. 206.

27. Lippit, "Economic Development in Meiji Japan."

28. K. Ohkawa, "Phases of Agricultural Development and Agricultural Growth," in K. Ohkawa, B. F. Johnston, and H. Kaneda, eds., *Agriculture and Economic Growth: Japan's Experience* (Princeton, N.J.: Princeton University Press, 1969); Lippit, "Economic Development in Meiji Japan."

29. Gustav Ranis, "The Financing of Japanese Economic Growth," in Ohkawa, Johnston, and Kaneda, eds., *Japan's Experience;* Ohkawa, "Phases of Agricultural Development."

30. B. F. Johnston, "The Japanese 'Model' of Agricultural Development: Its Relevance to Developing Nations," in Ohkawa, Johnston, and Kaneda, eds., *Japan's Experience.* See esp. p. 60.

31. Ranis, "The Financing of Japanese Economic Growth."

32. Johnston, "The Japanese 'Model' of Development."

33. Lippit, "Economic Development in Meiji Japan."

34. Johnston, "The Japanese 'Model' of Development"; A. R. Tussing, "The Labor Force in Meiji Economic Growth: A Quantitative Study of Yamanashi Prefecture," in Ohkawa, Johnston, and Kaneda, eds., *Japan's Experience;* Lippit, "Economic Development in Meiji Japan."

35. Yūjirō Hayami, *A Century of Agricultural Growth in Japan: Its Relevance to Asian Development* (Minneapolis: University of Minnesota Press, 1975).

36. Lippit, "Economic Development in Meiji Japan."

37. Hayami, *A Century of Growth.*

38. Albert I. Hermalin, "Empirical Research in Taiwan on Factors Underlying Differences in Fertility," in Ansley J. Coale, ed., *Economic Factors in Population Growth: Proceedings of a Conference* (New York: John Wiley and Sons, 1976).

39. Johnston and Kilby, *Agricultural Transformation,* p. 242.

40. Mellor, *New Economics,* p. 153.

41. Johnston and Kilby, *Agricultural Transformation.*

42. Ibid., p. 354 n.

43. Keith Griffin, *Land Concentration and Rural Poverty* (New York: Holmes and Meier, 1976), p. 269.

44. Ibid., pp. 271–72.

45. Nicholas R. Lardy, "Recent Chinese Economic Performance and Prospects for the Ten-Year Plan," in U.S. Congress, Joint Economic Committee, *Chinese Economy Post-Mao,* vol. 1, *Policy and Performance,* 95th Congress, 2d session, 1978.

46. Lippit, "Economic Development of Meiji Japan." By 1949 much of China's heavy industry had been destroyed by civil war and the departing Russian army. Russian aid, including technical aid, was important in rehabilitating and modernizing heavy industry, and even though the sudden withdrawal of Russian technical assistance in 1960 set industry back for a few years, this initial help provided a crucial base for China's future industrial development. (See various articles in U.S. Congress, Joint Economic Committee, *China: A Reassessment of the Economy,* 94th Congress, 1st session, 1975.)

47. See Chapter 3; Lippit, "Economic Development in Meiji Japan"; R. F. Dernberger and D. Fasenfest, "China's Post-Mao Economic Future," in U.S. Congress, *Chinese Economy Post-Mao.*

48. Henry J. Groen and James A. Kilpatrick, "Chinese Agricultural Production," in U.S. Congress, *Chinese Economy Post-Mao;* Lippit, "Economic Development in Meiji Japan."

49. John Gurley, *China's Economy and the Maoist Strategy* (New York: Monthly Review Press, 1976); Groen and Kilpatrick, "Chinese Agricultural Production"; Lippit, "Economic Development in Meiji Japan"; J. Wong, "Some Aspects of China's Agricultural Development Experience: Implications for Developing Countries in Asia," *World Development* 4 (1976): 485–97.

50. Alexander Eckstein, "The Chinese Development Model," in U.S. Congress, *Chinese Economy Post-Mao,* p. 74.

51. Wong, "Aspects of China's Agricultural Development."

52. Lippit, "Economic Development in Meiji Japan"; Groen and Kilpatrick, "Chinese Agricultural Production"; Gurley, *China's Economy.*

53. Alva Lewis Erisman, "China: Agriculture in the 1970s," in U.S. Congress, *China: A Reassessment;* A. Eckstein, *China's Economic Revolution;* Groen and Kilpatrick, "Chinese Agricultural Production"; Gurley, *China's Economy.*

54. Groen and Kilpatrick, "Chinese Agricultural Production"; Eckstein, "The Chinese Development Model"; Wong, "Aspects of China's Agricultural Development."

55. Eckstein, "The Chinese Development Model," p. 129; Gurley, *China's Economy.*

56. Nickum, "Labour Accumulation in Rural China."

57. Groen and Kilpatrick, "Chinese Agricultural Production"; Lardy, "Recent Chinese Economic Performance."

58. Groen and Kilpatrick, "Chinese Agricultural Production."

59. Lardy, "Recent Chinese Economic Performance"; Groen and Kilpatrick, "Chinese Agricultural Production"; U.S. Department of Agriculture, "Agricultural Situation: People's Republic of China, Review of 1978 and Outlook for 1979," supplement 6 to WAS-18 (Washington, D.C.: U.S. Department of Agriculture, 1979). The 1978 grain figures come from official Chinese statistics quoted in the *Los Angeles Times,* July 23, 1979, part 1, p. 1, and from "Agricultural Situation: People's Republic of China."

60. Lippit, "Economic Development in Meiji Japan"; Wong, "Aspects of China's Agricultural Development"; Eckstein, "The Chinese Development Model," p. 229.

61. Dernberger and Fasenfest, "China's Post-Mao Economic Future."

62. Berry and Cline, *Agrarian Structure.*

63. Two nations that have become socialist more recently, Cuba and Tanzania, are discussed briefly by Dudley Seers ("Cuba," in Hollis Chenery et al., *Redistribution with Growth* [London: Oxford University Press, 1974], pp. 262–68) and Reginald H. Green ("Tanzania," in Chenery et al., pp. 268–73).

64. Solon Barraclough, "Comment," *World Development* 4 (1976): 557–59.

CHAPTER 8

1. Felix Paukert, "Income Distribution at Different Levels of Development: A Survey of Evidence," *International Labour Review* 108, nos. 2 and 3 (1973): 97–125.

2. Paul Bairoch, *The Economic Development of the Third World since 1900* (Berkeley and Los Angeles: University of California Press, 1975); E. A. Brett, *Colonialism and Underdevelopment in East Africa* (New York: NOK Publishers, 1973); Andre Gunder Frank, *Capitalism and Underdevelopment in Latin America: Historical Studies of Chile and Brazil* (New York: Monthly Review Press, 1967); Andre Gunder Frank, *Dependent Accumulation and Underdevelopment* (London: Macmillan, 1978); Andre Gunder Frank, *Mexican Agriculture 1521–1630: Transformation of the Mode of Production* (Cambridge: At the University Press, 1979); Celso Furtado, *Economic Development of Latin America,* 2d ed., *Cambridge Latin American Studies* 8 (Cambridge: At the University Press, 1976); Clifford Geertz, *Agricultural Involution: The Process of Ecological Change in Indonesia* (Berkeley and Los Angeles: University of California Press, 1963); Rhoda Howard, *Colonialism and Underdevelopment in Ghana* (London: Croom Helm, 1978); Tibor Mende, *From Aid to Recolonization: Lessons of a Failure* (New York: Pantheon Books, 1973); Ann Seidman, *Comparative Development Strategies in East Africa* (Nairobi: East African Publishing House, 1972); Ann Seidman, *Planning for Development in Sub-Saharan Africa* (New York: Praeger, 1974); Eric Stokes, *The Peasant and the Raj: Studies in Agrarian Society and Peasant Rebellion in Colonial India* (Cambridge: At the University Press, 1978); Jean Suret-Canalé, *French Colonialism in Tropical Africa, 1900–1945* (London: Hurst and Co., 1971). G. L. Beckford, "The Economics of Agricultural Resource Use and Development in Plantation Economies," *Social and Economic Studies* 19 (1970): 435–65, and G. L. Beckford, *Persistent Poverty* (New York: Oxford University Press, 1972), have discussed colonies dominated by agricultural plantations.

3. Thomas R. Birnberg and Stephen A. Resnick, *Colonial Development: An Econometric Study* (New Haven, Conn.: Yale University Press, 1975).

4. Howard, *Colonialism and Underdevelopment in Ghana,* pp. 27, 28.

5. Frank, *Dependent Accumulation,* pp. 13, 14.

6. Ibid., pp. 14-17; Geertz, *Agricultural Involution;* Maurice Dobb, *Studies in the Development of Capitalism* (New York: International Publishers, 1963).

7. Mende, *From Aid to Re-colonization.*

8. Birnberg and Resnick, *Colonial Development,* p. 5.

9. Furtado, *Economic Development of Latin America,* p. 6. The account of Latin American colonialism is taken largely from this work by Furtado.

10. Furtado, *Economic Development of Latin America,* p. 29.

11. Frank, *Mexican Agriculture.*

12. Ibid.

13. Ibid.

14. Furtado, *Economic Development of Latin America,* p. 29.

15. Ibid., pp. 34-39; Birnberg and Resnick, *Colonial Development.*

16. Furtado, *Economic Development of Latin America,* pp. 44, 45.

17. Ibid., pp. 2, 3, 50-57, 194-208.

18. Frank, *Capitalism and Underdevelopment;* C. W. Reynolds, "Development Problems of an Export Economy: The Case of Chile and Copper," in M. Mamalakis and C. W. Reynolds, eds., *Essays on the Chilean Economy* (Homewood, Ill.: Richard D. Irwin, 1965); Brett, *Colonialism and Underdevelopment,* p. 71; Birnberg and Resnick, *Colonial Development,* p. 26.

19. Frank, *Dependent Accumulation,* pp. 17-24.

20. Stokes, *The Peasant and the Raj.*

21. Ibid., pp. 27, 28.

22. Tjin-Kie Tan, ed., *Sukarno's Guided Indonesia* (Brisbane, Australia: Jacarand Press, 1967); Stokes, *The Peasant and the Raj,* p. 35.

23. Birnberg and Resnick, *Colonial Development,* pp. 7, 8, 18.

24. Ibid., pp. 17, 18.

25. Stephen A. Resnick, "The Decline of Rural Industry under Export Expansion: A Comparison among Burma, Philippines, and Thailand, 1870-1938," *Journal of Economic History* 30 (1970): 51-73.

26. Birnberg and Resnick, *Colonial Development,* pp. 24-26.

27. W. B. Arthur and G. McNicoll, "An Analytical Survey of Population and Development in Bangladesh," *Population and Development Review* 4 (1978): 23-80.

28. Robert Eric Frykenberg, ed., *Land Control and Social Structure in Indian History* (Madison: University of Wisconsin Press, 1969).

29. Mahmood Mamdani, *The Myth of Population Control* (New York: Monthly Review Press, 1972); Frykenberg, ed., *Land Control.*

30. Alan Moorehead, *The White Nile* (New York: Harper, 1960).

31. K. Kjekshus, *Ecology Control and Economic Development in East African History: The Case of Tanganyika 1850-1950* (London: Heinmann, 1977); Seidman, *Planning for Development.*

32. Michael Crowder, *West Africa under Colonial Rule* (London: Hutchinson, 1968); Seidman, *Planning for Development.*

33. Kjekshus, *Ecology and Economic Development;* R.M.A. van Zwanenberg and A. King, *An Economic History of Kenya and Uganda 1800-1970* (London: Macmillan, 1975). The account of East African precolonial history presented here is based largely on Kjekshus.

34. Kjekshus, *Ecology and Economic Development,* p. 80 n; van Zwanenberg and King, *Economic History of Kenya and Uganda,* pp. 110-16, 119, 120.

35. Kjekshus, *Ecology and Economic Development,* p. 126 n, describes the breakdown of the East African economy at this time. See also p. 131.

36. Kjekshus, *Ecology and Economic Development,* p. 150.

37. Brett, *Colonialism and Underdevelopment;* Suret-Canalé, *French Colonialism;* Keith Griffin, *Land Concentration and Rural Poverty* (New York: Holmes and Meier, 1976).

38. Brett, *Colonialism and Underdevelopment,* p. 171.

39. Brett, *Colonialism and Underdevelopment;* Seidman, *Planning for Development;* Griffin, *Land Concentration.*

40. Kjekshus, *Ecology and Economic Development,* pp. 150-58.

41. Ben Wisner, "Man-Made Famine in Eastern Kenya: The Interrelationship of Environment and Development," *Institute of Development Studies Discussion Paper* no. 96, July 1976 (Brighton: University of Sussex); van Zwanenberg and King, *Economic History of Kenya and Uganda;* Brett, *Colonialism and Underdevelopment;* Kjekshus, *Ecology and Economic Development;* Suret-Canalé, *French Colonialism.*

42. Kjekshus, *Ecology and Economic Development,* pp. 70–78; John J. McKelvey, Jr., *Man Against Tsetse: Struggle for Africa* (Ithaca, N.Y.: Cornell University Press, 1973), pp. 43–57; John Ford, *The Role of Trypanosomiases in African Ecology: A Study of the Tsetse Fly Problem* (Oxford: Clarendon Press, 1971), pp. 146–52, 175 n, 268–71, 280.

43. van Zwanenberg and King, *Economic History of Kenya and Uganda,* p. 87 n.

44. Suret-Canalé, *French Colonialism;* Brett, *Colonialism and Underdevelopment.*

45. Suret-Canalé, *French Colonialism;* Brett, *Colonialism and Underdevelopment,* Seidman, *Comparative Development Strategies.*

46. Brett, *Colonialism and Underdevelopment,* pp. 75 n, 194; Kjekshus, *Ecology and Economic Development,* pp. 89, 108 n; van Zwanenberg and King, *Economic History of Kenya and Uganda,* p. 117.

47. Brett, *Colonialism and Underdevelopment,* pp. 191–98.

48. Brett, *Colonialism and Underdevelopment,* pp. 19–21, 76, 77; Wisner, "Man-Made Famine"; Howard, *Colonialism and Underdevelopment in Ghana,* pp. 181–219; Crowder, *West Africa under Colonial Rule,* pp. 381–85.

49. F. D. Lugard, *The Dual Mandate in British Tropical Africa* (1922; reprint ed., London: Frank Cars and Co., 1965), p. 611; Brett, *Colonialism and Underdevelopment,* pp. 19, 20, 39–41, 45; Seidman, *Planning for Development,* p. 66.

50. Brett, *Colonialism and Underdevelopment,* p. 18; Birnberg and Resnick, *Colonial Development.*

51. Frank, *Capitalism and Underdevelopment.* The emphasis throughout this chapter on structural features, rather than on the mere transfer of surplus (capital) from the colonies to the "central" nations, is crucial, for underdevelopment did not arise simply from a loss of capital but more fundamentally from the development of the class relationships reflected in these structural features (Robert Brenner, "The Origins of Capitalist Development: A Critique of Neo-Smithian Marxism," *New Left Review* 104 [1977]: 25–91).

52. Birnberg and Resnick, *Colonial Development,* pp. 13–15, 58–81, 250–57.

53. Lugard, *Dual Mandate,* pp. 404, 405.

54. Lord Hailey, *An African Survey* (London: Oxford University Press, 1957), p. 701, quoted in Seidman, *Comparative Development Strategies,* p. 30.

55. Birnberg and Resnick, *Colonial Development.*

56. Brett, *Colonialism and Underdevelopment,* pp. 89–103; Seidman, *Comparative Development Strategies.*

57. Beckford, "The Economics of Agricultural Resource Use"; Beckford, *Persistent Poverty.*

58. Beckford, *Persistent Poverty,* p. 9.

59. Tan, ed., *Sukarno's Guided Indonesia,* p. 17.

60. Bairoch, *Economic Development,* pp. 15, 16; Frederick C. Roche, "The Demographic Transition in Sri Lanka: Is Development Really a Prerequisite?" *Cornell Agricultural Economics Staff Paper* no. 76-5, January 1976, p. 9.

61. Samir Amin, *Neo-Colonialism in West Africa* (Harmondsworth: Penguin, 1973).

62. Gunnar Myrdal, *The Challenge of World Poverty* (New York: Pantheon Books, 1970), p. 72.

63. Myrdal, *The Challenge of World Poverty;* Brett, *Colonialism and Underdevelopment,* p. 77; Mende, *From Aid to Recolonization,* pp. 100–107; Crowder, *West Africa Under Colonial Rule,* pp. 381–85; Seidman, *Planning for Development.*

64. Keith Griffin, *The Political Economy of Agrarian Change* (Cambridge, Mass.: Harvard University Press, 1974); Furtado, *Economic Development of Latin America.*

65. Birnberg and Resnick, *Colonial Development;* Brett, *Colonialism and Underdevelopment;* Furtado, *Economic Development of Latin America.*

66. Mende, *From Aid to Re-colonization,* p. 22.

67. Birnberg and Resnick, *Colonial Development,* pp. 215–26.

68. Ibid., pp. 226–33; Furtado, *Economic Development of Latin America,* pp. 54–57.
69. Brett, *Colonialism and Underdevelopment,* pp. 38–41.

CHAPTER 9

1. Simon Kuznets, *Modern Economic Growth* (New Haven, Conn.: Yale University Press, 1966), pp. 445–60; by way of example, Keith Griffin, *Land Concentration and Rural Poverty* (New York: Holmes and Meier, 1976), pp. 178–82, describes economic classes in Ecuador.
2. Louis Lefeber, "On the Paradigm for Economic Development," *World Development* 2 (1974): 1–8; see also discussion of India in Chapter 7.
3. See Chapter 11 and Dudley Seers, "Indian Bias?: A Review Article on *Why Poor People Stay Poor: Urban Bias in World Development* by Michael Lipton," *Institute for Development Studies Discussion Paper* no. 116 (Brighton: University of Sussex, 1977); Raymond Vernon, *Storm over the Multinationals: The Real Issues* (Cambridge, Mass.: Harvard University Press, 1977).
4. Gunnar Myrdal, *The Challenge of World Poverty* (New York: Pantheon Books, 1970), pp. 72–75.
5. Alain de Janvry and Carlos Garramón, "Laws of Motion and Capital in the Center-Periphery Structure," *Review of Radical Political Economics* 9, no. 2 (1977): 29–38.
6. Ann Seidman, *Planning for Development in Sub-Saharan Africa* (New York: Praeger, 1974).
7. Ibid.
8. G. L. Beckford, *Persistent Poverty* (New York: Oxford University Press, 1972); Richard Weisskopf and Edward Wolff, "Linkages and Leakages: Industrial Tracking in an Enclave Economy," *Economic Development and Cultural Change* 25 (1977): 607–28. Agribusiness activities are discussed later in the chapter.
9. G. L. Beckford, *Persistent Poverty.*
10. Griffin, *Land Concentration,* pp. 178–82.
11. Michael P. Todaro, *Internal Migration in Developing Countries: A Review of Theory, Evidence, Methodology, and Research Priorities* (Geneva: International Labour Office, 1976), pp. 12, 65, 66.
12. Bruce F. Johnston and Peter Kilby, *Agricultural and Structural Transformation: Economic Strategies in Late-Developing Countries* (London: Oxford University Press, 1975); Gerald M. Meier, ed., *Leading Issues in Economic Development,* 3d ed. (New York: Oxford University Press, 1976), pp. 648–54; John W. Mellor, *The New Economics of Growth: A Strategy for India and the Developing World* (Ithaca, N.Y.: Cornell University Press, 1976); Hans W. Singer and Javed A. Ansari, *Rich and Poor Countries* (London: Allen and Unwin, 1977); various authors, "Special Issue: Latin-America in the Post-Import-Substitution Era," *World Development* 5, nos. 1 and 2 (1977); Michael P. Todaro, *Economic Development in the Third World: An Introduction to Problems and Policies in a Global Perspective* (New York: Longman, 1977), pp. 325–32.
13. Celso Furtado, *Economic Development of Latin America,* 2d ed., *Cambridge Latin American Studies* 8 (Cambridge: At the University Press, 1976), pp. 170–78. For details on the causes of the increase in inequality in income distribution in Brazil, see Edmar L. Bacha and Lance Taylor, "Brazilian Income Distribution in the 1960s: 'Facts,' Model Results, and Controversy," *Journal of Development Studies* 14 (1978): 271–97.
14. Meier, ed., *Leading Issues,* p. 653.
15. Various authors, "Special Issue"; E. L. Bacha, "Issues and Evidence on Recent Brazilian Economic Growth," *World Development* 5 (1977): 47–68; P. S. Malan and R. Bonelli, "The Brazilian Economy in the Seventies: Old and New Developments," *World Development* 5 (1977): 19–46; Gustav Ranis, "Employment, Equity, and Growth: Lessons from the Philippine Employment Mission," *International Labour Review* 110 (1974): 17–27.
16. W. Baer and L. Samuelson, "Editors' Introduction," *World Development* 5 (1977): 1–6.

17. See references in note 12 and World Bank, *World Development Report, 1979* (Washington, D.C.: World Bank, 1979), p. 51.

18. M. S. Ahluwalia, "Inequality, Poverty, and Development," *Journal of Development Economics* 13 (1976): 3-37; M. S. Ahluwalia, "Rural Poverty and Agricultural Performance in India," *Journal of Development Studies* 14 (1978): 298-323; Bacha and Taylor, "Brazilian Income Distribution"; Albert Fishlow, "Brazilian Size Distribution of Income," *American Economic Review* 62 (1972): 391-401; Griffin, *Land Concentration;* Mahbub ul Haq, *The Poverty Curtain: Choices for the Third World* (New York: Columbia University Press, 1976); Michael Lipton, *Why Poor People Stay Poor: Urban Bias and World Development* (Cambridge, Mass.: Harvard University Press, 1977); Meier, ed., *Leading Issues,* pp. 648-68; Felix Paukert, "Income Distribution at Different Levels of Development: A Survey of Evidence," *International Labour Review* 108, nos. 2 and 3 (1973): 97-125; T. N. Srinivasan, "Development, Poverty, and Basic Human Needs: Some Issues," *Stanford Food Research Institute Studies* 16, no. 2 (1977): 11-28; various authors, "Special Issue."

19. Keith Griffin and A. R. Kahn, "Poverty and the Third World: Ugly Facts and Fancy Models," presented at the World Bank Workshop on Analysis of Distributional Issues of Development Planning, Bellagio, Italy, April 22-27, 1977; Srinivasan, "Development, Poverty, and Basic Human Needs"; Nurul Islam, *Development Strategy of Bangladesh* (New York: Pergamon Press, 1978), p. 7; R. Nayyar, "Rural Poverty in Bihar 1961-62 to 1970-71," *Journal of Development Studies* 15 (1979): 194-201.

20. Dwight Y. King and Peter D. Weldon, "Income Distributions and Levels of Living in Java, 1963-1970," *Economic Development and Cultural Change* 25 (1977): 699-711; Lipton, *Why Poor People Stay Poor,* p. 150.

21. Lipton, *Why Poor People Stay Poor,* pp. 32-43; Seers, "Indian Bias?"

22. S. Lall and P. Streeten, *Foreign Investment, Transnationals, and Developing Countries* (Boulder, Colo.: Westview Press, 1977); various authors, "Special Issue."

23. Haq, *Poverty Curtain,* pp. 3-41.

24. Ibid., pp. 5, 6.

25. Richard Gott, *The Guardian* (London), September 15, 1977, p. 8.

26. Singer and Ansari, *Rich and Poor Countries,* pp. 37, 39, 50.

27. World Bank, *World Development Report, 1979,* pp. 16-19.

28. Singer and Ansari, *Rich and Poor Countries,* pp. 21, 22.

29. Ibid., pp. 32-35.

30. Ibid.

31. Seers, "Indian Bias?"; see also discussion of foreign investment, debt, and aid later in this chapter.

32. Paul Bairoch, *The Economic Development of the Third World since 1900* (Berkeley and Los Angeles: University of California Press, 1975), p. 98.

33. Singer and Ansari, *Rich and Poor Countries,* pp. 63-71; Seidman, *Planning for Development.*

34. Michael Lofchie, "Political and Economic Origins of African Hunger," *Journal of Modern African Studies* 13 (1975): 551-67; United Nations, Department of International Economic and Social Affairs, *Yearbook of International Trade Statistics,* vol. 1, 1977; Seidman, *Planning for Development,* pp. 30-33.

35. J. W. Sewell, *The United States and World Development 1979* (Washington, D.C.: Overseas Development Council, 1977), pp. 206, 207; United Nations, *Monthly Bulletin of Statistics* 30, no. 6 (1976): special table C.

36. Sewell, *The United States and World Development 1979,* p. 2.

37. Singer and Ansari, *Rich and Poor Countries.*

38. *The Guardian* (London), September 20, 1977.

39. A. B. Seira, "The World Economy, External Debt, and Prospects for Development Financing," *World Development* 7 (1979): 125-33; World Bank, *1979 Annual Report* (Washington, D.C.: World Bank, 1979); World Bank, *World Development Report, 1979.*

40. H. Hughes, "Debt and Development: The Role of Foreign Capital in Economic Growth," *World Development* 7 (1979): 95-112; M. S. Wionczek, "Editor's Introduction," *World Development* 7 (1979): 91-94.

41. Samir Amin, *Neo-Colonialism in West Africa* (Harmondsworth: Penguin, 1973);

Bairoch, *Economic Development*, pp. 111-34; M. G. Brown, *The Economics of Imperialism* (New York: Penguin, 1974), p. 249; Singer and Ansari, *Rich and Poor Countries*, p. 23; Sewell, *The United States and World Development, 1979*, p. 209; World Bank, *1979 Annual Report*, p. 12.

42. Seidman, *Planning for Development*, 38-41. Beckford, *Persistent Poverty*, provides a detailed discussion of the consequences, for Caribbean plantation economies, of vertical integration in oligopolistic companies.

43. Todaro, *Economic Development*, pp. 314, 315.

44. Unless otherwise indicated, the data on TNCs in this section are taken from Lall and Streeten, *Foreign Investment*.

45. Lall and Streeten, *Foreign Investment*, p. 15.

46. Ibid., p. 14.

47. Richard J. Barnet and Ronald E. Müller, *Global Reach: The Power of the Multinational Corporations* (New York: Simon and Schuster, 1974), pp. 142-46, 172-78.

48. R. S. Newfarmer, "TNC Takeovers in Brazil: The Uneven Distribution of Benefits in the Market for Firms," *World Development* 7 (1979): 25-43; Lall and Streeten, *Foreign Investment*.

49. Newfarmer, "Takeovers in Brazil."

50. Vernon, *Storm over the Multinationals;* D. Chudnovsky, "The Challenge by Domestic Enterprises to the Transnational Corporation's Domination: A Case Study of the Argentine Pharmaceutical Industry," *World Development* 7 (1979): 45-58.

51. Lall and Streeten, *Foreign Investment*, p. 40.

52. Constantine V. Vaitsos, *Intercountry Income Distribution and Transnational Enterprises* (Oxford: Clarendon Press, 1974): Lall and Streeten, *Foreign Investment*, p. 153; Vernon, *Storm over the Multinationals*.

53. Lall and Streeten, *Foreign Investment*, pp. 69, 145 n.

54. Vaitsos, *Intercountry Income Distribution;* Osvaldo Sunkel, "Transnational Capitalism and National Disintegration in Latin America," *Social and Economic Studies*, special number, 22 (1973): 135-70; James W. Howe, *The U.S. and World Development: Agenda for Action 1975* (New York: Praeger, 1975); Lall and Streeten, *Foreign Investment*, p. 178.

55. Lall and Streeten, *Foreign Investment*, pp. 169-80.

56. Andre Gunder Frank, *On Capitalist Underdevelopment* (London: Oxford University Press, 1975).

57. Beckford, *Persistent Poverty;* Howe, *U.S. and World Development;* Lall and Streeten, *Foreign Investment;* Newfarmer, "Takeovers in Brazil"; S. L. Parmar, "Self-Reliant Development in an Interdependent World," in Guy F. Erb and Valeriana Kallab, eds., *Beyond Dependency* (Washington, D.C.: Overseas Development Council, 1975); Vaitsos, *Intercountry Income Distribution;* Vernon, *Storm over the Multinationals;* A. J. Yeats, "Monopoloy Power, Barriers to Competition and the Pattern of Price Differentials in International Trade," *Journal of Development Economics* 5 (1978): 167-80.

58. Lall and Streeten, *Foreign Investment*, pp. 62-64.

59. Newfarmer, "Takeovers in Brazil"; Lall and Streeten, *Foreign Investment*, p. 44.

60. Newfarmer, "Takeovers in Brazil."

61. Lall and Streeten, *Foreign Investment*, pp. 27, 28, 37, 38, 44, 45; Vernon, *Storm over the Multinationals;* see Chapter 11 for discussion of CIA interference in Chile and elsewhere.

62. Hughes, "Debt and Development."

63. Ibid.

64. Bacha, "Issues on Brazilian Growth"; Malan and Bonelli, "The Brazilian Economy"; Seira, "The World Economy"; and Wionezck, "Editor's Introduction" are among the authors expressing concern over LDC debt. Hughes, "Debt and Development," and World Bank, *World Development Report 1979*, pp. 28-34, have been more optimistic about the ability of the LDCs to service their debts.

Public debt, whether from private or officials sources, is debt owed or guaranteed by the public sector (government or public institutions). It does not include nonguaranteed loans to private entities or individuals. Figures on LDC debt are from Sewell, *U.S. and World Development*, pp. 222-25, World Bank, *World Development Report, 1979*, and the United Nations Conference on Trade and Development (UNCTAD).

65. Barnet and Müller, *Global Reach*, p. 142; Howard M. Wachtel, "The New Gnomes: Multinational Banks in the Third World," pamphlet no. 4, Transnational Institute, 1977.

66. Cheryl Payer, *The Debt Trap: The International Monetary Fund and the Third World* (New York: Monthly Review Press, 1974); Wachtel, "New Gnomes," pp. 25–32.

67. Payer, *The Debt Trap*, pp. 25–49; the quotation is from p. 42.

68. Haq, *Poverty Curtain*, pp. 141–42.

69. Aid here is "net official development assistance." It is the total amount of government grants and low-interest loans from the developed countries, minus the amount paid by the LDCs in the same year to service previous aid loans. Hughes, "Debt and Development"; R. Jolly, *The Guardian* (London), May 8, 1978, p. 20.

70. Sewell, *U.S. and World Development;* Singer and Ansari, *Rich and Poor Countries,* pp. 174–79.

71. Singer and Ansari, *Rich and Poor Countries*, p. 143.

72. Singer and Ansari, *Rich and Poor Countries*, pp. 164, 178; Payer, *The Debt Trap*, pp. 79, 150–57.

73. Tibor Mende, *From Aid to Re-colonization: Lessons of a Failure* (New York: Pantheon Books, 1973); Parmar, "Self-Reliant Development"; Singer and Ansari, *Rich and Poor Countries*, pp. 165–68; Judith Tendler, *Inside Foreign Aid* (Baltimore: Johns Hopkins University Press, 1975); C. Peter Timmer et al., "The Choice of Technology in Developing Countries (Some Cautionary Tales)," *Harvard Studies in International Affairs* no. 32 (Cambridge, Mass., 1975).

74. R. E. Stryker, "The World Bank and Agricultural Development: Food Production and Rural Poverty," *World Development* 7 (1977): 325–36.

75. S. J. Maxwell and H. W. Singer, "Food Aid to Developing Countries: A Survey," *World Development* 7 (1979): 225–47.

76. The descriptions of aid presented in this section come from Tendler, *Inside Foreign Aid,* and Singer and Ansari, *Rich and Poor Countries,* pp. 157–92.

77. Tendler, *Inside Foreign Aid,* pp. 1, 2, 47, 48, 55–90; quotation from p. 75.

78. See note 73.

79. Seers, "Indian Bias?"

80. An important publication marking this change is Hollis Chenery et al., *Redistribution with Growth* (London: Oxford University Press, 1974). See also World Bank, *Assault on World Poverty* (Baltimore: Johns Hopkins University Press, 1975).

81. Stryker, "World Bank and Agricultural Development." The figure for 1979 lendings to agriculture is from World Bank, *1979 Annual Report,* p. 9.

82. World Bank, *Land Reform,* World Bank Rural Development Series (Washington, D.C.: World Bank, 1974), pp. 8–11.

83. United Nations, Food and Agriculture Organization/World Bank, *The Muda River Study: A First Report* (Rome: FAO, 1975).

84. Montague Yudelman, "Impact of the Bank's Rural Development Lending," *Finance and Development,* September 1979, pp. 24–28.

85. Raisuddin Ahmed, "Agriculture in Integrated Rural Development: A Critique," *Food Policy* 2 (1977): 140–47.

86. Stryker, "World Bank and Agricultural Development," p. 330.

87. Ibid.

88. Brian Bolton, "Agribusiness and FAO," *Food Policy* 2 (1977): 240–44; "Multinationals Face Attack Over Their UN Development Activities," *The Guardian* (London), November 9, 1978; Stryker, "World Bank and Agricultural Development," pp. 329–30; E. Feder, *Strawberry Imperialism: An Enquiry into the Mechanisms of Dependency in Mexican Agriculture* (The Hague: Institute of Social Studies, 1977); Lofchie, "Political and Economic Origins of African Hunger"; Frances Moore Lappé and Joseph Collins, *Food First: Beyond the Myth of Scarcity* (Boston: Houghton Mifflin Co., 1977); R. L. Ledogar, "Hungry For Profits: U.S. Food and Drug Multinationals in Latin America," *IDOC International Documentation* 70 (1976): 1–206. See also Chapters 6 and 10 for details.

89. Seidman, *Planning for Development,* p. 31.

90. Weiskopf and Wolff, "Linkages and Leakages."

91. Singer and Ansari, *Rich and Poor Countries.*

92. See, for example, Albert Fishlow et al., "The Third World: Public Debt, Private Profit," *Foreign Policy* 30 (1978): 132–69, and G. Barraclough, "Waiting for the New Order," *New York Review of Books,* October 26, 1978, pp. 45–53. This question is discussed in detail in Chapter 11.

CHAPTER 10

1. Donella H. Meadows et al., *The Limits to Growth* (New York: Universe Books, 1972); M. Mesarovic and E. Pestel, *Mankind at the Turning Point: The Second Report to the Club of Rome* (New York: E. P. Dutton, 1974); William Ophulls, *Ecology and the Politics of Scarcity* (San Francisco: W. H. Freedman and Co., 1977); J. W. Forrester, *World Dynamics* (Cambridge, Mass.: Wright-Allen, 1971), p. 12.

2. Meadows et al., *The Limits to Growth;* Lester R. Brown, *The Twenty-Ninth Day* (New York: W. W. Norton and Co., 1978).

3. Earl Cook, "Limits to Exploitation of Nonrenewable Resources," *Science* 191 (1976): 677–82; U.K. Dept. of the Environment and Transport, "SARUM 76," Global Modelling Project, Research Report no. 19, 1977; R. G. Ridker and E. W. Cecelski, "Resources, Environment, and Population: The Nature of Future Limits," *Population Bulletin,* vol. 34 (Washington, D.C.: Population Reference Bureau, 1979).

4. E. Cook, "Fossil Fuels: Benefits, Costs, and Future Supplies," in D. Pirages, ed., *The Sustainable Society* (New York: Praeger, 1977); J. P. Holdren, "Energy Costs as Potential Limits to Growth," in Pirages, ed., *The Sustainable Society;* Ridker and Cecelski, "The Nature of Future Limits"; H. E. Goeller and A. M. Weinberg, "The Age of Substitutability," *Science* 191 (1976): 683–89; World Bank, *World Development Report, 1979* (Washington, D.C.: World Bank, 1979), p. 11.

5. Paul Bairoch, *The Economic Development of the Third World since 1900* (Berkeley and Los Angeles: University of California Press, 1975), pp. 49, 50; United Nations, *Monthly Bulletin of Statistics* 33, no. 8 (1979): xiv.

6. H. H. Landsberg, "Materials: Some Recent Trends and Issues," *Science* 191 (1976): 637–40; Harrison Brown, "Population Growth and Affluence: The Fissioning of Human Society," *Quarterly Journal of Economics* 89 (1975): 236–46; S. V. Radcliffe, "World Changes and Chances: Some New Perspectives for Materials," *Science* 191 (1976): 700–708; Ridker and Cecelski, "The Nature of Future Limits."

7. Gerald Leach, *A Low Energy Strategy for the United Kingdom* (Atlantic Highlands, N.J.: Humanities Press, 1979); Demand and Conservation Panel of the Committee on Nuclear and Alternative Energy Systems, "U.S. Energy Demand: Some Low Energy Futures," *Science* 200 (1978): 142–52; Robert Stobaugh and Daniel Yergin, eds., *Energy Future: Report of the Energy Project at the Harvard Business School* (New York: Random House, 1979); Robert Stobaugh and Daniel Yergin, "After the Second Shock: Pragmatic Energy Strategies," *Foreign Affairs* 54 (1979): 836–71; *Los Angeles Times,* July 12, 1979, p. A-8, and July 17, 1979, p. IV-I.

8. Ronald G. Ridker and William D. Watson, Jr., *To Choose a Future: Resource and Environmental Problems of the U.S., A Long-Term Global Outlook* (Baltimore: Johns Hopkins University Press, 1980), summarized in Ridker and Cecelski, "The Nature of Future Limits."

9. The quotation is from Ridker and Cecelski, "The Nature of Future Limits," p. 29. See also *Science* 191 (February 20, 1976); Wassily Leontief et al., *The Future of the World Economy,* (New York: Oxford University Press, 1977); Cook, "Fossil Fuels"; Kingsley Dunham, "World Supply of Non-Fuel Minerals," *Resources Policy* 4 (1978): 91–99; "SARUM 76"; Interfutures, *Facing the Future* (Paris: Organization for Economic Cooperation and Development, 1979).

10. Goeller and Weinberg, "The Age of Substitutability"; Interfutures, *Facing the Future;* Ridker and Cecelski, "The Nature of Future Limits."

11. Ridker and Cecelski, "The Nature of Future Limits," p. 20.

12. H. Brown, "Human Materials Production as a Process in the Biosphere," *Scientific American* 223 (1970): 194-208.

13. Ridker and Cecelski, "The Nature of Future Limits," pp. 28, 29; Cook, "Fossil Fuels."

14. Interfutures, *Facing the Future*, pp. 26-41; Ridker and Cecelski, "The Nature of Future Limits."

15. N. Jéquier, ed., *Appropriate Technology: Problems and Promises* (Paris: Organization for Economic Cooperation and Development, 1976); A. Makhijani, *Energy Policy for the Rural Third World* (London: International Institute for Environment and Development, 1976); Arjun Makhijani and Alan Poole, *Energy and Agriculture in the Third World* (Cambridge, Mass.: Ballinger, 1975); R. Revelle, "The Resources Available for Agriculture," *Scientific American* 235 (1976); National Research Council, *U.S. Science and Technology Development: A Contribution to the 1979 U.N. Conference* (Washington, D.C.: U.S. Department of State, 1978); National Research Council, *Supporting Papers: World Food and Nutrition Study*, vol. 2, Study Team 4, *Resources for Agriculture*, and vol. 4, Study Team 12, *New Approaches to the Alleviation of Hunger* (Washington, D.C.: National Academy of Sciences, 1977).

16. Makhijani, *Energy Policy.*

17. Ibid.

18. Makhijani, *Energy Policy;* Revelle, "Resources Available for Agriculture"; National Research Council, *Science and Technology Development;* Elizabeth Cecelski, Joy Dunkerley, and William Ramsey, *Household Energy and the Poor in the Third World* (Washington, D.C.: Resources for the Future, 1979); Roy Meader, *Future Energy Alternatives* (Ann Arbor, Mich.: Ann Arbor Publishers, 1978); Vaclav Smil, *China's Energy* (New York: Praeger, 1976); Jyoti K. Parikh and S. Kirit, "Mobilization and Impacts of Biogas Technologies," *Energy* 2 (1977): 441-56.

19. Jéquier, ed., *Appropriate Technology.*

20. Ibid.

21. A. Gardano, *Technology and Desertification,* UN Document A/Conf. 74/6 (1977). See also A. Eggers-Lura, *Solar Energy in Developing Countries* (New York: Pergamon Press, 1979).

22. Leontief et al., *Future World Economy;* W. W. Murdoch, "Environment: Problems, Values, and Politics," in W. W. Murdoch, ed., *Environment: Resources, Pollution, and Society,* 2d ed. (Sunderland, Mass.: Sinauer, 1975); Ridker and Cecelski, "The Nature of Future Limits"; "SARUM 76."

23. E. P. Eckholm, *Losing Ground: Environmental Stress and World Food Prospects* (New York: W. W. Norton and Co., 1976).

24. United Nations, *Desertification: An Overview,* UN Document A/Conf. 74/1/Rev. 1 (1977), p. 84; Sterling Wortman and Ralph W. Cummings, Jr., *To Feed This World: The Challenge and the Strategy* (Baltimore: Johns Hopkins University Press, 1978), p. 64.

25. United Nations, *Desertification;* Interfutures, *Facing the Future.*

26. Gordon Conway, "Better Methods of Pest Control," in Murdoch, ed., *Environment: Resources, Pollution, and Society;* Carl Huffaker, *Biological Control* (New York: Plenum, 1971); National Academy of Sciences, *Pest Control: An Assessment of Present and Alternative Technologies* (Washington, D.C.: National Academy of Sciences, 1975); M. J. Way, "Integrated Control: Practical Realities," *Outlook on Agriculture* 9 (1977): 127-35; R. M. Perrin, "Pest Management in Multiple Cropping Systems," *Agro-Ecosystems* 3 (1977): 93-118; G. C. Wilkin, "Integrating Forest and Small-Scale Farm Systems in Middle America," *Agro-Ecosystems* 3 (1977): 291-302.

27. United Nations, *Desertification.*

28. United Nations, *Synthesis of Case Studies of Desertification,* UN Document A/Conf. 74/4 (1977), p. 24.

29. Ibid.; United Nations, *Desertification.*

30. Interfutures, *Facing the Future;* Eckholm, *Losing Ground.*

31. United Nations, *Desertification.*

32. Ibid.

33. United Nations, *Desertification* and *Synthesis of Case Studies.* There is little doubt

that most of those who died of starvation could have been saved if the aid agencies had acted more quickly, had made adequate plans when they first had news of the impending disaster, and if aid had been distributed more equitably (H. Sheets and R. Morris, "Disaster in the Desert," in M. H. Glantz, ed., *The Politics of Natural Disaster: The Case of the Sahel Drought* [New York: Praeger, 1976]). In Ethiopia at the same time 50,000 to 100,000 people died in droughts because Haile Selassie's government suppressed news of the famine and also because aid was slow (L. Wiseberg, "An International Perspective on the African Famines," in Glantz, ed., *The Politics of Natural Disaster*).

34. United Nations, *Desertification*, pp. 9, 10.

35. United Nations, *Desertification* and *Synthesis of Case Studies;* N. H. McLeod, "Dust in the Sahel: Cause of Drought?" in Glantz, ed., *The Politics of Natural Disaster*.

36. United Nations, *Synthesis of Case Studies*.

37. United Nations, *Desertification*.

38. United Nations, *Synthesis of Case Studies;* A. Warren and J. K. Maizels, *Ecological Change and Desertification*, UN Document A/Conf. 74/7 (1977). The quotation is from Warren and Maizels, p. 19.

39. R. W. Kates, D. L. Johnson, and K. T. Haring, *Population, Society, and Desertification*, UN Document A/Conf. 74/8 (1977).

40. Ibid.

41. Ibid.; McLeod, "Dust in the Sahel"; P. O'Keefe and B. Wisner, "African Drought: The State of the Game," in P. W. Richards, ed., *African Environment: Problems and Perspectives* (London: International African Institute, 1975); United Nations, *Desertification*.

42. Warren and Maizels, *Ecological Change;* Kates, Johnson, and Haring, *Population, Society, and Desertification*.

43. United Nations, *Desertification*, p. 17.

44. Gardano, *Technology and Desertification*.

45. Paul R. Ehrlich, Anne H. Ehrlich, and John P. Holdren, *Ecoscience: Population, Resources, Environment* (San Francisco: W. H. Freedman and Co., 1977), p. 621 n.

46. Eckholm, *Losing Ground*.

47. Ibid., p. 18.

48. Solon Barraclough and Juan Collarte, *Agrarian Structure in Latin America* (Lexington, Mass.: Lexington Books, 1973); United Nations, *Synthesis of Case Studies;* Kates, Johnson, and Haring, *Population, Society and Desertification*. See also Chapter 6.

49. United Nations, *Desertification;* Anthony C. Picardi and William W. Seifert, "A Tragedy of the Commons in the Sahel," *Technology Review,* vol. 78, no. 6 (1976): 42–51.

50. P. E. Lovejoy and S. Baier, "The Desert-Side Economy of the Central Sudan," in Glantz, ed., *The Politics of Natural Disaster*.

51. Jeremy Swift, "Disaster and a Sahelian Nomad Economy," in David Dalby and R. J. Harrison Church, eds., *Drought in Africa: Report of the 1973 Symposium* (London: University of London, 1973).

52. Lovejoy and Baier, "The Desert-Side Economy."

53. Ibid.

54. Ibid.

55. Jean Suret-Canalé, *French Colonialism in Tropical Africa, 1900–1945* (London: Hurst and Co., 1971).

56. Comité Information Sahel, *Qui se nourrit de la famine en Afrique?* (Paris: Comité Information Sahel, 1974). See also Chapter 9.

57. Frances Moore Lappé and Joseph Collins, *Food First: Beyond the Myth of Scarcity* (Boston: Houghton Mifflin Co., 1977); quotation from p. 261.

58. Lappé and Collins, *Food First;* Comité Information Sahel, *Qui se nourrit*.

59. Suret-Canalé, *French Colonialism;* United Nations, "Desertification."

60. Lovejoy and Baier, "The Desert-Side Economy"; Suret-Canalé, *French Colonialism*.

61. Dalby and Church, eds., *Drought in Africa;* United Nations, "Desertification"; Swift, "Disaster and a Sahelian Nomad Economy."

62. Ben Wisner, "Man-Made Famine in Eastern Kenya: The Interrelationship of Environment and Development," *Institute of Development Studies Discussion Paper* no. 96, July 1976 (Brighton: University of Sussex); O'Keefe and Wisner, "African Drought."

63. Charles Miller, *The Lunatic Express: An Entertainment in Imperialism* (New York: Ballantine Books, 1971).

64. E. Leys, *Underdevelopment in Kenya* (London: Heinmann, 1975), p. 31; Wisner, "Man-Made Famine," p. 8.

65. In 1954, 3,163 white farmers owned 20 percent of Kenya's best land, in the highlands; in 1970, 3,175 mainly African farmers owned this same land (R.M.A. van Zwanenberg and A. King, *An Economic History of Kenya and Uganda 1800–1970* [London: Macmillan, 1975]).

CHAPTER 11

1. By way of example, two writers for whom these principles have been important are H. E. Daly, "The Steady-State Economy," in D. Pirages, ed., *The Sustainable Society* (New York: Praeger, 1977), and William Ophulls, *Ecology and the Politics of Scarcity* (San Francisco: W. H. Freeman and Co., 1977).

2. Robert M. May, *Stability and Complexity in Model Ecosystems* (Princeton, N.J.: Princeton University Press, 1975); W. W. Murdoch, "Diversity, Complexity, Stability, and Pest Control," *Journal of Applied Ecology* 12 (1975): 795-807.

3. M. Huston, "A General Hypothesis of Species Diversity," *The American Naturalist* 113 (1979): 81-101; R. K. Peet and O. L. Loucks, "A Gradient Analysis of Southern Wisconsin Forests," *Ecology* 58 (1977): 485-99.

4. J. H. Connell, "Diversity in Tropical Rainforests and Coral Reefs," *Science* 199 (1978): 1302-10; H. Caswell, "Predator-Mediated Coexistence: A Non-Equilibrium Model," *The American Naturalist* 112 (1978): 127-54; P. L. Chesson and R. Warner, "Environmental Variability Promotes Coexistence in Lottery Competitive Systems," *The American Naturalist,* in press, 1980; Wayne P. Sousa, "Disturbance in Marine Intertidal Boulder Fields: The Non-Equilibrium Maintenance of Species Diversity," *Ecology* 60 (1980) in press.

5. Alain de Janvry, "Material Determinants of the World Food Crisis," *Berkeley Journal of Sociology* 21 (1976): 3-26; quotation from George Borgstrom, *The Food and People Dilemma* (North Scituate, Mass.: Duxbury Press, 1973), p. 14.

6. Garrett Hardin, "Living on a Lifeboat," *Bioscience* 24 (1974): 561-68.

7. Garrett Hardin, *The Limits of Altruism: An Ecologist's View of Survival* (Bloomington: Indiana University Press, 1977); William C. Paddock and Paul Paddock, *Famine '75* (Boston: Little, Brown and Co., 1967); Hardin, "Living on a Lifeboat"; W. W. Murdoch and A. Oaten, "Population and Food: Metaphors and the Reality," *Bioscience* 25 (1975): 561-67.

8. Hollis Chenery et al., *Redistribution with Growth* (London: Oxford University Press, 1974); first quotation from Richard R. Fagen, "Equity in the South in the Context of North-South Relations," in Albert Fishlow et al., *Rich and Poor Nations in the World Economy* (New York: McGraw Hill, 1978), p. 193; second quotation from C.L.G. Bell, "The Political Framework," in Chenery et al., *Redistribution with Growth,* p. 72.

9. Fagen, "Equity in the South."

10. Ibid., p. 199.

11. P. Chopra, *The Guardian* (London), July 10, 1978, p. 15.

12. Gerard Chaliand, *Revolution in the Third World* (Hassocks, Surrey: The Harvester Press, 1977), pp. xvi, 180.

13. James Petras, "Whither the Nicaraguan Revolution?" *Monthly Review* 31, no. 5 (1979): 1-22.

14. This view underlies IMF and World Bank policies. It is clearly laid out in World Bank, *World Development Report, 1979* (Washington, D.C.: World Bank, 1979) and in various chapters in Fishlow et al., *Rich and Poor Nations.*

15. Albert Fishlow, "A New International Economic Order: What Kind?" in Fishlow et al., *Rich and Poor Nations;* quotation from Fagen, "Equity in the South," p. 169.

16. Jan Tinbergen, *Reshaping the International Order* (New York: E. P. Dutton, 1976).

17. See references, note 14.

18. Albert Fishlow et al., "The Third World: Public Debt, Private Profit," *Foreign Policy* 30 (1978): 132–69.

19. Fishlow, "A New International Economic Order," p. 46.

20. World Bank, *World Development Report, 1979,* pp. 4, 5, 110–15; quotation from World Bank, *1979 Annual Report* (Washington, D.C.: World Bank, 1979), p. 12.

21. World Bank, *World Development Report, 1979,* pp. 16–19.

22. Ibid.; G. Barraclough, "Waiting for the New Order," *New York Review of Books,* October 26, 1978, pp. 45–53; G. Barraclough, "The Struggle for the Third World," *New York Review of Books,* November 9, 1978, pp. 47–58; Fishlow et al., "The Third World."

23. Mahmoud Mesteri, in a speech to the UN Assembly, quoted in Jane Rosen, *The Guardian* (London), October 22, 1979, p. 17; Fishlow et al., "The Third World," p. 141; Barraclough, "The Struggle for the Third World," p. 57.

24. S. Weintraub, "The New International Economic Order: The Beneficiaries," *World Development* 7 (1979): 247–58.

25. Fagen, "Equity in the South," p. 170.

26. The radical view presented here is based on an empirical review of international economic relations. The reader wishing to pursue a more theoretical, and neo-Marxist, viewpoint should consult Samir Amin, *Accumulation on a World Scale* (New York: Monthly Review Press, 1974); Alain de Janvry and Carlos Garramón, "Laws of Motion and Capital in the Center-Periphery Structure," *Review of Radical Political Economics* 9, no. 2 (1977): 29–38; Richard Brenner, "The Origins of Capitalist Development: A Critique of Neo-Smithian Marxism," *New Left Review* 104 (1977): 25–91; Andre Gunder Frank, *Dependent Accumulation and Underdevelopment* (London: Macmillan, 1978).

27. Dudley Seers, "Indian Bias?: A Review Article on *Why Poor People Stay Poor: Urban Bias in World Development* by Michael Lipton," *Institute of Development Studies Discussion Paper* no. 116 (Brighton: University of Sussex, 1977).

28. Fagen, "Equity in the South"; Richard Jolly, "An Overview," in Hollis Chenery et al., *Redistribution with Growth;* Dudley Seers, "Cuba," in Chenery et al., *Redistribution with Growth;* Reginald H. Green, "Tanzania," in Chenery et al., *Redistribution with Growth.*

29. Fagen, "Equity in the South," p. 205.

30. Fred W. Neal, Foreword to J. M. Aybar de Soto, *Dependency and Intervention: The Case of Guatemala in 1954* (Boulder, Colo.: Westview Press, 1978). See also Joyce and Gabriel Kolko, *The Limits of Power: The World and United States Foreign Policy, 1945–1954* (New York: Harper and Row, 1972); Walter LaFeber, *America, Russia, and the Cold War, 1945–1975* (New York: John Wiley and Sons, 1976); Daniel Yergin, *Shattered Peace: The Origins of the Cold War and the National Security State* (Boston: Houghton Mifflin, 1977).

31. Philip Agee, *Inside the Company: CIA Diary* (Harmondsworth: Penguin Books, 1975); F. Branfman, "The President's Secret Army: A Case Study—The CIA in Laos, 1962–1972," in Robert L. Borosage and John Marks, eds., *The CIA File* (New York: Grossman, 1976); Victor Marchetti and John D. Marks, *The CIA and the Cult of Intelligence* (New York: Knopf, 1974); R. Morris and R. Mauzy, "Following the Scenario," in Borosage and Marks, eds., *The CIA File;* David Wise, "Covert Operations Abroad: An Overview," in Borosage and Marks, *The CIA File.*

32. David Wise, "Is Anybody Watching the CIA?" *Inquiry,* November 27, 1978, pp. 17–21.

33. Barraclough, "The Struggle for the Third World"; J. MacManus, *The Guardian* (London), June 2, 1978; W. Schwartz, *The Guardian* (London), June 5, 1978.

34. Fagen, "Equity in the South."

35. Richard J. Barnet and Ronald E. Müller, *Global Reach: The Power of the Multinational Corporations* (New York: Simon and Schuster, 1974).

BIBLIOGRAPHY

Caldwell, John C., "Towards a Restatement of Demographic Transition Theory," *Population and Development Review* 2 (1976): 321-66, provides a particularly thoughtful survey of the major ideas.

Ehrlich, Paul R., Anne H. Ehrlich, and John R. Holdren, *Ecoscience: Population, Resources, and Environment* (San Francisco: W. H. Freeman and Co., 1977), provides thorough coverage of a large range of subjects and is an excellent sourcebook.

Haq, Mahbub ul, *The Poverty Curtain: Choices for the Third World* (New York: Columbia University Press, 1976), makes no attempt to be a complete analysis but is a stimulating and interesting book reflecting the author's extensive experience in planning for development.

Johnston, Bruce F., and Peter Kilby, *Agricultural and Structural Transformation: Economic Strategies in Late-Developing Countries* (London: Oxford University Press, 1975). This book, along with John Mellor's, is an important analysis of agriculture's potentially powerful role in development and the need for an appropriate agricultural strategy. They are especially useful works in providing detailed examples from major developing countries.

Lappé, Frances Moore, and Joseph Collins, *Food First: Beyond the Myth of Scarcity* (Boston: Houghton Mifflin Co., 1977), is a highly readable account of some of the misconceptions concerning world hunger and of some of the "structural" issues underlying low food production.

Lipton, Michael, *Why Poor People Stay Poor: Urban Bias and World Development* (Cambridge, Mass.: Harvard University Press, 1977), is an interesting and very readable analysis of how the suppression of rural society maintains poverty. It is based mainly on India's experience.

Mauldin, W. Parker, and Bernard Berelson, "Conditions of Fertility Decline in Developing Countries, 1965-75," *Studies in Family Planning* 9 (1978): 89-147, presents a detailed but clear and easily understood analysis of the major ideas and recent data concerning fertility decline. The authors have a strong bias toward family planning programs but give the data fair treatment.

Meier, Gerald M., ed., *Leading Issues in Economic Development,* 3d ed. (New York: Oxford University Press, 1976). This is a collection of excerpts from articles that present a great range of views on development, together with very useful comments by the editor.

Mellor, John W., *The New Economics of Growth: A Strategy for India and the Developing World* (Ithaca, N.Y.: Cornell University Press, 1976).

Singer, Hans W., and Javed A. Ansari, *Rich and Poor Countries* (London: Allen and Unwin, 1977), is a good introduction to the international aspects of the problem of development.

Todaro, Michael P., *Economic Development in the Third World: An Introduction to Problems and Policies in a Global Perspective* (New York: Longman, 1977). This excellent textbook combines standard economic analysis of development problems with a thorough and lively discussion of the major issues concerning poverty and development.

Weeks, John R., *Population: An Introduction to Concepts and Issues* (Belmont, Calif.: Wadsworth, 1978). This book provides a useful and easily understood introduction to the methods of demography and touches upon the main ideas concerning the demographic transition.

There is no single source that summarizes, in a readily accessible form, the studies that try to disentangle the relationships between fertility and socioeconomic variables. Useful reviews can be found in the journal *Population and Development Review.*

Wortman, Sterling, and Ralph W. Cummings, Jr., *To Feed This World: The Challenge and The Strategy* (Baltimore: Johns Hopkins University Press, 1978), provides an excellent account of the technical problems in food production, especially in the less developed countries.

Finally, there are three major sources of current information on population, food, and development. These are the United Nations, the Food and Agriculture Organization of the UN, and the World Bank. The Bank publishes each year a useful review called *World Development Report.*

INDEX

DATE DUE

DEC 0 5 1994			
DEC 1 4 2001			